THE BEST INTERESTS OF THE CHILD

THE BEST INTERESTS OF THE CHILD

Reconciling Culture and Human Rights

Edited by Philip Alston

United Nations Children's Fund

International Child Development Centre
Florence, Italy

CLARENDON PRESS · OXFORD

Oxford University Press, Walton Street, Oxford OX2 6DP

Oxford New York
Athens Auckland Bangkok Bombay
Calcutta Cape Town Dar es Salaam Delhi
Florence Hong Kong Istanbul Karachi
Kuala Lumpur Madras Madrid Melbourne
Mexico City Nairobi Paris Singapore
Taipei Tokyo Toronto
and associated companies in
Berlin Ibadan

Oxford is a trade mark of Oxford University Press

Published in the United States
by Oxford University Press Inc., New York

© Oxford University Press 1994

First published 1994

This is a special issue of the International
Journal of Law and the Family

British Library Cataloguing in Publication Data
Data available

Library of Congress Cataloging in Publication Data
The best interests of the child: reconciling culture and human rights
/ edited by Philip Alston.
p. cm.
1. Children—Legal status, laws, etc. 2. International relations and culture.
3. Human rights. I. Alston, Philip.
K639.B47 1994 341.4'81—dc20 94–16383
ISBN 0–19–825926–3

3 5 7 9 10 8 6 4 2

Printed in Great Britain
on acid-free paper by
Biddles Ltd, Guildford and King's Lynn

FOREWORD

THE 1989 United Nations Convention on the Rights of the Child is the world's most widely ratified international human rights treaty. In only four years, an extraordinary number of 155 nations, as of January 1994, have become States Parties to this Convention and others are expected to ratify shortly. The Convention thus provides an ideal context in which to examine the relationship between different cultural values and the international community's oft-stated aspiration to achieve universal human rights standards.

This volume focuses upon a widely accepted family law principle, reflected in Article 3 of the Convention, according to which 'the best interests of the child' shall be 'a primary consideration . . . in all actions concerning children . . .'. Since this legal principle has been applied largely in relation to family affairs, especially disputes concerning custody, adoption, maintenance, and intra-family abuse, many questions will naturally arise as the principle is further developed and interpreted in human rights law. Some observers will continue to argue that the 'best interests of the child' should remain a subject for state intervention only in specific cases of evident failure of the family, however defined, to protect the most basic interests of the child. An extreme formulation of this view reduces the legal issues virtually to a case-by-case determination of an individual child's 'best interest'. Another camp, closer to UNICEF's outlook on the world, finds the sheer survival prospects for children in many countries, as well as the deterioration of the living and learning environment of millions of children worldwide – North and South – sufficiently alarming to merit a reassessment of the traditional relationships between family, the state and the civil society in matters relating to children's health, nutrition, education, and general well-being. The question of the evolving role of the state, including its legislative and judicial roles, in protecting the interests of children, including future and intergenerational interests, may well be one of the basic social issues of our times. It is certainly pertinent to the issue of human rights law as applied to children.

The challenge of interpreting the 'best interest' principle is complicated by many powerful forces at work in the world, ranging from the extreme weakness of the state in resource-poor and conflict-torn societies of Africa to the bewildering legal and ethical concerns about the technological manipulation of human genes and the human reproductive system. No one study could hope to grapple with all these issues. A main objective of the contributors to this volume has been to demonstrate the importance of cultural values, across countries with widely diverse legal systems, as a major factor in the interpretation and application of the 'best interests' principle and, by extension, many other human rights norms. They have approached this task by combining broad theoretical analyses and country-specific case studies in a manner which links theory and practice more successfully than most efforts on this treacherous terrain.

The importance of culture, as well as (and related to) the diversity of legal systems in the world, provides cause for both hope and fear in national and international human rights communities. Culture, inevitably linked to customs, customary law, and 'tradition', provides an ethical and sometimes a political base, on the positive side of the ledger, for the protection, for example, of the rights of minority and indigenous groups, including children, to profess and practise their own religion, and to use their own language. Traditional extended family systems, moreover, provide essential social 'safety nets' in some cultures far more effectively than government programmes. Unfortunately, however, culture (usually combined with selective and self-serving interpretations of 'tradition') has also been used to defend such practices as the forced marriages of young girls and bonded child labour in parts of South Asia, female circumcision and other cruel and dangerous rituals in Africa and elsewhere, 'ethnic cleansing' in various regions of Europe, capital punishment for children under 18 in several jurisdictions in the United States and the beating of children as young as 5 as 'reasonable chastisement' by parents in the United Kingdom.

National and international human rights communities will have to continue struggling with social and legal issues relating to evolving cultural values, many of which are as ancient as the process of change in human societies. It is only very recently, however, that nearly all of our societies have agreed, at least in principle, to the primacy of the 'best interests of children', not just in judicial proceedings but 'in all actions concerning children, whether undertaken by public or private social welfare institutions, courts of law, administrative authorities or legislative bodies . . .', to quote the language in Article 3 of the UN Convention on the Rights of the Child. This volume has opened an intelligent and dispassionate debate on these issues, and it will undoubtedly guide the States which have ratified this Convention, human rights groups and other interested parties through the challenges and dilemmas involved, ultimately linked to a deceptively simple question: What do we mean by 'the best interests of the child'?

As the privatization of social services becomes an increasingly attractive policy to managers of hard-pressed governmental budgets in many countries, another aspect of Article 3 may acquire increasing significance. As Professor Alston notes in the first chapter of this volume, it is certainly a significant development of the 'best interests of the child' principle that it is related not just to official actions of governmental bodies but to 'all actions concerning children'. Although debates will (and should) undoubtedly continue about the extent to which this provision was intended to cover the actions (and which actions) of parents and guardians, Article 3 certainly leaves no doubt about its applicability to 'private social welfare institutions'. As more and more nations consider various forms of privatization of the delivery, even if not necessarily the financing, of social services directly affecting children, this expansion of the 'best interests' principle may acquire increasing relevance in international and national jurisprudence, as well as in other areas of public policy formulation relating to children.

The case studies in this volume focus on issues as varied as child custody in southern Africa, access to education in Egypt, the evolution from traditional customary law to modern family law in societies such as Tanzania and Burkina Faso, the status of children in South Asian societies, and the interpretation of what is considered to be in a child's best interests in France and Britain, the legal systems of which have had a profound influence throughout the world.

By examining the way in which different societies are likely to respond to one of the key provisions in the Convention, these detailed case studies help to provide a deeper and better understanding of the issues involved in the promotion of children's rights worldwide. On the one hand, they should help to strengthen the hand of reformers and human rights activitists seeking to change customs or traditional practices which are widely viewed as being detrimental for children. On the other hand, they support some of the arguments made by those children's advocates and others who have identified the need for culturally sensitive approaches to protecting children's 'best interests' and who recognize the importance of the flexibility required across diverse societies if the Convention is to be widely understood and respected, as well as effectively implemented.

This volume results from a project conducted by UNICEF's International Child Development Centre in Florence, as part of its programme on children's rights, which focuses much of its attention on implementation issues relating to key provisions of the Convention. The 'best interest of the child' project has been directed for the Centre by Professor Philip Alston of the Australian National University. Professor Alston, one of the leading authorities on the Convention as well as the Chairperson of the UN Committee on Economic, Social and Cultural Rights, has drawn on the insights and expertise of a range of distinguished researchers, child rights advocates and others directly involved in promoting greater understanding of, and respect for, the rights of the child. Professor John Eekelaar of Oxford University's Centre for Socio-Legal Studies made several important contributions to the project, in particular by preparing the papers for publication in the *International Journal of Law and the Family*.

UNICEF is gratefully indebted to all of the contributors to this effort. We would like specially to thank Professor Savitri Goonesekere, of the Open University of Sri Lanka, who served as a Senior Fellow at our Centre during part of the time she worked on her chapter. The contributors have succeeded in not only opening the debate and clarifying the issues but also in challenging us all to take these critical questions seriously – in the best interests of the world's children.

James R. Himes
Director
UNICEF International Child Development Centre

CONTENTS

NOTES ON CONTRIBUTORS

Philip Alston is Professor of Law and Director of the Centre for International and Public Law at the Australian National University. He is also currently Chairperson of the United Nations Committee on Economic, Social and Cultural Rights, and Discrimination Commissioner for Canberra. He has taught at Harvard Law School, University of Michigan Law School and the Fletcher School of Law and Diplomacy and has been senior legal adviser on children's rights to UNICEF since 1985.

Abdullahi An-Na'im is Executive Director of Africa Watch in Washington DC. He has degrees from the University of Khartoum (LL.B, 1970), University of Cambridge, (LL.B, 1973), and the University of Edinburgh (Ph.D, 1976). He has previously been: Associate Professor of Law, University of Khartoum; Visiting Professor of Law at UCLA, at the University of Saskatchewan, and at the University of Uppsala; and scholar-in-residence, the Ford Foundation, in Cairo. He is the author of *Sudanese Criminal Law* (Arabic, 1986); and *Toward an Islamic Reformation* (1990); Co-Editor of *Human Rights in Africa* (1990); and Editor of *Human Rights in Cross-Cultural Perspectives* (1992).

Alice Armstrong is the Regional Coordinator of the Women and Law in Southern Africa Research Trust (WLSA), which is a regional, non-governmental organization doing research on women's legal rights in the formal, customary and 'living' law in Zimbabwe, Zambia, Swaziland, Mozambique, and Lesotho. From 1981 to 1985 she taught at the Faculty of Law, University of Swaziland and from 1986 to 1990 at the Faculty of Law, University of Zimbabwe. She has a B.A. from Brown University, a J.D. from Boston University and a Ph.D. from the University of Copenhagen. Her most recent book is *Struggling over Scarce Resources: Women and Maintenance in Southern Africa* (1992).

Adel Azer is a Professor at the National Center for Social and Criminological Research (NCSCR) in Cairo, and is a consultant to UNICEF in Cairo. He is responsible for the Law and Social Policy project at NCSCR and his publications include: *Social Security in Egypt*, 2 vols. (1980/81); *The Rights of the Child in Egypt*, (1983); *Equal Opportunity in Education Policy in Egypt* (1991); *Child Labor in Egypt* (1991); and *Social Support Systems for the Aged in Egypt* (1992).

Fareda Banda has an LL.B from the University of Zimbabwe and a doctorate from Oxford University. In Zimbabwe she worked for the Harare Legal Projects Centre, a non-governmental organization specializing in the provision of legal services and information to rural areas. A Beit Fellowship at Oxford enabled her to write a dissertation entitled 'Women and Law in Zimbabwe:

Access to Justice on Divorce'. She graduated from Oxford in July 1989 and currently works with the English Law Commission.

Akila Belembaogo is Ministerial Delegate in charge of Social Action and the Family in Burkina Faso and, since 1991, Vice-Chairperson of the United Nations Committee on the Rights of the Child. Her degrees include a Master of Laws and a Diploma of Advanced Studies in Business Law. She has been Chief of the Legislation Service (1985), Director of Childhood (1986), technical adviser to the Minister (1988) and adviser to the Constitutional Chamber of the Supreme Court (1991).

John Eekelaar is Fellow and Tutor in Law at Pembroke College, Oxford and Reader in Law at Oxford University, specialising in family law. He has held a Research Fellowship at the Centre for Socio-Legal Studies, Wolfson College, Oxford, since 1976 and in this capacity has undertaken extensive empirical research in family law. He has collaborated in many international projects, the most recent of which was published as J. Eekelaar and P. Sarcevic (eds.), *Parenthood in Modern Society; Legal and Social Issues for the Twenty-First Century* (1993).

Savitri Goonesekere, LL.B (Cey), LL.M (Harvard), is an attorney-at-law, Professor of Law, and former Dean of the Faculty of Humanities and Social Sciences at the Open University of Sri Lanka. She has also taught at Ahmadu Bello University in Nigeria, and held visiting Research Fellowships at the School of Oriental and African Studies in London and the International Child Development Centre in Florence, Italy. She is a member of the SAARC panel. on Children's Rights and a member of the Sri Lanka National Committee on Children established under the Children's Charter of 1992.

Satoshi Minamikata is Professor of Law at Niigata University with research interests in divorce conciliation, counselling and child law. His recent publications include: 'Kaji Chotei: Mediation in the Japanese Family Court', in R. Dingwall and J. Eekelaar (eds.), *Divorce Mediation and the Legal Process* (1988), 'Custodial Fathers in Japan', in L. Weitzman and M. Maclean (eds.), *Economic Consequences of Divorce* (1992) and 'Lone-Parent Families in Japan', in J. Eekelaar and P. Sarcevic (eds.), *Parenthood in Modern Society; Legal and Social Issues for the Twenty-First Century* (1993).

Stephen Parker is a Professor of Law at Griffith University, Queensland. He was previously a Reader at the Australian National University and, before that, a lecturer at University College, Cardiff. His research interests lie mainly in family law and in legal ethics. He is author of *Cohabitees* (1991) and co-author of *Australian Family Law in Context* (1994).

Jacqueline Rubellin-Devichi is Professor of Private Law at the University of Lyon 3, director of the graduate programme in family law, and directs a family law research group. She was a member of the Barrot Commission on abused children and is currently rapporteur of a group on the protection of the child, organized by the Secretary of State for Human Rights of the Ministry of Foreign Affairs. She has also been appointed as rapporteur of the National Congress of French Notaries to be held in Tours in 1995 and is a Vice-President of the International Society of Family Law.

Bart Rwezaura teaches at the Faculty of Law, University of Hong Kong. Formerly he was Professor of Law at the Faculty of Law, University of Dar es Salaam. His major work deals with the link between economic change and the transformation of family relations in Africa.

THE BEST INTERESTS PRINCIPLE: TOWARDS A RECONCILIATION OF CULTURE AND HUMAN RIGHTS

PHILIP ALSTON*

ABSTRACT

The 'universality' to which international human rights standards aspire has been strongly contested in recent years. Nevertheless, the Convention on the Rights of the Child is likely to achieve near-universal ratification within the next year or two. This analysis uses the Convention, and especially Article 3(1), which incorporates the principle that, in all actions concerning children, 'the best interests of the child shall be a primary consideration', to examine the broader relationship between culture and human rights.

I. INTRODUCTION

The present analysis, like those that follow it in this collection, aims to explore the meaning and significance of the 'best interests' principle recognized in Article 3(1) of the United Nations Convention on the Rights of the Child.[1] It seeks to do so not only in relation to the Convention itself, or to children's rights, but also in the overall human rights context. Article 3(1) provides that:

In all actions concerning children, whether undertaken by public or private social welfare institutions, courts of law, administrative authorities or legislative bodies, the best interests of the child shall be a primary consideration.

The Convention represents, in a number of respects, the culmination of half a century of international efforts to set 'universal' standards in the field of human rights.[2] While the treaty is clearly consistent with the principles enshrined in the Universal Declaration of Human Rights some forty-five years ago, it has developed and built upon those principles in many ways. As a result, it is by far the most detailed and comprehensive (in terms of the rights recognized, as opposed to the categories of persons covered) of all of the existing international human rights instruments. Its importance is further underscored by the unprecedented rapidity with which States have ratified or acceded to it and

* Centre for International and Public Law, Australian National University, Canberra ACT 0200, Australia.

by the sheer number of states parties which it has attracted in the space of the four years since it was opened for signature on 26 January 1990. By December 1993 the Convention had 155 states parties, with the United States being the only major country remaining outside the treaty regime. The goal endorsed by the second World Conference on Human Rights, held in Vienna in June 1993, of achieving universal ratification of the Convention by 1995 would thus appear to be reasonably within the world community's grasp (with the United States as perhaps the only significant, potentially persistent, holdout).[3]

This prospect of universal ratification, combined with the objective of laying down universally applicable standards, also serves to place the Convention at the forefront of debates about whether human rights norms are capable of attaining 'universality' or are inevitably relative to each individual society. While the debates are, by their very nature, not susceptible of any definitive resolution, they raise vitally important challenges which cannot be ignored by the proponents of the international law of human rights, including the rights of the child. For much of 1993, those debates were played out in the context of the high-profile diplomacy surrounding the World Conference. The problems are far from being resolved, however, partly because of the level of generality and abstraction at which much of the discussion has occurred. One of the objectives of the present volume is to inject an element of specificity which will facilitate a much deeper appreciation of the complexity of the issues, at the same time as pointing the way towards approaches which involve neither the embrace of an artificial and sterile universalism nor the acceptance of an ultimately self-defeating cultural relativism.

II. PUTTING ARTICLE 3(1) INTO ITS BROADER CONTEXT

In addition to examining the content of Article 3(1), this article seeks to use that provision as a vehicle for exploring several different dimensions of the Convention as well as the broader relationship between culture and human rights. Such endeavours are important because, despite its prominence and the extent of the interest and support that it has generated, the full complexity of the Convention is not, as yet, well understood. It is sometimes presented (or, more accurately, misrepresented) as being a uni-dimensional document that reflects a single, unified philosophy of children's rights and contains a specific and readily ascertainable recipe for resolving the inevitable tensions and conflicts that arise in a given situation among the different rights recognized. Similarly the respective entitlements of the different actors involved, including the child, the parents, the family, the extended family, the local community, the society and the State are assumed to be clearly defined and delineated. This view is often encouraged by proponents of the Convention who wish to emphasize that a particular solution or outcome to a problem is mandated by the text; in this vision, certainty and consistency are viewed as indispensable values in a world-wide struggle against abuse and neglect. Ironically, a similar approach might also be adopted by some of the Convention's opponents whose various goals might include demonstrating its eurocentricity, portraying it as being anti-family or being opposed to child autonomy, parental rights or some other favoured agenda.

In fact, the Convention is far more complex and multi-dimensional than any of these characterizations would imply. As a result, if the Convention is to fulfil the aspirations of its drafters and of those who see it as providing an appropriate framework for addressing the entire range of major issues affecting children, it will be indispensable to develop a better appreciation of the nature of this complexity and of its implications at the global as well as at the national and local levels.

While the focus of the contributors to this volume is on Article 3(1) of the Convention, it should also be noted that the principle is mentioned in several other places within the Convention itself as well as in a number of other important international human rights instruments. Within the Convention the phrase 'the best interests of the child' appears in relation to the separation of the child from the family setting (Art. 9); with reference to parental responsibility for the upbringing and development of the child (Art. 18); in relation to adoption and comparable practices (Arts 20 and 21); and in the context of the child's involvement with the police and the justice system (Arts 37 and 40).

More generally, the principle has been reflected in international instruments since 1959 when it was included in the Declaration of the Rights of the Child.[4] It was subsequently reflected in two provisions of the 1979 Convention on the Elimination of All Forms of Discrimination Against Women.[5] Article 5(b) obligates States Parties to take all appropriate measures:

To ensure that family education includes a proper understanding of maternity as a social function and the recognition of the common responsibility of men and women in the upbringing and development of their children, it being understood that the interest of the children is the primordial consideration in all cases.

Article 16 (1)(d) of the same Convention provides that in all matters relating to marriage and family relations 'the interests of the children shall be paramount'. Similarly, Article 5 of the Declaration on Social and Legal Principles relating to the Protection and Welfare of Children, with Special Reference to Foster Placement and Adoption Nationally and Internationally,[6] provides that:

In all matters relating to the placement of a child outside the care of the child's own parents, the best interests of the child, particularly his or her need for affection and right to security and continuing care, should be the paramount consideration.

Although the phrase is not used specifically in the International Covenant on Civil and Political Rights,[7] the Human Rights Committee has nevertheless referred, in two of its General Comments, to 'the paramount interest of the children' in cases involving the dissolution of marriage.[8] But perhaps the strongest evidence of the extent to which the principle has gained general acceptance is the frequency with which it is used in legal analyses at the international level in general. This may be illustrated not only by reference to the jurisprudence under the European Convention on Human Rights[9] but also to the work of the Human Rights Committee in considering individual communications under the Optional Protocol. Thus, for example, in one notable instance, members of the Committee premised their Opinion on what they termed 'the undoubted right and duty of a domestic court to decide "in the best interests of the child" '.[10]

The principle is also reflected in the African Charter on the Rights and Welfare of the Child, Article IV of which provides that '[i]n all actions concerning the child undertaken by any person or authority the best interests of the child shall be the primary consideration'.[11] In relation to refugees, the Executive Committee of the United Nations High Commissioner for Refugees has formally 'stressed that all action taken on behalf of refugee children must be guided by the principle of the best interests of the child as well as by the principle of family unity'.[12]

But although the principle has often been recognized in international instruments it has yet to acquire much specific content or to be the subject of any sustained analysis designed to shed light on its precise meaning. The most important formulation is clearly that contained in Article 3(1) of the Convention on the Rights of the Child. There are several reasons for this. First, some of the other instruments do not purport to recognize the rights of children, but are concerned rather with those of women or others. Second, as used in the Declaration of the Rights of the Child it occurs in a context in which the child is more the object than the subject of rights. Third, Article 3(1) underlines the fact that the principle applies not only in the context of legal and administrative proceedings, or in other narrowly defined contexts, but 'in relation to *all* actions concerning children'.

This represents a very significant extension of a principle which was originally little more than a way of ensuring that the interests of any children involved would be taken into account in divorce or custody cases. But even in that somewhat specialized setting, the usefulness of the concept has often been challenged, as is indicated in the analyses by Stephen Parker and John Eekelaar in the present volume. Yet despite its very limited jurisprudential origins, the principle has come to be known in one form or another to many national legal systems and has important analogues in diverse cultural, religious and other traditions. This apparent commonality contrasts sharply, however, and potentially very revealingly, with the very diverse interpretations that may be given to the principle in different settings. Thus, to take one example, it might be argued that, in some highly industrialized countries, the child's best interests are 'obviously' best served by policies that emphasize autonomy and individuality to the greatest possible extent. In more traditional societies, the links to family and the local community might be considered to be of paramount importance and the principle that 'the best interests of the child' shall prevail will therefore be interpreted as requiring the sublimation of the individual child's preferences to the interests of the family or even the extended family.

Another example is the relationship between the rights of women and the children's rights recognized in the Convention. The text of the Convention does not, and indeed realistically could not, reflect any set formula for accommodating the competing interests that arise in this regard. Rather, it consists of a range of different principles, the balancing or reconciliation of which in any given situation will depend on a variety of considerations. This complexity needs, however, to be explored and illustrated in actual case studies. In the absence of the understanding that such studies could generate, it is very likely in the years ahead that the balance struck in the Convention will be misunderstood or misrepresented whether by those wanting to argue that the Convention elevates children's rights at the expense of those of women, or vice-versa, by children's advocates who wish to present a one-sided picture of the implications flowing from the Convention, or by other parties who would wish to mould the text to reflect their own particular value preferences.

The case studies that are presented in this volume use the 'best interests' principle as a lens through which to view the significance of certain aspects of the Convention in different societies, thus giving concrete expression to both the complexity of the principle and the extent to which it is inextricably linked to the cultural context in which it is invoked. The studies also enable us to better understand the ambiguities and ambivalences of the Convention and the flexibility which will be required for its effective implementation.

III.   THE RIGHTS OF THE CHILD IN THE CONTEXT OF THE CULTURAL RELATIVISM DEBATE

In their different ways both the Convention on the Rights of the Child and the debate over cultural relativism have been shaped to a very significant extent by the Cold War and the ramifications of its demise. One of the effects of that conflict, which dominated the period from the Second World War until 1989, was to suppress the debate over cultural relativism in favour of an ideologically dominated East-West dispute over whether civil and political rights should be accorded priority over economic, social and cultural rights, or vice-versa. The United Nations has always sought to resolve that issue by insisting upon the equal importance of the two sets of rights. Third World nations, a category which included virtually all of the governments most likely to argue that either the very notion of human rights, or at least certain specific rights, are eurocentric, were thus distracted by the 'need' to take the side of either the East or the West, rather than developing a more independent stance. It is thus not coincidental that one of the results of the ending of the Cold War has been the re-opening of the relativism debate, to which we shall return below.

Similarly, the evolution of the Convention on the Rights of the Child, both in its drafting phase and since its adoption, has been very significantly effected by the Cold War and its demise. While this is not the place for a detailed historical analysis of the politics of drafting the Convention, it is difficult in the absence of a brief overview of this aspect to appreciate fully just how the Convention came to be as comprehensive, as flexible, and as widely supported as it is. The submission of the original draft of the Convention to the United Nations Commission on Human Rights by Poland in 1978 constituted a quintessentially political gesture. While the formal occasion for the proposal was the twentieth anniversary of the Declaration of the Rights of the Child combined with the celebration (in 1979) of the International Year of the Child, the Polish Government was probably motivated more by a desire to seize at least some of the human rights initiative from Jimmy Carter. The rights of the child seemed to be the ideal topic for this purpose, not only because of a long association between Poland and the promotion of the concept at the international level, but more importantly because it was assumed that any such convention could justifiably be confined to the economic, social and cultural rights to which the Communist countries wanted to accord priority.

The initial response by the West was to downplay the importance of the initiative and to make the drafting process as slow and protracted as possible. But by the mid-1980s it had become apparent that the draft Convention was well on its way to garnering sufficiently widespread support to ensure its eventual adoption. In response, the Reagan Administration sought to ensure the inclusion in the text of a range of provisions reflecting the various civil and political rights that it accused the Communist countries of seeking to deny, or downgrade. The resulting initiatives seemed to be less motivated by a desire to accord rights such as those to freedom of speech, opinion, movement, religion and association to the world's children, than to render Poland's brainchild much less appealing to its original sponsors and their allies.

This strategy might have succeeded in bogging down the whole drafting process interminably but for the fortuitous intervention of various other factors. Most important was what proved in retrospect to be the beginning of the end of the Cold War at roughly the same time. In addition, since 1986 UNICEF had begun to play an active role in the preparation of the Convention, especially by encouraging and facilitating the more active participation of more developing countries in the drafting process. This in turn enhanced the eventual acceptability of the draft to those countries, enabled them to make a greater input than might otherwise, have been the case, and laid the foundations for the extraordinarily widespread support which was to be accorded to the Convention in the early 1990s. The replacement of Ronald Reagan by George Bush in January 1989 finally removed the likelihood of any attempt by the United States to prevent or delay the final push to adopt the Convention. At the same time, the former Communist countries, anxious to demonstrate their newfound attachment to a comprehensive package of international human rights norms, were eager to endorse the Convention.

One of the happy consequences of this combination of circumstances is that the Convention is not the product of a distorted or unduly contentious drafting process, as could well have been the case if some of the ingredients described above had been absent. Indeed the only permanent injury suffered by the Convention as a result of the dramatic political upheavals that occurred during its drafting, consists of a certain downgrading of a limited number of the provisions relating to economic and social rights, which was the legacy of the Reagan Administration's rejection of that category of rights. In cultural terms, however, the Convention, while by no means perfect, is probably more sensitive to different approaches and perspectives than most of the principal human rights treaties adopted earlier. Against that background, it is appropriate to inquire whether the Convention can withstand the attack launched upon human rights norms in general by the cultural relativists and whether the best interests principle has a significant role to play in that respect.

As noted above, the end of the Cold War gave a new lease of life to an otherwise surprisingly dormant debate over the merits of universal versus relative value systems, and the role of culture in their discovery and interpretation. Comparable debates have, of course, raged for centuries. It must suffice in this context to recall that even within the recent traditions of Western philosophy, the Enlightenment values which have often been closely associated with modern conceptions of human rights have been subject to spirited challenges almost from the outset. Thus, for example, Montesquieu supported a classical relativist position which insisted that that the moral acceptability of laws had to be evaluated according to the social, cultural and political context in which they were

found.[13] Similarly, Isaiah Berlin has drawn attention to the writings of
Giovanni Battista Vico who rejected many of the ideas of the French
philosophes such as Voltaire, Diderot, and Descartes on the grounds that
their doctrines were essentially ahistorical and proved to be 'utopian,
inflexible, deterministic, arrogant, unfeeling, homogenizing, intoler-
ant'.[14] As Lilla has noted in a brilliant recent analysis, Berlin especially
welcomed the fact that Vico, a Neapolitan writing in the early nineteenth century, 'unveiled a new approach to other cultures, permitting
us to understand foreign peoples in their own terms, rather than judging
them . . . in the high court of inflexible, eternal reason'.[15]

But rather than seeking to contribute to, or even resolve, such age-old
debates, the post-World War II international human rights regime has
been characterized by a determined, and often single-minded, commitment to universality on the part of the the treaty drafters, of most of
those responsible for the implementation of the norms at the international level and of the most active proponents of those norms among
the ranks of non-governmental organizations such as Amnesty International. Not surprisingly, this approach has drawn strong support from
the ranks of those victims of oppression living under regimes that have
sought to challenge the universality of the norms they stand accused of
violating. Indeed it is difficult to see how the human rights movement
could have survived as well as it did through the 1980s had a significantly different approach been adopted.

Nevertheless, the increasing success of that movement, especially in
terms of breaking down defences based on notions such as state sovereignty and domestic jurisdiction, and the increasingly effective threat
that it poses to governments which had assumed that they could remain
immune to international scrutiny and accountability, has endowed relativist arguments with at least two newly important constituencies. The
first consists of those, such as Abdullahi An-Na'im in the present
volume, who consider that efforts to promote respect for international
human rights standards are often likely to remain superficial and ineffectual until such time as they relate directly to, and where possible are
promoted through, local cultural, religious and other traditional
communities.

The other constituency consists of those governments which would
like for various, often selfish and culturally manipulative, reasons to
discredit the human rights concept. Thus in the lead-up to the 1993
World Human Rights Conference, Amnesty International, along with
various other groups, sounded alarm bells, warning *inter alia* of a 'back-
tracking on the ideals of universality'.[16] Some observers suspected that
these fears had been realized in the Bangkok Declaration, adopted at
the World Conference Regional Preparatory Meeting in April 1993, in
which the Asian states recognized 'that while human rights are universal
in nature, they must be considered in the context of a dynamic and

evolving process of international norm-setting, bearing in mind the significance of national and regional particularities and various historical,
cultural and religious backgrounds'.[17] While that statement was open
to competing interpretations, spokespersons for the South did little to
discourage negative assessments of its intent through comments such as
the following:

Cultural relativity keeps many countries in the South from embracing total
equality for women. . . . Similarly, the primacy placed upon the importance of
the individual or complete freedom of the press cannot be accepted completely
in the South, which places a far greater emphasis on the well-being of society.
Finally the developmental approach in the South would frown upon absolute
priority being given to civil and political liberties if they come in the way of
satisfying the basic needs of the people.

In sum, therefore, we have to recognize that while constantly upgrading
human rights, the countries of the South, rather than aping Northern models,
must work out their own norms and standards suited to their social, cultural
and economic conditions.[18]

It should also be noted that various types of relativist approaches to
human rights have continued to find considerable support among Western intellectuals in recent years.[19] Indeed, if the more extreme predictions of some political scientists and others are borne out, the Cold War
will be replaced by conflicts among and within cultures, religions and
ideologies at the expense of any further universalization of human rights
standards.[20]

At the end of the day, the World Conference adopted a perhaps
surprisingly unequivocal statement to the effect that '[t]he universal
nature of [all human rights and fundamental freedoms] is beyond question'.[21] While some of the wording of the Bangkok Declaration found its
way into the Vienna Declaration, it was accorded a rather different
thrust in the following formulation:

While the significance of national and regional particularities and various historical, cultural and religious backgrounds must be borne in mind, it is the
duty of States, regardless of their political, economic and cultural systems, to
protect all human rights and fundamental freedoms.[22]

But despite its undoubted importance in terms of rejecting what might
be termed crude relativist attacks, this diplomatic/legal vindication of
the principle of universality cannot be taken to have resolved the deeper,
more enduring challenge of ensuring greater openness and sensitivity
to different cultural contexts in the implementation of human rights
standards. This challenge is no less important in the promotion of
respect for children's rights. But since the Convention lacks any specific
provision to this effect much of the burden will be borne by the best
interests principle to which we now turn.

IV.   AN ANALYSIS OF ARTICLE 3(1)

1. An Overview of the Drafting History

The first draft of the Convention was in the form of a proposal made
by Poland in 1978 which only sought to adapt the provisions of the
formally non-binding 1959 Declaration of the Rights of the Child to
make them suitable for inclusion in a binding treaty. In essence, the
adaptation consisted of little more than the addition of appropriate
introductory and concluding clauses. As a result, the extensive best
interests provision contained in Principle 2 of the Declaration was
included in full in the following terms in the first version of the draft
Convention:

The child shall enjoy special protection, and shall be given opportunities and
facilities, by law and by other means, to enable him to develop physically,
mentally, morally, spiritually and socially in a healthy and normal manner and
in conditions of freedom and dignity. In the enactment of laws for this purpose,
the best interests of the child shall be the paramount consideration.[23]

This text has two particularly notable features. The first is that the
principle, far from being restricted to child custody arrangements, is of
very wide-ranging application. The second is that the child's best interests were not to be one one factor among several to be weighed, but
rather were to be 'the paramount consideration'. Initial reactions on
the part of some delegations were not favourable to this generosity and
an alternative draft was submitted in 1980 to the Working Group of the
Commission on Human Rights which was responsible for the drafting
of the Convention. It read as follows:

In all official actions concerning children, whether undertaken by public or
private social welfare institutions, courts of law, or administrative authorities,
the best interests of the child shall be a primary consideration.[24]

The revised text was first discussed in 1981. Despite the views expressed
by a number of delegations who considered the first version to be
broader in scope and to offer better protection to the child, the second
was adopted at the first reading stage. It was not discussed again until
seven years later, when the draft as a whole received a second reading.
At that stage a proposal to substitute the word 'the' for 'a' in qualifying
the term 'primary consideration' was put forward unsuccessfully. The
only change agreed to at this final stage was the addition of a reference
to 'legislative bodies' after the phrase 'administrative authorities'.[25]

2. 'The Best Interests of the Child'

It reflects rather poorly on the drafting processes followed in the preparation of international instruments such as the Convention to note
that although Article 3(1) was discussed at some length by the Working

Group, its meaning seems either to have been taken for granted or to have been considered unimportant. The extensive debates at the national level in various countries, and the misgivings expressed by many commentators, found no expression in the Working Group until 1988. But even then insightful contributions were largely confined to the observation by one representative that the phrase was inherently subjective and that its interpretation would inevitably be left to the judgment of the person, institution or organization applying it. This was said to be especially so because the Convention contained no prior stipulation that the 'best interests of the child' included his or her physical, mental, spiritual, moral and social development (as the first Polish draft had done).[26] In the ensuing debate, however, a number of delegations expressed satisfaction with the phrase as it stood, without either offering elaboration or seeking any more precise definition. By contrast, in the drafting of other provisions of the Convention in which reference is made to the child's best interests, the significance of the phrase in the particular context is generally more apparent.

In summary then, the drafters of Article 3(1) appear to have been sufficiently familiar with the phrase 'the best interests of the child' from its extensive usage in the domestic law of many countries as to conclude that it required no close analysis. On the other hand, they seem to have been unaware of the controversy over the principle in many of these jurisdictions and thus felt no need either to defend its open-endedness or to propose elements which might inject some particular content into it.

Oddly enough, no delegation focused specifically on the implications which would seem to follow from the inclusion of the principle in Article 3(1), as opposed to elsewhere in the Convention. This includes, in particular, the fact that the first five articles serve the function of providing an overall framework, or umbrella, under the shadow of which the remaining provisions of the Convention are to be applied. Because of the failure to address this aspect, the consequences of a clash between a particular right recognized later in the Convention and the interpretation of what is in a particular child's best interests, were never considered during the drafting process.

In interpreting the phrase under review, it is appropriate to place some emphasis on the term 'best' so as to exclude other factors which could arguably be in the child's overall interests but not his or her 'best' interests. This element could assume particular significance in jurisdictions in which the preferred statutory standard refers to the child's 'welfare' rather than his or her 'best interests'. The distinction between that which is considered to be consonant with the child's welfare and that which is not might thus be rendered more nuanced. But it is how those interests are determined that remains the principal dilemma in the application of the principle. It is suggested below that one advantage of the Convention over most domestic statutes in this regard is that the extensive catalogue of rights that it recognizes has the effect of providing at least a starting point in distinguishing primary interests (in the form of rights) from other types of interest.

3. 'A Primary Consideration'

It is noteworthy that there is no single version of the best interests principle reflected in other international instruments. To take but one example, the Convention on the Elimination of All Forms of Discrimination Against Women uses both the terms 'paramount' and 'the primordial consideration', albeit in somewhat different contexts. In the drafting of the Convention on the Rights of the Child the debate centred on whether the 'best interests' principle should be 'a primary', or 'the paramount' consideration, or might be better described in some other way. In 1981 some delegations in the Working Group expressed concern that the use of the word 'paramount' in the revised Polish draft was too broad. One speaker, for example, pointed out that the interests of the child should not be the overriding, paramount consideration in every case, since other parties might have equal or even superior legal interests in some situations, such as in a medical emergency during childbirth.[27]

The matter was again raised at the Working Group's final session in 1988. It was suggested in the context of a 'Technical Review' of the draft that 'a' primary consideration be altered to read 'the' primary consideration, on the basis that the latter would be more consistent with other international instruments.[28] The proposal was rejected, however, on the grounds that some of those instruments were concerned with a more limited range of issues (such as adoption and custody) than those covered by Article 3(1) and that there were situations in which the competing interests of, inter alia, 'justice and society at large, should be of at least equal, if not greater, importance than the interests of the child'.[29]

An alternative proposal to use the phrase 'a paramount' consideration (unsurprisingly) received no support.[30] Another proposal to the effect that the best interests of the child should be 'the' primary consideration only in actions involving his or her 'welfare' was opposed by various delegations who considered that it would unduly narrow the scope of protection afforded to children.[31] Given the extensive scope usually accorded to the term 'welfare' in such settings, this opposition reveals how broad many of the drafters wanted the scope of the principle to be.

It is clear that the drafters' preference for the indefinite rather than the definite article in this phrase is intended to indicate that the child's best interests are not to be considered as the single overriding factor. While this choice may be contestable in the context of custody decisions in which the principle is best known in domestic law, it could hardly have been otherwise in the context of an umbrella provision designed to be applicable in a very wide range of situations in which a vast array of competing considerations might arguably be both relevant and appropriate. The objective implicit in opting for the word 'a' is to ensure that there is sufficient flexibility, at least in certain extreme cases, to enable the interests of those other than the child to prevail. Nevertheless, the formulation adopted would seem to impose a burden of proof on those seeking to achieve such a non-child-centred result to demonstrate that, under the circumstances, other feasible and acceptable alternatives do not exist.

It should also be noted that while the indefinite article is used in this general, all-encompassing provision, other formulations are used in relation to more specific concerns elsewhere within the Convention. The strongest version of the principle is to be found in Article 21 which requires any system of adoption to 'ensure that the best interests of the child shall be the paramount consideration'. In Article 18(1) parents and legal guardians are enjoined, in exercising their primary responsibility for the upbringing and development of the child to have 'the best interests of the child [as] their basic concern'. Elsewhere, however, the formulation is more neutral, such as in relation to the forcible separation of a child from his or her parents (when 'necessary for the best interests' Art. 9(1)), the child's right to maintain contacts in the event of parental separation (except if 'contrary to the child's best interests' – Art. 9(3)), the removal of the child from the family environment (where it is not in the child's 'own best interests' to remain – Art. 20(1)), the separation of children and adults in custody ('unless it is considered in the child's best interests not to do so' – Art. 37(c)), or the right to a fair hearing in penal cases in the presence of one's parents or legal guardians ('unless it is considered not to be in the best interests of the child' – Art. 40(2) (b)(iii)).

The final element of this phrase that warrants analysis is the term 'consideration'. While it has the same meaning as 'element' or 'factor', it also has the additional significance of emphasizing that the the child's best interests must actually be considered. Such consideration must be genuine rather than token or merely formal and must ensure that all aspects of the child's best interests are factored into the equation.

4. 'In All Actions Concerning Children . . . Whether Undertaken by Public or Private Social Welfare Institutions, Courts of Law, Administrative Authorities or Legislative Bodies'

The first issue that arises in the interpretation of this phrase is how comprehensive the words 'action' and 'concerning' should be taken to be in domestic law. 'Action' is often used in contradistinction to 'omissions' but there is no indication in the context of Article 3(1) or in the relevant debates during the drafting process to indicate that such a restrictive usage was intended here. In any event, it is clear that certain types of omissions to act may be barely distinguishable from actions *per se*, as illustrated vividly in the United States context by the de Shaney case.[32]

The implications of the word 'concerning' would appear to be rather less clear. As long as an action has a direct impact upon a child, it would appear to be covered. But what about an action the impact of which is only indirect, such as the introduction of a new governmental benefits policy (assuming that a 'policy' of this nature would qualify as an 'action' for the purposes of Article 3(1))? There is clearly a point at which an action can be considered to be too general in nature, or too indirect in focus, to warrant its being considered to concern a particular child. But if we use the term 'children', as does the introduction to Article 3(1), then the difficulty of determining whether an action is so indirect as to no longer 'concern' children at large becomes somewhat greater.

A related question which arises is whether there is any contradiction between the reference to the best interests of 'the child' on the one hand, and on the other the provision at the beginning of Article 3(1) that this standard shall apply in all actions concerning 'children'. It would certainly have been possible from a grammatical perspective to have referred instead to 'all actions concerning the child'. The use of the plural would seem to indicate an intention to achieve broad rather than narrow coverage for the best interests principle. As noted earlier, an individualistic focus may be appropriate in relation to custody cases, but in the context of the range of issues addressed elsewhere in this Convention the failure to acknowledge some collective, distributive just-ice-type dimensions would have been artificial at best.

The other principal issue raised by this phrase is whether it was intended to cover private as well as public actors, and if so, whether there nevertheless remains a class of private actions which are excluded from the scope of the provision. In the drafting process two somewhat contradictory signals were sent in this regard. The first proposal put before the Working Group would have applied the 'best interests' principle to all actions concerning children, 'whether undertaken by their *parents, guardians,* social or State institutions, and in particular by courts of law and administrative authorities'.[33] An alternative proposal suggested that it should be applied '*in all official actions* concerning children, whether undertaken by public or private social welfare institutions, courts of law, or administrative authorities'.[34] While the latter version was preferred by the Working Group at the first reading stage, it specifically deleted the word 'official'.[35] At the second reading stage this version was maintained, with the addition of the phrase 'legislative bodies'.

The result would appear to have been a compromise between those who wanted private actors to be covered and those who did not want the provision to impose obligations on parents and guardians, at least not explicitly. That group had suggested that the provision should not regulate private family decisions but only official actions.[36] While their view was partly accommodated through the deletion of the reference to parents and guardians, this was achieved only at the cost of deleting the reference to 'official actions'. As a result, the scope of the provision as adopted, in respect to 'private' actions (particularly those by parents or guardians) would seem to be of a general nature.

In the first place, Article 3(1) does not seek to impose specific duties, but rather to state a general principle that should inform decision-making in relation to 'all actions concerning children'. Thus even though there may have been no intention to 'regulate private family decisions' as suggested during the drafting process, a general principle can still be made applicable in such contexts without amounting to regulation *per se*. This view is reinforced by reference to the terms used in Articles 18(1) and 27(2) of the Convention in relation to parental responsibility for the child.[37] Secondly, the deletion of the word 'official' is most plausibly interpreted as being intended to leave the door open to Article 3(1) being applied to non-official entities as well. Thirdly, this inference is reinforced by the inclusion of 'private social welfare institutions' among the list of entities specified, thus indicating that the provision is not exclusively confined to public undertakings.

This does not, of course, directly dispose of the remaining issue relating to the intended scope of the reference to 'private social welfare institutions'. Does it, for example, apply to the type of extended family arrangements described in this volume by Alice Armstrong and Bart Rwezaura? If we accept the broad interpretation advocated in the preceding paragraph, and in the absence of any stated objective during the drafting process of adopting a more restrictive approach, there would seem to be no reason not to include such arrangements whether on the grounds that they are covered by the all embracing reference to 'all actions', or whether on the basis that they are the cultural equivalent of private social welfare institutions.

V. THE ROLES TO BE PLAYED BY THE PRINCIPLE

It has already been suggested that the inclusion of the principle in Article 3(1) accords it an importance and prominence which it would not enjoy if it were merely included in a later, and more narrowly focused, provision of the Convention. It has also been characterized as an umbrella provision. But this does not adequately describe the role that the principle appears to be accorded by the Convention

In brief, there would seem to be three, rather different, roles which the formulation in Article 3(1) might play in the future in relation to children's rights. The first is in conjunction with other articles of the Convention in order to support, justify or clarify a particular approach to issues arising under the Convention. In this context, it is an aid to construction as well as an element which needs to be taken fully into account in implementing other rights. The second role is as a mediating principle which can assist in resolving conflicts between different rights where these arise within the overall framework of the Convention.

The third role is that suggested by Stephen Parker in this volume. He suggests that '[i]n all matters not governed by positive rights in the Convention, Article 3(1) will be the basis for evaluating the laws and practices of the States parties'. It remains to be seen, however, whether the principle will be accorded this role by international supervisory bodies or by national courts and authorities. In the Vienna Programme of Action, adopted by the 1993 World Conference on Human Rights, the best interests principle is placed on a par with the non-discrimination principle, in the following terms: 'In all actions concerning children, non-discrimination and the best interests of the child should be primary considerations and the views of the child given due weight'.[38] Leaving aside the unfortunate use of the merely hortatory verb 'should' rather than 'shall', the bracketing of these principles is potentially significant in the present context because of the different ways in which the principle prohibiting discrimination has been approached by the UN's Human Rights Committee and the organs established under the European Convention on Human Rights, respectively. Under the latter, the non-discrimination provision (contained in Article 14) has been held to apply only where the discrimination occurs in relation to one or more of the rights recognized in the other provisions of the Convention.[39] The Human Rights Committee, by contrast, has held that, for the purposes of Article 26 of the Covenant on Civil and Political Rights, it is sufficient if discrimination affects the enjoyments of any human right.[40] In general, there would seem to be strong policy reasons for following the latter approach in relation to the best interests principle.

VI.   THE BEST INTERESTS PRINCIPLE AS A WINDOW ON THE RELATIONSHIP BETWEEN CULTURE AND HUMAN RIGHTS

At a certain level, the debate over the nature of the relationship between international or 'universal' human rights standards and different cultural perspectives and contexts can never be resolved. Thus the very aspiration to achieve acceptance of certain universal standards invites continuing controversy and provokes the assertion of relativistic positions. At another level, however, the examination of the best interests principle as reflected in Article 3(1) of the Convention on the Rights of the Child provides insights which could help to respond to at least some of the criticisms that have been made of the universalist aspirations of human rights law.

1. Exploding the Myth of the Automatic Transferability of Domestic Jurisprudence

Analysis of the best interests principle sheds considerable light upon the relationship between international human rights norms and their apparent domestic counterparts. The eurocentrism of the international catalogue of norms is sometimes sought to be demonstrated on the basis that the formulations used in, for example, the Universal Declaration of Human Rights, have their origins and direct counterparts in American, English, or French law. But it is appropriate, and in many respects inevitable, that the drafters of international instruments will, wherever appropriate, draw upon formulations that have gained acceptance within domestic legal systems. Indeed it is the fact that this practice has been so widespread that justifies suggestions that a significant number of international human rights norms are binding upon States because of their status as 'general principles of law' within the meaning accorded to that phrase in Article 38 of the Statute of the International Court of Justice.[41]

But this process of drawing upon municipal law formulations does not imply the automatic transferability of the various interpretations that have been given to them by domestic courts and legislatures. Thus, for example, while the prohibition against cruel, inhuman or degrading treatment and punishment, which has now been reflected in innumerable international instruments, clearly has its origins in the United States Bill of Rights, it is already apparent that the international supervisory organs do not feel constrained in any way to follow the various interpretations of that norm adopted by the US Supreme Court in relation to issues such as the death penalty or solitary confinement. Similarly, the very extensive jurisprudential baggage accumulated by the best interests principle in both Anglo-Saxon and French contexts,[42] is not likely to be particularly influential, and will almost certainly not be determinative, in the interpretation of the principle by international bodies. Morever, the ways in which the Convention has both formulated and situated the principle should eventually result in the need for those domestic courts which seek to apply the Convention to adopt a rather different approach from that which they themselves have hitherto developed, primarily within the limited context of custody decisions.

2. The Indeterminacy of Children's Rights Norms

The corollary of this openness of international norms is a significant element of indeterminacy. Indeed it is one of the paradoxes of international human rights law that, on the one hand, the norms must be sufficiently clear, comprehensive and inflexible to provide the international community with some basis on which it might seek to constrain a government which undermines or circumvents minimum standards of decent behaviour. On the other, any enterprise which is avowedly universalist in its aspirations and aims to address a very wide range of issues involving, *inter alia*, the relationship between the state, the family and the child, must be characterized by a significant degree of flexibility and adaptability. As the European Court of Human Rights has observed in upholding a degree of indeterminacy even in laws at the national level: '[W]hile certainty is highly desirable, it may bring in its train excessive rigidity and the law must be able to keep pace with changing circumstances. Accordingly, many laws are inevitably couched in terms which, to a greater or lesser extent, are vague and whose interpretation and application are questions of practice'.[43] Thus the critics are correct to point out that indeterminacy is a characteristic feature of human rights norms[44] and not only of the more oft-disputed norms (such as the right to political participation or the right to food) but also of the so-called core norms (the right to life; the right to a fair trial; the right to be free from torture etc.). But, for the most part, such indeterminacy is no greater than in the case of other comparable broad-brush legal rules. Rather than leading to paralysis, it serves to emphasize the importance both of institutions as a means through which to pursue the interpretive enterprise and of the need to develop a better understanding of the different cultural dimensions of the relevant norms.

If human rights norms in general can be said to be inherently inde-terminate, the best interests principle is located by most of its critics at the most indeterminate outer margins even of that body of norms.[45] The inclusion of the principle in the Convention was the subject of criticism by academic commentators even before the drafting process had been completed. It was questioned, for example, whether the principle might not be able to be used as a justification for any decision taken affecting children, no matter how questionable it might otherwise seem.[46] Since the Convention's adoption, Joyal and others have questioned whether 'this notion of the child's best interest, conceived at a time when the child was perceived more as object than subject, retains its raison d'être within a context of rights?'.[47]

Indeed, the most commonly voiced scholarly criticism relates to the difficulty of identifying the criteria that should be used to evaluate alternative options that are open to a decision-maker seeking (or purporting) to act in the child's best interests.[48] In Mnookin's view:

The choice of criteria is inherently value-laden; all too often there is no con-sensus about what values should inform this choice. These problems are not unique to children's policies, but they are especially acute in this context because children themselves often cannot speak for their own interests.

. . .

Even if predictions [as to the consequences of policy alternatives] were possible, what set of values should a judge use to determine a child's best interests. . . ?

[H]e must have some way of deciding what counts as good and what counts as bad.[49]

But a study of the Convention on the Rights of the Child, and of the contributions to this volume, highlight two responses to such criticism. The first, elaborated upon below by Stephen Parker, and developed in other ways elsewhere by Carl Schneider,[50] is that this apparent indeterminacy can, in practice, be very significantly mitigated through the application of localized 'conventions' or understandings, in relation to such values, which are constructed by communities of rule users.

The second is that the Convention as a whole goes at least some of the way towards providing the broad ethical or value framework that is often claimed to be the missing ingredient which would give a greater degree of certainty to the content of the best interests principle. It provides a carefully formulated and balanced statement of values to which some 155 States Parties have formally subscribed. This is not to suggest that the Convention seeks to provide any definitive statement of how an individual child's interests would best be served in a given situation; any such pretension would obviously be misplaced. It does, however, provide a number of signposts capable of guiding those seeking to identify what is in the best interests of the child, and excludes from the equation, by implication, various other elements.

3. The Role of Culture in the Application of Human Rights Norms

In contrast to criticisms which tend to portray international human rights norms as being not only hostile, but also impervious, to non-Western cultural influences, the case studies in this volume demonstrate that there is enormous scope for such differences to be taken into account in the implementation of those norms at the domestic level. It is entirely appropriate for such scope to be provided; indeed it is in many ways a type of elastic glue which enables the overall human rights enterprise to be held together and remain coherent.

We can conceive of the different human rights in terms of concentric circles of increasing responsiveness or flexibility to cultural factors as we move further away from the central and less flexible norms. In the centre we might find norms relating to the physical and mental integrity of the human person. Thereafter might come norms relating to the treatment of detainees, freedom of thought, etc. In the field of children's rights a similar typology could readily be developed. While the best interests principle would be applicable across the board to all of the rights, its significance or influence will clearly be greater the further we are from the central core of survival and development rights.

This may be illustrated by reference to an example which relates closely to the articles by Adel Azer, Bart Rwezaura, Alice Armstrong and Fareda Banda in this volume. In various situations, the right to be

cared for by one's parents may come into conflict with the right to
education. The best interests principle might then serve as a mediating
principle which facilitates the conclusion that a degree of separation of
the child from his or her parents is the best way of securing access to
educational opportunities. But the ability of the principle to serve that
purpose will, in practice, depend quite heavily upon the relevant cultural
assumptions and practices that prevail within a given society. Although,
as noted below, culture cannot always be permitted to play such a
dispositive role.

Perhaps the best way to understand the role that culture can and
does play in this regard is by analogy to the concept of the margin of
appreciation within the jurisprudence developed under the European
Convention on Human Rights. That analogy also serves to emphasize
that the cultural dimension is a universal one and not only something
which comes into play when we are considering non-Western cultural
factors. The margin of appreciation concept is nowhere to be found in
the text of the European Convention. Rather, it is a doctrine which has
been developed by the European Commission and Court of Human
Rights to enable an appropriate degree of discretion to be accorded to
national authorities in their application of the provisions of the Convention. Cultural considerations have figured very prominently in the factors for which the European supervisory organs have been prepared to
make some allowance. Moreover, although many of the cases in which
the doctrine has been most clearly applied and explored have concerned
the notion of permissible restrictions upon rights, the organs have also
made considerable use of the doctrine in determining the actual scope
of many of the rights.[51]

4. The Limits of Culture

Just as culture is not a factor which should be excluded from the human
rights equation, so too must it not be accorded the status of a metanorm
which trumps rights. There are many cultural practices which, by
human rights standards, are difficult if not impossible to reconcile. Foot-
binding in pre-World War II China, child slavery or bondage, and
female infanticide in various societies are examples of practices in relation to which culture-based arguments have already had to yield (in
theory, if not always in practice) in favour of human rights norms. But
there are also many other cases in which cultural arguments continue
to be used today to justify the denial of children's rights. They include
arguments designed to defend the full range of practices relating to
female circumcision, to justify the non-education of lower class or caste
children, or to justify the exclusion of girls from educational and other
opportunities which would make them less sought after in marriage.

The best interests principle clearly has considerable potential to be
invoked in defence of cultural practices which are incompatible with

children's rights norms. One such case study has surveyed the extent to which the principle was applied by the Canadian judiciary to present a consistent preference in favour of 'the apprehension and placement of First Nations' children away from their families and communities as natural, necessary and legitimate, rather than coercive and destructive'.[52] In this respect, it must be accepted that cultural considerations will have to yield whenever a clear conflict with human rights norms becomes apparent.

5. The Individual Versus Collective Dimensions of Human Rights

Article 3(1) of the Convention also epitomises the artificiality of views which characterize international conceptions of human rights as being either wholly individualistic or predominantly collectivist. The very wording of the article, particularly through its juxtaposition of the words 'children' and 'child', brings out the interplay between these different, co-existing dimensions of human rights. While the individual element is clearly of quintessential importance and cannot be overridden by collective claims, the latter will inevitably, and indeed should, temper the way in which the individual right is exercised and interpreted. Denial of this interplay flies in the face of empirical evidence in case studies such as those contained in the present volume.

6. The Relationship Between Law and Social Change

There is one final observation which also emerges from the case studies of the best interest principle included in this volume. It relates to the limits of (human rights) law as a force for social change. This is in many respects the least well understood, and certainly one of the most neglected issues in the entire field. The expectations of diplomats, bureaucrats, international lawyers and others at the international level, the assumptions of domestic lawyers and of political scientists, the perspectives of philosophers, sociologists and anthropologists, the expectations of victims and of grass-roots groups, and the assumptions of nongovernmental human rights groups or of national-level bureaucrats and social workers, to name only a partial cross-section of those concerned, often seem to rest on radically different premises when it comes to characterizing and explaining the relationship between the international recognition given to certain norms by the United Nations or other comprable norm creators, and the processes through which those norms are given effect at the local level.

Although this issue has ramifications which go well beyond the field of children's rights, it manifests itself in many ways in this field. Thus, for example, one finds critics of the concept of children's rights who attribute numerous and far-reaching changes to the very fact of recognition.[53] Others see such recognition leading to the rapid 'legalization' of most issues concerning children. They object to an approach which, in their view, provides an automatic entry point for legalism in general and lawyers in particular to dominate all subsequent proceedings. They see the legal profession as importing various prejudices into the process which distort or prevent nuanced, sensitive and desirable outcomes.[54] They see an inevitably adversarial quality being introduced to the discourse surrounding children.[55]

Others argue that the mere recognition of rights is quite ineffectual, and perhaps even misleading and counter-productive. In this view children should not be accorded rights unless they are given the means to assert them effectively on their own behalf. It is therefore seen to be essential to an effective theory of rights to be able to identify the holders of specific duties that correlate with each right. From this Benthamite insistence upon effective legal remedies for the violation of any right, the move towards a narrowly constructed or Hohfeldian rights framework is readily made. Children's rights are then put on a par with legal rights in domestic legal systems, required to have all of the attributes thereof, and assumed to share all of their limitations and shortcomings.

Some of the critics even embrace different arguments that seem to imply the acceptance of competing conceptions of the nature and significance of (children's) rights and the discourse surrounding them. Katherine O'Donovan, for example, criticizes children's rights for, *inter alia*, the adversarial element they introduce, for their indeterminacy, and for their perceived inability to accord legal subjectivity to children, but then advocates an alternative approach based on 'an expanded legal concept of trust' under which 'care of the infant's person' would be held on trust by adults who would be liable for breaches of trust etc.[56] But it is not clear if, or how, her alternative model would, in practice, be less affected by the difficulties she associates with the rights approach. Similarly, Onora O'Neill rejects the concept of children's rights in favour of attributing appropriate obligations to adults and others responsible for the care of children.[57] But while her model definitively rejects the Hohfeldian approach to rights, it is not clear that it would operate in a significantly different fashion from that sometimes assumed under international human rights law.[58]

None of this is necessarily designed to rebut any particular approach to protecting the human dignity of children. Rather it underscores the extent to which an individual's approach to the concept and practice of children's rights is inevitably, and properly, influenced by his or her perception of the relationship between international norms and national law on the one hand and between national law and the cultural and other factors influencing social change on the other hand. The case studies in this volume provide powerful testimony to the fact that identical norms can lead to very different results, but results that may well be, in the light of the prevailing cultural and other circumstances, largely compatible with the international norms. Nor is the reference to these predominantly Third World-focused case studies intended to suggest that the situation in industrialized countries is radically different. Even within the common law tradition, American and English law have been shown to function very differently, in large part because of the different legal, political and institutional cultures in which the law operates.[59]

This is, in itself, a significantly relativist conclusion. Provided, however, that it is combined with an acceptance of the desirability of the quest for universally applicable standards it is potentially compatible with the existing approach to the promotion of international standards such as those recognized in the Convention on the Rights of the Child. It recognizes that no amount of universalist aspirations can cancel out the inevitable influence of cultural values and perceptions. This in turn is not to diminish in any way the important role of international institutions in mediating and encouraging more consistent approaches and interpretations to the relevant international norms. By the same token those institutions need to bear in mind both the heavy responsibility that they bear in terms of encouraging and facilitating greater consistency and the dangers of exaggerating their role and their potential influence.

NOTES

[1] General Assembly res 45/118 (1989), Annex.

[2] See generally Philip Alston, Commentary on the Convention on the Rights of the Child (forthcoming, United Nations Centre for Human Rights and UNICEF).

[3] Vienna Declaration and Programme of Action, Part II, para 46, UN doc A/CONF. 157/24 (Part I) (1993).

[4] General Assembly res 1386 (XIV) (1959).

[5] General Assembly res 34/180 (1979), Annex.

[6] General Assembly res 41/185 (1986).

[7] General Assembly res 2200A (XXI) (1966).

[8] General Comment No 17 (35), *Report of the Human Rights Committee*, UN doc A/44/40 (1989), Annex VI, para 6; and General Comment No 19 (39), *Report of the Human Rights Committee*, UN doc A/45/40 (1990), Annex VI, para 6.

[9] E.g. report of 8 March 1982, *Hendriks, Dec. & Recs* 1982, 5 (Where 'there is a serious conflict between interests of the child and one of its parents which can only be resolved to the disadvantage of one of them, the interests of the child . . . must prevail').

[10] Communication No 201/1985, Views of 27 July 1988, Appendix I (Individual opinion submitted by Mrs Higgins and Messrs Dimitrijevic, El Shafei and Zielinski), in *Report of the Human Rights Committee*, UN doc A/43/40 (1988), Annex VII, para 1.

[11] OAU doc CAB/LEG/153/Rev 2 (1987).

[12] Conclusion No 47 (XXXVIII) (1987) on 'Refugee Children', para (d), in *Conclusions on the International Protection of Refugees Adopted by the Executive Committee of the UNHCR* (Geneva, UNHCR, 1991), 105.

[13] Montesquieu, *The Spirit of Laws* (1750), Book I, Ch 3, S 12.

[14] See generally Mark Lilla, *G. B. Vico: The Making of an Anti-Modern* (Cambridge, MA, Harvard University Press, 1993), 4.

[15] Ibid 4–5.

[16] 'Issues at the UN World Conference on Human Rights', Amnesty International doc IOR 41/WU 02/93, 29 March 1993.

[17] A/CONF.157/PC/59, para 8.

[18] Statement by Satish Chandra, Ambassador/Permanent Representative of India to the United Nations Offices in Geneva, in *The South and Human Rights*, Proceedings of a Seminar Organized by the Sub-Committee on the South of the Special NGO Committee on Development (Geneva, 1993), 8 at 9. In a similar vein see also Kausikan, 'East and Southeast Asia and the Post-Cold War International Politics of Human Rights', 92 Foreign Policy (1993), 24.

[19] For a recent survey of some such challenges see Rhoda Howard, 'Cultural Absolutism and the Nostalgia for Community', 15 *Human Rights Quarterly* (1993) 315–38. See also Paul D. Carrington, 'Aftermath', in P. Cane and J. Stapleton (eds), *Essays for Patrick Atiyah* (Oxford, Clarendon Press, 1991), 113; ('Cultural relativism is the necessary basis for mutual respect in a pluralist world respecting rights of self-governance. Lengthening the lists of human rights . . . is a form of non-violent imperialism, depriving as it does the choice of social arrangements open to a self-governing state or community'. Accordingly, for Carrington, the Universal Declaration of Human Rights is 'a proclamation that the whole world should resemble as nearly as possible suburban middle-class America'. Ibid 114. See also Richard Rorty, *Contingency, Irony and Solidarity* (Cambridge, MA, Harvard University Press, 1989).

[20] See e.g. Samuel Huntington, 'The Clash of Civilizations?', *Foreign Affairs*, Summer 1993, 22–49. ('The people of different civilizations have different views on the relations between God and man, the individual and the group, the citizen and the state, parents and children, husband and wife, as well as differing views of the relative importance of rights and responsibilities, liberty and authority, equality and hierarchy'. Ibid 25).

[21] UN doc A/CONF.157/24 (Part I) (1993), Part I, para 1.

[22] Ibid Part I, para 5.

[23] Commission on Human Rights res. 2200A (xxi) (1966).

[24] UN doc E/CN.4/L.1542 (1978), para 44.

[25] UN doc E/CN.4/1989/48, paras 117–18.

[26] Ibid para 120.

[27] UN doc E/CN.4/L.1575, para 24.

[28] UN doc E/CN.4/1989/WG.1/CRP.1, 14.

[29] UN doc E/CN.4/1989/48, paras 121–2.

[30] Ibid para 119.

[31] Ibid para 123.

[32] *De Chaney* v *Winnebago County Department of Social Services*, 109 S.Ct. 998 (1989).

[33] UN doc E/CN.4/L.1575, para 19.

[34] Ibid para 20.

[35] Ibid paras 25–6.

[36] E/CN.4/L.1575, paras 23–4.

[37] Article 18(1), which is the most important in this respect, provides, *inter alia*, that: 'Parents or, as the case may be, legal guardians, have the primary responsibility for the upbringing and development of the child. The best interests of the child will be their basic concern'.

[38] UN doc A/CONF.157/24 (Part I) (1993), Part I, para 21.

[39] See generally Peter Van Dijk, and G. J. H. Van Hoof, *Theory and Practice of the European Convention on Human Rights*, 2nd ed (Deventer, Kluwer, 1990).

[40] See generally Dominic McGoldrick, *The Human Rights Committee* (Oxford, Clarendon Press, 1991).

[41] Bruno Simma and Philip Alston, 'The Sources of Human Rights Law: Custom, Jus Cogens, General Principles' 12 *Australian Year Book of International Law* (1992), 82–108.

[42] See the articles below by Parker, Eekelaar, and Rubellin-Devichi.

[43] *The Sunday Times Case*, Series A, No 30, para 49.

[44] See Klare, 'Legal Theory and Democratic Reconstruction: Reflections on 1989', 25 *University of British Columbia Law Review* 69 (1991).

[45] Thus according to Mnookin, society in general lacks 'any clear-cut consensus' as to the values which could be used to determine what is best for the child. Moreover, custody statutes provide neither content nor 'relative weights to the pertinent values'. Robert Mnookin, 'Child Custody Adjudication: Judicial Functions in the Face of Indeterminacy', *Law and Contemporary Problems*, Summer 1975, 226 at 260. Chambers takes this criticism even further by suggesting that even if the state did provide such values, its prescriptions would 'mindlessly refer to the majority's (or the judge's) preferences'. David Chambers, 'Rethinking the Substantive Rules for Custody Disputes in Divorce', 83 *Michigan Law Review* (1984), 477 at 491.

[46] Richard Lillich, (ed), *The Family in International Law: Some Emerging Problems* (Virginia, Michie Co, 1981).

[47] R. Joyal, 'The Notion of the Best Interests of the Child: Its Place in the United Nations Convention on the Rights of the Child', paper presented to DCI/ICJ Conference in Siracusa, September 1990, 2; and Katherine O'Donovan, *Family Law Matters* (London, Pluto Press, 1993), 100–5.

[48] One attempt to identify such criteria provides '(i) for children's views to be recognised; (ii) for it to be acknowledged that parents do usually represent those views; and (iii) for parents to be overridden by a court where it can be shown that they are (a) not representing a child's views or (b) representing a child's views which on criteria of maximisation of primary social goods are not in the child's best interests': M. Freeman, *The Rights and Wrongs of Children* (London, Frances Pinter, 1983), 271.

[49] R. Mnookin, *In the Interest of Children: Advocacy, Law Reform and Public Policy* (New York, W. H. Freeman & Co, 1985), 17–8.

[50] Carl Schneider, 'Discretion, Rules and Law: Child Custody and the UMDA's [US Uniform Marriage and Divorce Act, 1974] Best-Interest Standard, 89 *Michigan Law Review* (1991), 2215–98.

[51] See generally: J. G. Merrills, *The Development of International Law by the European Court of Human Rights* (Manchester University Press, 1988), 136–59; A. H. Robertson and J. G. Merrills, *Human Rights in Europe: A Study of the European Convention on Human Rights*, 3rd ed (Manchester University Press, 1993), 195–211; and Mireille Delmas-Marty (trans by C. Chodkiewicz), *The European Convention for the Protection of Human Rights: International Protection versus National Restrictions*, (Dordrecht, Martinus Nijhoff, 1992), 319–41.

[52] Marlee Kline, 'Child Welfare Law, "Best Interests of the Child" Ideology, and First Nations', 30 *Osgoode Hall Law Journal* (1992), 375 at 423.

[53] Laura M. Purdy, *In Their Best Interest?: The Case Against Equal Rights for Children* (Ithaca, Cornell University Press, 1992).

[54] See generally Michael King and Judith Trowell, *Children's Welfare and the Law: The Limits of Legal Intervention* (London, Sage Publication, 1992).

[55] O'Donovan, note 47 supra, 101.

[56] Ibid 100–5.

[57] Onora O'Neill, 'Children's Rights and Children's Lives', in P. Alston, S. Parker and J. Seymour (eds), *Children, Rights and the Law* (Oxford, Oxford University Press, 1992).

[58] See, for example, the emphasis placed upon the elaboration of duties in connection with the implementation of obligations relating to economic, social and cultural rights by G. J. H. van Hoof, in P. Alston and K. Tomasevski (eds), *The Right to Food* (Dordrecht, Martinus Nijhoff, 1984) at 97.

[59] Patrick Atiyah and Robert Summers, *Form and Substance in Anglo-American Law* (Oxford, Clarendon Press, 1987).

THE BEST INTERESTS OF THE CHILD – PRINCIPLES AND PROBLEMS

STEPHEN PARKER*

ABSTRACT

Those who make decisions about children are increasingly required by law to act in the child's best interests. At the same time, best interests standards are regarded as indeterminate, or worse. This article explores the indeterminacy argument and then turns to ways in which, in practice, a degree of predictable operation may still result. It focuses on the role played by localized conventions on values and understandings of the world.

I. INTRODUCTION

Many discussions of children law today refer to the indeterminacy, vagueness or open-endedness of its operating standard; the 'best interests'. or 'welfare' principle.[1] Scepticism about its usefulness seems to have affected the judiciary at the highest level in Australia. A High Court judge said in 1992 'it must be remembered that, in the absence of legal rules or a hierarchy of values, the best interests approach depends upon the value system of the decision-maker. Absent any rule or guideline, that approach simply creates an unexaminable discretion in the repository of the power . . .'.[2] It seems we are faced with an alarming situation. At the same time as the best interests standard is deepening its hold in domestic and international instruments, we hear that it provides a convenient cloak for bias, paternalism and capricious decision-making. Even worse, the open-endedness of the standard can legitimate practices in some cultures which are regarded in other cultures as positively harmful to children.

The purpose of this paper is to explore what it means to say that the best interests approach is indeterminate. This involves an examination of the major factors which make the results of its application unpredictable and which are productive of regional diversity. In the process of identifying the sources of indeterminacy we are also led to consider some matters which actually lead to a degree of *determinate* application.

Although in parts the paper deals with some rather abstract arguments, there is a practical aim to it all. Article 3(1) of the United Nations

*Faculty of Law, Griffith University, Queensland, 4111 Australia.

Convention on the Rights of the Child ('the Convention') seems to place a best interests standard at the heart of international children's rights law. In all matters not governed by positive rights in the Convention, article 3(1) will be the basis for evaluating the laws and practices of the States Parties. An understanding of the indeterminacy arguments helps us to know what can be expected from it. If, for example, the best interests standard is in truth a hollow concept then it provides no yard-stick by which a States Party's laws or practices can be criticized. The whole matter becomes a language game. If, on the other hand, we can understand the processes whereby content is given to the concept, we might glimpse also some moderately firm ground from which to praise or criticize.

I begin, in the next section, by cautioning against the assumption that there is only one best interests standard in currency. I suggest that the differences in formulation can be significant. I then go on to deal with two theoretical frameworks which highlight problems of indeter-minacy in the best interests approach. Lastly, I reverse the direction of the argument by suggesting that conventions (with a small 'c') are constructed by communities of rule users which can reduce uncertainties of application to a considerable extent. By understanding the role of these conventions, we may also understand how it is that quite divergent decisions with regard to children are made in different cultures all of which are plausibly justified by the best interests standard. The point of this is not to produce an analytical model which vindicates cultural relativism. On the contrary, if the international human rights movement is searching for positions from which it can criticize cultural relativism, it will be helped by a clearer sense of the different conventions which can supply meaning to the best interests standard. In this way, the argument focuses on the merits of the conventions themselves.

II.   BEST INTERESTS STANDARDS

The standard which normally applies in guardianship, custody and access matters in Western legal systems requires the best interests of the child to be the *paramount* consideration in any decision. As it appears in Australia, for example, in all proceedings in relation to the custody, guardianship, welfare of, or access to, a child, the court must regard the welfare of the child as the paramount consideration.[3] A weaker formulation of the best interests principle can be found in English adop-tion law. Section 6 of the Adoption Act 1976 provides that in reaching any decision relating to the adoption of a child, a court or adoption agency shall have regard to all the circumstances, *first* consideration being given to the need to safeguard and promote the welfare of the child throughout her or his childhood. A further weakening of the formu-lation is represented in Article 3(1) of the Convention:

In all actions concerning children, whether undertaken by public or private
social welfare institutions, courts of law, administrative authorities or legislative
bodies, the best interests of the child shall be a primary consideration.

The text of article 3(1) has been considered closely by Philip Alston in
this volume. I only need to emphasize that whilst the article binds a
broader group of decision-makers than typically do the stronger formulations, the best interests of the child are only 'a primary' consideration.
Clearly 'a' is weaker than 'the' and, arguably, 'primary' is weaker than
'paramount'.

Finally, the weakest formulation of all before the matter becomes one
of purely utilitarian calculation at large, is that the child's best interests
shall be a consideration. In the Australian Family Law Act, for example,
a set of principles applies to those courts exercising jurisdiction under
the Act. The courts 'shall . . . have regard to . . . the need to protect
the rights of children and to promote their welfare', inter alia.[4] The
requirement to 'have regard' to the child's welfare says only that welfare
is a necessary consideration. In the Family Law Act, this weak version
of the principle is displaced by ones of more specific application – for
example by the paramountcy version in custody decisions – but it can
operate in a residual range of decisions affecting children.[5]

The differences between these formulations are fairly obvious, but the
implications of the differences are not always so apparent. The role of
the child seems to change with successively weaker formulations. In the
paramountcy version, the attention is on the individual child, and that
child is the object of distribution. By the time one arrives at the version
in article 3(1) the context may be quite different. First, it is not clear
whether children *as a class* are intended to be the beneficiaries, or children individually. Note how the article begins by referring to 'all actions
concerning children' (in the plural) but ends with the requirement that
'the best interests of the child' (in the singular) be the primary consideration. It is hard to see how, practically, the article can have anything
other than a collective focus. Although courts of law often make
decisions about individual children, the other decision-makers embraced
by the article (public and private social welfare institutions, administrative authorities and legislative bodies) often make decisions about groups
of children. Resource allocation in education is a good example. Azer
in this volume refers to the difficult decision whether the school day
should be shortened so that scarce resources in Egypt can be used to
give more children some education, or whether it should be maintained
or lengthened so that the children who are actually in the education
system derive more benefit. If article 3(1) is given the same individualistic focus as the paramountcy formulation in family law, it will be of
no use in choices such as this.

The second difference in the typical operation of article 3(1), when
contrasted with the paramountcy formulation, is that groups of children

are as likely to be claimants *for* a distribution, in competition with other groups of children or with adults, as the object *of* distribution. This is significant because, amongst other reasons, conceptions of justice will be different. In the typical custody case there will be concerns about procedural fairness and, albeit less openly, the strengths of parental claims. In the typical decision covered by article 3(1), there will be concerns about distributive justice; about the moral arguments for a distribution to one group over another. One theme of this paper, as will be seen below, is that justice considerations are important components of conventions as to what a best interests standard is to mean. To grasp this, however, we must realize that there are various standards in operation and they call upon different justice considerations.

III. BEST INTERESTS STANDARDS AND INDETERMINACY

As I mentioned in the Introduction, there are two approaches, or pathways, which can drive home the indeterminacy of best interests standards. The first involves concentrating on what it means to make a rational choice in the first place. We look at the version put forward by Jon Elster, who openly draws upon Mnookin's earlier work.[6] The implication of this approach is that if people cannot practically make a rational choice about how a rule should be applied then outcomes will be widely divergent; either because, objectively, some decisions are made more rationally than others,[7] or because two or more decisions can equally plausibly be argued to be rational. The second approach, based in rule-scepticism, raises doubts about the ability of any rule to constrain outcomes.

Indeterminacy and Rational Choice.

According to rational choice theory, in any decision problem a determinate answer will in general require that the following knowledge conditions are satisfied:[8]

1. All the options must be known;
2. All the possible outcomes of each option must be known;
3. The probabilities of each possible outcome occurring must be known; and
4. The value to be attached to each outcome must be known.

It follows that objectively identical problems will be decided differently (ignoring coincidence) if the decision-makers have different knowledges *at any of the above stages*. The *italicized* words are important because the usual reason given for the indeterminacy of the best interests principle is based on 4 alone: ie, 'everything depends on one's values'. In fact, decisions on apparently similar facts by the same decision-maker, or by two decision-makers with similar values, may diverge because of matters in 1 to 3.

Even in a custody decision where, let us say, the only two feasible options (ie 1 above) are that the mother or the father will win, and even where the best interests of the child are the paramount consideration, not some weaker standard, it seems practically impossible to satisfy *all four* of these conditions in modern times.

First of all, the range of possible outcomes for the child are a matter of pure speculation, even if the world stood still throughout the child's minority.[9] Child custody cases involve the imprecise exercise of appraising peoples' characters and dispositions and then trying to work out how each possible decision might affect them and thus indirectly the child.

Next, even if two decision-makers happened to come up with the same range of possible outcomes,[10] they would then need to assign some probability to each outcome occurring. Finally, there is the problem of attaching a *value* to all of the possible outcomes (as weighted by the probability of them occurring). This is the most commonly given objection to the best interests principle and we need spend little time on it. An extended quotation from Mnookin suffices:[11]

> For many decisions in an individualistic society, one asks the person affected what he wants. Applying this notion to custody cases, the child could be asked to specify those values or even to choose. In some cases, especially those involving divorce, the child's preference is sought and given weight. But to make the child responsible for the choice may jeopardize his future relationship with the other parent. And we often lack confidence that the child has the capacity and the maturity appropriately to determine his own utility.
>
> Moreover, whether or not the judge looks to the child for some guidance, there remains the question whether best interests should be viewed from a long-term or a short-term perspective. The conditions that make a person happy at age seven to ten may have adverse consequences at age thirty. Should the judge ask himself (sic) what decision will make the child happiest in the next year? Or at thirty? Or at seventy? Should the judge decide by thinking about what decision the child as an adult looking back would have wanted made? In this case, the preference problem is formidable, for how is the judge to compare 'happiness' at one age with 'happiness' at another age.
>
> Deciding what is best for a child poses a question no less ultimate than the purposes and values of life itself. Should the judge be primarily concerned with the child's happiness? Or with the child's spiritual and religious training? Should the judge be concerned with the economic 'productivity' of the child when he grows up? Are the primary values of life in warm, interpersonal relationships, or in discipline and self-sacrifice? Is stability and security for a child more desirable than intellectual stimulation? These questions could be elaborated endlessly. And yet, where is the judge to look for the set of values that should inform the choice of what is best for the child? Normally, the custody statutes do not themselves give content or relative weights to the pertinent values. And if the judge looks to society at large, he finds neither a clear consensus as to the best child rearing strategies nor an appropriate hierarchy of ultimate values.

Rational choice theory is a useful device for pointing up the unlikelihood of two or more decision-makers coming to the same decision in identical circumstances. This seems to assume, however, that decision-makers are attempting to be rational choosers within the meaning of the theory, which is a major assumption, and quite possibly draws on an ethnocentric conception of rationality. The analysis seems also to rest on a belief that determinate decision-making is at least sometimes possible. Fundamentally, the indeterminacy debate in child custody law has relied upon the possibility of there *being* a rule that a decision-maker must act in a child's best interests: it has just stressed the computational problems that good faith decision makers face in applying it.

There are some, however, who doubt whether determinate rules can ever be said to exist. We need to burrow more deeply into this strongly sceptical position, partly as a way of appreciating further the problems there are with best interests principles, but partly also to move the discussion into ways in which indeterminacy is sometimes contained.[12] This second approach can be called the rule scepticism pathway.

Indeterminacy and Rule-scepticism.

Western legal scholars in the 1980s were introduced (or reintroduced) to certain forms of scepticism about their craft by the so-called Critical Legal Studies Movement ('CLS'). Perhaps the one claim on which CLS exponents agree is that law is indeterminate. Ironically, however, there is considerable disagreement over the meaning of the word 'indeterminacy' itself.[13] Sometimes the claim of indeterminacy is made in relation to selected individual rules,[14] whilst at other times it appears as a general conclusion about legal reasoning.[15] In its extreme form, the thesis amounts to the claim that legal doctrine is *never* able to provide a determinate answer with respect to any given fact situation.[16]

Adherents to a strong indeterminacy thesis have not been well-equipped to defend themselves against arguments from easy cases. That is, we all seem to know that there are some rules which can transparently be applied in a correct manner. Walking one's dog does not offend against competition laws. To put it differently, the adherents to a strong indeterminacy thesis have not been able to rebut the counter-argument that some legal rules are at worst only ever *under*determinate. Because one can say that some situations clearly fall outside a rule, when faced with a case where one situation does not fall outside it and all others do, the rule *is* capable of producing a uniquely correct answer.

What CLS has lacked is a theory about rules themselves. Such a theory may have existed throughout the time of CLS's heyday, although few members seemed aware of it. The philosopher Saul Kripke claims to have discovered an argument in Wittgenstein's *Philosophical Investigations* which has as its conclusion a profound scepticism about the existence of rules.[17] Although Wittgenstein and Kripke discuss mathematical rules, exactly the same argument applies to other kinds of rules such as rules of language.

Kripke's argument is simple enough to state. Imagine that I have not previously computed 68 + 57 but I do so now and obtain the answer 125. I am confident, says Kripke, that I have understood the plus function and that this example illustrates the fact. Along comes a sceptic and claims that I have misunderstood my own previous linguistic usage of the plus function and that I meant to give the answer 5. All that my past computations show, says the sceptic, is that I was deluded and was actually using something called the 'quus' rule, under which the correct answer is 5.

An obvious reply is to say something about the rules of arithmetic and the fact that plus means that function which gives me the answer 125! But the sceptic is not satisfied. She says that while you may *now* be talking about a new present usage of plus, in the past you meant 'quus'. After all, says the sceptic, what is it in the past that you have done that makes you so sure that it is the plus rule you dealt with? The fact that you have in the past carried out a series of computations does not establish anything, since any finite mathematical series can be used to support an indefinite number of rules or functions. The next number in the sequence '3, 6, 9, 12, . . .' is any number at all. If you want the answer to be 16 you can say that the rule was to jump by three until you reach 12 and then jump by 4.

The central point which Kripke's sceptic hammers home is that a statement of a rule like the plus rule can only be supported by a finite number of examples, and yet those examples are consistent with any number of rules, such as the quus rule. I am no more justified in picking the plus rule than the quus rule in a statement of which rule I can be said to be following by virtue of my past computations. There is no point in my furiously pointing to my past computations, such as '1 + 1 = 2, 2 + 2 = 4' and so on, for the sceptic will reply: 'Yes, and you were right under the quus rule to respond in that way, but now the quus rule requires you to say that 68 + 57 = 5 and you are not doing it. I might respond by counting out heaps of marbles and say that a heap of 68 and 57 equals 125. This does not help, for Kripke's sceptic simply says that by count I really meant 'quont' and now I should have a heap of 5 marbles in front of me. There is, in other words, no point in relying on *other* rules to support the plus interpretation since all rules are infected by the same problem; namely a reliance on a finite number of examples.

This, then, is the sceptical paradox. When I respond in one way rather than another to such a problem as '68 + 57', I can have no justification for one response rather than another. Since the sceptic who supposes that I meant quus cannot be answered, there is no fact about me that distinguishes between my meaning plus and my meaning quus.

Indeed, there is no fact about me that distinguishes between my meaning a definite function by plus (which determines my responses in new cases) and my meaning nothing at all.[18]

The consequences of this argument, if valid,[19] are shattering. Rules turn out to be no more than leaps in the dark and the whole notion of rule-following seems illusory. The apparent ability to communicate by language seems to lack any basis. *A fortiori*, the ability to express desired outcomes in legal rules is in doubt. Not surprisingly, Kripke does not leave the argument there and goes on to discuss a possible solution to what he calls this 'insane and intolerable' sceptical problem,[20] a solution which (he says) continues to be derived from Wittgenstein. The solution, Kripke says, starts by acknowledging that the sceptic's claims are unanswerable but that there is simply no *need* to provide the justification sought by the sceptic. The solution involves merely accepting that the practice of rule following is a matter of brute agreement.

IV.   BEST INTERESTS AND THE *REDUCTION* OF INDETERMINACY

Kripke's solution has been refashioned by the philosopher Phillip Pettit in a way that makes it more helpful. Pettit's approach to the sceptical dilemma is to focus on the capacity of previous *examples* to exemplify uniquely a rule for rule followers. While a set of examples potentially instantiates an infinite number of rules, that set may 'for a particular agent . . . exemplify just one rule'.[21] Examples, therefore, can produce an inclination in a rule follower, whether or not she is aware of the inclination or the process that led to it. The rule user may only be aware of seeing that one type of rule-governed response is appropriate in a given situation.

Crucially important in this strategy is the relationship between rules and inclinations. An account of this relationship has to avoid saying that rule-governed responses *always* match inclinations because that would make it impossible for rule followers to make mistakes in rule following. To allow for the possibility of human fallibility in rule-following, Pettit proposes the following *a posteriori* relationship between rules and inclinations:[22]

What other way is there for a rule to relate to my inclination? It can only relate as that which fits my inclination but only so far as certain favourable conditions are fulfilled: in particular favourable conditions such that I can discover that in some cases they are not fulfilled, and that I got the rule wrong.

This account of the relationship allows rule users to say that in certain cases they made a mistake in the application of some rule, because the particular response was not given as part of the usual or normal conditions of the inclination, but was rather influenced by some perturbing factor such as tiredness, drunkenness, lack of concentration and so on. As a result, the link that normally exists between inclination and rule is uncoupled and a 'mistake' is made.

An important consequence of arguing that inclinations select certain rules is that rule following becomes a highly interactive enterprise.[23] The reason for this lies in the qualification that the rule is selected *under normal conditions of operation*. In order to know what constitutes normal conditions we have to interact with *other* users of the rule.

Law is, in many respects, a paradigmatic example of the interactive nature of rule following. By virtue of their training within some given legal tradition, the court process, their allegiance to notions of precedent, hierarchy and authority, lawyers are continually confronted by the interactive nature of rule following. Yet this feature of rule following in law is often only subliminally perceived, or even completely displaced by a belief that legal rules are primarily a product of logical analysis and the grasping of objective meaning. This belief, captured and tagged either as formalism or conceptualism, has been rightly criticized but the deeper problem with formalism lies not so much in the inadequacy or inherent limitations of its rules of inference. It lies rather in the way it obscures the communal nature of the enterprise of rule following and decision-making within a given legal system.

Peter Drahos and I have argued elsewhere that the product of interactions amongst the legal community as to how legal rules should be applied in new situations can be called 'conventions'.[24] Because they function as part of the normal conditions of operation for other rules, conventions can be distinguished from those rules by the positional value they have in a given system of rules. They operate on other rules to produce stability of meaning and can only be understood as part of a system of interconnected rules.

Within legal systems, conventions help their users develop domains of understanding which makes those users internal participants within the system and provide the foundation stone for authority and influence within the system. A person who has mere rule *knowledge* stripped of the conventions which regulate it is more likely to be judged incompetent or deviant.

This response to Kripkean scepticism may seem comforting for those who want to believe that it is possible to apply law in a predictable fashion, but the comfort may be illusory. Using Pettit's formulation, previous examples can only be taken as instantiating the meaning of a rule if one shares an understanding of what 'normal conditions' are, and if one assumes that normal conditions were operating then and now. Particularly in contexts where a fine-grained analysis of the situation seems to be called for, such as where a decision needs to be made as to what is in a child's best interests, the scope for agreement on what are normal conditions is very narrow.

Moreover, it is clear that inter-subjective understandings about the applicability of previous examples may be highly localized, temporally specific and precarious. We can confine ourselves to the best interests principle to make this clearer. Assume a time in the West when adultery by a woman was regarded as highly immoral and disruptive to social stability. It could then plausibly be said that it was not in a child's best interests to live with her (at least where the alternative was to live with someone less blameworthy). After all, the child might not learn the value of personal restraint or the importance of social conformity.

To take another example, assume two custody disputes in different countries where the genetic make-up, characters, dispositions and abilities of all the relevant parties are identical in all material respects. Assume also that the decision-makers in each case attach the same value to individual happiness and believe that happiness is attained by maximizing a person's innate talents. Suppose, however, that the difference between the two cases lies in the wider societies in which they feature. In the first case, the life expectancy of a child is much shorter and the only opportunities likely to be available to the child do not require extensive preparation. In the second case, the life expectancy is greater and the opportunities are there, provided an investment of time and money is made in the child's education. The two cases might well be decided differently. In the first case, attention to short-term happiness would be warranted, and training a child beyond the opportunities available to her might only cause unhappiness through frustration. In the second, deferred gratification might be warranted because of the long-term gains. The difference between the two decision-*makers* is in their assumption as to what are normal conditions for the operation of the best interests principle.

If one relaxes the assumptions in the previous example then the scope for different results increases markedly. Suppose in the one case there is a strong political attachment to family autonomy and a restricted State. This is highly likely to operate as a formative condition in the construction of conventions as to how the best interests principle is to work. It may, for example, act to confine the pool of possibilities, so that the best interests principle then works upon a narrower set of possible outcomes. Parents might be favoured as against non-parents, even though no court is willing to say that there is a legal presumption in favour of parents. In another society where state intervention in the family is not treated with such suspicion, however, the pool of possibilities might be wider.

To make things simpler, I have so far contrasted examples across different societies. There is, of course, no need to do this. Within the same society there might be quite different assumptions about what being a boy and what being a girl means. An outcome for one might self-evidently be regarded as an inappropriate outcome for the other.

We can now begin to draw things together before moving on to related matters. We have seen two pathways, or chains of reasoning, which can lead us to conclusions about the indeterminacy of the best interests principle. The rational choice pathway emphasizes computational difficulties. Given the steps which rational choice theory requires, it is unlikely that anyone can say with justified confidence which outcome is in a child's best interests and it is quite likely that two decision-makers will reasonably come to different conclusions. In the passage quoted earlier, Mnookin says that deciding what is best for a child poses a question no less ultimate than the purposes and values of life itself. The second pathway, grounded in rule-scepticism, suggests that deciding whether the best interests principle even exists *as a rule* poses a question no less ultimate than the possibilities of co-ordinated and predictable human activity. The meaning of the words which make up the principle, and the meaning conveyed by the combination of words in it, are dependent upon inter-subjective agreements that are changeable in themselves and dependent on shared understandings of the normal conditions for their operation. We might be confident that if 68 + 57 had never been computed before, the answer 125 would still be given within a community of rule-users because of the strength of their conventions. Where the rules are not those of mathematics, however, but rules with highly general imputs, one could never be so confident.

In the discussion so far, the subject of values has been prominent. In the Mnookin/Elster pathway, it is value diversity which makes the fourth step in a rational choice so hard to take. In the sceptical pathway, value diversity can impede the construction of conventions as to how the rule should operate. In the West at least, this century has seen a collapse in consensus over certain kinds of values to do with conformism and individuality, material success and personal contentment, gender differentiation and so on. The gradual abandonment by judges of even rules of thumb as guidance in the application of the best interests principle in family law can be interpreted as an honest response to the collapse of a hierarchy of values in their own community.

One group of values, which does not exhaust the field but which is likely always to be important in law-governed decisions, are justice values.

V.   BEST INTERESTS AND JUSTICE

It was mentioned above that in the paradigmatic custody case, where the paramountcy principle typically applies, the child (or at least the child's time) can be seen as the object of distribution. To that extent, questions of distributive justice[25] are raised, as Elster shows,[26] even though the decision-maker may be more conscious of procedural justice issues. In the *weaker* formulation of the principle as it appears in Article

3(1), however, the decision-maker is concerned with how *other* goods (such as money, health care, education) are distributed *between children and between children and others*. Principles of distributive justice then become more central.[27] Some reference to a few of the basic positions on distributive justice underscores how widely divergent distributions can all plausibly be justified by reference to childrens' best interests.

As a way of finding our bearings, imagine to begin with that there is no best interests principle or any other criterion for making a decision about children. The starting point would presumably have to be equality because there is no basis for favouring one person's claims over those of another. So, in a standard custody dispute everyone with an interest in the outcome would have their claims considered equally. Without more, one might as well draw lots or resort to some other random means of selection. In reality, of course, working principles of distributive justice would quickly emerge. For example, parents' claims might ordinarily be given greater weight than non-parents'. One parent's claim might ordinarily be given greater weight than the other's. The parent who has done more for the child in the past might be favoured. The parent who needs the child more might be favoured. Or the parent who can best safeguard the child's welfare might be favoured.

If the context was not a custody dispute, but how some other resource should be distributed across the population or a group of it, again the default position would be one of equality. Children would not have stronger claims simply because they are children. Again, however, some working principles would emerge. Older people might be favoured in some kinds of distributions because they have contributed more. Some groups might receive more or less because their gender, race or social class is thought to give them more or less entitlement. Or distributions could be on the basis of need, future contributions to society and so on.

Each of these working principles might be traceable back, in a rough and ready way, to one of three broader kinds of theory about justice based in *welfare, fairness* or *rights*.[28] If, for example, the central idea was to increase the sum of human happiness, one would look first to some version of utilitarianism, although that does not exhaust the varieties of welfare consequentialist theories. If the central idea was to carry out a more complex exercise of balancing needs with possible gains, one might look first to a theory of justice rooted in substantive fairness.[29] If the central idea was to protect 'the family' from outside interference, or to shore up the position of men, or women, or a particular social group then one would look to a rights-based theory for justification.

Returning to the present world we *do*, of course, have some criteria to apply in cases concerning children. The strongest formulation of the best interests principle (ie the paramountcy standard) does not permit utilitarian calculation at large because, under the classical utilitarian approach, each is to count as one and no more than one. At most, the paramountcy standard is consistent with a restricted utilitarian approach. The justification for it might be that in order to maximize the welfare of a society over time, one should give greater weight to children's welfare.[30] The weaker the best interests standard, however, then the weaker are the prohibitions on general utilitarian calculation.

Elster has suggested that in local justice situations – ie, where distributions are being made by professional people locally rather than by central authorities – actual allocations can virtually never be reduced to a single criterion or mechanism[31] and that common sense conceptions of justice which mingle notions of welfare, fairness and rights are actually put into operation. For example, in Anglo-Australian family law, custody cases are in practice initially conditioned by ideas of rights and family autonomy. To appreciate this, imagine a place where it were not so. Imagine that those on the waiting list to adopt a child, in despair as to their prospects, wrote to the divorce court and asked to be considered as custodians in the next case where a young baby was the object of a dispute. In support, they say that they could promote the welfare of a child who was given to them at a young age better than some parents could. They argue that the paramountcy principle not only permits this, but actually *requires* the court to consider every option that is put before it.

My guess is that no court in a Western country[32] would compile the list or give equal consideration to the claims of people on it as compared with the claims of parents.[33] The reason is not simply because it might be unconstitutional or a breach of the Convention, but because it would threaten to unravel common assumptions about the family. No parent could feel secure because it would always be possible that a stranger would come along and demonstrate that they could do a better job.

We can also speculate that, contrary to what the Family Court of Australia has said,[34] there are cases where welfare considerations are evenly balanced, or almost so, and where other factors have to be invoked to tip it. These factors might, for example, be presumptions in favour of a mother, or individual calculations as to who would suffer most from not being awarded custody.

As one moves away from the standard custody case, so that a weaker formulation of the best interests principle applies, there is greater scope for the *explicit* invocation of justice considerations. Article 3(1) of the Convention, for example, only requires that the child's best interests be *a* primary consideration. Once that consideration is lodged firmly in the decision-maker's mind, some further resource must be drawn upon in order to arrive at a decision. For example, if the choice is between building a school or sheltered housing for old people then a deserts-based argument might be invoked in favour of the latter. They have contributed to society all their lives and deserve now to be looked after. If the choice is between different categories of children, such as between

medical resources to children with very rare illnesses or to general vac-
cination programmes different local theories of justice could tend one
way or another.

The point of all this is that, whilst some of the basic justice arguments
can be isolated and catered for, it is impossible to predict the precise
local formulation that will be applied to the case. As one moves away
from a strong best interests standard, prediction becomes progressively
harder. As with my discussion of rule indeterminacy above, however,
all hope of certainty need not be abandoned. There is no reason why
local, or even national, conventions on distributive issues should not
exist to provide some guidance. Even if they do not determine the exact
result, they may well operate to confine the pool of possible results. For
example, one might be able to say that no decision-maker in a particular
situation would apply ruthlessly one theory where the result strikingly
violates another theory.[35]

VI. CONCLUSION

I have used justice as a particular kind of value in order to make a
broader point. It is a variable which can lead to different interpretations
and applications of a best interests standard. I have drawn on two
frameworks, one based in rational choice and the other in rule scepticism, to demonstrate that the leeway of choice is inevitably there. In a
longer paper, many other variables could be developed, some of which
I have touched on. For example, although value diversity is the most
commonly given reason for the indeterminacy of the best interests standard, a more obvious illustration lies in differences about how the world
is, rather than how it ought to be. If one believes that there are spirits
in the world which will be offended by one arrangement rather than
another (as to which see Armstrong and Belembaogo in this volume)
then this belief will become part of the background understanding of
the best interests of the child. It will form part of the local convention
as to how a best interests standard should be operated. Alternatively,
if one takes a particular view about what the self is and how it develops,
then this will contribute to a particular local convention.

These arguments, despite some appearances to the contrary, are
designed to inject a note of realism into discussion about best interests
principles. Such standards are neither wholly useful nor wholly useless.
Their meanings, and the likelihood of any single meaning being adopted
by a decision-maker, can depend in large part on localized understandings or conventions. If any of the framers of article 3(1) expected more
of the best interests standard then they were mistaken. On the other
hand, the decision to *use* such a standard was not necessarily misguided
either. If sufficient attention is given to the many ways in which divergent interpretations can be arrived at, then debate can centre on each

of the variables. Most members of the human rights community would agree that both cultural domination and cultural relativism should be avoided in any pure forms. It would be wrong to assume that a wholly Western interpretation of the best interests of the child is necessarily preferable. It would be wrong also to assume that there is no basis at all for preferring one interpretation to another. It is suggested that by continuing to work away at the causes and cures of indeterminacy, we will have a clearer sight of what is at stake.

NOTES

[1] The inspiration for many critiques is Robert Mnookin's 'Child-Custody Adjudication: Judicial Functions in the Face of Indeterminacy' 39 *Law and Contemporary Problems* 226 (1975), referred to below. For other discussions, see M. L. Fineman, and A. Opie, 'The Uses of Social Science Data in Legal Policymaking: Custody Determinations at Divorce' *Wisconsin LR* 107 (1987); S. S. Berns, 'Living Under the Shadow of Rousseau: The Role of Gender Ideologies in Custody and Access Decisions' 10 *U. Tasmania LR* 233 (1991); A. G. LeFrancois, 'Children's Representation in Custody Litigation in America and Australia' 6 *Law in Context* 1 (1988) and A. Charlow, 'Awarding Custody: The Best Interests of the Child and Other Fictions' 5 *Yale Law and Policy Review* 267 (1987).

[2] Brennan, J in *Secretary, Dept of Health and Community Services,* v *JWB and SMB* FLC 92–3 at 79,191 (1992).

[3] Family Law Act 1975, s 64(1)(a). In England and Wales, the child's welfare is the court's paramount consideration in determining any question with respect to the upbringing of a child or the administration of a child's property or the application of any income arising from it; see Children Act 1989, s 1(1). For the New Zealand formulation, see Guardianship Act 1968, s 23, which follows the previous English version that the welfare of the child is the 'first and paramount' consideration.

[4] Section 43(c).

[5] The power is contained in s 66W of the Act and no criteria for its exercise are given.

[6] See *Solomonic Judgements: Studies in the Limitations of Rationality* (Cambridge, Cambridge UP, 1989) and Mnookin, above n 1.

[7] Using 'rationally' in the sense of attaining the standard of rationality embodied in the theory itself. It should be noted that Elster and Mnookin have different purposes, although similar lines of reasoning. Elster is concerned to show that the *costs* of trying to make rational choices are such that it can actually be more 'rational' not to embark upon the exercise at all. The costs thus saved might be devoted to improving the lot of children generally.

[8] This particular list is slightly adapted from Elster, *Solomonic Judgements*, above n 6, 134. A similar formulation can be found in R. H. Mnookin (ed) *In the Interest of Children,* (Freeman & Co, 1985) 2.

[9] In other words, I am referring to outcomes stemming only from the particular relationship that the child would have with the mother or the father in either outcome.

[10] Perhaps because they each adopt the reasonable strategy of acknowledging that they cannot tell the future and will therefore only work with a small number of factors which they know are likely to apply.

[11] *Law and Contemporary Problems,* above, 60.

[12] What follows is drawn from work I have done jointly with Peter Drahos. In particular, it is taken from P. Drahos and S. Parker 'The Indeterminacy Paradox in Law' 21 *U. Western Australia LR* 305 (1991) and 'Rule Following, Rule Scepticism and Indeterminacy in Law: A Conventional Account' *Ratio Juris* 109 (1992). I acknowledge Peter Drahos's major contribution.

[13] See W. J. Singer, 'The Player and the Cards: Nihilism and Legal Theory' 94 *Yale LJ* 10 (1984).

[14] G. A. Spann, 'Deconstructing the Legislative Veto' 68 *Minnesota* LR 473.

[15] D. Kennedy, 'Legal Formality' 2 *Journal of Legal Studies* 351.

[16] C. Dalton, 'An Essay in the Deconstruction of Contract Doctrine' 94 *Yale LJ* 999 (1986).

[17] S. Kripke, Wittgenstein on Rules and Private Language (Oxford, Blackwell, 1982).

[18] Kripke, above n 17, 21.

[19] Wittgensteinian followers are by no means united on whether Wittgenstein's own work can bear it: see G. P. Baker, and P. M. S. Hacker, *Scepticism, Rules and Language* (Blackwell, 1984).

[20] Kripke, above n 17, 60.

[21] Pettit, P. 'The Reality of Rule Following' (1990) *Mind* 9.

[22] Pettit, above n 21, 12.

[23] Pettit, above n 21, 17.

[24] In *Ratio Juris*, above n 12.

[25] I am being somewhat cavalier with this term. I mean only the justice issues which arise when distributions are in question. I appreciate that within political philosophy 'distributive justice' is often associated with a particular set of thinkers, such as Rawls; see T. Campbell, *Justice*, (Macmillan, 1988) ch 1.

[26] *Solomonic Judgements*, above n 12.

[27] I make no claim as to *how* prominent these considerations are. Officials with resources to distribute may be motivated by personal gain, unauthorized bias and so on.

[28] See J. Elster, *Local Justice: How Institutions Allocate Scarce Goods and Necessary Burdens* (Russell Sage, 1992), ch 6.

[29] Although some versions of utilitarianism would also be hospitable.

[30] I recognize the argument that promoting children's welfare is a matter of fundamental *rights* and not utility at all. Eekelaar has argued, convincingly I think, that there is something contradictory in the statement that a person has a right to have welfare done to them by others. My own position is that a restrictive form of utilitarianism is congenial to the idea of positive rights, but not to the idea of there being *fundamental* ones; see S. Parker, 'Child Support: Rights and Consequences' in P. Alston, S. Parker and J. Seymour, *Children, Rights and the Law*, (Oxford, Clarendon Press, 1992) 148.

[31] *Local Justice*, above n 28, 103.

[32] I confine my remark to Western countries simply because I do not know about others.

[33] Note the views expressed in the English Department of Health and Social Security report, *Review of Child Care Law* (HMSO, 1985) para 2.13 where the Committee noted that '[t]aken to its logical conclusion, a simple "best interests" test would permit the state to intervene whenever it could show that the alternative arrangements proposed would serve the children's welfare better than those proposed by their parents'. The Committee went on to say that 'it is important in a free society to maintain the rich diversity of lifestyles which is secured by permitting families a large measure of autonomy in the way in which they bring up their children'.

[34] See, for example, the decision of the Full Court in *Smythe* v *Smythe* (1983) FLC 91–336 at 78,287 where it was said that when 'matters are said to weight evenly in the balance all that has occurred is that the Court has not yet determined which of the factors of most relevance to welfare should be given pre-eminence over the others'.

[35] As Elster notes in *Local Justice*, above n 28, 149, 'the idea of differences in national character has a bad name' but '. . . most people nevertheless believe that national value differences are substantial and important'. Conventions on distributive issues might be far more localized than the nation state. An experienced lawyer or lobbyist may well be able to say with justified confidence that a particular court will not decide a case in a certain way or a local government will not make an allocation in a certain way, even though in a neighbouring town or city quite different predictions would be appropriate.

THE INTERESTS OF THE CHILD AND THE CHILD'S WISHES: THE ROLE OF DYNAMIC SELF-DETERMINISM

JOHN EEKELAAR*

ABSTRACT

The principal purpose of this paper is to explain how acting towards children with the objective of furthering their best interests may be reconciled with treating children as possessors of rights. The two bases for action require reconciliation if the argument is accepted that a right that another should have complete power to determine what is in A's interests and to direct A accordingly leaves A without any rights at all. The paper argues that the reconciliation can be effected through an understanding of the best interests principle which allows scope for the child to determine what those interests are: this is labelled 'dynamic self-determinism'. It is an account of what the best interests of the child means. Since most of the discussion of the 'principle' in Western legal literature occurs in the context of court decisions about children's upbringing, this discussion, too, is centred in that context. But the argument has implications which go beyond that context, and the final part of the paper considers briefly the implications of the concept within the framework of the UN Convention on the Rights of the Child.

I. INTRODUCTION

The principal purpose of this paper is to explain how acting towards children with the objective of furthering their best interests (which the UN Convention on the Rights of the Child says must be 'a primary consideration' in 'all actions concerning children') may be reconciled with treating children as possessors of rights (which the UN Convention clearly thinks they are). The two bases for action require reconciliation if the argument is accepted that a right that another should have com-

* Pembroke College, Oxford OX1 1DW, UK.

I acknowledge my debt to observations made by those who attended a Special Workshop at the Centre for Socio-Legal Studies, Wolfson College, Oxford, at which a summary of the first version of this paper was given. I am especially grateful to Dr David Jones, of the Park Hospital for Children, Oxford; Dr Helen Dent, of the Department of Psychology, University of Birmingham; Dr Danya Glaser, of the Bloomfield Clinic, London; Ms Donna Dickenson of the Open University and Ms Judith Timms, Director of Independent Representation for Children in Need (IRCHIN). I also record my appreciation for observations by other participants in the UNICEF project on the 'best interests' principle.

plete power to determine what is in my interests and to direct me accordingly leaves me without any rights at all.[1] The paper argues that the reconciliation can be effected through an understanding of the best interests principle (which, for convenience, I shall refer to as the 'principle') which allows scope for the child to determine what those interests are: this is labelled 'dynamic self-determinism'. This concept is not simply an application of the policy that, in applying the 'principle', decision-makers should, as Article 12 of the Convention requires, afford the child the right to express his or her views. Nor is it, at least, directly, a normative proposal of a course of action. Rather, the intention is to provide an account of what the 'best interests of the child' means.

Since most of the discussion of the 'principle' in western legal literature occurs in the context of court decisions about children's upbringing, this discussion, too, is centred in that context. But the argument has implications which go beyond that context, and the final part of the paper considers briefly the implications of the concept within the framework of the UN Convention on the Rights of the Child.

II.   MINORITY AS A STATUS

Western liberalism is very reluctant to confer the power on people in authority to use coercive means to *require* adults to act in certain ways simply because the authorities believe those actions to be in *those adults'* best interests (as distinct, say, from the general good of the community).[2] It is not my intention to explore that issue, however, but rather to start this paper by noting that, whatever view may be taken about paternalism towards adults, the central feature which traditionally marks minority as a legal status is that adults have a generalized legal power (exercisable either by parents or by legal authorities) to impose a course of action on minors on the basis of their assessment of the minors' best interests. No other individuals are normally subjected to this liability except in special circumstances (perhaps mental illness, or unconsciousness). We should, therefore, take a closer look at the status of minority in the common law.

In his monograph, *Status in the Common Law*, Ronald Graveson[3] described the origins of legal status as being a means of preserving the existing social order. 'Individual social progress', he wrote, 'took the form of rising to the top of one's own status rather than that of trying to climb to a higher place in the social scale'. This was as true for the status of infancy as for other statuses. Graveson noted that a guardian's interest in his ward was material, as was an employer's interest in his servants, which Graveson observed was based on the master's 'pecuniary right in the maintenance of a beneficial status',[4] illustrated by the availability of an action against anyone who should entice them from him. Such an action was also available to a father with respect to his children, although Graveson did not mention it.

Why did Graveson fail further to explore the nature of the parent-child status-relationship despite his recognition that a *guardian* had a material interest in his ward? After all, a father was the 'natural' guardian of his legitimate children. The answer might be lie in his perception of the status of infancy: 'Behind the legal status stands public policy, and there exists a strong social interest in the nurture and welfare of infants'. Infants, he averred, are 'special favourites of law and equity'. Graveson, it seems, conceived the status of infancy as (apparently always) grounded in the law's special solicitude for the well-being of children. How quickly we forget! In 1765 Blackstone explained the legal disabilities of married women as being 'for the most part intended for her protection and benefit. So great a favourite is the female sex of the laws of England.'[5] Dicey regarded this statement with amused contempt,[6] and even Graveson admitted that the status of the married woman followed that of 'guardianship', and 'the recognized feature' of guardianship 'was one of profit to the guardian'.[7]

In the case of the status of infancy, Graveson seems to have succumbed to the fatal bond that can arise between (imagined) protectionism and subjugation revealed by Blackstone's apologia for the legal status of married women at common law. But it is not proposed to engage in an historical investigation of the extent to which the law subordinated children's interests to those of their parents, or guardians. I have touched on this briefly elsewhere.[8] The point to be made is the simple one that the historical record shows that assertions that action is taken in the interests of women and children is consistent with an identification of those interests with those of others. Perhaps the clearest examples in the case of children are the nineteenth century cases in which fathers' rights to the custody of their legitimate children, as against those of their wives, was justified on the basis of the children's best interests.[9]

The point is hardly a novel one, however. It is well known that political oppressors (such as the architects of *apartheid* in South Africa) have been prepared to justify the rightlessness of the oppressed on the grounds that such deprivation is in their (the oppressed's) best interests. Nor is this necessarily conscious hypocrisy. The psychological pull to avoid guilt is strong and the general virtues of social stability loom all the larger when the social structure treats you kindly. In the case of young minors, of course, their incomplete personal development demands that decisions be taken on their behalf. The 'principle' therefore appears as a humane and natural guide. It is found in probably most family law systems throughout the world.[10] Yet legal philosophers have thought,[11] and the United Nations has proclaimed, that children have rights. An acceptable conception of the status of minority in modern conditions can only be achieved through a reconciliation between the 'principle' and children's rights.

III.   SOME CRITICISMS OF THE 'BEST INTERESTS' PRINCIPLE

Such a reconciliation must start by examining the 'principle' itself. The seminal article, from which modern critiques of the 'principle' draw inspiration, is that of Robert Mnookin in 1975.[12] Mnookin drew attention, first, to the 'indeterminacy' of the 'principle' (which he treats equivalently to the alternative formulation of the 'least detrimental alternative'). He argued that predictions of the effects of present dispositions on the future of children were necessarily speculative in the present state of knowledge and, even if they were not, there was no consensus in the values inherent in choosing between outcomes. These defects made the 'principle' inappropriate as a basis for child *protection* law, since 'the use of an indeterminate standard is inconsistent with the proper allocation of responsibility between the family and the state.'[13] This conclusion is predicated on the liberal perception of the relationship between state and citizen whereby state interventions in citizens' lives should be as far as possible clearly defined (so as to limit state power) and predictable. In this case, the objection would be that the allocation would make *parents* too vulnerable to unpredictable and largely unchallengeable[14] impingements on their upbringing of their children.[15]

In the sphere of private law, Mnookin suggested two 'intermediate' rules which could partially replace the 'principle'. One was that no action should be taken which would pose an immediate and substantial threat to the child's physical health and the other that, in disputes between parents, the court should prefer the adult 'who has a psychological relationship with the child from the child's perspective'. Subject to these, natural parents should be preferred to strangers in blood. However, these would not dispose of all cases, and for the remainder the 'principle' was the 'least detrimental' guide to apply.

Since Mnookin's article, many others have added their critiques of the 'principle'. The United States literature is reviewed by Carl Schneider[16] and Stephen Parker makes a further analysis in this collection[17] Parker draws attention to the fact that even the following of *rules* depends on accepted conventions, while Schneider concludes that the indeterminacy of the 'principle' is reduced in practice because its application is strongly influenced by community standards. Martha Fineman[18] has complained that the 'principle' has allowed the values of the 'helping' professions to capture the decision-process in child placement cases, to the detriment of women's interests, while Michael King and Christine Piper[19] have advanced the contrary position that the determinations of children's best interests reached by those professions are corrupted by their 're-construction' in the legal arena. It seems unlikely that perceptions of children's best interests can remain uncoloured by notions of justice, and Parker examines the important relationship between the 'principle' and conceptions of justice, which this paper will also touch on later.

Mnookin's critique, as we have seen, worries about the incompatability between the indeterminacy of the 'principle' as a decision standard and the role of the law in restraining official behaviour and predicting decision outcomes, although Parker observes that such concerns may also be present even in the case of rule-guided decision-making. But my focus is different from these arguments within liberalism, which are mostly about the relationships between adults and legal authorities. It is on the way in which perceptions about the best interests of children are reached and applied and, in particular, the extent (if at all) that they are distinguished from other interests. For example, it has been suggested that American legislation concerning the placement of tribal Indians reflects a model whose premise is 'that the existence of the subgroup essentially operates to the child's detriment unless the child is firmly anchored in the framework of the subgroup itself. On this analysis, the interests of the child and those of the group are symbiotic. Here the preservation of of the group identity in and of itself advances the child's interests'[20] Fineman appears to provide another example. The rule allocating a child after divorce to the custody of the 'primary caretaker' is justified in terms of 'rewarding' the time devoted to child care by the primary caretaker. There would be no 'speculation' about the emotional bonding of the child: it would be 'assumed' that this existed with the primary caretaker.

IV. A RECONSTRUCTION OF THE 'BEST INTERESTS' PRINCIPLE

I will now attempt to rebuild a concept of the 'principle' in such a way as to reveal the extent to which is may be reconcilable with treating children a rightholders. The first step is to imagine what the decision-making process would be like if the 'principle' were completely removed. Decisions about children could be made without reference of any kind to their 'interests'. The first value of the 'principle' is, then, that it injects a set of issues into the decision-making process which is independent of other concerns. But, as we have seen, perceptions and evaluations of these issues are ambiguous and unstable. We need to analyse how this set of issues may be approached. I will suggest that perceptions of a child's best interests may be formed in accordance with two distinct methods which I call *objectivization* and *dynamic self-determinism*.

(a) Objectivization

By this method the decision-maker draws on beliefs which indicate conditions which are deemed to be in the child's interests. The beliefs might derive from the claims of welfare professionals confident in their predictive capabilities, such as the influence exercised by Goldstein, Freud and Solnit towards the view that contact with an absent parent, unless approved by the caregiving parent, would be damaging to children,[21] or the (related) view, now attenuated, that disruption of attachment at an early stage of bonding would have serious deleterious effects.[22] More often, the decision-maker relies on his or her social beliefs. The law reports are replete with examples. It has been deemed to be in a child's interests to grow up in a 'normal' family (as distinct, say, from a lesbian household),[23] that a baby is better off with its mother than a father with a nanny;[24] that it is better for a boy to grow up with a father who is an 'honest hard-working and conscientious citizen' than in a home with his mother and a step-father with a criminal record;[25] that it was harmful for a girl to withdraw from the intellectual and social training provided by school.[26]

These perceptions of children's interests presuppose various states of affairs the experience of which are thought to have beneficial or adverse results for the child. The 'principle' therefore makes implicit reference to (1) *consequences* which are believed to follow from the experience (or non-experience) of the state of affairs and (2) the preferability of those consequences to *different* consequences which would follow from their experience (or non-experience). Orthodox modes of evidence and calculation of probablities may be used in making these judgements. Reasonable deductions about the consequences of non-attendance at school (especially when not accompanied by an alternative socialization process) may be drawn, and reasons for believing these consequences will cause disadvantage in the long term can be advanced. Conversely, evidence might be produced that upbringing in a lesbian household is *unlikely* to have the consequences claimed by unsubstantiated prediction,[27] or even that the school system is having adverse consequences for a particular child or group of children.[28]

One should not therefore lightly dismiss the possibility of making objective assessments of children's interests. But their reliability is difficult to determine. First, they depend on a large measure of consensus over values. Second, even where such consensus exists, the range of social experience which may follow from a specific determination can be very diverse and the personality of children, and its interaction with social experience, is variable. It is therefore necessary to introduce a second element into the decision-making process.

(b) Dynamic Self-Determinism

The additional element is 'dynamic self-determinism'. This severely blurs the normally sharply focused conclusions of an objectivized determination. Instead, the child is placed in an environment which is reasonably secure, but which exposes it to a wide range of influences. As the child develops, it is encouraged to draw on these influences in such a way that the child itself contributes to the outcome. The very fact that the outcome has been, at least partly, determined by the child is taken to demonstrate that the outcome is in the child's best interests. The process is dynamic because it appreciates that the optimal course for a child cannot always be mapped out at the time of decision, and may need to be revised as the child grows up. It involves self-determinism because the child itself is given scope to influence the outcomes.

A characteristic feature of this strategy is that initial dispositions may often not be determinative. The court decrees no *final* outcome, a feature to which Fineman[29] objects on the grounds that it damages the interests of the caregiving parent. Instead, the directions in which the child's relationships may move are left open-ended. A welfare professional may be positioned to monitor changes in the family dynamics and to assess the receptiveness of the child to possible developments. Examples are now appearing in the English reported cases[30] and an instance was recently reported from the Netherlands[31]. The movement to greater openness in adoption, now occurring in the United Kingdom, is part of this trend. On the issue of post-adoption contact, an Interdepartmental Working Group Consultation Paper observed.[32]

It should be up to the agency to work with the child, parents and relatives, and prospective adoptive parents to work out arrangements for contact and, if necessary, for the court to confirm these arrangements. The child's wishes and feelings as regards contact may in any case change quite significantly as he or she grows up: the child may come to feel overwhelming commitment to his or her new family and draw back from contact; or he or she may decide several years after placement to seek contact with a relative for the first time.

Another example is the growth in the belief that children should, where possible, maintain contact with the absent parent after parental separation, or that the possibility of such contact should be kept alive. These attitudes reflect greater sensitivity to the ongoing character of family dynamics and an appreciation that, on parental separation, children are at risk of losing contact not only with one parent, but the possibilities opened out through interaction with that parent's kin network. Martin Richards, a developmental psychologist has gone as far as to suggest that where parents separate it should be a rule that children are placed with the parent most likely to allow the children good contact with the absent parent.[33] Within child protection law, the policy of the Children Act 1989 to discourage coercive intervention and the increased emphasis placed on *reviews* when such intervention occurs are further examples.

As applied in some of the cases, this approach may put considerable strain on resources. But that will only be so in the most conflicted of cases, where the costs are high in any case, and more open-ended solutions may simply displace costs from the court process to welfare budgets. More importantly, these solutions may find their way into the informal settlements reached between parents. The recent large-scale study by Maccoby and Mnookin[34] illustrated that there was a good deal of adjustment in arrangements regarding children and separated parents while the children grew up.

V.   DYNAMIC SELF-DETERMINISM: AN ANALYSIS

(a) Related ideas

Although the above discussion identified the emergence of dynamic self-determinism within the specific legal context of court determinations over children's upbringing, the concept is loosely related to a variety of social, political and pyschological theories. One of these is the subjectivism to be found in the social philosophy of Friedrich von Hayek.[35] Like the critics of the 'principle', Hayek considered social phenomena to be of such complexity and our knowledge so limited, that prediction, at least by collective social reformers, is impossible. One conclusion from this was that an individual should be guided in his actions by those immediate consequences which he can know of and influence rather than by what is thought appropriate 'by somebody else who is supposed to possess a fuller comprehension of the significance of these actions to society as a whole'[36] (or, one might add, to the individual concerned).

But more direct influences must have come from strong strands in developmental theory. In 1960, Anthony Storr summed up what he then took to be the common aims of the different schools of psychotherapy to be the 'self-realization' of the individual, by which he meant: 'to be oneself, to realize one's own personality to its fullest extent.'[37] This reflects the 'humanistic psychology' of Abraham Maslow and Carl Rogers, who saw the self-actualizing process occurring throughout an individual's lifetime. Reviewing the relationship between these psychologists and developmental theorists, like Arnold Gesell and Maria Montesorri, Crain observed:

According to Gesell and others, children, filling their own inner schedule and timing, are eminently wise regarding what they need and can do. So, instead of trying to make children conform to our own set of schedules and directions, we can let them guide us and make their own choices – as Maslow proposed.[38]

He continued:

Developmental theorists. like the modern humanistic psychologists, have tried to uncover instrinsic growth factors that stand apart from pressures toward social conformity.

Chess and Thomas adopt a related view in their claim that optimal development results from a 'good fit' between a child's 'temperamental' disposition and the environmental demands placed upon the child; and that where there is dissonance between them, maladaptive functioning may occur.[39]

Dynamic self-determinism may also be described in terms of the form of liberalism advocated by Joseph Raz. Although Raz's is a political theory, it has similarities with the psychological theory of identity of E. H. Erikson, and the relationship between the two will be explored later. Raz sees virtue in the value of autonomy which is the condition which allows each individual to determine his or her goals or life-plan.[40] One ground for embracing this form of individualism is that various life-goals are incommensurable. There is no necessarily 'best', or even 'better', choice between certain life-goals (being a lawyer or being a musician; a mother or a nun), just as there may not be any way of determining the best or better interests of a child by comparing one possible outcome against another.[41] The value for the individual lies *in the individual's embracing whichever goal is chosen, and the way the goal is embraced*. So, just as (for Raz) the task of political community is to ensure a reasonably wide range of available goals to be chosen, and to create conditions for choices to be made, so dynamic self-determinism extends the range of possible outcomes for children and enhances their capability of choosing between them.

(b) Objections to Dynamic Self-Determinism

The concept of dynamic self-determinism, as applied to children, can be further elucidated through consideration of objections that might be made to it. One variant, the self-determination of peoples, may have led to overthrowing the colonial yoke; but in its place may have come other social divisions and economic collapse. Yet another variant, individual self-fulfilment, may be one cause of the growth of family instability, leading to liberation from domestic constrictions, but also to economic and emotional impoverishment. Can this idea be safe for children?

The objections break down into the following types: (i) self-determinism implies *licence*; (ii) self-determinism privileges *impulse*; (iii) self-determinism is *self-destructive*.

(i) Self-determinism implies licence

The reply to this objection is that self-determinism is not a *moral* theory in the sense that a moral theory dictates or guides how people should behave towards one another. Nor is it a variant of that form of utilitarianism which holds that the greatest good is to be attained by satisfying, as far as possible, every individual's wants.[42] It is only a way of discovering what is good for an individual, not how that individual should behave to others. A child's 'goods' cannot be bought at any cost, and without regard to the rights and interests of others.[43]

But, conversely, appreciation that children are to be socialized within society's moral framework should not result in annihilation of any scope for self-development by children. The contribution of dynamic self-determinism lies in the creation of *space* for such self-development. A perception of which *totally identifies children's well-being with acting in conformity with an existing moral code* effectively treats children as objects and is inconsistent with viewing them as rightholders. This exposition cannot produce a formula according to which a 'balance' between self-determinism and the imposition of a moral code should be struck. Probably none could be found. Yet consciousness that such a balance must always be found is probably enough to ensure that dynamic self-determinism will be permitted to play a realistic (ie, not trivial or merely formalistic) role in determinations of children's best interests.

(ii) Self-determinism privileges impulse

The fear that dynamic self-determinism favours impulsive, or egoistic, conduct, which is damaging to the individual as well as others, is met in two ways. The first involves an examination of what impulsive conduct may mean in this context. The second places an important external constraint on dynamic self-determinism, especially in the case of children.

(a) Raz argues that if one has goals, or desires, one has reasons for them: and, if the reasons are mistaken, 'one does not wish merely not to have mistaken desires; one also does not wish to have them satisfied'[44] He makes the same point about goals.[45] Put perhaps over-simply: your immediately felt desires may lead you astray from goals which you know you have, the achievement of which constitutes your ultimate well-being. So, if we can identify some of our desires as 'mistakes', we are protected against impulse: following such desires is not true self-determinism.

Raz's rationalistic and schematic presentation relating desires to goals may be useful for adults, who might be able to articulate or rationalize their ultimate goals and introspect their well-being. But such self-analysis is bound to be more difficult for a younger person. The reason may be found in Erikson's analysis of identity formation. Adolescents, he thought, were in the process of establishing their identity, which, when achieved, comprised a perception of the *continuity* and *unity* of the self. The process is for most people a gradual and unconscious synthesis of experience and selection, but three types of deviation might occur. The individual might impose a 'moratorium', delaying identity achievement; there might be 'foreclosure', where the individual fixes on a premature identity dictated from some authority figure; or there might be 'diffusion', where the individual drifts between identities[46] During such times, how is an individual to know if the satisfaction of a desire is a mistake? The position is even harder for younger children. The experience of child psychiatrists requires distinctions to be made between

verbal expressions of wishes and deeper 'feelings'. A young child's statements may be momentarily influenced by a specific context. Where
articulation is unreliable and self-identity incomplete, can the individual's 'true' self be reliably identified? How is it possible to speak of
self-determinism?

Those are ultimately philosophical questions which need not be
addressed here because dynamic self-determinism is a practical process.
It demands an unravelling of the child or young person's presenting
attitude so that *what seems important to the individual* can be separated from
the merely incidental or transitory. For it is precisely in the exploration
of matters that are of importance to the individual that identity can be
built up and the individual enabled to piece together his or her self-
portrait: to know what his or her goals may be.

(b) Raz identifies another constituent of goals which at first sight
might seem to pose considerable problems to applying self-determinism
to young people. He argues that an individual's goals can only be
achieved through socially defined activities, which he calls 'social
forms'.[47] The implications of this are that, even for adults, autonomy
does not *simply* mean the impulsive satisfaction of wants experienced in
the abstract; for the ultimate goals of humans are embedded in social
life. Social activity can both expand and restrict our goals. Quite apart
from any external restraints which should be imposed on our conduct
on moral grounds, this shows that recognition of the demands of social
interaction are necessary for our individual well-being. An adult will
have experienced the interaction between 'social forms' and his or her
aspirations, and in this way settled on ultimate goals. A child will have
had little such experience.

This factor must be a severe qualification on any claim that a child's
wants should, without more, be satisfied. But dynamic self-determinism
does not make that claim. The child is, as it were, 'fed into' a shifting
social matrix. Its wants must be viewed against that matrix and, if
unrealistic, modified. A primary role of parenting is, indeed, to mediate
between the developing personality of the child and the social world.
Decision-making for children can therefore be characterized as reconciling children's wants (viewed cautiously, as explained above) with the
actual and prospective social relationships surrounding them.

(iii) Self-determinism is self-destructive

The final objection to self-determinism is that children's decisions may
be contrary to their own interests. As Coady has pointed out, desires
and interests do not necessarily coincide.[48] But nor do reflected life-goals
necessarily coincide with a person's interests, unless it were to be stipu-
lated that achievement of life-goals *must* by definition be in a person's
interests. Raz, however, uses 'self-interest' in a narrower sense, as representing an individual's biologically determined needs: essentially,

physical well-being (including longevity). So promoting one's well-being, following one's goals, is not necessarily equivalent to promoting one's self-interest. It may be your life-goal to risk health or life in exploration, war service or helping others, in which case you are risking your self-interest (as perceived by Raz) for the sake of your goals. This helpful perception allows us to see that the satisfaction of perfectly admirable desires can threaten one's self-interest as much as less acceptable ones (like taking certain drugs).

How does dynamic self-determinism for children cope with this? A variety of solutions could be adopted. The most satisfactory is to say that if the child's self-interest, in Raz's sense, would be threatened by following self-determinism, it should be simply disapplied. The rationale for such a restriction is that the *purpose* of dynamic self-determinism is to bring a child to the threshold of adulthood with the maximum opportunities to form and pursue life-goals which reflect as closely as possible an autonomous choice. Life and, on the whole, health are essential preconditions for the exercise of such choice. But here I wish to add an element to Raz's perception of self-interest. It may extend to matters of the mind. Mental illness, utter ignorance and the fear born of oppression may all frustrate the capacity to pursue goals as much as biological deprivations. As in the case of the constraint of a community's morality, it is not possible to provide a sharply focused formula for drawing a line objectively between such narrow self-interest and wider interests. Essentially, self-interest refers to the capacity to formulate and achieve any goals at all. The significance of dynamic self-determinism lies in its ability to open up perceptions that such lines can be drawn at all.

VI. DYNAMIC SELF-DETERMINISM AND THE CHILD AS DECISION-MAKER

(a) Dynamic Self-Determinism does not imply Delegation of Decision-making to Children

The preceding analysis of dynamic self-determinism should make it clear that the concept is far from a recommendation that decision-making concerning children should simply be delegated to children themselves. Nevertheless, children do seem to be playing a more important role in decisions concerning their upbringing, at least in the United Kingdom,[49] and practitioners have observed a tendency for some disputing parents to ask courts to turn to the children for a decision. There are, however, many objections to setting up children as decision-makers in cases in which they are involved.

Such children will be vulnerable to pressure from the disputing adults to decide in their favour; they risk being burdened with the guilt of an adverse outcome, and the hostility of the adult against whom they decide. There are also formidable practical problems in interpreting the child's decision. Assuming the child is capable of deciding at all, the decision may be affected by the quality of the information provided and the subjective biases of the provider. The articulation of a decision by children may be influenced not only by age, but also by how they think the decision will be received, whether they think it is likely to be accepted, whether they have made promises about what they should or should not say, whether they have support from a friend or sibling, where the interview occurs and how it is conducted. An even more serious problem arises, more usually in child protection cases, where it is difficult to convey to a child the nature of the alternatives available.

It is, however, essential to understand that dynamic self-determinism does not stipulate that decisions should simply be delegated to the child. For one thing, unless the child is competent (to be discussed below), there can be no *question* of the child's opinion being determinative. But more importantly, the method does not primarily seek to elicit *decisions* from children. Nor does it primarily seek the child's *views*, insofar as this implies a balanced evaluation of the whole situation,[50] though if a child wishes to offer such an opinion, it should surely be listened to.[51] Rather, it aims to establish the most propitious environment for the child further to develop the personality growing within him or her and in this way to fashion the outcome. It is for the adults to decide what that environment might be, and their responsibility to seek to realize it.

The child's wishes, if articulated, are likely to be a significant factor in the adults' decision. But in view of the complexity of self-determinism and the problems involved in interpreting such wishes, statements made by children to judges or lawyers may often not be reliable bases for grounding a decision based on dynamic self-determinism. A *guardian ad litem* or court welfare officer, interviewing a child, is in a better position to structure an environment in which the child's competence and personality can be assessed. Applying dynamic self-determinism, this assessment should include their interpretation of the child's expressed wishes (if any), their stability and their consistency with the process of self-realization occurring within the child.[52]

(b) Legal Competence

It is important to relate dynamic self-determinism to the question of legal competence. A legally 'competent' child can enter transactions for which his or her competence equips him or her and control (by consenting or witholding consent) another person's dealings with him or her within the area of the competence. For example, the English Children Act 1989 states that when an Emergency Protection Order contains a direction as to the medical or psychiatric examination or assessment of a child, the child may, 'if he is of sufficient understanding to make an informed decision, refuse to submit to the examination or other assessment'.[53] More generally, Lord Scarman, in the *Gillick* case,[54] said that a parent's right to determine whether or not a child will have medical treatment terminates 'if and when the child achieves a sufficient understanding and intelligence to enable him or her to understand fully what is proposed' which includes the 'maturity to understand what is involved'. This may well extend beyond medical treatment. Subsequentally, however, and very controversially, Lord Donaldson and Balcombe LJ have expressed the opinion that this does not apply to *refusals* to consent to treatment.[55]

The English courts have, however, taken the view that when they make a decision concerning a child's upbringing governed by section 1 of the Children Act 1989, they are bound to make it on the basis of their assessment of the child's best interests, whether or not the child is legally competent in the issue.[56] They must have regard to the child's wishes but need not address the question of the child's competence because those wishes are not necessarily determinative. But in other contexts, the child's wishes may be determinative if the child is 'competent'.

When, then, is a child 'competent'? It is important to try to fill out Lord Scarman's references to 'intelligence', 'understanding' and 'maturity'. Raz provides a guide, but not a complete one. His concern is not, of course, with legal competence but with what he considers to be the constituents of a fully autonomous decision. Yet the analysis provides a useful structure for a view of competence. For Raz, an autonomous decision is one wherein the desires chosen to be followed are consistent with (and intentionally so, not by accident) the individual's ultimate goals. Furthermore, the goals in which the desires are realized must be achievable within attainable social forms. Finally, a decision may be autonomous even if inconsistent with the decision-taker's self-interest.

The requirement that an autonomous decision must be achievable within the social forms is helpful in constructing a concept of legal competence for children. Children's decisions may be incompetent because whatever goal they aspire to may simply be unrealistic, at least at present. We may express this element of competence thus: a child's wish or aspiration will not be competently expressed if it could not be realistically implemented or if its realization is extremely improbable in the time frame contemplated by the child. Social realization requires knowledge and prediction of the behaviour of other social actors and also that of the child and therefore comprises primarily cognitive ability. It falls to adults to make these assessments. It may be that those occasions where adults seem to be saying that their assessment of a child's maturity (competence) depends on the degree to which the child's views coincide with their own evaluation of the child's best interests are often those where they think that the child's preference *is* consistent with social reality.[57] So in one case a judge agreed with a nine-year old girl's objections to going to live in France with her mother in these terms:

It seems to me that the view she has put forward, looking at the whole circumstances of her life, is a mature and rational view which seems to be based on genuine and cogent reasons. I would go further and say that I think it is probably in her best interests . . . in deciding whether the views are mature, if they coincide with what seems to me to be the best interests of the child, I am entitled to take that into account in assessing her maturity.[58]

For reasons already given, the requirement that the wish or decision be reconcilable with the individual's life-goals raises much harder problems in the case of children. Following Erikson's theory of identity formation, it will be usual for such life-goals to be unsettled during the formatory period. Nevertheless, competence should not be denied for that reason alone. But serious deviations within the process, whether through 'foreclosure' or 'diffusion', could inhibit the achievement of competence. Similarly, some children's feelings, such as those expressed through personal attachments, might be seriously unstable especially if they are disturbed or traumatized. We might say that a decision is incompetent if it reflects a feeling or aspiration which is so seriously unstable or where there is such grave disjunction between it and others held by the individual that to give effect to the decision risks serious conflict within the individual at a later stage of development. It is necessary to stress the degree of seriousness which should be present because, as has been explained, there will usually be some degree of instability and incoherence during the process of identity formation. In the case of certain pathological conditions, where the individual is consistent and (within his or her own terms) coherent, but the behaviour reflects a severely deviant view of reality, incompetence may lie in the degree of disjuncture between the child's perceptions and social reality, including the effects of the behaviour on the child, as explained earlier.[59]

It may be argued that, even if a child has a coherent desire/goal which is socially realizable, competence should be denied on the ground that the decision is really that of (say) a parent and not of the child. This was one basis upon which Ward J, ordered the blood transfusion for a fifteen-year-old Jehovah's Witness in *re E*.[60] Because he had been brought up in a strict religious household, the young person was, the judge said, 'not fully free'. Yet, as Raz observes, 'the completely autonomous person is an impossibility'.[61] From the point of view of political theory, Raz confines the ambit of coercion to cases where A intentionally causes B to act (or refrain from acting) otherwise than he would have done due to fear of adverse consequences in circumstances where A's behaviour is wrong and provides B with an excuse for so acting (or refraining from acting). Such coercion if applied to a child would render its decision incompetent, but the case arguably does not cover the circumstances of *re E*, because it is not socially unacceptable for parents to inculcate their children with a religious belief which is tolerated among adults. If one is to hold a person incompetent because his decision reflects socially tolerated values ingrained in his upbringing, competence could hardly ever be achieved by anyone.

Those, then, seem to be the main determinants of legal competence for children. If a child is found to be competent on this basis, acceptance of dynamic self-determinism implies that the child's decision should determine the outcome, subject to two constraints. The first is, of course, its compatability with the general law and the interests of others. The second might be more controversial. It is conceivable that a child might competently take a decision which is contrary to his or her *self-interest*, as narrowly defined, above, in terms of physical or mental well-being and integrity. It was suggested there that dynamic self-determinism should be disapplied where this interest was threatened. One can imagine that a legal system might decline to recognize decisions of competent children in the same circumstances, although it might require special procedures (for example, application to a court, except in emergency situations) for overriding them.

VII.   WIDER ISSUES

The UN Convention on the Rights of the Child proclaims a series of rights which children have. It also proclaims the 'principle' as a 'primary consideration' in all actions concerning children. The 'principle' can operate as an interpretive device in the application of the 'rights' and also as a residual standard in areas unaffected by express rights. In arguing that the element of dynamic self-determinism in the conception of the 'principle' is subject to various constraints, in particular the constraint of social morality, I do not mean to suggest that those elements of children's interests which are explicitly enshrined as rights within the Convention must be subordinated to such morality. Such rights can be viewed as objective determinations by the international community of what children's interests are. One would expect them to protect children's *self*-interests (as understood above), though they can cover wider ground. But the Convention is not cast in iron, and societies and ideas change. The background principle of the best interests of the child provides a passage by which such changes can be accommodated within the framework of rights established by the Convention.

However, as can be seen from the other contributions to this collection, conceptions of children's best interests are strongly rooted in the self-images of world cultures. These objectivizations of children's interests will inevitably largely constitute the way the 'principle' is viewed in those cultures. But the introduction of dynamic self-determinism has something important to add. It is not equivalent to collective self-determination. It appeals directly to *each individual child within each culture* and demands that such a child, as it develops, be allowed space *within the culture* to find its own mode of fulfilment. This may imply adjustments to that culture, though the extent to which this can or should be achieved through the 'principle' cannot be laid down with precision. But it is essential that a dialogue should take place within the culture about the scope to be given to self-determinism. Where it is given little or no scope, the adults take of a heavy responsibility for imposing a replication of their own order on the succeeding generation.

In contrast to dynamic self-determinism, objectivisation is often a process of crude generalization of how children's well-being will nor-mallity be realized within the society in which they will live, founded on a global view of socialization or the demands of organizational necessity. The view, for example, that education, effected through compulsory school attendance, will self-evidently promote their well-being may be seen as such a generalization. It would be impossible to consider the attitudes of each child towards school attendance and to determine, in each case, what kind of socialization would give the fullest expression to the emergent life goals of the child. Compulsory school attendance will do this reasonably well for most children. However, the insensitive operation of such a generalization does carry the danger of damaging individual children, or groups of children, and a good education system must be responsive to this. The greatest danger of objectivization is, however, that it can be a vehicle for the furtherance of the interests or ideologies of others, not of the interests of children.

But objectivization is inevitable and necessary. It operates most appropriately in the protection of children's self-interest, in which case dynamic self-determinism may in any case not apply. The two modes should operate in parallel. Dynamic self-determinism proceeds from a sceptical attitude which narrows the scope of the determinitive force of objective assessments of children's interests made at one point of time but intended to project into the future. Decisions tend to be more tentative and open-ended. The presumption is that the best response to whatever issue has arisen may lie within the child, even though the child may need direction to an accommodation with the social world surrounding it, rather than in a manipulation of that social world to which the child is left to respond. Self-determinism is a mode of optimally positioning children to develop their own perceptions of their well-being as they enter adulthood: not of foreclosing on the potential for such development. Perceived in this way, the best interests principle is not a threat to children's rights, but becomes a mode of enhancing them.

NOTES

[1] John Eekelaar, 'The Importance of thinking that Children have Rights' (1992) 6 *International Journal of Law and the Family* 221.

[2] The most influential contemporary exposition of this ideology, classically expressed by J. S. Mill, is probably found in H. L. A. Hart, *Law, Liberty and Morality* (Oxford University Press, 1965).

[3] R. H. Graveson, *Status in the Common Law* (London, 1953); see especially 13–14.

[4] Above, n 3, 14.

[5] Blackstone, *Commentaries on the Laws of England*, vol 1, 445.

[6] A. V. Dicey, *Law and Opinion in England in the Nineteenth Century*, 375.

[7] Above, n 3, at 21.

[8] John Eekelaar, 'The Emergence of Children's Rights' (1986) 6 *Oxford Journal of Legal Studies* 161.

[9] See especially the discussion by Susan Maidment, *Child Custody and Divorce* (1984). For a similar view about the position in Japan, see Yukiko Matsishima in *Annual Survey of Family Law 1990*, 32 *Journal of Family Law* at 351 (1991).

[10] Extensive examples would be tedious. A few are: Argentina (Civil Code of 1985): see Cecilia P. Grosman in *Annual Survey of Family Law 1990*, 32 *Journal of Family Law* at 250 (1991); the Netherlands: see P. Vlaardingerbroek, 'The rights of Parents and Children in the Netherlands: Seeking a New Balance' in J. Eekelaar and P. Sarcevic (eds), *Parenthood in Modern Society: Legal and Social Issues for the Twenty-First Century* (1993), ch 31; Switzerland: see Oliver Guillod, *Annual Survey of Family Law 1989*, 31 *Journal of Family Law* at 450 (1990). It is a central pillar of the Children Act 1989 (England and Wales): see section 1(1) of the Act.

[11] For a full discussion see P. Alston, S. Parker and J. Seymour (eds), *Children, Rights and the Law* (1992).

[12] R. H. Mnookin, 'Child-Custody Adjudication: Judicial Functions in the Face of Indeterminacy' (1975) 39 *Law & Contemporary Problems* 226.

[13] Id 268.

[14] The difficulty of challenging a decision based on the 'best interests' principle is illustrated in *G* v *G*, [1985] 2 All ER 225 (HL).

[15] This view was taken in the reform of English child care law which led to the Children Act 1989.

[16] Carl E. Schneider, 'Discretion, Rules and Law: Child-Custody Decisions and the Best Interest Standard' in K. Hawkins (ed), *The Uses of Discretion* (1993).

[17] Stephen Parker, at 26 in this volume.

[18] Martha Fineman, 'Dominant Discourse, Professional Language and Legal Change in Child Custody Decision-making' (1988) 101 *Harvard Law Rev.* 727.

[19] Michael King and Christine Piper, *How the Law thinks about Children* (1990).

[20] David S. Rosettenstein, 'Custody Disputes involving Tribal Indians in the United States: A Case Study of the Problems Inherent in Custody Adjudications involving Non-Isolated Semi-Autonomous Population Sub-Groups', chapter 40 in J. Eekelaar and P. Sarčevic (eds), *Parenthood in Modern Society: Legal and Social Issues for the Twenty-First Century* (1993).

[21] J. Goldstein, A. Freud and A. J. Solnit, *Beyond the Best Interests of the Child* (1975); for a fuller discussion of professionals' views, see Judith Masson, 'Contacts between Parents and Children in Long-Term Care: an Unresolved Dispute' (1990) 4 *International Journal of Law & the Family* 97.

[22] See John Bowlby, *Child Care and the Growth of Love* (2nd edn, Penguin, 1965); *Attachment and Loss: vol 1: Attachment* (The Hogarth Press, 1969). Compare Michael Rutter, *Maternal Deprivation Re-assessed* (Penguin, 1972).

[23] *C* v *C* [1991] 1 FLR 223

[24] *Re W (a minor) (residence order)* [1992] 2 FLR 332

[25] *Re G (a minor) (custody)* [1992] 2 FCR 279

[26] *Re O (a minor) (care order: education: procedure)* [1992] 4 All ER 905.

[27] As indeed occurred in *B* v *B* [1991] 1 FLR 402, where, unlike the court in *C* v *C* (above, n 23) the judge had the benefit of evidence of an expert in the effects of homosexual parentage and consequently came to a conclusion different from that in the earlier case.

[28] See Adel Nazer at 226 in this volume.

[29] See above, n 18.

[30] In *re B (minors: access)* [1992] 1 FLR 140 children aged twelve and eleven found visits with their socially awkward and uncommunicative father uncomfortable. Nevertheless, the court held they should continue, on a supervised basis four times a year, because this would give them the opportunity of 'gradually understanding' their father and 'perhaps even coming to accept and appreciate (his characteristics) as something of which neither he nor they need feel ashamed'. Similarly, in *re S (minors) (access: religious upbringing)* [1992] 2 FLR 313, where children of thirteen and eleven, living with their athiest mother, indicated they did not wish to retain contact with their devout Roman Catholic father, the Court of Appeal thought it would be wrong for them to

lose all contact with him and that they were too young to 'decide their religion was no longer for them'. They did not *require* contact to be maintained, but gave the father the right at a later date to approach the Official Solicitor who could advise whether, in the light of the children's development, contact should be resumed.

In another case the court was prepared to contemplate the possibility that the father's claim might be kept alive in case circumstances changed. 'Though existing circumstances may demand that his children see or hear nothing of him, and that he should have no influence upon the course of their lives for the time being, their welfare may require that if circumstances change he should be re-introduced as a presence, or at least as an influence, in their lives': *re C (minors: parental rights)* [1992] 1 FLR 1, per Waite J. These developments had been foreshadowed in a remarkable adoption case in 1973 *(re J (a minor) (adoption order: conditions)* [1973] Fam 106) where the court inserted a condition into the adoption order allowing the natural father, at a later date, to approach the Official Solicitor who would decide whether it would be advisable to make contact with the child 'at the right time and in the right manner'. See also *Re R (a minor) (contact)* [1993] 2 FLR 762.

[31] This appears also to be a new development in Dutch law: see Madzy Rood de Boer, 'The Netherlands: New Legal Facts', 31 *Journal of Family Law* 389 at 392.

[32] See Department of Health and Welsh Office, *Review of Adoption Law, Consultation Document* (1992), para 5.3.

[33] Martin Richards, 'Private Worlds and Public Intentions – the Role of the State at Divorce' in A. Bainham and D. Pearl (eds), *Frontiers of Family Law* (Chancery Law Publishing, 1993). Fineman, above no 18, is particularly scathing about such a rule. It seems that Fineman's critique is so rooted in gender conflict that it fails to appreciate that such approaches are designed to fulfil the best interests principle when objectivization fails.

[34] Eleanor Maccoby and Robert H. Mnookin, *The Divided Child* (Harvard, 1992), especially at 169.

[35] For a general account, see Norman P. Barry, *Hayek's Social and Economic Philosophy* (Macmillan, 1979).

[36] F. Hayek, *Individualism and Economic Order* (1946) 14.

[37] Anthony Storr, *The Integrity of the Personality* (Pelican Books, 1960) 26–7.

[38] William C. Crain, *Theories of Development: Concepts and Applications* (Prentice-Hall, 1980), 262. For both Montessori and Piaget, 'true learning is not something that comes from the teacher but something that comes from the child': 98.

[39] S. Chess and A. Thomas, *Origins of Evolution of Behavior Disorders* (NY, Brunner/Mazel, 1984); Laura C. Berk, *Child Development* (Boston, Allyn & Bacon, 1989) 439.

[40] Joseph Raz, *The Morality of Freedom* (1986).

[41] See Raz, *The Morality of Freedom*, ch 13; John Finnis, 'Natural Law and Legal Reasoning' in Robert P. George, *Natural Law Theory* (1992).

[42] See Raz, op cit, 138.

[43] This is an aspect of the 'justice' issues raised by Parker at 36 in this volume.

[44] Raz, op cit, 142.

[45] Op cit, 300.

[46] E. H. Erikson, *Identity: Youth and Crisis* (N. Y. Norton, 1968); Laura E. Berk, *Child Development* (Allyn & Bacon, Boston, 1989) 476.

[47] These include all kinds of social interaction: Raz, op cit, 311.

[48] C. A. J. Coady, 'Theory, Rights and Child: A Comment on Campbell and O'Neill' in P. Alston, S. Parker and J. Seymour (eds) *Children, Rights and the Law* (1992), 48.

[49] See Sally Jones, 'The Ascertainable Wishes and Feelings of the Child' (1992) 2 *Journal of Child Law* 181.

[50] The Scottish Law Commission preferred seeking the child's 'views' to its 'wishes and feelings' precisely for this reason: Scottish Law Commission, *Report on Family Law*, Scot Law Com No 135 (1992). To make a child's views, in this sense, the primary objective could involve eliciting judgements by the child of the merits of the behaviour of others which could be suspect and damaging.

[51] Thus Article 12 of the UN Convention on the Rights of the Child requires States to assure the child who is capable of forming his or her views a right to express those views freely 'in all matters affecting the child'. The Article does not impose a duty to *seek* those views.

[52] Under English procedures, if a local authority brings proceedings for a care order, a *guardian ad litem* is usually appointed for the child and may be represented in court through a lawyer. But if the child is competent to give instructions, and these differ from those of the guardian, the lawyer should take instructions from the child. However, in such circumstances, the guardian may use another lawyer. See *re H. (A Minor) (Care Proceedings: Child's Wishes)* (1993) 23 *Family Law* 200. But

the Court of Appeal has held that, if a *child* who is adjudged competent to instruct a lawyer brings 'family proceedings' in its own right, such as, for example, an application for the court to decide with whom it is to live, the child is entitled to have his or her case presented by the lawyer and the court should not make the child a ward of court simply to bring in a guardian to give an independent assessment of the child's interests: *re T* [1993] 4 All ER 518. But there seems no reason why a court should not, in such a case, ask for a report by a court welfare officer: Children Act 1989, s 7(1). That might be important because, although the court ultimately decides on the child's fitness to give instructions, the lawyer lacks the opportunity fully to contextualize the child's expressed wishes. Courts need to develop consistent practices in applying self-determinism soundly in cases where children are independently represented. See also *re H. (a minor) (role of Official Solicitor)* [1993] 2 FLR 552.

[53] Children Act 1989, s 44(7).

[54] *Gillick v West Norfolk and Wisbech Area Health Authority* [1986] AC 112. I take Lord Scarman's judgement to represent the majority opinion, although this view is not universally accepted.

[55] *Re W (a minor) (medical assessment: court's jurisdiction)* [1992] 3 WLR 758.

[56] *Re W (a minor) (medical assessment: court's jurisdiction)*, above n 55.

[57] See the test, drawn from American law, applied by Weithorn and Campbell in evaluating children's competence in medical decision-making: this required that the choice made by the child to correspond to that which an hypothetical 'reasonable' person might make: Lois A. Weitborn and Susan B. Campbell, 'The Competency of Children and Adults to make Informed Treatment Decisions', (1982) 53 *Child Development* 1589. In their tests fourteen-year-olds performed almost as well as adults, and nine-year-olds did not do much worse.

[58] *S v S (child abduction)* [1992] 2 FLR 31, per Ewbank J. In *re E* [1992] 2 FCR 219 Ward J. ordered a blood transfusion to be carried out against the wishes of a fifteen-year-old Jehovah's Witness. One reason for the decision was that the judge did not believe the child adequately appreciated the suffering he would undergo. We may add such failures to comprehend the consequences of a decision for the child itself (if firmly established) alongside inadequate appreciation of social consequences as grounds for incompetence.

[59] This would be a ground for holding that a girl afflicted by *anorexia nervosa* is incompetent to make certain decisions, as in *re W*, above n 55; or where a child is severely mistaken as to the effects of a course of action on his or her body, as was held to be the case of the fifteen-year-old Jehovah's Witness who refused a blood transfusion in *re E (a minor) (wardship: medical treatment)* [1992] 2 FLR 219.

[60] See above n 59.

[61] Op cit, 155.

CULTURAL TRANSFORMATION AND NORMATIVE CONSENSUS ON THE BEST INTERESTS OF THE CHILD

ABDULLAHI AN-NA'IM*

ABSTRACT

The premise of this analysis is that normative universality in human rights, including the rights of the child, should neither be taken for granted nor achieved through the 'universalization' of the norms and institutions of dominant cultures, whether at the local, regional or international levels. In relation to the definition and implementation of the best interests of the child principle, the paper emphasizes the need to maximize opportunities for contesting the nature and rationale of action regarding children from as many different perspectives as possible. This should include rigorous analysis to see who is taking the action in question, on what basis and for whose benefit, how does it affect children at large or groups thereof, and so forth. Particular attention should be given to understanding the nature, context and dynamics of power relations between and among the various actors and subjects of the action in question, and possibilities of altering or adjusting those power relations.

Thus, the essential feature in developing specific strategies for substantive normative consensus is the need to enable alternative perceptions and interpretations of cultural norms and institutions to emerge and compete with dominant ones. Such procedural universality, the paper concludes, is both readily achievable and conducive to the realization of genuine normative consensus on the definition and implementation of principles such as the best interests of the child.

I. INTRODUCTION

The Convention on the Rights of the Child (the Child Convention) reflects sensitivity to the impact of contextual factors and cultural considerations on the norms it purports to set. As noted by Philip Alston in the introductory paper above, the Convention is a far more complex and multi-dimensional instrument than is implied by characterizations which would, whether in support or criticism, portray its text as man-

* Africa Watch 1522 K Street, Suite 910, Washington DC 20005, USA.
I prepared the first draft of this paper while holding the position of Scholar-in-residence at the Ford Foundation Office in Cairo, Egypt, for 1992–3. I am most grateful for the support of the Ford Foundation and its Cairo staff; and wish to thank, in particular, Emma Playfair for her very useful comments and suggestions.

dating a particular solution or outcome to global problems of child abuse or neglect. It could be argued, on the other hand, that flexibility and recognition of diversity may either hide an unbridgeable normative schism or lead to a slippery slope of persistent indecision and confusion. In the end, it might be said, there may be much apparent consensus on very little substance.

For example, all would readily agree that the child must be protected from 'all forms of physical or mental violence' (Art 19.1), that school discipline should be 'administered in a manner consistent with the child's human dignity' (Art 28.2) and that the child should not be subjected to 'torture or other cruel, inhuman or degrading treatment or punishment' (Art 37.a). How should these 'universal norms' be interpreted and implemented in relation to certain types of corporal punishment which are routinely used by parents and school teachers in many parts of the world, with the complete approval of their local cultures? Are these provisions of the Child Convention intended to prohibit the use of all forms of corporal punishment, and if so, how can such prohibition be enforced in practice?

This sort of tension between the requirements of contextual diversity and cultural specificity, on the one hand, and the dangers of normative ambiguity or confusion, on the other, is inherent to any project which purports to set truly universal norms, especially in relation to a subject like the rights of the child. Without due regard to the consequences or implications of such diversity and specificity, there is little prospect of global normative consensus, but if the dangers of ambiguity or confusion are not addressed, the consensus thereby achieved might be superficial and perfunctory. While maintaining that this inherent tension cannot be eliminated altogether, I would argue that it can and should be mediated and somewhat contained through certain procedures and processes. The basic thesis of this analysis may be summarized in the following propositions:

1. Generally speaking, it is important to seek to formulate, interpret and implement all internationally-recognized human rights in proper cultural context. While precluding arbitrary imposition of a specific definition of principles such as 'the best interest of the child', respect for cultural and contextual diversity should not lead to normative indecision and confusion. This tension can and should be mediated through the requirement of certain features and safeguards in the process by which this clause is defined and implemented in any setting at a given point in time.

2. Although clearly identifiable and distinguishable from each other, human cultures are also characterized by their own internal diversity, propensity to change and mutual influence. These characteristics can be used to promote normative consensus within and among culture through processes of cultural transformation.

3. Given the inherent diversity and contestability of cultural attitudes towards matters such as the best interest of the child in particular, the meaning and implications claimed for this principle in a certain society at a given point in time should not be taken as final or conclusive. Rather, the meaning and implications of the best interests principle in any society should be open to challenge, reformulation and refinement through the processes of internal discourse and cross-cultural dialogue.

4. In due course, these processes of discourse and dialogue will promote genuine international consensus on the meaning and implications of the principle of the best interests of the child. Thus, the rigorous implementation of agreed *procedures and processes* for defining this clause in various contexts will lead to a substantive common standard or level of achievement in relation to the best interests of the child without violating the integrity of local cultures or encroaching upon the sovereignty of the various peoples of the world.

5. Although participants in the processes of definition and specification of this clause will probably have their own normative agenda, they can all share a commitment to agreed procedures and processes which are conductive to developing international consensus in this regard. Thus, my commitment to the principles set by the Child Convention, as I understand them, should be distinguished from my advocacy of the proposed methodology. While the former would be the subject of my personal contribution as a participant in the process, I see the latter as necessary for the integrity and efficacy of consensus-building among all participants. My wish that the process would lead to the adoption of my views on this issue should not detract from my commitment to the procedure and its safeguards. If accepted, however, this or any other proposed methodology should be institutionalized and protected against violation by those who may not like its outcome at any given point in time.

To explain the application of this thesis to the principle of 'the best interests of the child', I will discuss what might be called the 'paradox of normative universality', and possible ways of resolving it in a given setting or context. In light of that discussion, I will review some relevant studies on the Arab world, propose a tentative model for defining the best interests principle in cultural context and illustrate its application in relation to child labour, corporal punishment and female circumcision.

II.   THE PARADOX OF NORMATIVE UNIVERSALITY

Modern international human rights, such as the rights of the child, are premised on the assumption of universal normative consensus on who is a human being, and what is due to a human person by virtue of his or her humanity, without distinction on grounds of race, gender, religion and so forth. This notion and assumption are certainly very attractive and comforting for all of us. Upon reflection, however, one can see that genuine normative universality is a somewhat paradoxical concept which is yet to be realized in real and concrete terms.

To appreciate the paradoxical and problematic nature of such normative universality, it is important to distinguish it from purely formal agreement between governmental delegates who 'negotiate' international human rights treaties. Delegates are usually more concerned with negotiating the official positions of their governments into 'expedient ambiguity' than with achieving conceptual clarity on the basis of the realistic beliefs, attitudes and practices of their national constituencies. Moreover, it is important to note that the circumstances under which even this level of 'official universality' is pursued are normally far from consistent with its purported premise of the equal sovereignty and proportionality of the negotiating positions of the parties.

The delegates of governments from the South who flocked to New York and Geneva since independence to take part in the drafting, adoption and implementation of 'universal' human rights norms were not only late participants in a predetermined process, but also operated with a fraction of the human and material resources available to their counterparts from the North.[1] Delegates from the North, moreover, operated with concepts and mechanisms which evolved from their own political, cultural and ideological history, and enjoyed the wide support of their national governments and populations in this regard. In contrast, delegates from the South not only lacked that sense of familiarity, authenticity and support at home, but may also have had no alternative positions to present since their national constituencies did not have the chance to articulate different proposals out of their indigenous experiences and in response to the realities of their own contexts.

Although the situation may have been relatively better for some countries, or recently improved for others, serious inequality in negotiating positions and other concerns still persist for the majority of countries from the South. As a matter of international law, of course, all states are bound by duly ratified treaties, but one must look beyond formalistic obligation in order to appreciate the realistic prospects of implementation of those treaties.

The elusiveness of universal normative consensus can readily be appreciated in view of the diversity of cultural and contextual realities which condition people's beliefs and behaviour in daily life. With respect to the rights of the child, there are bound to be significant differences between the perceptions of childhood, and circumstances affecting behaviour regarding children, in the South and the North, as well as within these regions. The issue here is not a value judgement on which is the more humane perception of childhood or better way of treating children. Rather, it is simply to emphasize that different perceptions and circumstances are bound to impact on people's beliefs and behaviour in this regard. This is very relevant, for example, in relation to the responsibilities, rights and duties of parents and others to provide direction and guidance for the child, recognized by Articles 5, 14.2 and 18.1 of the Child Convention.

Parents in the South would probably try to have as many children as they can because of the risk, almost certainty, of loss through infant and child mortality. In contrast, parents in the North would probably plan to have the number of children they wish (for personal, financial or life-style reasons), in the expectation that their children will survive and receive good education, health care, and so forth. To parents in the South, children are to be prepared for taking care of members of the extended family – that is, to provide private 'social security' for many against sickness and old age. Children of the Northern 'nuclear family' are expected to 'move out and make their own lives' when they grow up, leaving their parents to enjoy the privacy and independence of retirement on their pension and/or life-savings. These stereotypes are obviously not universal models of the situation in the South or North, but they certainly reflect dominant sociological norms and assumptions which appear to underlie public policy in these regions.

There are also bound to be significant differences between perceptions of how to raise children to uphold and live by which values, depending on the world-view and religious beliefs of parents, or the cultural norms of their societies. What would be important for Muslim parents to instil in their children is likely to differ in some significant ways from that of Buddhist, Hindu or agnostic parents. Within each religious or cultural group, economic, educational and other differentials will probably influence parents' objectives and expectations for their children, thereby affecting child-rearing practices.

Given the wide range of contextual specificity and cultural relativity between and within various regions of the world, how can normative universality be achieved on the rights of the child in general, or the best interests principle in particular? In view of the above-noted need for emphasis on the actual beliefs and behaviour of parents and other people concerned with children throughout the world, this issue raises questions about where to look for, and how to verify claims of, such universality. By whose criteria or according to which philosophical framework can the universality of the norms in question be declared or verified? To the extent that they can be shown to exist at any point in time, how can such norms be elaborated and specified for daily implementation in different contexts?

Part of the basic problem here is that any conceptualization of the issues will probably be limited by the cultural conditioning and/or intellectual and professional orientation of its author. It is unrealistic, for example, to expect a Western lawyer to know and account for the implications of Islamic jurisprudence to his or her analysis, or an Islamic jurist to appreciate and apply an analysis rooted in liberal thought and European or Anglo-American legal theory. This does not mean that the project of normative universality on the best interests principle should be abandoned because of the difficulty of cross-cultural communication and understanding. Rather, my objective here is to emphasize the need to take that difficulty into account in seeking to achieve normative universality in this regard.

III.   UNIVERSALITY AND CULTURAL TRANSFORMATION

As suggested elsewhere,[2] the paradox of normative universality can be mediated through processes of internal discourse and cross-cultural dialogue to broaden and deepen genuine and substantive consensus over the formulation, interpretation and implementation of international human rights norms. The basic premise and concept of this approach may be briefly summarized as follows:

Global cultural diversity reflects the dominance of certain interpretations of the major norms and institutions of each culture at a given point in time. Although the proponents of dominant interpretations would normally purport to present them as *the only* 'authentic' or 'legitimate' position of the culture on the issue in question, different positions can usually be presented within a certain range of possibilities. This is due to the fact that cultural norms and institutions are characterized by varying degrees of ambivalence and flexibility in order to cater for the different needs and circumstances of the population. Cultures also change and evolve over time in response to external influence as well as internal demands.

There would therefore always be other perspectives which can be articulated to challenge dominant interpretations, and thereby present alternative views of the position of the culture on a particular issue at any given point in time. The prevalence of one perspective or another is therefore open to challenge through change or adjustment in the dynamics of power relations within the culture. It should be noted here that the struggle over cultural resources can take place through action or behaviour as well as verbal articulation. The absence of particular manifestations of such struggle, or the lack of certain forms of challenge and contestation of prevailing interpretations, does not mean that cultural transformation is not happening at any point in time.

To be effective in changing the beliefs, attitudes and behaviour of the relevant population, the proposed alternative perspective must be perceived by that population to be consistent with the *internal* criteria of legitimacy of the culture, and appreciated as relevant to their needs and expectations. It would therefore seem to follow that the proponents of change must not only have a credible claim to being *insiders* to the culture in question, but also use internally valid arguments or means of presentation. In other words, the presentation and adoption of alternative perspectives can best be achieved through a coherent *internal discourse*.

This does not mean that outsiders to the culture have no influence on the processes of internal discourse. Outsiders can influence an internal situation through, for example:

– engaging in their own internal discourse, thereby enabling participants in one culture to point to similar processes taking place in other cultures,

– supporting the right of the internal participants to challenge prevailing perceptions, while avoiding overt interference because this will undermine the credibility of internal actors,

– engaging in a cross-cultural dialogue to exchange insights and strategies of internal discourse.

Cross-cultural dialogue can also seek to promote universality at a theoretical or conceptual level by highlighting moral and philosophical commonalities of human cultures and experiences. For example, the Golden Rule of treating others as one would wish to be treated by them – which is found in some formulation or another in all the major cultural traditions of the world – can be presented as a universal moral foundation of human rights norms. This principle of reciprocity could provide universal rationale for human rights as those rights which one would claim for himself or herself, and must therefore concede to others. However, efforts to articulate shared values and principles must be founded on mutual respect and sensitivity to the integrity of other cultures, especially in view of colonial and post-colonial power relations between the North and South.

The Dynamics of Internal Discourse

As applied to the principle of the best interests of the child, this approach would emphasize criteria and procedural safeguards for the *process* by which the best interests of the child are specified, challenged and changed or refined within a specific culture, or between different cultures, at a certain point in time. Given the multiplicity of perspectives and options regarding the meaning and implications of the best interests principle within each culture, the main issue is how to regulate the processes of discourse and dialogue over the meaning and implementation of this principle in various policy and decision-making settings. The sharing of insights and experiences of such internal discourses will, I suggest, over time help to mediate cultural and contextual differences and thereby produce common standards on the principle of the best interests of the child. In pursuing these processes, the following considerations should be taken into account.

First, the scope and dynamics of the popular participation envisaged by the premise and concept of internal discourse are problematic in several respects. For example, while it may appear that there should be no limits on participation, it is unlikely that all segments of the population would have even relatively equal or proportionate capacity to participate in this discourse in the normal course of events. To maximize participation, discourse should include non-verbal formulations since wide segments of the population are disinclined to verbal articulation of their beliefs and attitudes. The question is therefore how to bridge the communication gap between the *words* of the intellectuals and the *world* of their less articulate constituencies whose behaviour is the central concern of this analysis.

Moreover, the nature and dynamics of internal discourse would suggest that the most effective strategy is to promote change through the transformation of *existing folk models* rather than seeking to challenge and replace them immediately. This strategy is successfully applied, for example, by Islamist groups in several Islamic countries today. The Islamists are effective because they apparently confirm the existing beliefs and practices of their constituencies, and seek to unite and mobilize them into 'radical' action in order to effectively realize what the Islamists claim to be already the goals and expectations of their audience. Although the Islamists are, in my view, actually seeking to transform the beliefs and practices of their constituencies in this process, that objective is skilfully hidden in the rhetoric of 'continuity of tradition' and 'return to the Golden Past'.

In contrast, the liberal intellectuals of Islamic societies appear to be, or are presented as, challenging the folk models of their societies and seeking to replace them by alien concepts and norms. This negative perception may be partially due to the rather abstract verbal articulation employed by those intellectuals, and their own life-style which is often distant from the daily realities of the population at large. It may well be true that the substance of the message of the liberal intellectuals is not as far removed from the essence of the 'tradition' as it is often presented by their Islamists opponents. But this may not be easily appreciated by the masses of Muslims in the present dynamics of verbal and non-verbal discourse.

The point of this slight digression is to emphasize that the more one is *perceived* to be confirming existing beliefs and practices rather than challenging them, the better would be the prospects of wide acceptance and implementation of one's proposals. Since perception is of the essence here, it is possible to achieve the gradual transformation of the same folk models toward greater conformity with international standards through internal discourse and cross-cultural dialogue as explained above. Does this mean that folk models, or elements thereof, can always be reconciled with some minimum standards set by the Child Convention or required by the best interests of the child principle? What should happen when reconciliation is clearly not possible through the proposed methodology?

Process and Purpose

It is certainly true that there is an underlying tension between process and purpose in this proposed approach. The rationale of internal discourse and cross-cultural dialogue presupposes that these processes should freely define their own purpose. If they are allowed to take their full course, however, it is conceivable that these processes may lead to conclusions at variance with international concepts and norms of the rights of the child in general, or the best interests principle in particular. Should the processes of internal discourse and cross-cultural dialogue be allowed to define and specify this principle freely, whatever that may lead to in each context, or are these processes only expected to operate within the framework of certain standards already set by the Child Convention?

It may be argued that it is possible to modify or clarify the objectionable aspects of the folk model through internal discourse in order to bring it into greater conformity with the Convention's minimum standards. This argument is premised on the belief that more conformity will in fact be achieved through close analysis and imaginative reinterpretation of the folk models in question, and more sensitive presentation of the relevant standards of the Convention. However, since there is no way of verifying whether this will actually happen in practice except through the actual application of this methodology over time, one must admit the possibility of irreconcilable differences between folk models and the standards set by the Child Convention.

Alternatively, it may be argued that folk models should be made the point of reference for any standards which are believed to be set by the Child Convention because the former are the basis of the legitimacy of the latter. From this point of view, the standards of the Convention should be defined in terms of folk models rather than the reverse. However, one may then wonder about the utility of an international treaty on this, or any other human rights subject, if all it can do is to conform with existing folk norms and practices. To make folk models the point of reference for international standards is also problematic in other respects. For example, those who make such a 'folk-centric' claim would readily concede, I suspect, that folk practices should be discontinued if they are clearly shown to be harmful to the physical health of children. The problem, they might respond, is that it is difficult to demonstrate the universal validity of a determination that a folk practice is 'harmful' to children when the alleged negative consequences are psychological or sociological rather than physical. This line of thinking is flawed, in my view, for two reasons. First, it draws too sharp a distinction between various types of harm which in fact tend to interact and overlap. How can one distinguish, for instance, between psychological, sociological and physical consequences of circumcision for the girl child? Second, the folk-centric position assumes that folk models do in fact provide settled and definitive criteria for evaluating international standards while this is unlikely to be the case in practice. What criteria does a practice such as female circumcision set for evaluating international standards, and according to which alleged rationale of the practice?

Instead of a simplistic dichotomy between folk models and international standards, which instals one as the definitive norm by which the other is to be judged, I propose a dynamic interaction between the two. On the one hand, international standards should be premised on fundamental global ethical, social and political values and institutions, and thereby have an inspiring, elevating and informative influence on popular perceptions of existing folk models. These models and their rationale, on the other hand, should be seen as a source of the values and institutions which legitimize the international standards. Both aspects of this dynamic interaction, I suggest, should be mediated through the processes of discourse and dialogue outlined earlier.

IV.   THE BEST INTERESTS PRINCIPLE IN ARAB DISCOURSE

It is misleading, especially in view of the premise and analysis of this paper, to speak of the cultural context of the best interests principle in terms of regional or even national classification. There is very little cultural uniformity in countries like the Sudan, or between, for example, Somalia, Syria and Morocco which are all said to be parts of the so-called Arab world. Even characterizing these or other countries as Arab may be objectionable to some segments of their population. Yet official policies are usually drawn, and purported to be implemented, on national and/or regional basis. The following review may therefore be useful, but is presented as subject to this caveat, and pending more discriminating analysis than I can offer here.

Issues of Description and Characterization

Any intelligent attempt to analyse an issue or propose a solution for a problem must, of course, begin with a clear and accurate description and characterization of the issue or problem in question. However, such description and characterization would themselves be premised on a certain conceptual framework, or influenced by a particular intellectual or cultural orientation. For example, a major Arab League study of the basic needs of the child in the Arab world, by Ismail Sabri Abdalla, is premised on the view that the child is born into an economic, social and cultural environment which determines to a great extent his or her capabilities at the time of birth. These capabilities develop subsequently in accordance with the same determinants. Thus, Abdalla maintains that the situation of the child should not be discussed in isolation from general economic, social and cultural backwardness (the term he uses) of the family and society in Arab countries.[3] The study then proceeds to describe, on the basis of twenty country case-studies from the region, aspects of the social environment of the child and family in terms of, *inter alia*, rural, nomadic and urban settings, income levels, physical and cultural environments, social conditions of mothers and the family in general, and questions of basic services for the child.[4]

On the basis of these studies, Abdalla summarizes the state of the Arab child (as of 1980) as being that where children constitute a high percentage of total population, but are normally born to illiterate parents and suffer a high rate of mortality. Growing urbanization and modernization is diminishing the role of family in child-rearing, and there is a very low degree of social awareness about problems of childhood.[5] He then concludes that Arab development efforts to date were characterized by the adoption of a Western concept which did not differentiate between development and Westernization. Consequently, the concepts and methods of the basic needs of the child in the Arab world are drawn in essence from Western societies, despite the clear difference between the conditions of advanced industrialized societies and the actual conditions of under-development of the Arab world, including the oil-rich countries. Westernization exposed children to the shock of conflict between traditional family values and Western modern values which are encouraged by the mass media and reflected in increasing consumerism. Even if they pretend to do otherwise, Abdalla maintains, the effect of the local media is to instil these Western values.

Following a critique of the methods of delivering basic services to children, Abdalla emphasizes the need for innovative new models of basic services founded on a realistic evaluation of real needs of society and primarily relying on its own resources.[6] In his view, basic services should be presented in an integrated comprehensive manner and provided through popularly legitimate institutions which are frequented by people in their routine daily lives, such as schools, hospitals and mosques. He suggested that the assumption that prevailing norms of 'under-developed' or poor societies are necessarily archaic and obstacles to development would be valid only if development is completely identified with Westernization, a view which he rejects.

On the question of child labour, for example, Abdalla notes that, despite the existence of laws which prohibit child labour below a certain age and restrict it at other ages, many children continue to work out of economic and social need. In his view, this discrepancy is due to the fact that official standards are based on Western views, although strict separation between education and work is neither desirable nor realistic in Arab societies. Rather than calling for its total abolition, he suggests that official policies should only be directed at preventing child labour from being exploitative or dangerous to the physical and psychological health of the child. Child labour should be directed towards enhancing the capabilities and skills of children and linked to academic education. Education itself should seek to end the dichotomy between manual and intellectual work.[7]

As clearly shown in another Arab League study by Tahir Labib, however, the very concept of 'basic needs of the child' should be clarified. For example, people assume that the needs of the child are obvious, but they are in fact thinking of services (which are the means for satisfying needs) rather than the needs themselves.[8] Some of the needs ascribed to social groups are, in fact, the needs of supervisory bodies. The 'establishment', in its various social, economic and political forms and levels, tends to neglect those needs which it is incapable or unwilling to satisfy while purporting to create needs which it claims to satisfy. It is therefore important to distinguish between real needs as perceived by the people concerned and artificial or invented needs identified or specified by others.

Children, and maybe even their parents, have no voice to articulate their own needs, *as perceived by themselves*, and do not constitute pressure groups to demand the satisfaction of those needs as so defined. The child does not determine his or her own needs. Instead, his or her needs are defined by the needs of others (parents, school, the State and so forth), and by the need of those others for the child. Thus, if the need of others for the child is weak or inadequate, that would be reflected in perceptions and articulation of the 'needs of the child', thereby leading to neglect or other adverse effect on the child. The unsatisfactory state of the child in Arab societies might therefore raise questions about the real need of these societies for the child, despite claims that the needs of the child are a first priority.

Labib argues that bureaucracy in the Arab world lacks intellectual initiative, and might even be anti-intellectual, on the grounds that its work is administrative and directly practical, not allowing for conceptual thinking. The typical bureaucrat may not therefore appreciate the complexity of the issues involved in making and implementing sound policies on the needs of the child. Moreover, with the persistent political instability of the region, each new government tends to modify priorities and amend lists of needs of, and services for, the child in order to show how different it is from the previous government. In this way, the needs of the child are 'modified' while the status quo remains unchanged.

The relationship between the needs of the child and those of others is unavoidable, but one should be aware of the nature and implications of this relationship in evaluating formulations of the needs of the child, and their corresponding projects and services. For example, Labib wonders whether child-care facilities are part of the needs of the child or of his/her mother, whether or not she is working regular hours out of the home. I take this question as indicating that a confusion between the two perceptions of 'needs', or between need and service, would affect the prospects of satisfaction. Thus, the perception that child-care facilities are a need of mothers who work regular hours outside the home, coupled with a social attitude or policy that mothers should stay at home to take care of children, will probably diminish the prospects of the provision of adequate child-care facilities. In contrast, if child-care facilities are accepted as a genuine need of the child, independently from that of the mother, and regardless of whether or not she works regular hours outside the home, the situation might be different.

According to Labib, since needs have a contextual social content, it is important to know who determines that content. Children are not a social sector or a coherent group as such because they have different social origins and relationships. Thus, what is taken to be needs of children might in fact be class or sectarian needs. While essential needs, such as health and food, appear universal (though they too have their social and political content), the objectives, content and forms of other needs, such as those relating to education, literature and arts, cannot be divorced from the social and political structure of society. Since differentiation and its causes or basis are present in all human societies, and the child must bear the consequences of such differentiation within the framework of his or her family and social group, the question arises: the needs of *which* child are we talking about? Unless this question is taken into account and addressed, some social groups would be allowed to determine the needs of the children of other groups in ways which would in fact be for the benefit of the determining group and its own children, rather than of society in general, or of all children at large.[9]

In another study, Mahmud Ahmed Musa discusses what he calls the problematic of the negative characteristics of the Arab person, and reviews the debate over the desired alternative.[10] According to Musa and the authors he cites, negative Arab characteristics include determinism, excessive submission to authority figures, being backward looking, emphasizing the form rather than substance, copying rather than creating, close-mindedness, learning by heart rather than understanding, analysis and discussion. While some authors speculate on ideal alternative models, others emphasize the need for popular participation in the development of appropriate models. All agree that the reconstitution of the Arab person must primarily rely on the nature and objectives of education.

Musa criticizes Arab educational systems as essentially defined by former colonial administrations, expanded after independence without radical change in objectives, structures and content. Massive quantitative expansion led to lowering of standards and highly competitive formal academic education. There is also little attention to building character and qualities of organization, discipline, love of knowledge, enjoyment of work, appreciation of art and beauty, independence and initiative. All of this is a reflection of Arab societies and their political regimes, and impacts negatively on the orientation and character of educated people, for instance, by creating unrealistic and inappropriate work expectations and leading to a tendency to refuse manual labour and migrate to cities to look for office work.[11]

The author links that to a critique of social value systems as reactionary or backward-looking and deterministic, defensive (seeking refuge in the past) rather than evolutionary and forward-looking, dominated by tribal patriarchal systems based on the values of unquestioning obedience and submission. All of this is reflected in the educational system which emphasizes submission and obedience, uncritical acceptance of the views of others without real conviction. What is required is therefore reforming the educational system so that it can resist dominant value systems.[12] Musa calls for education for an independent view of total development which emanates from a unified national perspective and rational methodology. Social transformation should be achieved through socialization processes either by enhancing the efficacy of existing educational systems or reforming them.[13] He calls for the intelligentsia to engage the masses and popular institutions to challenge 'false-consciousness' created by dominant social and political systems to perpetuate their own power. The author reviews several studies on education and false-consciousness in Arab countries (analysis of content of text-books and school syllabi) and notes the negative impact of oral traditions in perpetuating stereotypes of male and female – father and mother – role models, and the influence of the mass media in creating false consciousness.[14]

The studies by Abdalla and Musa (which are regionally significant and representative) reflect a tension between commitment to indigenous perspectives and self-reliance, on the one hand, and the realities of under-development and dependency of the region on Western intellectual and technical resources and expertise, on the other. For example, while national and regional analysis of Abdalla's study emphasizes contextual and cultural specificity and the need for indigenous solutions and expertise, the 'scientific' information on which he relies is Western.[15] This is perhaps why the measures he proposes for satisfying the basic needs of the child sound so abstract and unrealistic.[16] Authors from the region are cited in Musa's critique of Arab educational systems, but when it comes to alternative models and theories, his point of reference becomes the work of Western scholars.[17] One may therefore wonder how will the reform of educational systems be achieved in terms of an 'independent view of total development', as advocated by Musa, especially in view of his negative characterization of Arab society.

In my view, descriptions and characterizations of issues should take into account the fact that 'independence' is, by definition, born out of a state of dependency, and can only be achieved through a realistic appreciation of the *possibilities* as well as constraints of the situation. It is also important to appreciate that dependence and independence are relative terms, especially in view of the present globalized political, economic, social, cultural and intellectual relations. The politics of the basic needs of the child discussed by Labib should therefore be seen in international as well as local or national contexts. For example, the consequences of structural adjustments and economic liberalization, and their impact on poor families and their children, can neither be understood nor redressed at a purely local or national level.[18] This need for a global approach would emphasize the importance of promoting an international overlapping consensus on human rights norms and their implementation through the dynamics of internal discourse and cross-cultural dialogue, as suggested earlier.

I have devoted much space to reviewing these studies because their 'basic needs' analysis provides a useful background for developing a tentative model for defining and specifying the principle of the best interests of the child in the region. Many of the 'actions concerning children' envisaged by Article 3.1 (where the best interests of the child are required to be a primary consideration), as well as other aspects of the Child Convention and related concerns, can usefully be analysed in terms of what might be called basic needs of the child.[19] As briefly explained below, the premise and main features of the following tentative model can apply to basic needs analysis in relation to, for example, child labour. The model may also be useful in mediating normative consensus on the issue of corporal punishment and female circumcision mentioned earlier.

V. A TENTATIVE MODEL FOR DETERMINING WHAT CONSTITUTES THE BEST INTERESTS OF THE CHILD

It might be helpful to reiterate here that this paper is concerned with the nature and dynamics of the process by which actions (including norms-setting and decision-making) are taken in relation to, or as rationalized by, best interests of the child considerations. Since, as indicated earlier, there are always different perspectives and options regarding each type of action, the main issue is how to regulate the processes of discourse and dialogue over the interpretation and application of the best interests principle in each case. I would therefore recall here my earlier analysis and proposal for promoting genuine normative universality on the best interests principle in relation to the following elements of a tentative model for regulating the process of defining this principle:

1. Clear and accurate description and characterization of the action to which the best interests principle is applicable, whether in terms of a basic needs approach or in some other way. In this regard, as indicated earlier, one should

know who is making the description and characterization and according to which framework or orientation.

2. Rigorous analysis of the action in question in order to identify its type or nature, who is taking it, on what basis and for whose benefit, who are the immediate and consequential subjects of the action and how are they affected.

3. Understanding the nature and dynamics of power relations between and among the various actors and subjects of the action, and of the situation in local or broader contexts, as appropriate.

4. Appreciation of the possibilities and constraints of changing or influencing the nature and dynamics of power relations between and among actors and subjects, as well as in the situation at large.

5. In all of the above, the fundamental guiding principle should be to maximize opportunities for contesting the nature and rationale of action regarding children from different perspectives and presenting alternative positions.

Given the integral and dynamic relationship between form and substance, these and related elements should be applied in devising (reforming) and implementing the *procedures and processes* through which action is taken, as appropriate for each type of action. For example, procedure and process in a private child custody case would be different from those of setting and/or implementing a policy on basic needs (food, shelter or health) or with regard to child labour, and so forth. But the purpose in each case should be not only to determine (through procedures and processes consistent with the proposed model) which action is in the best interests of the child under the circumstances, *but also to allow for the subsequent contestation, revision or change of the initial action.* The model is applicable to both aspects, and with respect to procedural as well as substantive matters because valid ends cannot be achieved through invalid means.

The application of this tentative model may be illustrated with respect to the question of child labour. It is not possible to discuss here various causes and consequences of child labour,[20] or to review possible explanations and responses to the serious discrepancy between theory and practice in this regard. Instead, I wish briefly to discuss how the proposed model might be applied in relation to Abdalla's suggestion, noted earlier, that rather than seeking the total abolition of child labour, official policies should be directed at preventing it from being exploitative or dangerous to the physical and psychological health of the child.

This proposition reflects the fundamental dilemma of balancing and reconciling apparently conflicting basic needs as well as raising the question of who defines those needs and for whom. On the one hand, child labour is essential for his or her immediate and long term survival in certain situations where such labour also constitutes a vital educational and socialization institution. The nature and circumstances of labour, on the other hand, may not only threaten the physical and mental health of the child, but also deprive him or her of the basic needs of academic education. The very reasons for child labour, and/or conditions under which it is likely to happen, tend to expose children to excessive exploitation and abuse.

Like all dilemmas, the only solution in situations where child labour is justifiable or necessary is to seek to achieve its 'benefits' while safeguarding against its dangers and negative consequences. This sort of simple and obviously reasonable formula, however, is only a broad framework for developing and implementing a resolution of the dilemma. Many questions need to be answered before specific strategies for action can be devised and implemented, subsequently evaluated, and so forth, in order to resolve the dilemma at any given point in time. For example, the rationale of the formula seems to suggest that child labour, or certain types thereof, should be prohibited altogether if it is not possible to safeguard effectively against its dangers or negative consequences (or if the risks outweigh the benefits). What does this mean in specific cases? Who makes these determinations and on what basis? How is 'mental health' or 'exploitation' of the child defined and by whom?

Successful resolutions of the dilemma will probably be too much conditioned by the social, political, cultural and other circumstances of its context to be readily applied elsewhere. That is to say, the manner in which the formula is specified and implemented (how are terms defined and determinations made and by whom), are unlikely to be transferable to a different setting. It is therefore important to focus on essential pre-requisites for, and essential features of, the *process* by which appropriate resolutions are developed more than on specific solutions, although the latter are no doubt useful in understanding which similar issues might be addressed in other settings.

Since the process through which the dilemma of child labour may be resolved should occur at various official and non-official levels and from different perspectives, the proposed model must be specified separately for each level and perspective. In all cases, however, the model calls for maximizing opportunities for contesting prevailing descriptions and characterizations of the action in question, allowing for alternative analysis, and so forth. The experiences and insights of such an internal discourse can be influenced and exchanged through cross-cultural dialogue as explained in section 3 of this analysis.

A similar process can also promote normative universality on the question of corporal punishment. As suggested at the beginning of this paper, apparent normative universality in the relevant provisions of the Child Convention may in fact hide serious schism and ambiguity with regard to corporal punishment for children. Nevertheless, I would not recommend that one should try to rule on the admissibility of this form of punishment on the basis of records of preparatory works for the Convention or declarations of official positions on the issue. Rather, I call for internal discourse and cross-cultural dialogue in order to develop genuine universal consensus on the normative implications of the relevant provisions of the Convention. The questions to be addressed include: Should the Convention's prohibition on 'all forms of physical or mental violence' against the child be absolute? Can corporal punishment ever be justified, in some cases or under certain circumstances, 'in the best interests of the child'? Do all forms of corporal punishment necessarily violate 'the child's human dignity', or constitute 'torture or other cruel, inhuman or degrading treatment or punishment'?[21]

In accordance with the proposed model, discourse and dialogue might present alternative descriptions and characterizations of corporal punishment in debating whether to contest or confirm its cultural legitimacy. Rigorous analysis might either substantiate or repudiate the classification of such punishment as physical or mental violence – a necessary stage in prohibiting or exempting it under some formulation of a 'best interests' rationale. An appreciation of the nature and dynamics of power relations between proponents and opponents of corporal punishment is necessary for deciding whether or not to seek to influence and change the situation, and how can that be achieved. To the extent that universal consensus on prohibiting corporal punishment cannot be achieved, or until it is realized, the processes of discourse and dialogue can be useful in developing and implementing effective safeguards.

As applied to female circumcision, the proposed model would provide those who oppose this practice with opportunities for contesting prevailing perceptions of the nature, rationale and consequences of the practice, while presenting alternative ways of responding to sociological, psychological and other needs the practice might be believed to satisfy. My concern here is not particularly with reasons for repudiating female circumcision in principle, and seeking its total abolition in practice. Rather, I am concerned with the manner in which that determination is made, and consequent action taken, *in the most effective, lasting and legitimate manner.* Many programmes seeking to eradicate this heinous practice, I suggest, have failed to achieve their objective because of the arbitrary, intrusive and elitist (top-down) manner in which those programmes were conceived and implemented.

VI.   CONCLUSION: TOWARD A STRATEGY FOR SUBSTANTIVE CONSENSUS

This paper is premised on the view that normative universality in human rights should neither be taken for granted, nor abandoned in the face of claims of contextual specificity or cultural relativity. Human rights scholars and activists throughout the world must recognize that a universal project, for the rights of the child in this case, cannot be legitimately achieved through the 'universalization' of the norms and institutions of dominant cultures, whether at a local, regional or international level. Such recognition does not mean that one should condone or concede the apologetic or manipulative abuse of contextual specificity or cultural relativity of the type attempted by some governments and elites, especially in certain parts of Africa and Asia today. On the contrary, taking cultural diversity seriously is the best way to combat such abuse by challenging its basis in the consciousness of the relevant constituencies.

With respect to the principle of the best interests of the child, the paper proposes the establishment of procedures and processes to ensure not only dynamic diversity of perspectives, as appropriate, in taking initial action regarding children, but also opportunities for subsequent contestation, revision and change of such action. Procedural universality, in my view, is both readily achievable and conductive to the realization of genuine normative consensus on the definition and implementation of the principle of the best interests of the child. This approach should be applied to issues of daily implementation as well as the articulation of broad standards regarding the best interest principle.

NOTES

[1] The terms 'North' and 'South' are used here subject to the observation made by Clarence Dias (of the International Center for Law in Development, New York) in various conference presentations that they refer to concepts rather than geographical regions. There are pockets of the North within the South, and of the South within the North.

[2] See, generally, A. An-Na'im and F. Deng (eds), *Human Rights in Africa: Cross-Cultural Perspectives* (Washington DC, The Brookings Institution, 1990); and A. An-Na'im (ed), *Human Rights in Cross-Cultural Perspectives* (Philadelphia, University of Pennsylvania Press, 1992).

[3] I. S. Abdalla, 'Elements of a Strategy for the Development of the Arab Child', in General Secretariat of the Arab League, Social Affairs Administration (ed), *Al-ihtiyajat al-Assasiya lil-Tifl fi al-Watan al-Araby* (Arabic: The Basic Needs of the Child in the Arab Homeland), (Tunis: The Arab League 1982), 22–8.

[4] Ibid, 22–35.

[5] Ibid, 37–8. For more recent information on these indexes, for example, S. Miladi and H. Serag El Din (eds), *The State of the Child in the Arab World 1990* (Jieza, Egypt, Arab Council for Childhood Development, 1990); and the UNICEF/Oxford University Press annual series on *The State of the World's Children*.

[6] Abdalla, 'Elements of a Strategy for the Development of the Arab Child', 39–40.

[7] Ibid, 40.

[8] Tahir Labib, 'The Arab Child: Between the Needs and the Institutions', in General Secretariat, Administration of Social Affairs, the Arab League (eds), *Al-Tufula wa al-Tanmiya fi al-Watan al-Araby* (Arabic: Childhood and Development in the Arab Homeland: Proceedings of the Conference on Childhood and Development (Tunis, 13–15 November 1986), Part II, 375–9.

[9] While Labib's analysis generally supports the rationale of child self-determinism of the type suggested in John Eekelaar's chapter in this book, it would also raise valid concerns regarding the diversity of the 'self' of the child, the circumstances under which it is supposed to exercise 'self-determinism', and the process by which that might be articulated and implemented.

[10] Mahmud Ahmed Musa, 'Arabic: The Role of Education in the Rearing of the Arab Child', in General Secretariat, Administration of Social Affairs, the Arab League (eds), *Al-Tufula wa al-Tanmiya fi al-Watan al-Araby* (Arabic: Childhood and Development in the Arab Homeland:

Proceedings of the Conference on Childhood and Development (Tunis, 13–15 November 1986). Part I, 215–19.

[11] Ibid, 224–9.

[12] Ibid, 229–31.

[13] Ibid, 233–7.

[14] Ibid, 238–45.

[15] Abdalla, 'Elements of a Strategy for the Development of the Arab Child', 2–3 and 14.

[16] Ibid, 16–18.

[17] Musa, 'The Role of Education', 227–9.

[18] See, generally, UNICEF, *The State of the World's Children 1992* (Oxford University Press for UNICEF, 1992). For a discussion in relation to Egypt see, K. Kuriym, 'Athar Siyasat al-Islah al-Iqtisady ala al-Usar Mahdudat al-Dakhl wa al-Atfal bi-Masr' (Arabic: The Impact of Policies of Economic Reform on Limited-income Families and Children in Egypt), Study prepared for Third World Forum, Middle East Office, and UNICEF, Egypt, not dated.

[19] See, for example, UNICEF, *The State of the World's Children 1993* (Oxford University Press for UNICEF, 1993), 37–49.

[20] See generally, for example, A. Azer and N. Ramzy, *Child Labor in Egypt* (Cairo, The National Center for Social and Criminological Research and UNICEF Egypt, 1992).

[21] Cf A. An-Na'im, 'Toward a Cross-Cultural Approach to Defining International Standards of Human Rights: The Meaning of Cruel, Inhuman, or Degrading Treatment or Punishment', in An-Na'im (ed), *Human Rights in Cross-Cultural Perspectives*, 19–43.

THE CONCEPT OF THE CHILD'S BEST INTERESTS IN THE CHANGING ECONOMIC AND SOCIAL CONTEXT OF SUB-SAHARAN AFRICA

B. RWEZAURA*

ABSTRACT

The international Convention on the Rights of the Child has been commended by many states and welcomed with much enthusiasm. What remains now is to consider the extent to which the principles contained in the Convention can be applied to all state signatories. The task of evolving universal definitions of the many principles and concepts contained in the Convention is crucial to the wider acceptability of the Convention. One of the key concepts in the Convention is the concept of the best interests of the child. It is argued in this paper that the way this concept is to be interpreted and applied by states will be influenced to a large extent by the social, political and economic conditions of those states. The main objective of this paper is to show how economic and social factors give meaning to this concept in the sub-Saharan region of Africa. My aim is not to give a comprehensive definition of the concept. Rather, the paper tries to provide a general exposition of the factors which do play a role in the process of defining and applying this key concept of the Convention. This paper is concluded by noting that the worsening economic conditions of Africa have led to the narrowing of the best interests concept to mean simply the satisfaction of the child's material needs.

I. INTRODUCTION

After nearly a decade of preparatory work the United Nations adopted in 1989 the Convention on the Rights of the Child. The adoption of this Convention represents a welcome recognition on the part of the international community that the rights of certain categories of people are best protected in a single instrument designed for that purpose. It is also important to mention here that this particular convention has been given unprecedented support by many member states. One indication of this support is shown by the speed at which it has been ratified. Alston and Parker have noted, for example, that no other treaty espe-

---

* Faculty of Law, University of Hong Kong, Pokfulam Road, Hong Kong

cially in the field of human rights has 'been ratified by so many states in such an extraordinarily short period of time'.[1] Muntarbhorn has also noted to the same effect that 'nearly 140 countries have become parties to this Convention, making it one of the most widely accepted international treaties'.[2] The Convention has also gained further support in Africa where a regional initiative in the form of a charter has been adopted to provide a specific regional complement to the Convention. This is the African Charter on the Rights and Welfare of the Child, adopted in 1990 by the Organisation of African Unity (OAU).[3] Whereas we must acknowledge that this is an important development with immense potential for the eventual creation and growth of widely accepted standards of international protection of children and their rights, and further that the international community shares a common desire to create a new and better world for all its children, we must also recognize that there is not yet an agreed standard by which compliance can be measured. One important reason for lacking this common standard is that the international community is very diverse. It is neither homogeneous politically, culturally, nor economically. There are regions with varying religious beliefs, social systems and economic organizations. These differences are in turn reflected in the varying world-view of the people, their approach to life, their strategies for survival and what they will do for their children. An effective framework for the implementation of the Convention cannot ignore these factors.

What is even more compelling is the fact that there are certain regions like Africa where the introduction of European colonialism, new marriage laws and foreign religions like Christianity and Islam, have resulted in a complex interaction between indigenous systems and those originating from outside the continent. This has sometimes led to conflicting social identities and values, much of which are still in the process of mutual accommodation. Thus the introduction of western ideas of individualism into pre-capitalist communal societies as well as the partial and often distorted penetration of capitalism into these economies have led to many social conflicts and insecurity all over Africa.

These factors make it impossible for states, and even communities within a single state, to have a common conception and understanding of vital provisions of the Convention such as the concept of the child's best interests, as well as a common strategy for achieving its objectives. Hence, in devising strategies for implementation and for measuring compliance, such factors must not be ignored.

The aim of this paper is to provide the reader with a context in which questions concerning the position of the child in Africa can be examined and analysed. Although the paper will focus on issues which are closely related to the key concept of the best interests of the child there are other issues such as the status of women in marriage which will force their way into the discussion. This is largely because it is difficult to separate issues of children's rights from concerns for the status of women.

The second point which should be made at the outset is that, despite its title, this paper is not intended to give a comprehensive analysis which is applicable to the whole of sub-Saharan Africa. It is fully recognized that Africa is also diverse much like the rest of mankind. But it is also true that Africa has experienced major historical processes such as European colonialism and the penetration of capitalist relations. These historical processes have generated comparable transformations in the social and economic systems of Africa and this makes it possible to attempt a general analysis of these changes so that common trends and patterns can be identified. In order to attain this objective, the paper has drawn from a range of sociological sources as well as from the more recent field research conducted in Africa.

This paper is divided into five parts of which the first is this introduction. The second part gives a brief and general overview of the social and economic systems of pre-colonial Africa. This part forms the context in which the changing concept of the best interests of the African child is to be located. It stresses the economic and social importance of children to the whole community and how property transfers in the form of marriage payments (ie bridewealth) were intended to ensure the filiation of children to the kinship group from which the property came. It is within this social and economic context that the community made provision for the material and moral welfare of its children.

The third part of the paper looks at the effects of economic and social transformation which occurred during the colonial period. It is argued here that the penetration of the market economy weakened the African kinship system by transforming the economic basis of most social groups. Thus the responsibility for children tended to be concentrated on individual families rather than the whole community. This process was buttressed by colonial laws which gave support to individualist values thereby accelerating the process of change.

In the fourth part, the paper raises some of the issues identified above and tries to give a broad explication of the possible factors which go into parental decision about the future of their children. The general thrust of this section is that economic factors do play a major role when parents make decisions about their children's future and that in the majority of cases the interests of the children and those of their parents are hardly distinguishable. But whereas this observation remains generally true for all children, this paper draws attention to the differential treatment between male and female children. In many cases such treatment has tended to be favourable to male and unfavourable to female children. Although such discriminatory treatment of children is in conflict with the provisions of the Convention and other treaties such as the OAU Charter its persistence does reflect existing social beliefs and cultural norms in African communities. This part also argues that although the State in Africa has intervened as early as the colonial period to protect what it defines as the interests of the child, its role is highly circumscribed by its lack of a strong resource base as it continues to depend upon families to provide for all children. The fifth part concludes this paper.

II.   THE ECONOMIC AND SOCIAL SYSTEMS OF PRE-COLONIAL AFRICA

Three major aspects are to be noted about the economic and social systems of pre-colonial Africa. These are the kinship system; the role of property in creating and maintaining kinship ties; and the dominant political role occupied by male elders in the community. In many societies of pre-colonial Africa people were socially and economically bound together by enduring kinship ties. The kinship system provided the framework for social organization and economic co-operation between individuals within a given social group. Status relations were assigned on the basis of either kinship or marriage. Thus an individual had status as a parent, a child, a spouse or more generally, as a member of a kinship group. To these statuses were attached certain responsibilities as well as entitlements or claims which individuals could make upon other members within the group. Thus kinship ties were created and reinforced by constant transfer of property and services between members. The exchange of property, apart from meeting people's material needs, served also to integrate and to reinforce social ties. In many respects therefore, status relations served to express but also to mask underlying property relations within these communities.[4]

In most societies subsistence agriculture and animal husbandry constituted the major economic activity. Production was carried out by the most basic tools and this, therefore, necessitated the deployment of large numbers of people in the fields and pastures. The household was in many societies the basic unit of production and of consumption. Marriage formed a fundamental institution for the recruitment of new members of the group as well as for natural reproduction. Through marriage also social and economic alliances were formed and maintained with other neighbouring groups by regular transfers of goods and services.

Political leadership in these groups was vested in the senior male members who performed political roles on behalf of the group. For example, elders negotiated marriages for the young members, decided disputes between family members and acted as the spokesmen to the ancestors. Elders thus combined the political as well as religious roles which gave them a special place in the community.[5] These foregoing values and social arrangements, as we shall see, were expressed in various traditions and religious beliefs. Traditional law also performed the function of legitimizing as well as supporting the entire social formation.

(a) African Marriage; Bridewealth and the Status of Children

Marriage in Africa, as in many societies of the world, is still considered to be the socially approved relationship within which the birth of children takes place. But perhaps what makes the African marriage distinct from marriages in other contemporary cultures is the fact that in most patrilineal African societies marriage is effected by the transfer of resources known generically as bridewealth.[6] The transfer of bridewealth from the family of the husband to the family of the prospective bride has two main functions. The first is to validate the marriage. The second is to effect a transfer of the bride's procreative capacity from her family to that of her husband. This transfer entitles the husband and his family to claim all the children the wife bears whether or not he is the biological parent. Because patrilineal societies consider that all children born during marriage belong to the husband and his family, custody of children at the time of separation or divorce is claimed as a matter of right by the father. This rule of allocation of rights in children may be called the 'patrilineal principle'.[7]

Radcliffe-Brown has noted that in accordance with the patrilineal principle, 'the rights of the father and his kin over the children of the marriage are so preponderant as to be nearly absolute and exclude any rights on the part of the mother's kin'.[8] He argues that the rule is comparable to the Roman law concept of *patria potestas*. Indeed, it may be added here that the concept is known to many European and other legal systems.[9] For example, until 1886 the English common law made comparable provisions.[10] Much has been written about the significance of bridewealth and its role in the validation of marriage. It is not necessary to review the literature here. A few illustrations from well known sources will suffice. According to Schapera, in order for a marriage to be valid, under Tswana law, 'two essential conditions must be satisfied: (a) a formal agreement . . . must be made between the two family-groups concerned, and (b) the bridegroom's family must give cattle to the family of the bride'.[11]

Max Gluckman makes the same point concerning the legal effect of bridewealth among the Zulu of Natal. He notes that the payment of cattle makes a marriage valid and the husband becomes legal father to all his wife's children, whether or not he is their genitor. He cites the Zulu saying that 'cattle beget children' and adds that what the saying means is that 'the marriage cattle given for a woman indicate the giver (usually her husband) to be the pater of her children'.[12] Studies made in many other African societies confirm the above findings.

It should be stressed here that where sufficient bridewealth is not given, the children, unless subsequently redeemed, belong to the maternal side. It is irrelevant that they were sired by the husband. This is mainly because the reproductive rights in the wife were not transferred to the family of the husband. In some societies there are certain crucial instalments which have to be paid in order to effect this transfer. Perhaps a powerful illustration of the rule is found among the Swazi. According to Swazi law, when a man obtains cattle from a chief for his marriage, 'the first daughter of the union is then spoken of as the chief's child, and cattle received on her marriage go to [the chief or] his heir'.[13] And the custom of the Kuria of northeastern Tanzania requires that where cattle are borrowed from a co-wife's 'house' to pay for the marriage of another co-wife's son, they must be returned, otherwise the children arising from that marriage will belong to the house from where the cattle came.[14]

So much importance is placed on the power of bridewealth to validate a marriage and affiliate its offspring that in some African societies which practice levirate marriages,[15] children born after the death of the first husband will be counted as legitimate issue of the dead man and his lineage and are entitled to inherit from his estate.[16] Ghost-marriages[17] are also based on the same jural postulate in that bridewealth is paid on behalf of the dead relative and another man, usually a kinsman, is appointed to perform the role of genitor to the children but the resulting children belong to the dead man.[18]

In sum, it can be said that bridewealth, while serving to validate marriage, had also the capacity to determine the status of children. It was possible for a man to marry without assuming any rights in the children of the marriage. This occurred typically in matrilineal societies where children belong to the maternal side and where the amount of bridewealth payable was small. It also occurred in cases where insufficient amount of bridewealth was paid and no transfer of the woman's reproductive potential was effected.[19]

Whereas the role of property (as bridewealth) in creating status relations and determining the kinship affiliation of the children is significant in traditional Africa, it is important not to lose sight of the fact that it was the birth of children that stabilized marriage and thus made it possible for bridewealth to remain where it had been 'deposited'. As the Swazi people say, 'the marriage cattle are closed by the carrying sling in which the baby is tied on the mother's back'.[20] This saying suggests that birth of children is essential for the stability of marriage. We must therefore, briefly turn our attention to the role of children in promoting the stability of marriage in traditional Africa.

(b) Children and Marriage Stability

The birth of children was and still is an important factor in the stability of marriage. Children enhance the social status of the mother and secure her position in the husband's lineage. In many communities a marriage was not viewed to be an event which occurred in a single day but a process which unfolded over many years during which time the two affinal groups got to know one another better. One major reason for the slow process of marriage is the fact that until children were born, the marriage was not considered to be well established. As noted already, since one of the functions of marriage in traditional societies was to establish an alliance between two families or kinship groups and children were seen as the essential link between the two social groups, the alliance could not be complete without there being many children.

Referring to the importance of children among the Dinka people of the Sudan, John Makec notes that 'the offspring of the union stand in the middle of the two families. They hold both sides of the marriage . . . together'.[21] He adds that a marriage which is childless in Dinka society lacks a 'sound foundation'.[22] Welch and Sachs also stress that the parents of the bride in the Manica province of Mozambique would not take the whole marriage payment until children had been born to the couple.[23] The Ndebele people of Zimbabwe also refrain from paying all bridewealth until children have been born.[24] And in the Batimbaru community of Tarime District in Tanzania, a father-in-law would ask for an additional cow called Nyabirundu (the cow of the birundu plants) which, according to Ruel, is given as a recognition that the marriage has held together. But the request for Nyabirundu was made only after a daughter had given birth to two or three children.[25]

Thus where a wife delayed in conceiving, both sides would make efforts to find a solution. A traditional doctor would be contacted to look into the reasons for the delay. If it were found that an important relative had not got his share of the bridewealth cattle, this would be given immediately. Referring to the Barbaig, a pastoral community of Tanzania, George Klima[26] notes that a 'husband's refusal to send his wife to a ritual specialist in order to be cured of infertility or frequent miscarriages is the second major complaint of women wishing a divorce'. And Weinrich observed in Zimbabwe that where 'fertility was unobtainable by either medical or religious means, social customs allowed a substitution of an infertile spouse by either a relative or an additional wife'.[27]

In the case of the Igbo of Eastern Nigeria, if a senior wife was unable to bear a child for her husband she could, by personally paying bridewealth, 'marry' for her husband another wife. The new wife would cohabit with the husband and the resulting children belonged to the senior wife with her husband. In such cases the junior wife could not establish her own independent house because she was a surrogate mother.[28] Writing about the Swazi, Kuper notes that where a wife is unable to bear children, 'her husband is entitled to a co-wife from her family to produce children, and they are spoken of as the children of the older woman as well as of the younger'. The latter practice is described as putting 'into the womb of another'.[29]

Also the Kuria of Tanzania permitted a wife who was unable to bear a son in her second marriage, but had sons in a previous marriage, to ask her former husband to give her a son for her new marriage. In such a case the new husband was required to give a head of cattle to the father in return for the child. Yet where the wife had no other children there was another possibility. She could form what is called *mokamona* marriage ie 'daughter-in-law marriage' with the help of her husband. In such a case she would 'marry' a young wife for her 'house' so that this young wife could bear a son for her.[30] Commenting on the prevalence of the practice of widow inheritance among the Nyakyusa of Tanzania, Monica Wilson notes that many non-Christian widows 'agree to be inherited because they wish to remain with their children; if they refuse the heir, they are parted from their children like divorced women'.[31]

All this goes to show that great importance was attached to the birth of children and their role in promoting the formation and stability of marriage. Hence, Weinrich puts the point well when he states that in Zimbabwe a man without children would not be accorded adult status. Social pressure and traditional religion were used to add weight to this highly regarded community obligation. The Shona say that 'without children a man will be forgotten because only sons can pour libations for them.'[32]

So far we have looked at bridewealth and its role in validating marriage as well as its function of determining the status of children. We have also considered the importance of children in promoting the stability of marriage and how certain forms of marriage are, to a large extent, motivated by the desire to have and retain children. It should be clear by now therefore, that the position of the child in Africa can only be appreciated by locating him in this matrix of wider social and economic ties. In order to complete the overview, we need to look finally at the economic role of children in Africa.

(c) The Economic and Social Role of Children

The economic and social roles of children in Africa have been written about by a number of ethnologists who studied many societies during the colonial period and after. One common theme running through the literature is that children perform important economic roles by directly engaging in production from a very early age. These roles tend to follow existing gender based division of labour and to reflect the dominant economic activities of the particular group.[33]

Writing about the Kipsigis of Kenya, Ian Orchardson notes that as the male children 'get a little older, it is [their] task to look after the lambs and kids, to bring them to their mothers in the evening and to put them away under their upturned baskets for the night'. The boys continue performing these tasks until they reach the age of initiation when they are assigned more responsible duties in the fields and pastures. As for the girls, Orchardson found that although they also herd sheep and goats when the boys are not around, their main tasks include looking after babies, 'whom they often have to carry about on their backs or hips before they are old and strong enough for such a weight'.[34] During the weeding season Kipsigis girls also partake in farmwork by going around in small groups 'hand weeding the fields of their neighbours or relations'.[35]

Similar observations were made by George Klima among the Barbaig, a pastoral community of central Tanzania. He observed that children start to engage in production from an early age and as they grow up they are assigned more tasks relative to their age. According to Klima, 'boys and girls of three years are given the task of herding small stock such as calves, sheep, and goats, in the vicinity of the kraal [and] as they get older, [they] are allowed to herd large animals'. Here again, like the Kipsigis, girls in the Barbaig community may partake in herding with the boys but their main duties lie with their mothers whom they help with child care and other domestic chores such as grinding maize meal and drawing water. Klima observed little girls, some of them less than four years old, accompanying their mothers back from the river with small water gourds placed on their backs as they staggered and struggled back to the homestead. He adds that these little girls must feel 'a sense of accomplishment when the water in their tiny gourds is used to prepare the evening meal'.[36]

In Liberia, Bledsoe found that Kpelle children do not only perform economic roles, such as those illustrated above, but they are also politically important to their families. Boys may be sent to the homes of important political leaders to work there during which time these children are expected to acquire political skills and to establish important political connections for themselves and for their families. The Haya people of the Kagera region of Tanzania had a comparable practice whereby young men were sent to the chief for military training and service and if they distinguished themselves there, they could be rewarded with a political office or be given cattle or wives to marry. Similar practices are known to have existed in the Lake Victoria region of Uganda and in other parts of Africa.

In times of dire economic hardship, child-pledging was viewed as a solution for the survival of some families. According to Holleman's research in Zimbabwe, conducted during the late 1940s and early 1950s, a marriage by child-pledging developed out of economic hardships arising from droughts and famine where heads of families who had few options for survival would pledge their daughters in return for grain or cattle. He also noticed that some fathers pledged their infant daughters in order to meet a sudden bridewealth claim caused by a son's unexpected elopement with a girl from another family.[37] The practice of child-pledging among the Chagga of Tanzania occurred in a variety of ways. Any child could be given as collateral for an unpaid debt and in case of a female, if she attained the age of marriage before the debt was paid, the creditor could receive the bridewealth as an interest on the debt.[38] In pre-colonial times, Chagga children were also used as security in cattle transactions. This occurred where a family, having taken cattle for grazing from another unrelated family, was required to give a child to the cattle owners as security. In Zimbabwe, even today, in cases of homicide, custom requires that a child must be given to the family of the deceased to placate the spirit of the dead. This practice, like marriage by child-pledging, has been abolished, but some of its elements remain.[39]

At another level, children in Africa, even today, are still 'given' to other relatives to enhance kinship relationships. For example, a young married woman may be given a child to look after because she is lonely [see Armstrong in this Volume]. A married sister without children of her own could ask her brother to give her a child to look after. And a grandparent living apart from adult married children has a right to ask for a child from his son to help her to make a fire, run errands and perform all the tasks appropriate to his age. In 1989 during my field research in Tanzania, I interviewed an old Kuria lady who complained that her married sons had refused to give her children to look after, noting with concern that 'an old woman without grandchildren to look after, would be considered a witch by her peers'.[40] Sometimes children are sent to live with relatives in urban centres to assist them with housework or to train for a career. In the 1974 census conducted in rural Sierra Leone, women aged between 25–29 reported that 40 per cent of their children were living away from their mother.[41]

Although the main objective underlying the engagement of children in various economic activities was to train them for future adult roles, there is no doubt that tangible economic benefits accrued to parents and the household members from the work of children. As we shall see, although children play such a vital economic role their participation is played down as insignificant. What the adults stress is the fact that they cared for the child, gave him food and proper upbringing. All this is leads to an accumulated debt to be repaid by the child with a lifetime of unquestioning obedience and loyalty. In those cases where children were pledged, this was viewed as service to the greater good of the family.

In sum, the economic and social roles of children can be viewed as part of a self-propelling system of inter-generational dependence whereby children were cared for by adults in return for future support. Hence as they grew older their economic roles also increased and changed. The girls become brides thus linking their natal families with the families of their husbands. They also initiated a movement of resources in the form of marriage cattle or other property which in due course would be applied to the marriage of their own brothers through a system of linking. Occasionally such cattle could also be used to marry additional wives for the bride's father. This system of mutual dependence between generations has been described as a 'wealth in people' system.[42] The system provides an incentive for the adults to look after the young in return for future material as well as other form of support.

We can sum up the foregoing section, therefore, by noting that no matter how we look at the values and beliefs of most African societies, great importance was attached to having children. This is short of saying that the entire social system as well as its survival was organized around and geared towards the objective of acquiring as many children as the community could get. In modern Western cultures such a desire for children might be viewed as irrational as well as economically unwise. However, if we consider that these economic systems did not have advanced technology but depended on human labour, it will become clear that the survival of the entire community largely depended upon how efficient they were in reproducing themselves. Moreover, the fact that many children died during infancy and others were miscarried during pregnancy did not reduce the desire to have more.

In the next section we turn out attention to some of the effects arising from the introduction of colonial rule and the penetration of capitalist relations and how these in turn have impacted on children.

III.   SOCIO-ECONOMIC CHANGE AND ITS EFFECTS ON CHILDREN

Much has been written about the economic and social transformation of Africa. Only a brief overview will be given here. Most of Africa south of the Sahara fell under European colonial rule from about the end of the nineteenth century. Although the British and the French took most of the Continent, some other parts were occupied by the Dutch, Belgians, Germans, Italians and Portuguese. For the first time a powerful state apparatus was established to prevail over various indigenous political systems and social groups which were located within its jurisdiction.

The economies and social systems of Africa which for many generations had been autonomous and oriented to meet subsistence needs became part of a wider political and economic order of the colonial state. Through a range of administrative and legal techniques such as compulsory taxation, forced sale of livestock and enforced cultivation of cash crops, the colonial state created a need for European money. Households soon became partially dependent upon the market for their recurrent needs and this implied also a degree of vulnerability to the economic crises of the world economy.

Some parts of Africa, especially those neighbouring mining towns and large commercial farming regions lost many economically active males who were drawn into wage employment. Molokomme notes for example, that 'as early as 1943 . . . almost half of the young Batswana men between the ages of 15 and 44 years were employed away from their homes, and 28 per cent of all adult Batswana males were absent working in South Africa'.[43] In these regions wives and children were mostly left in the rural villages without male support. There was therefore, a growing number of female-headed households with dependent children.[44] But the pull to the urban centres, though carefully regulated, also attracted some women who moved into mining towns in search of jobs and independent income.[45]

The monetization of these economies had its impact on social relations as well. For example, kinship ties which had provided the framework for production and distribution of essential goods and services weakened as individuals began to produce for the world market and others migrated into urban centres for wage employment. Land rights which had been more generally vested in the community and widely shared, underwent rapid transformation due to the growth of commercial farming. There was a growing market for land in certain parts of Africa which in turn led to problems of land shortage.

In this process of change, Christian missions also played a crucial role in promoting individualist ideas. Marriage was defined as a union of one man and one woman and the nuclear family was projected as the ideal type. The payment of bridewealth was condemned as a form of wife-purchase and practices like widow inheritance, sororate and levirate marriages were discouraged.[46] These changes had very specific impact on marriage payments as well as on the status and welfare of children. We shall examine these in greater detail below.

(a) Changes in Bridewealth and Marriage

When looking at the nature of bridewealth[47] and its legal effect in modern Africa, we have to confront the complex issue of whether we are dealing with a traditional economic exchange or with an individualized economic transaction. Indeed the same applies to marriage both in its form, that is, how it is negotiated and celebrated and in the relationships arising from marriage. This dualism also appears at the conceptual level when the same vocabulary is used by individuals to describe a marriage payment or any other property transfer as if it is still traditional.[48] Notwithstanding these conceptual difficulties there are certain qualitative transformations in the institution of marriage and bridewealth which have impacted on the status of children. These transformations are considered below together with their effects.

Research and even casual observation show that bridewealth in most parts of Africa has taken a new economic and social character. To-day cash has become a major component of most bridewealth transactions in Africa. In the past, marriage payments in pastoral and semi-pastoral communities comprised mainly livestock. In other communities they consisted of agricultural subsistence goods and services. Locally made iron hoes and even gold bars were given as part of the bridewealth. All this has now largely changed into European money, industrial consumer goods, or a combination of all these.[49] This development is so prevalent in Africa that it does not require illustration here.

In many parts of Africa this process may have begun when a small cash component was added to bridewealth in order to assist the bride's father, for example, in paying colonial poll tax, or in buying a new dress for the girl's mother or sending a child to a local school. The Shona people of Zimbabwe described these additional payments as the 'little things' ie *zviduku*.[50] In due course, the little things ceased to be little and as the practice became socially accepted the cash component also increased. In some parts of Africa cash became the major item payable on marriage.[51]

On the other hand, in matrilineal societies where bride-service was common, this was also gradually transformed. Thus the son-in-law, instead of going to reside with his wife's family and working for them for a number of years, got an exemption by paying cash. But this clearly deprived the wife's family of an opportunity to cultivate a close relationship with the man to whom their daughter would be married. Co-residence with one's in-laws must have been crucial in creating a basis for future understanding between the husband and the wife's family to whom the children of the marriage belonged.

Another significant transformation which is noticeable in most parts of Africa is that the obligation to pay for one's marriage has also narrowed. It has become the obligation of the prospective husband alone and if he is fortunate he may get assistance from his father especially if it is his first marriage. Thus writing about the Kpelle of Liberia Bledsoe notes that, 'young men seeking bridewealth funds [t]ry to define these as their due patrimony [b]ut their older male kin are equally determined to define bridewealth as a debt that the young man must repay with labour and loyalty'.[52]

The new ethos of individualism and the emerging property relations were enhanced by colonial law and state and given a new legitimacy. Thus when a Tanzanian son applied to the court for an order to compel his father to pay bridewealth for him, the court rejected the application on the ground that to allow such an application 'would be dangerously encroaching on the individual rights to property'.[53] Yet as noted above, in pre-colonial Africa the obligation to pay bridewealth was not placed entirely on the husband or his family. It was the community concern to see to it that its young men got wives for the economic prosperity and continuity of the whole community. But now things were changing.

Young men working in urban centres and mines were able to earn enough money to pay for their marriages. They could even ignore the views of elders and select wives whom they desired.

It can be argued, therefore, that one effect of the transformation of bridewealth into items such as cash, which were outside the control of male elders, led to the gradual weakening of the authority of the elders in initiating the process of marriage. Furthermore, individuals who could pay for their own marriages gained a degree of autonomy from the wider family in initiating their marriages. But there were other consequences which were far-reaching. One of these was that the cost of marriage now fell upon one family or, indeed, on the prospective husband. Thus in societies where bridewealth was high, the poor famil-ies could no longer afford to marry and have children. For example, in a case decided in 1967 at Mwika, Tanzania, a son-in-law who was sued by his wife's father for the balance of the unpaid bridewealth (being six cows and four goats) defended that 'he had no assets and no job'.[54] Kirwen's calculations, using the cattle prices of 1973, led him to con-clude that 'the purchase of twelve cows by an average [Tanzanian] man would require his total income for a period of two years'.[55] In the Tarime district of Tanzania where the average bridewealth is much higher, the same wife would have been worth five years of wage labour.[56]

The focusing of bridewealth liability on the single family or indi-viduals encouraged some young men to abscond with brides without paying for them and others to marry 'on credit'. Bledsoe notes that among the Kpelle of Liberia a man without relatives to lend him money or resources with which to marry could borrow a woman from a rich man by pledging his services. Such men have no legal rights in their children and are referred to as 'wife borrowers'.[57]

The large number of court cases which have been reported throughout Africa where fathers-in-law have sued their sons-in-law for the unpaid balance of bridewealth reflect both the inability of the husband to pay as well as the fact that the husband is considered to be the person legally liable to discharge that obligation. Hence in Lesotho, four researchers found that bridewealth negotiations had become long and acrimonious. Sometimes these negotiations led to what these researchers described as 'absurd requirements'. They were of the view that some of these prob-lems arise because 'bohali agreements have become enmeshed in a cash economy'.[58] On the question of the intensity of litigation concerning unpaid bridewealth, Cutshall's research in Zimbabwe reveals that bridewealth claims brought in the community courts 'constituted the fourth largest category of all complaints processed'.[59] My own investi-gations in the Lake Victoria regions of Tanzania reveal similar trends.[60]

Yet as might be appreciated, the transformation of bridewealth could not have occurred without having a corresponding impact on the posi-tion of children. Aspects of this impact are considered next.

(b) 'Children or Cattle'?: Competition Over Scarce Resources

In what was described above as court disputes between 'debtors' and their 'creditor' fathers-in-law, the children of the marriage become implicated as well. Many local courts in Africa even today still consider the birth of children to be the measure by which to determine the amount of bridewealth refundable on divorce.[61] In the case of an outstanding balance of payment, a father-in-law who may have been hesitant to press a claim for additional payment felt more confident to make a demand after a few children were born to the couple. And in the case of a son-in-law who did not pay up on demand, his wife and children could be recalled to their natal home for a while until the son-in-law had produced an acceptable instalment.[62]

Where a maternal grandfather did not wish to sue for payment, he could exercise the option of taking away the children from his son-in-law in order to force him to 'redeem' them by paying more cattle. Should such pressure be ignored and the son-in-law fails to pay up, the children would stay with the maternal family. Ultimately the maternal grandfather would be able to reimburse himself by arranging marriages for the female children. But if the father wished at a later time to 'redeem' his children, he would find himself paying a large amount of money as child-rearing fees. The purpose of such payment is to compensate the maternal family for raising the child. An additional amount might be added as child-redemption fee. Cutshall found in Zimbabwe that 'when fathers claim custody they may also face a counter-claim for outstanding *lobolo* or rearing fees'.[63]

Suits for child-rearing are quite common everywhere in modern Africa. They are the most practical means available by which maternal grandfathers can recover their costs from a former son-in-law who claims a child left there for many years after divorce or a wife's long desertion. This is more so when the father does not voluntarily send to his wife's parents any maintenance money or cows for milk. Similar child rearing fees can be claimed by a natural father who cohabits with a woman and has children with her. Such children are often claimed by a former husband of their mother who has not had his bridewealth refunded to him. Here again, children become implicated in the various disputes in which men compete over money and other scarce resources.

It should be noted here that although traditionally most African cultures recognize a kind of payment for child-rearing, this amount was neither large nor ever used as a bargaining chip for holding on to the child against the wishes of his family. Among the Sambaa of Tanzania, for example, such payment was known as *mtonge* and constituted one cow. Moreover, as we have noted, in traditional times, and indeed even today, children do perform important economic roles for the families with whom they live. Thus one might ask the question why are those for whom the children have served entitled to any compensation at all? Why should the child not be entitled to compensation for the service he has rendered?[64]

There are three possible explanations for this. The first is that in traditional times all the needs of children as well as those of the adults were met from the subsistence economic sector in which also the children actively participated. Today, children's needs can no longer be satisfied without cash. Children need clothes, school fees and medicine when they fall sick. Those who incur these costs expect to reimburse themselves when the child grows up and either gets a paid job in the city or, in case of a female child, when she gets married. Therefore, anyone who wishes to take away such an asset, must compensate the family which has invested in the child. These claims are framed in a manner perfectly acceptable to the state courts and are usually allowed. In Tanzania, legal fathers who fail to claim their children for many years by leaving them with the their maternal families are not viewed in a good light. It is thought that such claims are motivated by the desire for the daughters' bridewealth. Courts say that when daughters grow up and the time for their marriage is near, a father begins to remember a forgotten girl child who was not claimed after she was weaned.

The second reason why child-rearing fees are claimed is the fact that no monetary value is attached to the tasks which children perform, however onerous these may be. Their labours are viewed within the pre-capitalist economic context where money is not a measure of expended labour time. Moreover, the status relations of kinship are also deployed here to mask the underlying property relations. State courts share this notion of attaching different values to goods and services from the non-traditional sector so that when a person spends hard cash on the child, this cost tends to overshadow the economic contributions of the child in the farm or pastures. Indeed, in some parts of Africa, fathers charge a higher bridewealth for an educated daughter, partly because hard cash has been spent on her education but also because it is assumed she will earn money for her husband.

The third reason is that the system of 'wealth in people' is dependent on the degree to which a person is able to keep others indebted to him. In the case of a child, the system ensures that the child is not free from the obligation to support his parents. In order to do this successfully, the contribution of the child has always to be undervalued otherwise, it is feared, the child will be free of any future obligation.[65]

Another consequence of the transformation of bridewealth is the phenomenon of forced marriages. Forced marriages can be associated with the rise in the cost of marriage and with the inability of some men to pay for marriage. Although the problem of forced marriages has much to do with the wider social transformations, it is also true that the desire of certain parents to maximize returns from their daughter's marriage or to alleviate economic hardship, are some of the causes responsible for forced marriages. Many cases have been reported, both during the colonial period and after in which fathers have compelled their daughters to marry selected men who could afford to pay a large bridewealth.[66]

Economic need also underlies certain forms of marriages such as infant betrothal and child pledging. Many of these marriages come about as a result of factors completely unrelated to the wishes of the girl to marry. The result is that many of these marriages end up with the young wife running away to another district or to the city. In either case, several children would be sired by other men during the woman's desertion. If no formal divorce had been granted and bridewealth refunded, these children will be claimed by the deserted husband.[67] These events may lead to a cycle in which a girl child who was forced to marry ends up losing her children to a man whom she rejected.

While doing research in northeastern Tanzania, I came across many such cases. The most notable of these was the case of *Morabu Chacha*. In this case a man aged about sixty-years gave fifty-six head of cattle to marry a young woman aged about twenty years. Despite the woman's protests she was nonetheless compelled by her father to marry the chosen husband. Shortly after the wedding she 'escaped' to live with another man with whom she had eight children. Yet because the second 'husband' did not have the fifty-six cattle to refund to the first husband, his wife could not obtain a valid divorce under customary law. The consequence was that all the children she had with her second husband were taken by the first husband, as they became available.[68]

It is quite possible that the second husband, in the above case, was unable to get the assistance of his kinsmen who could have contributed cattle to enable him to redeem his wife and children. The relatives could have recovered their contribution on the marriage of their kinsman's daughter.[69] Thus we see again that the shifting of the obligation to pay bridewealth from the wider community to the husband resulted in a complete inability of some husbands to lay any claim over their own children; much like the wife 'borrowers' of Liberia reported by Bledsoe. The reverse consequence was that the rich husband could lay a claim on children fathered by other men. When the same argument is put from the child's point of view, it can be said that the father's inability to pay bridewealth denies a child the right to 'belong' to his natural parents and compels him to be 'owned' by the man who paid cattle to marry his mother. Thus commenting on the case of *Morabu Chacha* a High Court Judge in Tanzania wondered why the appellant:

Instead of challenging the respondent's right to take away his children, he goes to court to claim costs he incurred in maintaining his own children ... It is clearly against the interests of these children to be taken away from their mother and natural father and be given to a strange old man whose only interest in them is as possible sources of more cattle wealth (per Mfalila J).

Yet as noted in this paper, the narrowing of the obligation to pay bridewealth also shifted the balance of power and authority in the marriage relationship from the community to the husband. As Seeiso and her colleagues found in Lesotho, 'payment of *Bohali* gives the husband very strong and almost absolute rights over his wife'.[70] Thus the role which the community had played in the formation of marriage was gradually assumed by the husband. And the children arising from that marriage also became the sole responsibility of the husband.

Sally Moore found that in 1957 local courts of Kilimanjaro, Tanzania, were prepared to compensate a Chagga father for providing care to his married daughter who happened to be temporarily living at her natal home owing to a marital dispute.[71] And in the cases where married daughters returned to their natal homes for childbirth, courts in Kilimanjaro ordered husbands to pay to their families the cost of feeding and caring for the said wives during their post-partum periods. Comparable cases occurring about the same time in other parts of Tanzania confirm this trend. Thus the duty to maintain a wife or a child became more narrowly defined and was increasingly shifted from the wider family and placed on the shoulders of the husband and father.

As noted above, this change was supported by the colonial state in a variety of ways. For example, in disputes over the guardianship and custody of children between various claimants it became necessary to determine precisely the specific individual who was to be held liable to discharge certain obligations. Although this was the way European law viewed the allocation of rights and obligations between individuals, it was also the way social relations were developing at this time. In this case the law reinforced the changes which were already taking place.

In sum, these illustrations which are by no means exhaustive or confined to one region of Africa show how the status of the child was seriously altered by change. As we noted already, the narrowing of the obligation to pay bridewealth weakened the community participation in the marriage of individual members of the group. This development had a corresponding effect on the responsibility of the wider community towards children. As husbands struggled to raise the necessary resources to marry, they began to feel entitled to exercise authority over their wives as well as over their children. This authority was given blessing by the colonial state which began to order husbands to meet the cost of child rearing. Besides the obvious inclination for men to maximize returns from a marriage relationship, there was also the problem created by the weakening of kinship ties which created insecurity and thus motivated men to expand their immediate families by having more children. In this way conflicts over scarce resources such as livestock and cash became inextricably intertwined with competition over rights in children.

IV. THE BEST INTERESTS OF THE CHILD: WHO DEFINES THEM?

Before moving on to consider in greater detail the points raised above, it is necessary to spell out the two senses in which the term 'best interest of the child' is used in this paper. The first is derived from Anglo-American family law (see Parker in this Volume) which state courts and quasi-judicial tribunals apply when determining questions concerning children particularly in the context of matrimonial proceedings, but also in proceedings for adoption of children and guardianship of minors. This is the first sense which state courts in Africa apply in comparable proceedings. Thus the term 'best interests of the child' or 'welfare of the child', with its various levels of weighting, is to be found in received statutory provisions of many African countries. It is not a principle of African law but came to Africa via the colonial received law but has now been accepted as part of the local law.

There is a second sense in which the term 'best interests' is used in this paper. This encapsulates a much wider notion of what the community or family consider to be in the interest of a given child or children. As this paper has so far shown, there is often no clear separation between the interests of the child or children on the one hand and the interests of adult members of the family or any relevant social group on the other hand. The main reason for this lack of separation lies in the way the traditional society was organized economically as well as socially. As this paper has tried to show briefly, the pre-capitalist communities of Africa were not organized on individualist lines and hence they tended to subsume individual interests into group interests.

What seems to be happening in contemporary Africa is a continuing conflict between the wider and the narrow version of the term 'best interests'. As would be expected, the wider (or pre-capitalist) version might be used as a means of exploiting the child (in the modern context of individualism) by those who are in a position to benefit from maintaining that interpretation. But these efforts are likely to be shortlived as they seem to run against the tide of individual autonomy (or self-determination of the child; see Eekelaar in this Volume). The narrow version is likely to become dominant as states continue to bind themselves to implement international treaties on the rights of the child. Indeed even the OAU Charter on the Rights and Welfare of the African Child stresses in Article 1 (3) that 'any custom, tradition, cultural or religious practice that is inconsistent with the rights, duties and obligations contained in the present Charter shall to the extent to such inconsistency be null and void'. Having noted these two meanings of the term 'best interests' we must now turn to the discussion of how parents make their choices and what constraints they have put into account when determining what is in the best interests of a child in the changing social and economic context of Africa.

(a) The Child's Best Interests: Formal Education or Marriage?

In this section, the paper raises some of the issues identified above and considers the possible factors which parents put into account when making decisions concerning what is in the best interests of their children. Included in these factors is the role of the state and law in shaping the outcome by imposing its own version of the best interests principle. The general thrust of this section is to show first, that economic factors do play a major role in the decisions of parents, whether this is to do with sending a child to school or opting instead for a child's marriage or indeed even giving up custody (in the case of mothers) to the father; second, that in the majority of cases the interests of the children and those of their parents are not considered to be separate; and lastly, that although the state in Africa has intervened since the colonial period to protect what it defines as the interests of children, its role remains highly circumscribed by its lack of resources. In certain cases, however, this is due to the State's allocation of scarce resources without seriously considering the needs of children. Consequently, most African governments have continued to depend upon families to make provisions for their own children. Hence, for those children who are without families or those whose families are unable to support them, no tangible institutionalized arrangements exist to provide for such children.

The family in rural Africa today has limited choices concerning what future it must prepare for its young members. Formal education in private or government schools is one such choice. Yet, unlike informal training in agriculture and animal husbandry, formal education costs money which many parents lack. Even where education is offered free, some parents may fail to pay for school uniforms and other invisible costs like travelling expenses.[72] The decisions which parents will have to make regarding the future of a given child depend upon a range of factors as well as the parents' own conception of what is best for the child. Rarely is a child consulted on such matters.

A number of strategies have been devised by some parents to overcome their economic inability to educate their children. For example, a child may be sent away to assist a relative in doing housework in return for tuition money and a place at a neighbouring school. In most cases there is an expectation on the part of parents that their child will be treated as a member of the family. This is because the entire arrangement is viewed in an African traditional framework. But times have changed and reality sometimes points to a different direction. Such a child may never be enrolled at a school or, having been enrolled, he/she may be burdened with housework and thus never get adequate time to do private study. This burdening may lead the child into failing examinations.[73]

On the other hand, where resources are scarce and a choice has to be made, it is most probable that a son will take precedence over a daughter. Although this is clearly discriminatory, it is nonetheless rational in the eyes of many parents. Take the patrilineal communities in which a bride leaves her natal home and follows her prospective husband. In these communities, daughters are viewed largely as potential wives for another family. It is expected that in such cases the woman will make economic contribution to the family of her husband. As for sons, it is believed that they will stay to provide for their parents during their old age. Sons are also viewed as the future heads of the paternal family. Their success in educational or career goals will be shared by the whole paternal family.

Anyone who has visited African institutions of higher learning such as universities or other training institutions at tertiary level will be struck by the lack of a healthy balance between female and male students. There is indeed a huge body of literature on this subject and statistics from government ministries all over Africa show this imbalance clearly.[74] Whatever other explanations exist for this phenomenon, it cannot be denied that in a society where female children are viewed as future sources of bridewealth and where marriage and child bearing are seen as the major vocation for women, formal education will not be considered a top priority for them.

Even in cases where a daughter is sent to school, it is expected that she will drop out to attend female initiation rites which in some cases take several months to complete. In other societies the end of the rite is the beginning of marriage because the girl is ready to bear children. Here again, because it is believed that initiation for a woman is more important than formal education, the choice is made in favour of initiation. Some African communities believe that a girl who does not go through the ritual cannot bear children. Few parents would be willing to take the risk of having no grandchildren.

While researching in northeastern Tanzania (in 1979), I came across an interesting instance of conflict and accommodation between the demand for formal education and female initiation. During interviews with Kuria elders of northeastern Tanzania, I found that the age for female circumcision had dramatically dropped, in the preceding couple of decades, from around fourteen to about eight years. Parents were apprehensive that their daughters would come into contact with men before undergoing an important puberty rite. Pregnancy before initiation among the Kuria, or indeed even mere sexual intercourse, is considered to be a serious breach carrying adverse ritual consequences for the whole family. As one old man told me, 'we could not take chances' with our daughters.[75] Thus, although the importance of formal education may be appreciated, parents are still inclined to weigh these new advantages against existing values and other interests of the child.

But other parents have an interest in withdrawing their daughters from school before they become too difficult. Caroline Bledsoe found in Liberia that although many Kpelle girls 'go to the nearby public schools, few are graduated even from the sixth grade. Their parents usually take them out of school, insisting that girls with too much education become hard to handle and leave for greener pastures in the city – often an accurate perception'.[76]

There is here a strong connection, therefore, between economic and cultural factors on the one hand and the discrimination of a girl child in the sphere of higher education on the other. This, as noted before, is part of a larger question concerning gender relations and the status of women in contemporary African societies. Although some states in Africa have passed legislation to prohibit parents from withdrawing their daughters prematurely from schools, this has not been always effective. Either governments have simply failed to police families or parents have exploited certain conflicts in state policy to attain their objectives. One example from Tanzania will be used here to illustrate the point. It is an offence in Tanzania for a parent or guardian to fail to register a child who has attained the age of seven years. It is also an offence to withdraw a child from primary school before that child has completed seven years of formal education.[77]

Since 1977 primary education in Tanzania is technically free for all children between the ages of seven and thirteen years. It is also a rule in all primary and secondary schools that a pupil who becomes pregnant is automatically expelled from school. During interviews, I found that some parents who were too scared to withdraw their daughters from primary schools, for fear of prosecution, had them married secretly to men while they continued to attend school until they became pregnant. Then, predictably, they would be expelled by the school authorities at which point they became full time wives.[78]

There were also other stratagems which I uncovered during interviews. For example, I was told that because the system of transfer of school children from one district or region to another is imperfect, it was common for parents who wanted to withdraw their daughters from school to initiate a fake transfer whereby, instead of the daughter going to the designated school, she went to a designated husband in a distant village. Because it is assumed by school authorities that parents will follow up such transfers, in the interests of their children, it was not thought that anyone could use this device to evade the law.

But formal education, besides costing money, also takes children away from home where they are productively employed in the fields and in

cattle rearing. As noted already, female children are very useful in looking after their younger siblings while their mothers are away in the
fields. It is indeed instructive to note here that in 1978, soon after the
law for compulsory school attendance was enacted in Tanzania, it was
reported by the Ministry of Education that the largest number of children who remained unregistered or missed classes often were from pastoral communities. There is a possible correlation here between the
essential functions of children in pastoral communities and their absence
from schools.

Even those girls who are lucky to remain in school a bit longer are
still not free from the constraints of sexual division of labour or family
poverty. For example, female day students who return home every evening after school with a quantity of homework assignments to do may
find themselves asked instead to fetch water from a distant river or to
prepare an evening meal while their brothers go free to do their own
private study. In the urban areas, mothers who cannot make ends meet
with the housekeeping money use their daughters to assist them in the
preparation and sale of pastries and other foods. Other children come
straight from school to the market or small shop to relieve their mothers
so that the latter can return home to prepare the family evening meal.[79]

Studies in urban centres in parts of Africa show that the participation
of children in the economic undertakings of the family has increased
relative to the worsening economic situation of families. For example,
in her research in Tanzania, Aili Trip found that the economic role of
women had changed drastically over the last two decades. Whereas
surveys conducted in Dar es Salaam in the 1970s showed a large percentage of women (ie 66 per cent) had no source of income, surveys conducted in the same city ten years later showed a remarkable change. In
a Dar es Salaam survey conducted in 1987–1988 Trip found that many
of the surveyed women (ie 66 per cent) had income-generating projects
in which they sold food-stuff, charcoal, secondhand clothes and local
beverages.[80] Research in other urban centres elsewhere in Africa shows
similar trends.[81]

The engagement of children in the economic undertakings of the
family, however detrimental to their school work, is often viewed as an
extension of the traditional practice whereby, as noted above, children
were active participants in the subsistence economy. Yet, unlike the
traditional era where future career and training were synchronized, the
extracurricular activities of the pupils clearly conflict with the objectives
of formal education. And yet, on the other hand, these activities are in
many cases vital for the economic survival of the family. Here again we
see that the economic difficulties of the family are shared between its
members notwithstanding the fact that the long term perspective indicates that the child pays a higher price.[82]

The above are but a few illustrations of the conflict between the values of the modern world symbolized by formal education as a desirable goal for the child and the competing values of the old order made more complex by economic constraints and the harsh realities of modern living. Before completing this section we should take up another theme which also reveals the various ways in which values promoted by the state might conflict with the parents' view of what is in the best interests of the child.

(b) Economic Factors Affecting Child Custody Today

A number of African countries have passed legislation in which it is expressly stated that in all cases involving the guardianship and custody of minor children, the best interests of the child shall be first and paramount.[83] Whereas in a few countries this requirement has not been extended to cases where customary law is the only law applicable, many jurisdictions in Africa apply this rule to all children irrespective of the system of law applicable. Moreover, even in those states where the principle of the best interests of the child is not mandatory, courts have drawn inspiration from the general law and in practice have applied the principle in its broad form. It can be argued therefore, that in view of the growing pressure for reform of family laws in Africa, the best interests of the child principle, as understood in Anglo-American law, is likely to be more widely applicable. This is more so now that many African states have ratified the United Nations Convention on the Rights of the Child as well as the African Charter on the Rights and Welfare of the Child.

This trend makes it important to begin looking at the factors which might play a part in influencing the application of the principle as well as the extent to which these are taken into account by courts in the application of this principle. Research on the way recently introduced family legislation is applied in some African states has shown that, despite the fact that the new laws are designed to improve the status of women by legislating for equality of rights in the family, the women, especially those in rural areas, appear not to have shown as much eagerness to claim their new rights.[84]

One of the new rights which seem not to be claimed is the right to custody of children at the time of divorce or separation. The major question is why this should be so. First, it must be emphasized that with minor exceptions, most mothers would like to have custody of their minor children after divorce or separation.[85] Therefore, indifference to the needs of the child or over-confidence as to the ability of the father to fulfil those needs cannot be the main reasons why mothers do not claim custody of children. In this section I shall stress the economic reasons which seem to be the most significant in the decisions in which mothers do not claim custody. Indeed, by way of contrast and emphasis, I shall try to show also that where these economic factors are removed, women do seek and are awarded custody of their children by courts.

I shall begin with a general statement that in societies where vital economic resources such as land, livestock, and money are held by husbands and fathers, it is inevitable that separating the child from the holder of such resources is detrimental to the short term as well as the long term interests of the particular child and indeed even the mother.

Many rural women in Africa do not have independent land rights and are therefore dependent on men as husbands, parents or adult sons, to allocate to them land on which to grow food for themselves as well as their minor children.[86] Indeed one can say that a substantial number of unhappy marriages today are maintained primarily for the sake of children. As we have noted, the system of levirate and widow inheritance is partly grounded on economic provision for the widow as well as for the children.[87] Thus many rural mothers are reluctant to separate from their children but are also equally unwilling to take them away from their source of economic support.

One might ask, for example, why the law which requires parents to provide maintenance for their children should not be invoked to compel a father to make such provision. This is almost a joke for the majority of poor families in Africa whether they reside in the rural or urban centres. An ordinary peasant who relies on home grown food and has small cash obtained from the sale of cash crops or a stipend from his labouring migrant son cannot be ordered to make a monthly payment to court for children staying with another family. Moreover, it will be assumed by the father that these children are economically profitable to the family where they reside. Why, therefore, should a person who does not benefit from their services be compelled to pay for their maintenance?

There is also the fear, often justifiable, that if a mother takes away a child, particularly a son, the father might lose interest in the child and this may endanger the child's future chances of whatever little inheritance he can expect, let alone the opportunity of getting a bridewealth contribution for a first wife.[88] This fear is not only entertained in relation to the father but also to the extended family of the father who might resent the fact that the child has been taken away from them to grow up with his maternal relatives as if the paternal family owed any bride-wealth for his mother.

Perhaps realizing this danger but also anxious not to isolate the child from both parents, local court justices in Zambia have now developed a pragmatic policy of ordering that 'children are for both parents'. This imaginative approach, as Himonga's recent study shows, has been taken in order to stress the fact that both parents whether married or divorced have 'joint responsibility to support and maintain their children'. The justices were apprehensive that if they were to make custody orders which gave custody to one parent, 'the parent who did not get the children would not feel any responsibility to support them'.[89] The point therefore, is not to isolate any parent but to encourage them to pool their resources together, 'in view of the high cost of educating and feeding children in the modern society'.[90]

But there may be other reasons more personal to the mother. In cases of a young mother, she may wish to remarry or indeed to move on into the urban centre to get a job. This factor will weigh against any attempt on her part to press for custody of children. Many husbands will not be too keen to marry a wife and let her come in with an entourage of children from a previous marriage. This may have been acceptable in the pre-colonial era when the cost of maintaining children was more widely spread and little or no cash was involved. Hence the Zimbabwean traditional view that 'if you pull a branch you pull it together with its leaves' is now cracking under the weight of economic imperatives.[91]

In the case of working class urban families, life is such that members of the family live literally from hand to mouth, not knowing whether or not they will get their next meal. We have noted in the previous part how women have moved into the informal economic sector in order to survive. Their contribution to the household budget must be considerable. However, their economic position is not yet strong enough to give them the confidence necessary to mobilize for their custodial rights. They still lack all those things they would wish for their children. Indeed as Rwebangira found in Dar es Salaam, Tanzania, some non-custodial mothers are prepared to 'support their older children clandestinely either at school or by preparing meals which children regularly stop by to have on their way to school and sometimes on [their] return'.[92] And those mothers who have tried to seek custody still face some difficulty in proving to the court that they have a reliable income and decent accommodation with which to support the children.[93]

Families within this economic bracket have next to nothing left to give to the children who may be living with another family. Mothers who know the real economic situation in the home are not likely to view with enthusiasm any law giving them a right to custody. Hence, as noted above, they may be prepared to offer to their children some additional economic support even if this may sometimes be done secretly. Hence, as Armstrong has correctly noted in her aptly titled report on the maintenance research, the rather large number of claims for maintenance in Zimbabwe and Botswana reflects the fact that in both states there is some money to be shared owing to high levels of employment. But in Mozambique, where the economy is in poor shape, only a small number of people claim maintenance.[94]

But even here, where the husband has a job and, hence, an income which can be garnisheed, there are two problems. The first problem is that the amount of maintenance ordered by courts is often unrealistic relative to the actual cost of maintaining a child in any setting, whether rural or urban. The second is that, once ordered, fathers are too slow to comply with the court order. Cutshall's study in Zimbabwe community courts shows that court awards for child maintenance were much less than the amount originally claimed. This finding has been confirmed by a more recent study by Women and Law in Southern Africa (WLSA) research team.[95]

But what is even more revealing is Cutshall's finding that community courts were more inclined to reduce the maintenance claim when respondents fell in the upper-income category than when they fell into the lower-income category, thus tending to ignore the 'means test'. He concluded that the community courts' claim-reduction strategy was aimed at reducing high-value claims, even when such claims might be reasonable or justified in view of the respondent's income. The reason for this rather arbitrary reduction was because the courts were aware of the people's opposition to such orders.[96] Indeed even after these claims were considerably reduced, the rate of non-compliance was still high. In neighbouring Zambia, until 1990, the maximum amount of maintenance which subordinate courts could order for a wife and a child was a mere Kwacha 120 and even more laughable was the K.12 maximum amount for a child born out of wedlock. This amount has been raised now to K.8,000 and K.1,000 respectively, but as Armstrong has pointed out, these amounts are still grossly inadequate. In Lesotho, because most husbands work in the South African mines, and until now no reciprocal maintenance agreements exist between the two states[97] a married woman who needs maintenance has to travel to South Africa to petition in the court. Small wonder therefore, that WLSA researchers found only a negligible number of women who applied to the court for maintenance.[98]

Throughout the entire southern Africa region, except perhaps Zimbabwe, WLSA researchers found a general reluctance on the part of women to seek maintenance in court against their husbands or even lovers with whom they had children. These findings are not peculiar to that region nor indeed is the tendency for courts to order unrealistic amounts of maintenance. Research in Tanzania has revealed similar problems.[99] The maintenance orders for children are extremely out of step with the current or indeed even past economic realities. As in Zambia, the Tanzania Affiliation Ordinance fixes a maximum amount of child maintenance at Tshs.100 per month which is about US$ 0.20 and in neighbouring Kenya the Affiliation Law was repealed because it was believed that many women would become wealthy by receiving less than US$1.00 per month for every child conceived out of wedlock with various men.[100]

Perhaps to conclude this section I need only to refer to a few studies where courts have granted custody to mothers who are economically capable of supporting their children. Based on her recent research in Tanzania, Rwebangira has concluded that 'when custody claims are contested, women are disadvantaged by their weak economic base. The prime consideration for an award of custody as practised by the court currently, other things being equal, is the economic ability to provide for the child'. Thus where a mother can show that she has a steady income as well as reasonable accommodation, 'she has good chances of getting custody'.[101] This conclusion is supported by our own findings in other parts of Tanzania where we found in 1987 a small but growing number of women in professions and business who were keen to apply for custody of children and were invariably successful.[102] Himonga's findings in Zambia also show that where a former wife has means or where her parents are able and willing to support her, she seeks custody and sometimes does not even bother to apply for maintenance.[103]

What we learn from the above illustrations is that the law may provide that a mother has equal rights to the custody of the children but there are many other factors which will work to render the provisions of the law rather nugatory. The economic argument, even though quite strong, as we have seen, is not the only one to be considered by the mothers in the balancing act which they have to perform in the best interests of their children. In sum, one can argue that the patrilineal principle, which unquestioningly conferred on the father the rights of physical custody and guardianship (as we know these concepts under state law today), was largely supported by an economic power base which, even though weakening, continues to be largely in the hands of men.

V.   CONCLUSION

This paper has shown that the concept of the best interests of the child is best appreciated by locating it in the wider social and economic matrix of any community. In the case of sub-Saharan Africa, I have shown that the social and economic systems of most communities were organized in such a way that the interests of the child were inseparable from those of other members of the group. Through the system of economic exchange which obtained between members of the group the economic and social security of the members was safeguarded. Male elders were the principal managers of these societies and held property and other scarce resources and ritual powers in trust for the whole community.

During the nineteenth century most of Africa south of the Sahara came under European colonial rule. This marked the beginning of a new era. Capitalist relations penetrated the traditional system with the assistance of the colonial state and colonial law. This development transformed the communal mode of production along with the relations which it sustained. Traditional marriage which had been formerly the major means for the formation and maintenance of social cohesion between two groups or families was transformed and its individual character emphasized.

As the cost of marriage escalated while also becoming concentrated in a single family or individual males, husbands now viewed themselves as the owners of wives and their children. Competition for the acquisition of rights in children intensified but often without corresponding ability on the part of fathers to provide adequately for families. The ethos of individualism concentrated the obligation to maintain children on one family while the subsistence economy was yielding to the dissolving effects of the world economy. In their efforts to maintain economic viability as a family, many individuals devised a range of strategies in which also children became inextricably involved. As in the pre-colonial period, the interests of the child and those of the adults remained intertwined.

But while this lack of separation between the interests of family members had been necessary as part of the social structure during the pre-colonial era, it became much harder to maintain it in the era of capitalism. The push towards individualism which the state, law and economy promoted, tended to atomize the traditional family. The consequences were that the interests of the individual members attracted the attention of the State. It is in this context that the State moved in to protect what it viewed to be the best interests of the child. But state intervention, as we have seen, is ineffective because of its incapacity to provide economic support to families. In the light of growing economic deprivation in most of Africa, the concept of the best interest of the child has come simply to mean the satisfaction of material needs. Although state courts may be criticized for putting too much emphasis on who can provide materially for the child, this reality is not lost sight of by mothers who are hesitant to embrace their new rights on child custody. The contemporary economic realities, at least for the majority of Africans, require that the principle of the best interests of the child be construed rather narrowly to mean the satisfaction of material needs of the child.

This paper has concentrated on the typical African family with average income and mainly based in the rural areas. This is a choice dictated by my concern for giving a representative picture of Africa. However, by so doing the paper inevitably leaves out significant groups of children, especially those living dangerously in harsh conditions such as war, famine, political repression and police brutality. There are also economically deprived children living in the streets of urban Africa sometimes begging alongside their disabled (or able) parents. There is another growing category of African children living in AIDS-ravaged areas of Africa. The economic burden of supporting these children has fallen on their aged grandparents and other relatives. But the latter have also lost the economic support originally obtained from the dead parents of these orphans. For the majority of these children sheer survival is their major goal and if asked the proverbial question: 'What would you like to be when you grow up?' Most of them will answer: 'I would like to be alive.'

REFERENCES

Eshiwani G. 1985, 'Women's Access to Higher Education in Kenya: A Study of Opportunities and Attainment in Science and Mathematics Education', *Journal of Eastern African Research and Development*, Vol 15, 91–110

Robertson C. 1986, 'Women's Education and Class Formation in Africa, 1950–1980' in Claire Robertson & Iris Berger (eds), *Women and Class in Africa* African Publishing Co, New York 92–113

NOTES

[1] P. Alston and S. Parker, 'Introduction'; P. Alston, et al (eds), *Children, Rights and The Law* (Oxford, OUP Clarendon Press, 1992), vi–xii at viii.

[2] Vitit Muntarbhorn, 'The International Convention on the Rights of the Child: Universalization, Localization and Transnationalization'; Paper presented at the *First World Congress on Family Law and Children's Rights* Sydney, Australia (4–9 July 1993) 1.

[3] B. Thompson, 'Africa's Charter on Children's Rights: A Normative Break with Cultural Traditionalism'; *ICLQ*, 41, 432–444 at 432.

[4] M. Gluckman, 'Property Rights and Status in African Traditional Law' in M. Gluckman (ed), *Ideas and Procedures in African Customary Law* (International African Institute and Oxford University Press, 1969), 252–65 at 252.

[5] B. A. Rwezaura, 'The Changing Community obligations to the elderly in contemporary Africa'; *Journal of Social Development in Africa* (1989) 4, 1, 5–24; J. S. Mbiti, *African Religion and Philosophy* (New York: Preager, 1969).

[6] Many African societies have a specific name for it. For example, it is called lobola and roora (in Zimbabwe), bogadi (in Botswana), bohali (in Swaziland), mahari (in Tanzania).

[7] The term 'patrilineal principle' is used here to express a general rule or principle of traditional law under which a head of family or husband was entitled, on behalf of his kinship group, to have all the children born to his wife irrespective of who was their genitor, provided that sufficient bridewealth had been transferred to the family of the wife. B. A. Rwezaura, *Traditional Family Law and Change in Tanzania* (Baden Baden: Nomos Verlagsgesellschaft, 1985) at 101.

[8] A. R. Radcliffe-Brown, 'Introduction'; in Radcliffe-Brown and D. Forde (eds), *African Systems of Kinship and Marriage* (London, International African Institute and Oxford University Press, 1950), 1–85 at 50.

[9] S. Goonesekere, 'Women's Rights and Children's Rights: The United Nations Conventions as Compatible and Complementary International Treaties'; *Innocenti Occasional Papers* (Florence: ICDC, 1992) at 1.

[10] The Guardianship of Infants Act 1886 abolished the absolute and virtually exclusive right of the father to the guardianship of his legitimate children by the introduction of the principle of the welfare of the child and equal right to child custody between both parents.

[11] I. Schapera, 'Kinship and Marriage Among the Tswana', in Radcliffe-Brown and D. Forde (eds) (op cit, 1950), 140–65 at 150.

[12] M. Gluckman, 'Kinship and Marriage among the Lozi of Northern Rhodesia and the Zulu of Natal', in Radcliffe-Brown and D. Forde (eds) (op cit, 1950), 166–206 at 184.

[13] H. Kuper, 'Kinship among the Swazi', in Radcliffe-Brown and D. Forde (eds) (op cit, 1950), 86–110 at 88.

[14] The term 'house' in certain African societies signifies an idea going beyond the wife's physical shelter. It has two elements, ie the economic; as a unit of production, of distribution and of consumption within the household. It has also a metaphysical/spiritual element of continuity beyond the life of the particular wife through her own or adopted children (for details see Rwezaura, above, n 7, 11; and also P. Rigby, *Cattle and Kinship among the Gogo; A Semi Pastoral Society of Central Tanzania* (New York: Cornell University Press, 1969), at 172.

[15] The levirate form of marriage is based on the principle that the death of the husband does not dissolve the marriage. The widow remains married to her dead husband while a male relative is appointed to cohabit with the widow and raise children with her. All the children born post-humously are considered to be the children of the dead husband from whose estate they are entitled to inherit (see Gluckman, above, n 12, 183–93).

[16] Shapera, above, n 11, 153; and Gluckman, above, n 12, 183.

[17] Ghost-marriages occur when a man dies childless and his relatives, being anxious to continue his line, decide to find a wife for him so that she may bear children for his lineage. Such marriages have been reported to exist in Southern Sudan among the Nuer and Dinka people but are not unknown in other African societies (see E. E. Evans-Pritchard, *Kinship and Marriage Among the Nuer* (Oxford: The Clarendon Press, 1951).

[18] Evans-Pritchard, above, n 17, 89.

[19] A. P. Cheater, *Social Anthropology: An Alternative Introduction* (Gweru: Mambo Press, 1986), at 224.

[20] Above, n 13, 89.

[21] J. W. Makec, *The Customary Law of the Dinka: A Comparative Analysis of an African Legal System* (Khartoum Sudan: St. George Printing Press, 1986), at 50.

[22] Above, n 21, 53.

[23] D. Welch and A. Sachs, 'The Bride Price, Revolution, and the Liberation of Women', *International Journal of the Sociology of Law* 15 (1987), 369–92, at 374.

[24] A. K. H. Weinrich, *African Marriage in Zimbabwe* (Gweru: Mambo Press and Edinburgh: Holmes McDougall, 1982), at 54.

[25] M. J. Ruel, *The Social Organization of the Kuria; Field Work Report* avail. at University of Nairobi Library Nairobi, at 104.

[26] G. J. Klima, *The Barbaig: East African Cattle-Herders* (New York: Holt, Rinehart & Winston, 1970), at 77.

[27] Above, n 24, 105.

[28] C. O. Akpamgbo, 'A "Woman to Woman" Marriage and the Repugnancy Clause: A Case of Putting New Wine into Old Bottles', *African Legal Studies* 14 (1977), 87–95, at 87; and above, n 7, 161.

[29] Above, n 13, 89.

[30] Rwezaura, above, n 7, 143; H. Huber, 'Woman Marriage in Some East African Societies', *Anthropos* 63/64 (1969), 745–52, at 745; and E. Cotran, *Casebook on Kenya Customary Law* (Abingdon Oxford: Professional Books Ltd and Nairobi University, 1987), at 185.

[31] M. Wilson, 'Nyakyusa Kinship', in A. R. Radcliffe-Brown and E. Forde (op. cit, 1950), 111–39, at 123.

[32] Above, n 24, 105.

[33] Rwezaura, above, n 7, 152–4; and E. C. Baker, *The Bakuria of North Mara Tarime Tanganyika Territory* Ms in Lib East African Inst of Social Research, also at Rhodes House, Oxford (1935), at 100.

[34] I. Q. Orchardson, *The Kipsigis* (Nairobi: East African Literature Bureau Nairobi, 1961), at 49.

[35] Above, n 34, 49.

[36] Above, n 26, 54.

[37] J. F. Hollemann, *Shona Customary Law* (Cape Town: Oxford University Press, 1952), at 116–117).

[38] S. F. Moore, *Social Fact and Fabrications: 'Customary Law' on Kilimanjaro, 1880–1980* (Cambridge: Cambridge University Press, 1986), at 60, 107.

[39] Above, n 24, 62.

[40] Rwezaura, above, n 7, 159.

[41] C. Bledsoe, 'The Effect of Child Fostering on Feeding Practices and Access to Health Services in Rural Sierra Leone', *Soc Sci Med* Vol 27 No 6 (1988), 627–36, at 627–8.

[42] C. Bledsoe, 'School Fees and the Marriage Process for Mende Girls in Sierra Leone', in P. R. Sandy and R. G. Goodenough (eds), *Beyond the Second Sex: New Directions in the Anthropology of Gender* (Philadelphia: University of Pennsylvania Press, 1990), 283–309, at 46–80; also B. A. Rwezaura

and U. Wanitzek, 'Family Law Reform in Tanzania: A Socio-Legal Report', *International Journal of Law and the Family* 21 (1988), 1–26, at 5–24; and also H. Schneider, 'People as Wealth in Turu Society', *South Western Journal of Anthropology* 24 (1968), 375–95.

[43] A. Molokome, *'Children of the Fence': The Maintenance of Extra-marital Children under Law and Practice in Botswana* (Leiden: Center for African Studies, 1991), at 52.

[44] S. M. Seeiso, et al, 'The Legal Situation of Women in Lesotho', in J. Stewart and A. Armstrong (eds), *The Legal Situation of Women in Southern Africa* (Harare: University of Zimbabwe Publications, 1990), 47–73, at 53.

[45] J. M. Ault, 'State Power and the Regulation of Marriage in Colonial Zambia', *Theory and Society*, 12, 2 (1983), 181–210.

[46] M. C. Kirwen, *African Widows* (Maryknoll, NY: Orbis Press, 1979); and also above, n 19, 145.

[47] The term 'bridewealth' as used in this section includes bride-price; dowry and marriage payments. These terms describe the transfer of property, such as livestock, money, agricultural and industrial consumer goods and or services from the prospective son-in-law or his family to the father of the prospective wife or her family. Such payment can be done either in a single lump sum or by instalment during the life of the married life of the couple and sometimes, posthumously by the couple's children.

[48] The use of the term 'traditional' to refer to any social processes in contemporary Africa is fraught with conceptual dangers. This is because the term is sometimes used in ways that try to project social stability and therefore, to underplay any transformations which have radically altered social relations and social institutions. But also because the nature of social change is such that there is no clear divide between the old and the new or between the indigenous and the foreign one can be selective by stressing those elements which seem to reflect one's perception or political goals. Moreover, as often happens in Africa, change has sometimes strengthened existing relations while at the same time undermining others. These issues are complex but they have to be acknowledged in order to appreciate the process of social and economic transformation in Africa.

[49] Above, n 19, 145.

[50] Above, n 24, 52.

[51] Rwezaura, above, n 7, 70–94; and also C. R. Cutshall, *Justice for the People* (Harare: University of Zimbabwe Publications, 1991), at 57–74.

[52] C. H. Bledsoe, *Women and Marriage in Kpelle Society* (Stanford, Ca.: Stanford University Press, 1980), at 57.

[53] See Kimicha J in *Masero Mwita* v *Rioba Masero* (1969) HCD 199.

[54] Above, n 38, 198.

[55] Above, n 46, 93.

[56] Rwezaura, above, n 7, 86.

[57] Above, n 52, 97.

[58] Seeiso, above, n 44, 52.

[59] Cutshall, above, n 51, 57.

[60] Rwezaura, above, n 7, 90.

[61] An example from Tanzania relates to a former husband sued in 1973 for the return of forty-one head of cattle which he had paid as bridewealth. The marriage had lasted for seven years and a daughter was born to the couple. The District Court allowed the refund of thirty head of cattle after putting into consideration the period of marriage and the birth of one child (Tanz. CLDO Rules 52–61). But the former husband was unhappy with the order and appealed to the High Court. In order to improve on his case, the appellant denied that the couple had any children of the marriage. Although this strategy badly backfired on the appellant (because the High Court disallowed the entire claim), his expectations were that by denying the birth of the child he could get an order for full refund of the cattle. This in effect amounted to saying that the daughter should now belong to the maternal side which was allowed under the parties' customs. (See *Paulo Nyatutu* v *Marwa Mwita*, Mwanza High Court (PC) Civ App 177 of 1975 per Mfalila J).

[62] In 1977 a group of ninety-eight Tanzanian men and women sitting for a pre-University entrance examination were asked to write a short essay commenting on a recommendation made by a women's seminar that bridewealth should be abolished by law. Although only eleven suggested its abolition, the majority who did not recommend its abolition were nonetheless opposed to it. Of these, forty respondents stated that the payment of bridewealth was a source of marriage instability because it encouraged parents to force their daughters to marry rich men whom they did not love. And where a daughter insisted on a man of her choice, then she had to put up with constant interruptions of her cohabitation by parents who kept recalling her in order to enforce bridewealth payment (Rwezaura, above, n 7, 87).

[63] Above, n 51, 102.

[64] In 1979 I came across a case in Tarime District, Tanzania where a husband sued his wife claiming child rearing fees (malisho) in respect of two of her daughters born in an earlier marriage and having accompanied their mother from neighbouring Kenya when they were about ten years old. The main cause for the dispute was that the wife had secretly arranged marriages for her daughters and kept the bridewealth for herself. The husband, who felt that he had been unjustifiably denied a share decided to sue for child rearing. The magistrate who perfectly understood the nature of the dispute and the economic manoeuvres of the claimant husband, rejected the claim on the ground that the claimant was not entitled to apply for 'malisho' because the two daughters along with their mother had maintained themselves and also maintained the claimant because he was too old to work.

[65] A revealing expression of this notion was made by a Zambian Member of Parliament who in 1989 stated in opposition to the Intestate Succession Bill, that it would be against people's customs and traditions to allow children to inherit 50 per cent of their father's estate because if this were to be done the children 'can never come back to the relatives of the deceased to plead for help' (Parliamentary Debates, 4 April 1989, 273, cited in C. N. Himonga, *Family Law and Succession Law Reform and Socio-Economic Development in Zambia* Research Report (Bayreuth: University of Bayreuth, 1992), at 64.

[66] M. L. Chanock, 'Making Customary Law: Men, Women and Courts in Colonial Northern Rhodesia' in M. Kay and M. Wright (eds), *African Women and the Law: Historical Perspectives* (Boston, 1982); M. L. Chanock, *Law, Custom and Social Order* (Cambridge University Press, 1985); also M. Mbilinyi, 'Runaway Wives in Colonial Tanganyika: Forced Labour and Forced Marriage in Rungwe District 1919–1961' *International Journal of the Sociology of Law* 16, 1–29 (1988); and also Rwezaura, above, n 7, 63.

[67] For a discussion of the case of Morabu Chacha see Rwezaura, above, n 7, 112.

[68] *Morabu Chacha* v *Marwa Wambura*; Mwanza High Court Matr Civ App No 25 of 1976.

[69] In pre-colonial times it was possible for a debt to remain unpaid for many years. As long as it was not denied, no one bothered to ask. Debt was part of the wider social insurance for the people. After all, theoretically everyone owed something to the other. But change destroyed the mutual trust and the uncertainties of the future compelled people to live in the present. Indeed this was one of the reasons why fathers preferred to be paid the whole bridewealth instead of the old system of instalments.

[70] Above, n 44, 52.

[71] Above, n 38, 202.

[72] A parent who has to raise money for school fees by selling his cattle or part of his land makes a hard choice between depleting his capital savings which are essential for family survival, and the mere hope and expectation of his child completing school and getting a good job and eventually supporting him.

[73] A case in point concerns a young Sierra Leonean woman who was put to hard work by her guardian family and when she accidentally spilled some food before serving it, she was denied food for four days. This punishment was not only too harsh but it also led to more detrimental consequences for the young woman. Driven by hunger, she sought help from a local shopkeeper in return for sexual favours and as Bledsoe put it, 'not surprisingly, she soon became pregnant and was forced to drop out of school'; Bledsoe, above, n 42, 294.

[74] See for example, Claire Robertson (1986); George Eshiwani (1985). In Tanzania women account for 19 per cent of all University students and 20 per cent of all registered students in Diploma courses at various institutes and vocational training centres and 5 per cent of registered students at the three technical colleges; Tanzania, United Rep of; and UNICEF, *Women and Children in Tanzania: An Overview* (Tanzania: Dar es Salaam, 1990), at 59.

[75] The side effect of all this was that despite the rather young age at which these girls were circumcised, the initiates tended to believe that they had in fact matured and were ready for marriage. Hence in a discussion with teachers in two primary schools in the area, it was revealed that a number of female students behaved as if they were adult women. The teachers thought that the conduct of these female pupils was bordering on indiscipline.

[76] Above, n 52, 153.

[77] See the Public Primary Schools (Compulsory Enrolment and Attendance) Order, (Govt Notice No 150 of 1977) made under section 35 of the Education Act (No 50 of 1969).

[78] There are criminal prohibitions against infant marriages and sexual intercourse with underage females but the potential for the prosecution of offenders largely depends on someone reporting to the police.

[79] Aili Trip found in Dar es Salaam that 'as many as 61 per cent of self-employed women said they were helped by their children, and according to teachers and principals, small family enterprises had become a single most important reason for poor school attendance and unsatisfactory progress in the classroom'. According to Trip, some children worked so late into the night, selling fish, chips, peanuts, or helping their parents in brewing beer, that the next day morning when they went to school they would be too tired to concentrate: A. M. Trip, 'Women and the Changing Urban Household Economy in Tanzania' *Journal of Modern African Studies* 27, 4 (1989), 601–623.

[80] On 10 July 1993 a Radio Tanzania commentary after the news (Mazungumzo Baada ya Habari) stressed the magnitude of the problem by noting that many children between the ages of ten to twelve do not go to school and are instead engaged in income-generating activities which are seen by their parents to be essential for the economic survival and welfare of the entire family. The commentator stated that although this practice was strongly opposed by the Tanzanian government as well as international organizations such as the ILO and UNICEF and many NGOs, there is a need to launch a massive national campaign of educating the population about their parental duties as well as on the effects of 'child labour and child exploitation' [recorded by author]. A. M. Trip, 'Responses of Urban Women to Economic Reforms and Crisis in Urban Tanzania: New Role of Women's Organization', Paper Presented at African Studies Association Conference, 1–4 Nov 1990, 7.

[81] See Uzodike (1990), 89.

[82] It is fully recognized that the exploitation of child labour can be perpetrated under the guise of either tradition or even poverty. As Uzodike (1990) has clearly shown from her research in Nigeria, the use of children in street hawking and other capitalist enterprises is a growing problem in Africa. Another related question is the problem of defining and policing child abuse and the likelihood that tradition and culture can be used to hide crime against children (see B. Thompson, 'Child Abuse in Sierra Leone: Normative Disparities', 3 *International Journal of Law and the Family* (1991), 13–23 at 13). These issues however, cannot be discussed in a general piece such as this whose main aim is to provide a socio-economic overview which can shed light on specific studies.

[83] For Zimbabwe see Section 3(4) of the Customary Law and Primary Courts Act No 6 of 1981 and a detailed discussion by M. Maboreke, 'The Love of a Mother: Problems of Custody in Zimbabwe', in A. Armstrong and W. Ncube, *Women and Law in Southern Africa* (Harare: Zimbabwe Publishing House, 1987), 137–63; for Tanzania see section 125 of the Law of Marriage Act No 5 of 1971; for Kenya see section 17 of the Guardianship of Infants Act (Cap 144); for Botswana see section 6 Customary Law (Application and Ascertainment) Act; for Zambia section 42 Matrimonial Causes Act. In the case of Zambia Subordinate Courts do apply the best interests principle even though there is no direct statutory provision to that effect (see Himonga, above, n 65, 145).

[84] There are many reasons for the reluctance of women to rush for their rights. Some of these reasons are based on cultural considerations while others are a result of simple ignorance or the inaccessibility of remedies due to costs and time. These issues will not be considered here. A. K. Armstrong, *Struggling Over Scarce Resources: Women and Maintenance in Southern Africa*, Women and Law in Southern Africa Trust; Regional Report (University of Zimbabwe Publications, 1992). See also Rwezaura and Wanitzek, above, n 42, 1; Himonga, above, n 65; R. T. Nhlapo, 'The Legal Situation of Women in Swaziland and Some Thoughts on Research' in J. Stewart and A. Armstrong (eds), *The Legal Situation of Women in Southern Africa* (Harare: University of Zimbabwe Publications, 1990), 97.

[85] As the Sotho proverb says: 'namane ya kanyesetetsa e bonala ka ho ota' ie a motherless child is not well cared for (cited in Armstrong & Ncube, above, n 83).

[86] J. Davison, 'Who Owns What? Land Registration and Tensions in Gender Relations of Production in Kenya' in J. Davison (ed), *Agriculture, Women and Land: The African Experience* (Boulder: Westview Press, 1988), 157–76, at 157.

[87] Maboreke, above, n 83, 137.

[88] See also M. K. Rwebangira, *Women Seeking Redress in Courts of Law in Tanzania* (A Survey of Mbeya and Dar es Salaam Regions) Research Report, Dar es Salaam (1992), at 37.

[89] Himonga, above, n 65, 112.

[90] Ibid.

[91] A. K. Armstrong, 'School and Sadza: Custody and the Best Interests of the Child in Zimbabwe', at 150 in this volume.

[92] Above, n 88, 30.

[93] Above, n 88.

[94] Armstrong, above, n 84, 119.

[95] Armstrong, above, n 84, 102.

[96] Above, n 51, 111.

[97] This matter is currently being negotiated with the help of the Harare based Women and Law in Southern Africa Research Project.

[98] The case of Fatima illustrates the predicament of most rural women. Fatima, a Zimbabwean wife and mother of four children, was not getting maintenance from her husband until she got to know from the WLSA researchers that she could make a claim against her husband in a community court. When she took the case to court she discovered that she had to pay money to effect service of summons. When she obtained a court order, she found that she could not get the cash without opening a bank account. Yet the account had to be opened with money which she did not have. Moreover she needed an identity card and in order to get the ID she had to have a birth certificate. The latter had to be obtained from her natal home which was a good distance away and therefore she needed money for her bus fare. Fatima was lucky to get a loan from her mother-in-law who supported her efforts. The entire process took a period of nearly five months before she could receive any money in her new bank account (see Armstrong, n 84, 97–8).

[99] Rwezaura and Wanitzek, above, n 42.

[100] Under sec 5 of the Kenya Affiliation Act (Cap 142) a court was empowered to order a putative father to pay a sum of KShs 50 per month to the mother for the maintenance and education of her child but in 1969 the Affiliation Act was repealed by the Kenya Parliament to 'prevent women so inclined, from freely collecting illegitimate children and then sit in legal receipt of custom' per Miller J in *Peter Hinga* v *Mary Wanjiku* (High Court of Kenya Civil Appeal No 94 of 1977) reported in Cotran, above, n 30, 62–63.

[101] Above n 88, 29.

[102] Rwezaura and Wanitzek, above, n 42, 20.

[103] Himonga, above, n 83, 159–67.

THE BEST INTERESTS OF THE CHILD: A SOUTH ASIAN PERSPECTIVE

SAVITRI GOONESEKERE*

ABSTRACT

This paper examines the effect of the introduction of the 'best interests' concept into the law of the countries of the Indian sub-continent. It shows how the received colonial laws partly coincided with, and partly differed from, the indigenous laws of the region. Initially, the received laws, like the indigenous laws, gave prominence to paternal rights, but they also introduced the 'best interests' concept, which was used by the courts and certain legislation to introduce a degree of uniformity which undermined the pluralism of the region. To-day, religious and ethnic awareness is threatening that uniformity. However, the paper concludes by indicating that constitutional norms are showing signs of playing a similar role to the earlier colonial principles of equity and may maintain some uniformity based on constitutional standards in the region.

Article 3 (1) of the Convention on the Rights of the Child sets a general standard that must be observed by the major agencies of government, the legislature, the executive, Courts of law and private social welfare institutions within a country that is a party to the Convention. When taking any action concerning children, these agencies are all required to make the best interests of the child a 'primary consideration'. All the countries which belong to the South Asian region, namely Bangladesh, Bhutan, India, Maldives, Nepal, Pakistan and Sri Lanka, have ratified the Convention. They have therefore taken on a commitment to realizing this standard in their domestic jurisdictions.

I. BEST INTERESTS AS A 'PRIMARY' CONSIDERATION AND THE 'PARAMOUNTCY' PRINCIPLE

When the Convention states that the best interests of the child shall be a 'primary' consideration it is departing from a standard of 'primordial' or 'paramountcy' that has already been incorporated into international law, English law, case law and some legislation on religious law in this region.[1] The Convention's article 21 (on adoption) also uses the term 'paramount' rather than 'primary' consideration, and draws attention to the difference between these expressions.

The fact that these terms can be interpreted differently in custody litigation has been highlighted in a dictum of Lord McDermott in *J v C*:

* Department of Legal Studies, Faculty of Humanities and Social Sciences, The Open University of Sri Lanka, Nawala, Colombo, Sri Lanka.

'these words' said his lordship, referring to the 'paramountcy' concept, mean 'more than that the child's welfare is to be treated as the top item in a list of terms relevant to the matter in question . . . They connote a process whereby when all the relevant facts, relationships, claims and wishes of the parents, risks, choices, and other circumstances are taken into account and weighed, the course to be followed will be that which is most in the interests of the child's welfare. That is . . . the paramount consideration, because it rules upon or determines the course to be followed'.[2] In this particular case, the House of Lords decided to give the care and custody of a child to foster parents rather than natural parents, despite the fact that the parents were unimpeachable, on the basis that the child's interest in remaining with the foster parents outweighed any other concern. The welfare of the child therefore became the sole consideration.

Giving paramountcy to the child's welfare in guardianship litigation has sometimes been criticized as too child-rights oriented, and as undermining the need to consider the interests of parents and other children in the family.[3] On the other hand, it has also been argued that the concept of the 'child's welfare' is only ostensibly child-centred because courts in fact use it as a tool for making decisions based on adult perspectives whether religious, moral or social, rather than the needs of children.[4]

Domestic courts may perceive the child's interests or welfare as a 'paramount' consideration so as to provide a different standard to that envisaged in the Convention. This would not be in conflict with the Convention, since Article 41 gives the benefit of a domestic standard if it is seen as higher than the Convention's standard. On the other hand, the perception of best interests as a 'primary' standard of concern can encourage the exercise of discretion with awareness of the dynamics of the child's own environment. Making children's interests a 'primary' consideration will thus be useful in creating sensitivity to the need for a holistic perception of the child's interests, without the child's interests becoming the sole concern. However, the emphasis on an open-ended concept of 'child welfare', combined with an interpretation of best interests as a primary rather than paramount concern, can undermine commitments to realize the ideal standards on child rights articulated in the United Nations Convention, unless the concept itself is interpreted within the framework of those rights and international standards.

II.   PERCEPTIONS OF THE CHILD'S 'BEST INTERESTS' IN SOUTH ASIA: COMPARATIVE APPROACHES

Countries of South Asia have a variety of indigenous social and legal traditions that came to be viewed as 'customary' or religious personal laws in the British Colonial period. They were, and are still, perceived as 'personal law' since they are based on norms that deviate from uniformly applicable state or received colonial laws. The latter, together, are the 'dominant' legal regimes, while the indigenous systems apply as personal laws to particular ethnic or religious communities within these countries. It is relevant to compare the child-centred concerns in these indigenous systems with colonial laws, particularly in a context where the 'best interests' concept in the Convention can be interpreted as a tool for exposing values and ideologies that may conflict with the basic rights guaranteed to children by the Convention.

The Colonial Laws

English Common law has been described as a system which showed 'brutal indifference to the child's fate'.[5] Early English common law recognized the superior parental right of a man in a family unit created within marriage, and was more concerned with safeguarding his paternal rights than the interests of children. A child born out of wedlock by contrast was considered '*filius nullius*' or the child of no one. Blackstone remarks on this difference between marital and non-marital children, and the exclusion of the mother of marital children from parental status. Parental power and authority over minor marital children were identified by him with paternal power 'for a mother as such is entitled to no power, but only to reverence and respect'.[6] Not surprisingly, at common law, the father's legal right of custody over a marital child was so absolute that he could claim the physical custody of a child who was being nursed at the mother's breast. The right to physical control was the essence of the paternal right, and the procedure for enforcing the right was the writ of habeas corpus.

Child-oriented developments in English law took place initially through the intervention of the Court of Chancery, which exercised a special jurisdiction in Equity distinct from the ordinary jurisdiction of the Common law courts. The Court of Chancery was authorized to intervene on behalf of children in the exercise of the prerogative power of the Crown to act as '*parens patriae*'. This jurisdiction provided a procedure for intervening between parent and child by making a child a 'ward of court'. It also allowed the court to make and enforce a variety of orders concerning matters such as the education of the child. The impact of Equity eventually led to a modification of the position in Common law, so that the 'best interests' or welfare of the child came to be perceived by the English courts as the first and paramount consideration in any litigated dispute involving the care and custody of children born within lawful marriage. By the beginning of this century, the concept that the child's welfare and best interests should be the paramount consideration had a strong impact in the determination of custody disputes in English law.

The child-centred approach that developed through the intervention of Equity was also endorsed in legislation in England from the early part of the nineteenth century. The Common law concept of the father's custodial right was qualified by a series of nineteenth century statutes which empowered the courts to give the mother custody of a legitimate child. The Guardianship of Infants Act 1925 was the culmination of the process and introduced the basic principle that courts called upon to make decisions on the custody and upbringing of children must regard 'the child's welfare as the first and paramount consideration'.[7]

English law provided a value base for countries in the subcontinent of India which experienced British Colonial rule. Sri Lanka, which was a British Colony, also experienced another received colonial system, Roman-Dutch law. This system, which combined Roman Law with Germanic custom, recognized the husband's marital power over his wife and his natural guardianship over minor children. His protective authority over the wife and marital children was deeply entrenched in the system. However, Roman-Dutch law accepted the overriding responsibility of the Princeps and later the courts to act as *parens patriae* and safeguard the interests of children. The courts, acting as 'upper Guardian of minors', could deprive the father of any or all of the incidents of paternal power. Roman-Dutch law, like English law, did not have the institution of adoption. Yet, unlike English Common law, it emphasized the importance of mutual obligations of support between parents and children, and imposed a duty on a man to maintain his marital and non-marital children. Though the distinction between marital and non-marital children was accepted in Roman-Dutch law, and the latter suffered disabilities, duties of support were conceded and the concept of 'upper guardianship' could be used to safeguard the interests of such a child in guardianship or custody litigation.[8]

The Indigenous Systems

These perceptions of the child's best interests in the received colonial heritage were in some respects similar to and in others different from some indigenous legal traditions in South Asia. This is apparant in an overview of concepts in Hindu and Islamic law and in Buddhist values which affected Sri Lankan indigenous law.

It has sometimes been suggested that child-rearing practices in medieval Islamic societies revealed a greater concern for the child's needs than in early European societies.[9] However, the concept of paternal power was just as strong in that system, and enabled adult interests to prevail over the health and developmental needs of children. Thus the controversial concept of marriage guardianship recognizes that a father may impose the status of marriage on a minor child. There is no minimum age of marriage, and the male guardian (*wali*) becomes the contracting party to the marriage. These norms have encouraged the practice of child marriage in Islamic societies. Yet Islamic law permitted an 'option of puberty' or the right to annul a marriage contracted by a guardian contrary to the interest of a child, gave a child bride a right to her marriage portion (*mahr*) and placed constraints on unilateral repudiation by the husband seeking to divorce his wife by pronouncing *talak*. A woman's separate property rights were recognized by Islamic law.

There are no specific injunctions in the Koran stating an order of guardians. However, jurists of different schools concede that the mother has a preferential right to the custody of a child of tender years. The child's nurturing needs were considered important enough to permit using the exceptional and limited doctrine of independent juristic reasoning to modify the Islamic law on hire. The consideration normally required for hire of a person was an object like gold or silver. However, Islamic law permitted a wet nurse to be hired in return for her food and clothing.[10] Unlike English Common law, which did not create an enforceable legal duty of maintenance, Islamic law imposed parental obligations to support marital children.

Islamic law, like English Common Law, considered a non-marital child *filius nullius*, and did not recognize adoption. Yet adoption is practised by some Islamic communities in South Asia, and has been described as a practice which is not prohibited, but an act that is *mubah* – 'towards which religion is indifferent'.[11]

The approach of Hindu law to children reflected a similar dualism between child-centred concerns and disregard for the needs of the child.[12] Child care and nurturing were recognized in various principles of Hindu Law. The State (represented by the king) and members of the joint family had rights and responsibilities in regard to the child. Various legal protections focused on the Kings' power to protect and safeguard the child's proprietary interests. Since family authority was distributed among several elders, an order of guardians was not clearly identified. Hindu law also recognized the paternal obligation to maintain both marital and non-marital children, irrespective of the nature of their parents' union. Nevertheless, unlike Islamic law, this system was marked by an all-encompassing concept of male protection over females that encouraged a perception that a woman had no rights and belonged to her father or husband. According to the interpretation of texts of Manu, 'the father protects a woman in childhood, her husband protects (her) in youth, and her sons protect (her) in old age; a woman is never fit for independence'. This perception of the female is combined with strong son preference, or a concept of 'sonship'. The scriptural texts declare that 'through a son one conquers the world. Through a grandson one obtains immortality, and through the great grandson one ascends to the highest heaven'.[13]

There is some indication in the scriptural texts that marriage was not perceived as sale. Thus Manu states that 'no father who knows (the law) must take even the smallest gratuity for his daughter; for a man who through avarice takes a gratuity is a seller of his offspring'.[14] Nevertheless the idea of a father gifting his daughter to a husband was all pervasive. This was combined with a later development in Hindu law which suggests that she could be given in marriage before puberty. Consequently Brahmin girls could be married between the ages of eight to ten years.[15]

The practices of child marriage and dowry that are current in India, and expose young girls to physical violence and abuse, are legitimized by the scriptural sources on age of marriage, and the concept of a parental right to gift a bride. Despite the constraint on bride sale, the perception of the right to own and gift 'a daughter decked with ornaments and jewels' conflicts with a perception of the girl as someone with her own human identity. The customary practice of female infanticide which is known to be common in parts of Tamil Nadu,[16] appears to be as much a response to the need to provide dowry as lack of concern for the individual identity of a girl child.

Some of the indigenous laws of Sri Lanka, of the Sinhala and Tamil Communities,[17] reflect child-centred concerns as well as ideas of parental power and family authority which tend to deny the identity of the child. The Tesawalamai Code of the Tamils of the North, which applies even today, originally contained several sections in the part on sales which referred to the sale of children. Child marriages were familiar to these Tamil Communities. Nevertheless, the provisions in the Tesawalamai Code also reflect the values of Hindu law and do not recognize an order of guardians, but make an assumption of wider family responsibilities for nurturing a child. For instance, the Tesawalamai Code declares that 'if a father wishes to marry a second time, the mother-in-law or nearest relation generally takes the child or children (if thy are still young) in order to bring them up'. Similarly the code contains a provision which states that 'if the father and mother die . . . and their surviving children are infants under age, then the relations of both sides assemble to consult to whose care the children are to be entrusted; and a person being chosen, the children are delivered to him'. There is no corresponding statement of an order of guardians. Some concept of family support and family provision after death from inherited property is found in isolated provisions of the Code. Adoption is also permitted, and there are detailed provisions which were subsequently removed from the code by legislative intervention.

A similar perception of wider family responsibilities for the care and nurture of children can be seen in the early records of the law of the Sinhala Community in the Central (Kandyan) provinces of Sri Lanka. Kandyan (Sinhala) law does not indicate a specific order of guardians, except in the event of dissolution of marriage. A surviving mother is preferred over other relatives, but there are instances in which paternal relatives are preferred. The focus on guardianship only in the event of dissolution suggests that, as in Hindu law and Tasawalamai, imposition of authority on a single parental or paternal guardian was not considered important in a situation where the wider family assumed responsibility for the child's nurturing and other needs.

The perception of individual family responsibility is, however, reflected in an important Buddhist text on the responsibilities of the layman or woman. According to the Mangala Sutra 'caring for mother and father, and the cherishing of spouse and children' are important obligations in lay life. The high value placed by Buddhism on individual human potential and individual responsibility affected social and legal values in the pre-colonial period. These values were strengthened by the impact of South Indian matriarchal social influences of later centuries. Kandyan law and indigenous laws in Kerala share concepts on gender and family relations that suggest a common legal heritage.

Kandyan law recognizes the separate legal identity of men and women, and did not allow parental authority to impose marriage on minor children of either sex. This system also appears to have accepted that a child of sufficient understanding could leave a guardian and 'commit himself to the guardian of another relation'. Kandyan law emphasized the importance of family obligations in providing support to children, and held that inheritance rights could be claimed on the basis of 'familial assistance' or support provided during a person's lifetime. Rights of inheritance and support extended to both marital and non-marital children, and Kandyan law did not distinguish between these two categories sharply. This was consistent with a legal and social system that had a liberal view of sexual relations, and recognized consensual divorce and the reality of marriage breakdown.

Early British administrators and residents appreciated the difference in the approach to family relations in Sri Lanka and remarked on what seemed to be to them a striking egalitarianism. Accounts of the country note that 'the natives of Ceylon are more continent with respect to women than other Asiatic nations and their women are treated with more attention'.[18] Nineteenth Century Victorian British administrators found it remarkable that 'as fathers and mothers and sons and daughters' . . . 'family attachments were strong and sincere', infanticide even among the very poor seemed to be rare, and 'natives' treated children 'with utmost' kindness and 'too often spoiled them by over-indulgence'.[19] It was thought equally strange that a child should be adopted by persons who wanted merely to provide care and nurturing, and accepted him/her as a full member of the family with legal rights within it. A child who was considered 'unlucky' in one family could be given to another, who would 'take such child and bring them up with Rice and Milk' as a natural child of the adoptive family.[20] This type of indigenous adoption was different from adoption for succession and was perceived by the British administration in the early years as fostering, without legal consequences.

Despite these nurturing traditions, extensive parental authority was also recognized in Kandyan law. Parents had the right to sell or pawn children when they could not afford to maintain them or in order to discharge their own liabilities. Nevertheless, feudal patronage could be benevolent; children received in affluent families could be cared for as members of the household.

III.   RECEPTION OF COLONIAL VALUES AND THEIR INFLUENCE ON LAW AND POLICY

Hindu law, Islamic law, and systems which represent the indigenous socio-legal culture on children thus reflect perceptions of parental authority and the position of children which were familiar to Common law, Roman-Dutch law and European law, several centuries ago. These indigenous systems did not operate in isolation from the centuries of colonial influence. It has been observed how trading contacts with the Byzantine and Persian Empires resulted in aspects of Islamic law absorbing influences from Roman and Jewish law, and that Greek ideas influenced the attitude to child care and nurturing in some early Islamic societies.[21] This process has taken place in the colonial period in South Asia.

A comparison of the received and indigenous legal heritage in South Asia shows that indigenous systems reflected some child-centred concerns that were not found in the early English Common law and Roman-Dutch law. On the other hand, there are also similarities of perceptions in regard to parental or family authority. The focus on these adult interests impinged on the capacity to address a child's individual needs. While English and Roman-Dutch law developed in their own environment, the indigenous systems of South Asia were denied the opportunity to grow and develop on their own momentum. The South Asian experience of the application of the 'best interests' standard in law and policy as well as future interpretations of that standard must therefore be understood in the context of the received, rather than the indigenous heritage. The 'best interests' concept derived from the colonial legal heritage has influenced law and policy in the post-independence period, and set child-centred standards. These come into conflict with norms in indigenous systems which do not reflect current social realities. For instance, the focus on wider family responsibility and authority and the value placed on care and nurturing are not reflected in today's reality of sweeping paternal authority, exploitation of girl children, child marriage and infanticide. Infanticide and child abandonment are reported in the press and by social welfare authorities, even in Sri Lanka, which has comparatively high social indicators for children.[22]

Guardianship Law in the Subcontinent

(a) The development of the welfare principle

Guardianship law in the subcontinent of India has been influenced greatly by the Guardianship and Wards Act 1890, introduced in the colonial period. This legislation is said to have originated in the difficulties the British administration experienced in determining guardianship disputes concerning royal children in the Indian states. Nevertheless, the Act was introduced as a uniform law applicable to all communities, and has been retained in Bangladesh, Pakistan and India. None of these countries has chosen to deviate from this legislation in the post-independence period. The 1890 Act is applied today in all these countries as a uniform law in custody and guardianship litigation. The Act reflects the English law of the time and therefore concedes the superior paternal right of the father which will prevail unless he is 'unfit' to be a guardian. Nevertheless, the Act also requires a court to determine custody according to the 'welfare of' the minor child.[23]

We have observed that Hindu law did not specify an order of guardians. Yet very early judicial decisions in British India held that the father was the superior and preferred guardian. In *Skinner* v. *Orde* (1871)[24] the Privy Council stated that a child in India must be presumed to have the father's religion. The Guardianship Act made it easier for the courts to state, as in the leading case of *Besant* v. *Narayaniah*,[25] that 'there is no difference in this respect between English and Hindu law. As in this country, so among the Hindus, the father is the natural guardian of his children during their minorities'.

During the colonial period the father's preferred right of guardianship became a fundamental legal principle in the uniform law of guardianship through a combination of legislative and judicial intervention. The child's welfare, however, provided the court with a tool to interfere with the paternal right. That principle was often used to introduce a child-centred approach into judicial decision-making in custody disputes, even as the colonial legislation entrenched a concept of a 'natural' paternal rights of guardianship.

In India, the 1890 Act envisaged that the courts would give due recognition to the 'personal law' of the parties. Thus it declared that the court had the power to appoint guardians according to 'the law of which the minor was subject'. They should interpret the welfare of the child 'consistently with the law to which the minor is subject' and have regard to 'the religion of the minor'[26] Yet judicial developments on guardianship in the subcontinent indicate that the child's welfare has been given paramountcy even though the 1890 Act did not give the child's welfare that significance.[27] They show how the Courts have modified even parental rights conferred by the personal laws on the basis that consideration of the child's welfare cannot be undermined by these laws.[28]

There are many Indian court decisions holding that the father is the preferred guardian and that the onus is on the party seeking to displace those rights to show that he is 'unfit' and that it would be contrary to the child's interests to recognize that custody. These decisions identify the paternal right to custody with the child's interests. The guardianship of the father has been described by the courts as a 'sacred trust', a right which should not be denied unless he is 'utterly unfit'.[29] Thus courts have sometimes ignored the fact that a child might be happier or more comfortable with other relatives.[30] In a competing claim between the father and maternal relatives, the latter have been considered as not 'expected to evince the same interest in the health, welfare and upbringing of the minor that a natural parent or a step parent may take'[31] The sentiments contrast sharply with the perception of the role of relatives in the indigenous systems discussed earlier. These decisions clearly identify the paternal right to custody with the child's best interests, and accept that it is in the child's best interests to be with the father whose legal rights law recognizes. But the Indian courts have not been consistent in this approach. There are many judicial decisions indicating a willingness to use the child's best interests to award custody to the mother or a foster parent.

The parent who has given custody to a third party will not therefore be allowed to assert natural rights and the dispute will be decided on the basis of what is best for the child. The focus on the child's welfare has also enabled some courts to confer custody rights on the mother.[32] In *Saraswatibai* v *Shripad* (1941)[33] the court stated that 'if the mother is a suitable person to take charge of the child, it is quite impossible to find an adequate substitute for her, for the custody of a child of tender years'. The idea that the welfare of the child creates a right in the mother of an infant is reflected in the dictum that 'the mother's lap is God's own cradle', and in many judicial pronouncements.[34] A mother's poverty has not been considered a reason for denying the child's nurturing needs, although it has also resulted in a denial of the mother's custody.[35]

These judicial views were subsequently entrenched in statute law. The mother's preferential right as custodian parent was upheld by the Hindu Minority and Guardianship Act 1956 which codified Hindu law. Section 6(a) declared that 'the custody (as distinct from guardianship) of a minor who has not completed the age of five years shall ordinarily be with the mother'. Section 13(1) made the welfare of the minor a 'paramount' consideration. This provision has enabled courts to focus more clearly on the child's need to retain a close relationship with the mother. It has been pointed out that the father's 'right is not absolute; nor is it indefeasible in law; it is circumscribed by the consideration of the benefit and welfare of the minor'.[36] Although Indian courts continue to afford preferential status to the father, there are adequate precedents to support awarding custody to the mother in the child's interests.

A provision in the 1890 Act sets certain guidelines for determining whether an order is in the best interests of the child. The court must have regard to certain considerations such as the age, sex and religion of the child and the character and nearness of kin to the child.[37] These guidelines have encouraged courts to give weight to factors such as kinship relationship of wider family members, and the 'morals' of a parent, particularly of the mother,[38] Nevertheless, in general the major consideration has been whether giving custody to the mother is conducive to the general well-being of the child, or whether the paternal right should be conceded.

(b) Islamic principles

We have observed that the 1890 Act envisaged the application of the personal law of the child, a perception strengthened by reference to the need to take account of the child's religion. The Indian courts have adopted an ambivalent approach to Islamic-law principles on guardianship, when they come into conflict with the court's perception of the child's welfare. We have observed that the Koran does not set an order of guardians, but that different schools of Islamic law recognize specific rules in regard to the custodial rights of either the father or the mother. Early cases on Islamic law in India considered these custodial rights to be subordinate to the the child's welfare.[39] However, there are cases where courts have applied only the personal law, sometimes stating that 'the Guardianship and Wards Act 1890 does not permit the court to subordinate the law to which the minor is subject to the consideration of what will be for the minor's welfare'.[40] But in 1983 Anand J. in the Jammu and Kashmir High Court interfered with custodial rights under Islamic law by applying the concept that the child's welfare is the paramount consideration.[41]

The approach to Islamic law principles in the context of the 1890 Act, which applies as a uniform law in Bangladesh and Pakistan, indicates that the child's welfare can be used to deny the custodial rights confirmed by that law. One view is that in Pakistan the concept of the child's welfare is the sole criterion when a guardian is being appointed, but due consideration must be given to personal law when a guardian is being removed.[42] Pakistan Courts have sometimes departed from the traditional principles of Islamic law on the basis that there are no Koranic rules on the subject. Thus it has been stated that 'it is permissible for Courts of law to depart from the rules of custody as stated in the textbooks . . . since there was no Quranic or Traditional texts on the point, and courts which have taken the place of Quazis can, therefore, come to their own conclusions by process of Ijtihad (exposition) . . .

Therefore it would be permissible to depart from the rules stated . . . if on the facts of a given case its application is against the welfare of the minor'.[43] Courts apply an initial presumption that the child's welfare is identified with custodial rights, but show willingness to interfere with them. In *Atia Waris* v. *Sultan Khan* (1959) Mahmud J stated that 'initially the minor's welfare lies in giving custody according to the dictates of personal law, but if circumstances clearly point that his or her welfare dominantly lies elsewhere, or that it would be against his or her interest, the court must act according to the demand of the welfare of the minor'.[44] Factors such as the mother's apostasy or remarriage which prejudice her custodial rights in Islam may also be disregarded in the interest of safeguarding the child's welfare, though these rules are presumed initially to be in the child's interests.[45]

The open-ended nature of the best interests concept has led to the exercise of a wide judicial discretion in Pakistan. As in India, this has resulted in conflicting judicial decisions where judges' attitudes and personal perceptions determine the choice between recognizing traditional rights and deciding the issue without any preconceived notions of a 'suitable' guardian. One writer has commented that 'despite exceptional judgements to the contrary, the law to which the minor is subject is assigned a relatively subordinate position to that of the rules of welfare', and that courts have been willing to grant custody to the mother. However she comments that, with the recent trend towards expanding the significance of Islamic law as a source of family law in Pakistan, guardianship cases between 1981 and 1988 indicate a preference for the father.[46]

(c) Access

The Guardianship Act 1890 has certain other aspects relevant to the best interests of the child. Although that Act and the Hindu Guardianship Act 1956 do not refer to rights of access, Indian courts have considered such rights to be an aspect of the child's welfare. Access rights of the non-custodian parent are therefore recognized as a matter of course. Denial is an exceptional measure that can be justified on the basis that allowing access will be prejudicial to the child. A relative may also be granted rights of access in the interests of the child. The Supreme Court has pronounced that courts must give full and clear directions on access, and avoid practical difficulties as far as possible.[47]

(d) Non-marital children

The Hindu Guardianship Act now accepts that the mother is the preferred natural guardian of non-marital children, followed by the father. The Act has therefore modified the traditional law, which gave the father preferential status. In these cases, the welfare of the child has been used to award custody to the mother or other relatives. The mother's 'immorality' has sometimes been considered relevant in these cases, but has also been ignored.[48] Though the 1890 Act permits the courts to consider the 'character' of the guardian, an early Indian case held that 'an immoral father has just as good a right to his own children as a moral man and in many cases . . . is likely to see that his children are properly brought up'.[49]

(e) The child's wishes

The child's best interests have been used in custody and guardianship litigation in India to give significance to the child's wishes and preferences. The Guardianship and Wards Act 1890 states that the child's welfare must be determined in the context of the age of the child and that 'if the minor is old enough to form an intelligent preference the court may consider that preference'.[50] This has been used by the Indian courts to focus on the maturity of the child, rather than his or her age. Indian courts have sometimes been influenced by the early English law's concept of an 'age of discretion' at which the writ of habeas corpus could not be brought to question 'the detention' of a girl over the age of sixteen and a boy over the age of fourteen. However, the predominant view of the Indian Courts is to approach the issue of the child's wishes flexibly, considering the ages of discretion too artificial to be applicable in the Indian context. Reported cases also show that, in the absence of some guideline as to the weight to be attached to the child's wishes, there is a great deal of subjectivity in decision making, leading to a situation where a teenager's wishes are disregarded, while young children have been considered competent to express an 'intelligent preference'.[51]

(f) Religion

The father's right to control religion appears to be given special significance in India and Pakistan in some cases, so as to determine the issue of guardianship and custody, irrespective of other considerations. One commentator therefore notes that in India the 'parental (father's) right to control the religion of his children has not been tested on the touchstone of the welfare of children'.[52] Thus the child's preferences may be deemed subordinate to the importance a court attaches to enabling the father to control the child's religious upbringing. Since Islamic and Hindu law presume that children will follow the religion of their father, public policy appears to make it difficult to depart from this view. Nevertheless, we have observed that the 'best interests,' concept has been used to displace rights under personal law. This willingness to depart from the personal law strengthens the argument against attaching special significance to the father's rights in this regard where they conflict with other considerations.

Section 17 (2) of the Guardianship and Wards Act merely mandates the court to consider the religion of the minor when making its decision on what is in the child's welfare. However, the judicial approach goes further than that in identifying the parental right over religion with the child's interests. If the parental rights in this regard are given greater significance in the current environment of religious fundamentalism, further rationales are likely to be developed to justify interpreting the child's interests in terms of the father's parental rights. This could even-tually lead to erosion of uniformity and resurgence of principles of per-sonal law.

The Convention requires States parties to realize the right of the child to 'freedom of thought, conscience and religion,' and to respect the 'right and duty of guardians to provide direction to the child' in the exercise of this right 'in a manner consistent with the evolving capacity of the child'. The Convention's approach to religious upbringing is therefore consistent with its general value system in regard to parental responsibil-ity and protection and autonomy rights. The Constitutions of India, Bangladesh and Pakistan also recognize the right to freedom of con-science and of religion[53] These provisions and the Convention's value system are difficult to reconcile with the existence of a parental right to control the religious upbringing of a child in circumstances where the wishes of a child are disregarded to accommodate the parent's interests.

(g) Child marriage

The application of the Guardianship Act 1890 and the child welfare concept has clearly helped to introduce uniformity into personal law and also resulted in judicial modifications of personal law. They have also contributed to developing a uniform body of legal principles that have benefited women by modifying personal law.[54]

Despite these developments, child marriage remains an area where the child's welfare has not been used to modify values of the personal laws. We have observed that Hindu and Islamic law permit child mar-riage. Uniformly applicable legislation, the Child Marriage Restraint Act, was introduced in the subcontinent of India in 1929. This legisla-tion has been amended to increase the minimum age in the post-independence period in India, Bangladesh and Pakistan. Yet child mar-riages solemnized in violation of the law have not been declared void. Despite the policy stated in the Act, provisions in the Guardianship and Wards Act 1890 and the Hindu Marriage Act 1956 continue to refer to the 'husband's guardianship of his minor wife'.[55] This ambivalence in legal policy encourages social and legal legitimacy for the practice.

Indian cases thus discuss the issue of the 'child's interests' in the context where they are considering whether or not to award the guar-dianship of a child bride or a child widow to a husband or father-in-law. The courts use the welfare of the child to interfere with the husband's

or male relatives' right of physical custody and control of a child wife.[56]
There are, however, occasions when this is not done. In *Poras Ram* v
State (1960)[57] the Allahabad High Court permitted the father-in-law of
a minor widow and other persons forcibly to remove her from her
mother's house and contract a subsequent marriage for her against her
wishes.

Research has revealed the extent of the abuse of girls in child marriage. Its connection with child trafficking is apparent from the fact that
girls are taken across national borders for prostitution or marriage. The
case of Ameena (1991), a child bride discovered travelling on an international flight to Saudia Arabia with her sixty-year-old husband, attracted
media attention, and is one case among many which reveal the new
dimensions of the problem of child marriage.[58]

IV. BEST INTERESTS OF THE CHILD IN A MIXED JURISDICTION: THE SRI LANKAN EXPERIENCE

The concept of the child's 'best interests' entered Sri Lankan law
through the combined influence of Roman-Dutch law and English law.
The early Dutch jurists proclaimed that courts were 'upper guardians
of minors' and could intervene to deprive a parent of any or all of the
different components of parental power. These principles applied in Sri
Lanka in a context where the colonial British administration established
a legal system based on English law. Thus, as in the Indian subcontinent, the Superior Appeals Courts could grant relief in custody disputes
by the writ of habeas corpus, while the civil courts, known as District
Courts, were given a special jurisdiction to appoint guardians of minors.

In the absence of specific guardianship legislation, as in the Indian
subcontinent, from an early date applications for custody in Sri Lanka
were made in the Supreme Court by writ of habeas corpus, on the
ground of the child's wrongful detention. These applications became
the common method for litigating custody disputes, and provided an
avenue for introducing English legal values. The initial focus was thus
on parental rights and especially on the rights of the father. Court intervention was constrained, as it had been in India, by the fact that he
had to be proved to be 'unfit'. We have noted how indigenous laws did
not have an order of guardians. Yet court decisions and statutes in the
colonial period introduced exclusive paternal authority.[59]

In Sri Lanka, the child's best interests are identified with the parental
rights of the father or mother and the concept has been developed
entirely by the judiciary without any legislative intervention. The courts
have invariably focused on the preferential right of the father to custody
and guardianship, deriving inspiration from early cases in English law,
and more recently from the Roman-Dutch law. The leading South
African case of *Calitz* v *Calitz*,[60] on the award of custody in the modern

Roman-Dutch law, has been followed in utilizing the court's jurisdiction to intervene into parental rights as 'upper guardians of minors'. Court interference with the father's preferential right on the basis of prejudice to the 'child's life, health and morals' has been established by many cases which interpret the child's welfare within the framework of paternal rights, and require proof of his 'unfitness'. The general view is that the courts 'will recognize the father's prima facie right except when the element of danger or detriment is positively established'.[61] Sri Lankan law is in this regard similar to Indian law developed under the Guardianship and Wards Act.[62]

Isolated judicial decisions in the Supreme Court have interpreted the child's welfare as a paramount consideration, so as to recognize the mother as preferred custodian of the child. Weeramanatry J said in *Fernando* v *Fernando* (1968) that 'there is a rule commended by law and ordinary human experience that the custody of very young children ought ordinarily to be given to the mother'.[63] Nevertheless, in the absence of statutory reforms which focus on the mother's custodial rights, and a paramountcy principle, the current trend in Sri Lankan courts focuses on the need to interpret the child's best interests within the framework of the Roman-Dutch law's preferential paternal right. This legal position cannot be faulted because both Roman-Dutch law and Sri Lankan statute law in other areas emphasize the father's natural guardianship and his preferred position as custodian parent. In recent years Sri Lankan Courts have not followed the earlier cases which used a paramountcy principle to confer preferential custodial rights on a mother.

The modern Roman-Dutch law as interpreted in the South African case of *Calitz* authorizes the court to make the interests of the child the sole criterion when a divorce or judicial separation is granted in court proceedings. Early Sri Lankan cases ignored this, interpreting the best interests of the child in the context of the preferential right of the father, even in matrimonial disputes. Recent cases, however, have emphasized that the sole consideration is the child's welfare.[64] A strong commitment to interpreting the child's best interests in the context of the natural parents' rights continues, however, to be reflected in custody disputes with foster parents. Courts have stressed that 'one starts with the assumption that the natural parent has a natural right'. Strict and clear proof of 'danger to the life, health or morals of the child' is required to displace parental rights, even in circumstances where informal arrangements for custody have been made with caring foster parents or grandparents.[65]

Judicial decisions reveal that 'danger to life, health or morals of the child' is interpreted flexibly to refer to any indications of prejudice to the child's welfare. Factors such as parental neglect and indifference, even due to poverty, are given weight. However, poverty or immorality in themselves have not been considered relevant if there is evidence of concern and care. Nevertheless, the focus on the natural parents' rights, and the presumption in their favour, means that the courts take the view that they are 'called upon to adjudicate in the best interests of the child but the adjudication must be reached within the framework of the law' on parental rights.[66] The generally held view is that 'the rights of the father will prevail if they are not displaced by considerations relating to the welfare of the child . . . (and) the petitioner who seeks to displace those rights makes out his or her case'.[67]

The same focus on parental status is seen in regard to access rights. Sri Lankan judicial decisions invariably refer to the 'access rights' of a non-custodian parent. There is judicial authority that 'natural ties ought not to be completely disregarded and denied unless the interests of the children are likely to be substantially prejudiced'.[68]

Consequently, courts awarding custody during a de facto separation or in matrimonial litigation usually make an order giving 'reasonable access' to the other parent. Since the parents of a marital child share the parental power as natural guardians, subject to the father's preferential status, access rights under Roman-Dutch law are considered an aspect of guardianship that continues even when custody has been granted to one parent. The legal position is that access rights are available to a non-custodian parent unless a court order on custody has either limited or denied them in the child's interests.

The idea of legally recognized parental rights in regard to 'non-marital' children in Sri Lanka has determined the parameters within which the concept of 'best interests' functions. Sri Lankan indigenous law, as represented in principles of Kandyan law, accepted that some non-marital children could be acknowledged and acquire legal rights in the father's family. The parental status of both father and mother was recognized. Yet modern law, influenced by English law, principles of Roman-Dutch law and statutes, perceives the mother as the exclusive guardian of these children. Custodial status can be conferred on the biological father on the basis that there is good reason to deny the mother's parental rights, and award custody to him in the child's interest. He has no right of access, though access may be claimed on the basis that he has a continuing relationship with the child, and it is the child's interest to maintain that association.[69]

Roman-Dutch law, as we have observed, gives the courts a wide discretion to determine the issue of custody in the child's interests. Nevertheless, Sri Lankan courts have often applied the English law concept of the 'age of discretion' and decided that the wishes of a girl of sixteen and a boy of fourteen are conclusive in determining the issue of custody. There is also a judicial pronouncement in an early case in support of the view that a court must respect the wishes of an adolescent girl under sixteen who wishes to leave her parents and reside elsewhere.

These decisions accord with the Convention's perception that parental rights must diminish in significance with the evolving capacities of the child. Yet they do not reflect the balance that the Convention seeks to achieve. The emphasis on particular and different ages for assessing the maturity of boys and girls, and the constraints on judicial discretion, are out of harmony with the court's responsibility to act as upper guardian to protect the child's interests.[70] The absence of guidelines on the exercise of this discretion is felt especially in this area, where the courts often apply the 'age of discretion' mechanically.

A basic problem in any event in ascertaining the wishes of a child in Sri Lanka lies in the absence of a procedure for ensuring that this information is available to court. Since there are no facilities for a court welfare officer's report, nor independent representation for a child in custody and guardianship litigation, the courts must rely on the lawyers for the parties. A judge sometimes interviews a child in his chambers, a procedure that is not conducive to determining what is best for the child. A formal brief interview in a judge's chambers can be traumatic for the child, and hardly an atmosphere in which to ascertain his or her wishes. A child-centred focus in the law clearly requires facilitating the child's wishes being presented to court in a manner that is truly geared to finding out what the child's view is on the matter of his or her custody and guardianship. Sri Lankan court decisions on guardianship indicate that a balance between protection and participation has not yet been worked out by allowing the child's wishes to be considered as an important but not conclusive factor.

PLURALISM IN PERSONAL LAW IN SRI LANKA, GENDER EQUITY, AND BEST INTERESTS

The fact that the development of the child's best interests came through English or Roman-Dutch law, and not the indigenous systems, has undermined pluralism in the subcontinent. In an early case on custody decided in the colonial period, the Supreme Court of Sri Lanka declared that it was committed to making the child's welfare and interests a paramount consideration, irrespective of parental rights recognized in indigenous laws. The court stated that it 'decides nothing here about Moors and Sinhalese, about followers of Buddha and disciples of Islam'.[71] In the post-independence period, Sri Lanka's Supreme Court has utilized its jurisdiction as upper guardian to intervene on the basis that 'under any system of law, a paramount, indeed a valid consideration . . . is the interests of the child, any other consideration being subordinate to it'.[72] The use of a common procedure by an application for a writ of habeas corpus and the absence of a distinct procedure exclusively for determining custody disputes in the only 'customary court' (the *Quazi* Court), has affected the substantive law. In the law on custody and guardianship, principles of indigenous systems have to be applied within the context of the uniformly applicable norm of the child's best interests. Parental rights recognized in the indigenous systems have been displaced by the 'best interests' concept. The mother's custodial status has been recognized on the basis that it is in the child's best interests to award her custody. The child's right to express his/her preference has been conceded on the basis of the 'age of discretion'.

Statutory policies in regard to child marriage, as well as judicial decisions, recognize the right of a girl child not to be given in marriage against her wishes, even when this conflicts with perceptions of the personal law. The experience of Sri Lanka in regard to child marriage provides interesting insights into the way in which the best interests have been used to articulate legal values designed to protect girl children against exploitation in marriage, even where there has been a tradition of social and legal legitimacy for child marriage.

The Sri Lankan legislation on non-Muslim marriages is derived from British Colonial legislation and still stipulates the age of legal capacity to marry as twelve years for girls. This was the original age in early English law, which reflected the influences of Roman law in this regard. Marriages contracted below the statutory age are void. The need for restraints on abuse of parental authority to give a child in marriage have been accepted in legislation and in court decisions. Legislation permits the court to give consent in circumstances where parental consent is unreasonably withheld. Similarly, a person under the age of majority who contracts a marriage is considered to have acquired the status of majority by entering into this relationship. A parent or husband has no rights of guardianship over a married woman and there is no concept of guardianship of a widow or divorcee. Also, consent of the parties is a basic requirement for marriage. There is judicial authority that agreements by parents to give minors in marriage before a certain date are invalid and contrary to public policy. Such an agreement has been viewed as 'an embarrassment upon the absolute freedom to consult the best interests of this child which parents possess'.[73] The consent of parents is therefore not a substitute for the consent of an under-age child; it is an additional requirement and can be dispensed with by court in the child's interests.

The Islamic law on marriage in Sri Lanka reflects a different scale of values in this respect because of the wide power conferred on the father and male relatives as marriage guardians. However some statutory restraints on early marriage have been introduced even in this system, and the concept of the 'option of puberty' is recognized as a principle that can restrict abuse of marriage guardianship. The need to introduce statutory reform on requiring the consent of the bride has been raised by the Muslim Law Research Committee in a published report, and by Muslim Women's groups. There are reported cases in which adverse comments have been made on the practice of child marriage, and courts have emphasized the importance of obtaining the bride's consent.[74] Statistics reveal a low incidence of child marriage in Sri Lanka in general and also in the Muslim community. While other factors, such as accessible educational opportunities have contributed to this situation, it is clear that the legal value-system has moved away from a traditional approach to the permissibility of child marriage just as English Common law moved from acceptance of child marriage and an option to repudiate the marriage at puberty, to enactment in 1929 that such marriages were void and the idea that a parent's refusal to consent could be overruled by a court.

The undermining of pluralism by the 'best interests' concept has recently met resistance in the recent resurgence of religious and ethnic consciousness which has resulted in a new willingness to exclude uniformly applicable laws, even in Sri Lanka. In *Abdul Cader* v. *Razik* (1952)[75] the Privy Council refused to determine whether a girl could change her religion without her father's consent, but there are Supreme Court decisions in Sri Lanka which support the view that the father may control religious upbringing even when he is not the custodial parent. This situation can clearly expose the child to conflicts, but courts and the legislature in Sri Lanka have been unwilling to interfere with this right on the basis of the welfare of the child. Thus early cases and the Education Act 1939 consider the father as the parent with the right to control religious upbringing.[76]

The right to freedom of 'thought conscience and religion' is now articulated as a fundamental right in the Constitution,[77] and conflicts with the concept of a paternal right to control religious upbringing. The Constitutional provisions also support a balance between parental responsibility for providing religious instruction, and the need to accept the right of a child of sufficient maturity to determine his or her own religious convictions. The child's wishes should receive priority depending on age and maturity.

A recent case on adoption under a uniformly applicable statute shows how the trend towards uniformity may be undermined when the 'best interests' concept is not used to give a child-centred orientation, even when a religious or ethnic law applies. Although Islamic law does not know adoption, Sri Lanka Muslims have adopted children under a uniformly applicable statute introduced in 1941. In *Ghouse* v. *Ghouse* (1988)[78] relatives challenged the adoptive child's right to inherit property according to principles of Islamic law. The Supreme Court of Sri Lanka, dissenting from the decision of the Court of Appeal, decided that the principles of Islamic law prevented Muslim parents who had validly adopted under the uniform statute conferring rights of inheritance. At no point was it argued, nor did the court consider, whether it was correct to hold that Muslims could utilize the general law of adoption without conferring rights of inheritance on adoptive children despite provisions in the adoption statute which require the Court to permit adoption only if it is in the child's interests and clarify that an adopted child shall be considered to be a legitimate child of the adoptive parents. The highest court of the country thus ignored the cardinal principle that the child's best interests should guide any court in adoption proceedings. In focusing on the right of inheritance of Muslims under personal law and the Constitutional provision recognizing fundamental rights regarding religion, the Supreme Court undermined the judicial duty to take a child-centred approach in all adoption applications. The Constitution has in this case served to erode, rather than support, commitment to uniform legal values.

V.   ADOPTION AND PLACEMENT OF CHILDREN 'IN CARE'

Legal policies in India in regard to adoption and 'in care' proceedings indicate perceptions of the best interests concept. Adoption in Hindu law originated in religious ritual and the right of adults to perpetuate their lineage, and did not develop in a context of concerns with child care and nurturing. This perception was not modified in the codifying Hindu Adoption Act 1956.[79] The statute has given a court the discretion to consider the suitability of adopters and the child's preference only when a person other than the parents desires to give the child in adoption. These provisions contrast sharply with the child-centred modifications introduced into the codified Hindu Guardianship Act 1956.

Some provisions intended to reflect gender equity in adoption have been introduced into codified Hindu adoption law. Adoption by females and adoption of a girl or non-marital children is now permitted, while a man cannot give a child in adoption without his wife's consent. However, the Act has not introduced safeguards to protect the interests of children in the adoption process, thus creating in some sense a conflict between women's rights in adoption and the child's interests.

We have observed that Islamic law does not recognize adoption. Yet the Sharia Act 1937 recognized that Muslims may adopt according to customary practice. Social activists have not been able to persuade the Government to enact a uniform secular law on adoption in the interests of children. Therefore existing procedures in the Guardianship Act 1890 continue to be used in inter-country adoption to appoint a guardian authorized to take the child abroad. The child's welfare may be used to deny guardianship. But once the order is issued, the child is taken overseas and adopted under the procedures of the foreign country.

Concern over abuses in this procedure resulted in the Supreme Court decision in the leading Indian Case *Lakshmi Kant Pandey* v. *Union of India*.[80] The Supreme Court assumed fundamental rights jurisdiction by writ petition on a letter from a lawyer alleging malpractice by social and voluntary organizations offering children for foreign adoption. The court referred to the primary objective of safeguarding the welfare of the child, and set the guidelines and standards which must now be followed in inter-country adoptions. India does not perceive inter-country adoption in an alien environment as contrary to the interests of children. As the court stated, 'if it is not possible to provide (children) in India a decent family life where they can grow up under the loving care and attention of parents and enjoy the basic necessities of life, . . . there is no reason why such children should not be allowed to be given in adoption to foreign parents'. Guidelines developed by the court are meant to set regulatory procedures which can prevent trafficking and child exploitation.

The Sri Lankan policy on inter-country adoption is similar.[81] Although restrictions on inter-country adoption have been introduced progressively with a view to prevent trafficking, Sri Lankan law permits foreign adoption under uniform legislation enacted in 1941. This statute is not part of Guardianship law, as in India, but is based on the first Adoption Act of 1926 in England. It requires the court to obtain the consent of a child over ten years old, and also consider the welfare of the child. Under recent amendments aimed at controlling child trafficking, new offences have been created. Also, adoption requires the consent of the Commissioner of Probation and Child Care, and is confined to children from State receiving homes. The 'open policy' on inter-country adoption fosters the sense of legitimacy for the practice. In two recent cases the trial court gave permission for inter-country adoption of a child who was not in a state home. The decision of the trial court was reversed in an appeal supported by the Attorney-General, on the ground that the constraints were mandatory and in the interests of children.

Bangladesh[82] also permits adoption under the Guardianship Act 1890, and this procedure is used as in India for inter-country adoption. An 'Abandoned Children's Order' promulgated in 1972 permitted a child to be declared 'abandoned' by the Director of Social Welfare, so that a custody order could be made in this officer's favour. This was a response to the need to provide foster care for children born to victims of violence in war. Since the Director could delegate custody the regulation was subsequently used for inter-country adoption. However, the Government subsequently prohibited this procedure for foreign adoption in response to objections to a child's alienation from an Islamic environment.

None of these countries which regulate foreign adoption have addressed the need to safeguard the interests of the child in local adoptions. There are no procedures for home study reports and other devices to ensure adequate and proper placement. Though child abuse in adoptive situations is known to take place, courts, social welfare and probation authorities do not give sufficient attention to the issue of placement, nor to its monitoring. This has much to do with the lack of adequate administrative services to link with judicial processes and the legislation regulating child abuse and children in conflict with the law.

The social welfare authorities in all countries perform a dual role in working both with children in conflict with the law as well as adopted children and child victims of neglect and abuse. The laws of the region on children in need of care originated in juvenile justice laws in England, or a colonial Children and Young Persons Ordinance. Several countries have also enacted specific legislation on juvenile justice after independence, and articulated the welfare concept. These laws have clearly been introduced with the intention of safeguarding children's interests. The Sri Lankan statute on juvenile justice was perceived as a 'children's charter . . . to give them their right place in society . . . and to prevent them from being exploited in money making'.[83] Indeed this legislation was introduced in 1939 as one of a series of child welfare enactments. Adoption was combined with registration of custodians, and seen as an intervention to prevent exploitation of children in domestic service.[84] The Juvenile Justice Act in India provides for decision-making in regard to neglected or abused children by Juvenile Welfare Boards in a non-adversarial and child-centred environment. The Act has several innovative features, such as limiting access to lawyers, and limiting the time for completing inquiries. Despite these efforts, adequate resources have not been allocated to ensure carefully considered child-centred placement in adoption, or child centred decisions on victims of abuse.

The criminal overtones of the legislation encourage the perception that victims of abuse or 'neglected juveniles' who are placed in 'state receiving homes' 'observation homes' or in foster care are detainees whose liberty has been restrained. The criminal approach is strengthened by the absence of an adequate cadre of trained probation officers or social workers who can perform their roles in representing the child's interests and assist the court to make a decision in the interests of the child.

It has been found in Sri Lanka that victims of abuse are transported to and from court in prison vehicles, while all those involved in court proceedings refer to an order on the child victim as an order for 'remand'. There is no facility for independent representation for a child, unless a parent is able to obtain representation or a legal aid organization or lawyer offers these services voluntarily. Intervention into family privacy and decisions on adoption are made in an environment which does not reflect an appropriate combination of judicial and administrative procedures. The fact that Family Courts and special Juvenile Justice tribunals have been established has not altered the adversarial overtones.

Besides, even in Sri Lanka, where courts have an overriding jurisdiction to act as upper guardian, it is not clear whether they can act in that capacity outside the traditional types of custody, guardianship or adoption litigation. Thus 'in care' legislation can be used insensitively by judicial authorities, law enforcement agencies and even social service or probation officials without realizing that they are making vital decisions denying a 'neglected' or 'abused' child's right to personal liberty. The emphasis on 'protection' and safeguarding the child's welfare in that regard leads to a denial of the participatory concepts recognized in other areas of law, where the child's wishes and preferences are consulted.

Uniformly applicable adoption and juvenile justice laws articulate a general concern with the child rather than the adult. With effective resources for training judicial and administrative personnel, they can be used to achieve their articulated policy. They are in that sense different from guardianship laws which are used for adoption, and maintenance laws. These are areas where concern with an adult family member's rights or values on legitimacy colour a court's decisions on what in best for the child.

VI.   THE NATIONAL CONSTITUTIONS

The Constitution of India has inspired national constitutions in South Asia. Created from a populist political movement, this constitution articulates a vision of social, economic and political justice for 'the people' based on democratic and egalitarian values. It recognizes international norms on human rights and individual dignity. This constitution's perceptions on children are contained in several provisions, which link with the general human rights standards in the document.

These standards have been absorbed into or have influenced other constitutions in the region. Thus the right to equality and freedom from discrimination is articulated in all constitutions as a fundamental right which is only qualified by the right of the State to take affirmative action or make 'special' provision for women and children.[85] The Bangladesh and Pakistan Constitutions refer to 'protection' while the Sri Lanka Constitution refers to the 'advancement' of women and children. Though the scope of affirmative action may vary because of the difference, there is a consensus on the need for policy intervention on behalf of children in order to realize equality and redress historical injustices. The Constitutions of India and Pakistan also state a fundamental right to protection from trafficking, bonded labour and (in the case of children under fourteen years) hazardous employment. The Bangladesh Constitution refers to a right to protection from 'all forms of forced labour'.[86] These provisions clearly confer special rights on children.

All countries have provisions on Directive Principles of State Policy which are not enforceable but have been used by the Courts in interpreting fundamental rights. The Indian Constitution refers to the States' duty to 'endeavour to provide within a period of ten years (from 1949, the date of the Constitution) free and compulsory education for all children up to the age of fourteen years'. Similar but more general provisions are found in some other countries.[87] General provisions in the Indian Constitution refer to the obligation of the State to provide children with opportunities for growth and development 'in conditions of freedom and dignity' and receive protection from exploitation.[88]

Provisions of this kind have not been articulated in other countries. However, Sri Lanka's Constitution has a Directive Principle of State Policy which refers to the duty to 'promote with special care the interests of children and youth, so as to ensure their full development . . . and to protect them from exploitation and discrimination'.[89] Though education is dealt with under unenforceable Directive Principles, Nepal's recent independence Constitution identifies education as a fundamental right. Interestingly this is stated as a group right – the right of 'a community . . . to establish schools for imparting education in the mother tongue'. The Indian Constitution has a similar fundamental right in regard to minorities.[90] These provisions appear to impose on the state of duty not to prevent (and at most to facilitate) education rather than a duty to realize the right by positive policies.

The constitutions of the region therefore clearly reflect a perception of 'best interests' which conforms with the UN Convention's standards on child development, protection, and participation. Although development and protection are more clearly defined values, there is a general assumption that a child has a right to identity and dignity. Some constitutions recognize a right to life. However, even when a right to life is not generally recognized, the rights to personal liberty, freedom from torture and freedom of expression may be construed as carrying an implication of a right to life, development and participation.[91]

The legislative record of realizing the fundamental rights in regard to child labour, the Directive Principles of State Policy in general and on compulsory education indicates that these perceptions of 'best interests' have not been translated into policy interventions. Recent statutes on child labour in Pakistan and India[92] are almost copies, and they legitimize use of child labour in areas other than those specified as 'hazardous' occupations under these Acts. This means that even a child under ten years old can be legally employed as a worker in industrial production.

The perception that child labour is a logical outcome of poverty, and a necessary survival strategy for the child and the family, has perpetuated over the years a policy view that child labour is in the best interests of low-income children. Even the Supreme Court of India in 1991 considered it permissible for low-income children to work because 'although (under the Constitution's Directive Principles) all children up to the age of fourteen are supposed to be in school, economic necessity forces

... children to seek employment ... and children can therefore be employed'.[93] This argument of the child's 'interest' in working has masked the reluctance to move children out of the labour force, allocate more resources for primary education, and replace children with adult male and female labour. One advocate of the 1986 child labour legislation publicly referred to the conflict of interest. 'One has to see this child first of all as a child requiring all those things that a child needs for growth and development and a complete childhood', she said, and added: 'But this child is also part of the labour force, and has to be seen as a worker contributing to the economy of the country'.[94]

Antislavery child rights activists in India and international lobbying groups inspired the Harkin Bill in the USA which bans the import of products made by child workers. These activists have lobbied for realization of constitutional values and human rights standards in South Asia which recognize every child's right to a childhood. They argue that other interests can never compete against the fundamental right of every child to grow and develop and experience childhood. Recent initiatives to revise the child labour laws in India are as much a response to these pressures as the critique from within the system in regard to enforcing the new laws.[95] Neither India nor Pakistan has enacted and enforced compulsory education laws nationally, and the argument of lack of resources has been used to postpone indefinitely the introduction of such policies. However Bangladesh has recently introduced an affirmative action policy, and made education free and compulsory for girls in rural areas, up to Grade eight.

The development in India of public interest litigation, sometimes described as social action litigation, has been a response to executive and legislative apathy in realizing fundamental rights and the rights and interests of children in particular, guaranteed by the Constitution. This effort to 'take suffering seriously'[96] has resulted in radical judicial activism. The Supreme Court has dispensed with usual formalities of writ procedures and initiated action to consider violation of fundamental rights on the basis of a letter addressed to the court by concerned members of the public, organizations, or victims of violations. Traditional concepts of *locus standi* have been modified to permit non-governmental organizations or concerned individuals such as journalists, social workers and professionals to petition for redress, even without identifying an individual affected by the violation. The court has appointed commissions of inquiry to report on the allegations, and assumed a continuing monitoring role. There are many cases involving children in which the Supreme Court of India has mandated State action to realize constitutionally guaranteed rights. These include cases of child labour where the court has directed that the right to protection requires state action to provide facilities for education.[97] Other cases have directed that conditions in State homes for children and juvenile offenders be improved.[98] The Court has intervened to prevent establishment of separate schools and hostels for children born to prostitutes on the ground that it is not in their interest to be isolated from the community.[99]

Justice Ranganath Mishra's judgment in *Mehta* v. *State of Tamil Nadu* (1990)[100] conflicts with this concern with the child's need for growth and development. The court considered that the employment of children in the match industry in Sivakasi was not in violation of the constitution because 'the tender hands of children are more suited to the sorting out of the manufactured product, and processing it for purposes of packing'. The need for child labour for these tasks seems to have outweighed the court's concern for children working in the 'hazardous' match-manufacturing industry. However, two recent cases in the Indian Supreme Court have interpreted the 'right to life' in the constitution in the context of the non-enforceable Directive Principles of (social and economic) State Policy, so as to recognize a fundamental right to education.[101]

The social action litigation developed by the Indian Supreme Court has influenced judicial activism in the region. There are instances of such litigation in Pakistan in relation to child workers and children in prison.[102] In his inaugural address as President of SAARC LAW, a regional organization of judges and lawyers, the present Chief Justice of Pakistan referred to the judgment of the Supreme Court in the *Nawaz Sharif* case, and stated that the scope of social action litigation must be expanded in South Asia to realize fundamental rights, and provide access to justice for the people. 'The judiciary in Pakistan' he said 'has in response to the demands of society begun to play a positive role to undo the injustice done to the people. This is being attempted through the technique of Public Interest Litigation . . . this is an effort to eradicate social evils and undo injustice through the agency of law . . . consistently with the provisions of the Constitutions . . . There is no limit or condition imposed on the Supreme Court (in Pakistan) except that the appropriate order which is made should be for the enforcement of fundamental rights'.[103] Such judicial activism can be perceived as a response to the need for a 'new equity' to realize constitutional guarantees and values on justice. The courts of the subcontinent used the concept of 'equity and good conscience' in the colonial era to introduce uniform legal values and undermine legal pluralism between different systems of personal law. The activist role of the to-day's judiciary can be seen as a continuation of that legal tradition. This is related to the wide power of judicial review under the constitutions of India, Pakistan and Bangladesh.

The situation is different in Sri Lanka where the courts do not have the power to challenge past laws.[104] The Supreme Court exercising fundamental rights jurisdiction reviews state action rather than inaction, and has not accepted the expanded doctrine of locus standi. The recent decision in the adoption case[105] also shows how religious and cultural rights guaranteed under the constitution can be used to undermine perceptions of 'best interests' in terms of the other fundamental rights, such as equality before the law and gender equity, guaranteed by the constitution.

If the subcontinent has a tradition of judicial activism and legislative and administrative apathy in realizing constitutional guarantees, Sri Lanka's impressive social indicators for children are the product of legislative and executive action. A strong social welfarism which originated in the British colonial administration, linked with egalitarian Buddhist values and a populist political and trade union movement, introduced important child-oriented measures in health and education.[106] The link between child marriage, child labour and education was perceived very early. A developed system of registration of marriage and accessible free state health and education services focused on the low-income child and the community. The education reforms of the middle of this century were based on the right of every child, rural or urban, to receive a good education. Consequently, education policies were aimed at establishing rural schools and good, state-managed provincial Central Schools. These schools succeeded in providing upward mobility for rural low-income children, and catalyzed parental and adult interest in using educational opportunities for children. The failure to persist with those policies, combined with policies on language and a regulated economy, has contributed to ethnic and political violence. Sri Lanka's dissatisfied and 'educated' rural youth population is as much a product of its successes as its failures in the area of education.

National Policies on Children of this decade (particularly in the post-UN Convention period) have created a new interest in child-centered policy planning in South Asia.[107] Sri Lanka has recently promulgated a Charter on Children's Rights, although this is not a law but a policy document. There are some provisions in the Charter which dilute the international standards that Sri Lanka has ratified.[108] On the other hand the Charter prohibits recruitment of children under eighteen years old into the armed forces, setting a higher standard than the Convention[109] and already confining recruitment into the armed services to adult citizens. The Cabinet has also approved new uniform legislation on child abuse and prostitution. In order to strengthen enforcement, the law will be enacted as amendments to the Penal Code. It has yet to be seen whether these child abuse laws will evoke a negative response in Parliament.

VII. CONCLUSION

The colonization of countries in South Asia is part of their historical experience. This period saw the significant modification of personal law.

The entrenchment of new values makes it difficult to justify an interpretation of 'the best interests of the child' in terms of 'traditional' or 'cultural values.' It is necessary to recognize that the colonial experience contributed to secularism and uniformity in important areas of child law and policy in these countries. That tradition has been child-centred, to some extent, and placed a value on internationally recognized human rights standards of individual dignity and gender equity.

The recent judicial initiatives and activism as represented by social action or public interest litigation has potential for creating a new environment of access to justice and community participation in the realization of rights. These developments have in general been beneficial to disadvantaged sections of the child population, and can be used creatively to ensure that all children benefit from uniformly applicable policy approaches. It seems important for children that rights associated with the practice of religion or culture should not be used to resist reform ·and reverse the trend towards uniformity and setting human rights standards in policy making.

The national constitutions represent a powerful value framework that should be used to link with international standards on child rights that have been accepted by all countries through ratification of the UN Convention. Rather than using the 'best interests' as a relative concept for interpreting child rights, these rights can be used to provide the framework for laws and policies on children. In a recent decision in the Supreme Court of India, the constitutional guarantee on the right to life was used to apply the child's welfare and resist and application for custody based exclusively on parental rights.[110] We have noted how this right has been used to imply a right to education. If the Constitutional and international standards could be used to set the guidelines for determining what is in the best interests of the child, it will be possible to reduce the current subjectivity in decision making both by judges and policy makers.

While there appears to be awareness of the child's right to provision and protection, South Asian countries will find it difficult to develop participatory rights. Although the child's wishes and preferences are relevant in guardianship litigation, legal procedures do not in general provide that access. The lack of interest in participation is reflected in policy statements and SAARC resolutions which do not refer to these rights.[111] It is not unusual for official statements to declare that 'children are a valuable asset and all development activities should be focused on recognizing their worth', and to proceed to observe that children are not adults, and should take 'an oath of obedience to their elders' on children's day. Sri Lanka's Children's Charter replaces the 'evolving capacities of the child' with a reference to parental guidance.[112] Yet adolescent and youth unrest particularly in schools and Universities in South Asia over the last decade indicate that children have not learned to handle adult life and responsibility. Unless children are afforded participation rights, the perception that children suddenly move from childhood to majority will continue to pervade parenting in the family, and policy planning.

  Indigenous laws and tradition in many areas such as adoption and family support reflect values which are more consistent with international child rights standards than those of the received English or Roman-Dutch law. Consequently the rights perceptions of the UN Convention can be used to revive those traditional values which will conform with the framework accepted as an international standard for all countries in South Asia. It is, however, important for the children of South Asia that countries in the region do not obscure the realities of ignorance and social and economic deprivation and resurrect questionable 'indigenous' values, so as to undermine basic standards already accepted and developed further by the UN Convention. Their cause will not be promoted unless the national constitutions which link to international standards are used to address the inherent inadequacies in both the colonial and indigenous laws. The *Shah Bano Case* in India and the case of *Tennekoon* v. *Tennekoon* (1986)[113] in Sri Lanka indicate how values of the personal laws can be distorted and misrepresented as basic religious or customary norms. The words of the late Muhammad Ali Jinnah in the debate on the Child Marriage Restraint Act 1929 have relevance for South Asia today. Supporting the legislation, he said:

I cannot believe that there can be a divine sanction for such evil practices as are prevailing and that we should give our sanction to the continuance of those evil practices. . . . If we are going to allow ourselves to be influenced by the public opinion that can be created in the name of religion when we know that religion has nothing whatever to do with the matter, I think we must have the courage to say 'No we are not going to be frightened by that'.[114]

NOTES

[1] Convention on the Elimination of All Forms of Discrimination Against Women (1979) Art 5 (b) ('primordial'); Convention on the Rights of the Child (CRC) Art 21; Declaration of the Rights of the Child (1959) Principal 2; Hindu Minority and Guardianship Act (1956) India S 13 (1) Children Act (England) 1989 s 1(1) ('paramount')

[2] *J* v *C* [1970] AC 668 at 710

[3] P. M. Bromley and N. V. Lowe (eds), *Bromley's Family Law* (London: Butterworths, 1987), 315–16.

[4] Ibid at 318, citing Maidment *Child Custody and Divorce*, 149.

[5] J. C. Hall, 'The Waning of Parental Rights' (1972) 31 *Cambridge LJ* 248, 265.

[6] W. Blackstone, *Commentaries on the Laws of England* (London: A. Strahan, 1825), 452, 458.

[7] Talford's Act 1839, Custody of Infants Act 1873, and Guardianship of Infants Act 1925, cited Bromley op cit 312.

[8] S. Goonesekere, *Sri Lanka Law on Parent and Child* (Colombo: Gunasena, 1987), 206; E. Spiro, *Law of Parent and Child* (Cape Town: Juta and Co. Ltd, 1985), 4, 257.

[9] Giladi Anver, 'Concepts of Childhood and Attitudes Towards Children in Mediaeval Islam', 32 *Journal of the Social and Economic History of the Orient*, 121.

[10] David Pearl, *A Textbook on Muslim Personal Law* (Kent: Croom Helm Ltd, 1987), 15.

[11] Bromley, op cit 588; M. Hidayathullah (ed), *Mulla's Principles of Mahomedan Law* (Bombay: Tripathi Pvt Ltd, 18 ed reprint 1986), 383; Pearl, ibid, 91.

[12] Paras Diwan, *Law of Adoption, Minority, Guardianship and Custody* (Allahabad: Wadwa & Co., 1989), 152–3, 334.

[13] Ibid. 178, and 191, L. Rocher, 'The Theory of Matrimonial Causes According to the Dharmasastra' in J. N. D. Anderson (ed), *Family law in Asia and Africa* (London: George Allen and Unwin Ltd, 1968), 90 at 96;

[14] Rocher, op cit 93 note 3; Paras Diwan, op cit 27.

[15] B. Mathew and others, *Cases and Materials on Family Law I* (Bangalore: National Law School of India, 1990), 0.1.5.

[16] A. Bajpai, 'The Girl Child and the Law', *Report of Seminar on Rights of the Child* (Bangalore: National Law School of India, 1990), 118.

[17] Goonesekere, op cit 200–3; Niti-Nighanduwe (Colombo: Government Printer Ceylon 1880), 44, 46, 25.

[18] Robert Percival, *An Account of the Island of Ceylon* (London, 1803), 116.

[19] *Major Forbes Eleven Years in Ceylon* (London: Richard Bentley, 1840) Vol II 98–9; John Davy, *An Account of the Interior of Ceylon* (1821) (Colombo: Tisara Publishers, 1969), 216.

[20] Robert Knox Robert, *An Historical Relation of Ceylon* (1681) (Colombo: Tisara Publishers Ltd, 1966), 178.

[21] Anver, n 9 above.

[22] Bangladesh Abandoned Children (Special Provision) Order 1972; A. Bajpai, 'The Girl Child and the Law,' in *Report of a Seminar on the Rights of the Child* (Bangalore: National Law School of India, 1990), 118; R. Panicker, 'The Child and the Indian State' in Fortuyn and de Langen (eds), *Towards the Realisation of Human Right of Children* (Amsterdam: D.C.I., 1992), 76; Administrative Report of the Commissioner of Probation and Child Care Services Sri Lanka (1983) and press and television interviews by the current Commissioner; S. Goonesekere, *Child Labour in Sri Lanka* (Geneva: ILO, 1993).

[23] Guardianship and Wards Act 1890 s 19 (b), ss 7, 17.

[24] (1871) 14 MIA 309, 323.

[25] (1914) ICR 38 Mad 807 at 819.

[26] Ss 6, 19(1)(2).

[27] Paras Diwan, op cit; H. Jilani, 'Legal Status of Women, Country Study Pakistan' (Bangkok: ESCAP 1993 unpublished paper); Ghazi Shasur Rahman, *Laws Relating to Children in Bangladesh* (Dacca: Bangladesh Shishu Academy (1981); *Bhat v Bhat*, AIR 1961 Jam & Kash 5.

[28] Paras Diwan, op cit 319 ff, 323; Jilani, op cit 25–7; *Bhat v Bhat*, AIR 1961 Jam & Kash 5.

[29] *Besant v Narayaniah*; Paras Diwan, op cit 322, citing *Kumaraswami v Rajammal*. AIR 1957 Mad 563 per J. Ayer; *Ansari Sajeeda*, AIR 1983 AP 106 (Muslim Father).

[30] Ibid, *Andiappa v Nalliendram*, ILR 39 Mad 473.

[31] *Singh v Kaur*, AIR 1974 P & H 124.

[32] *Bai Tara v Mohan Lal*, AIR 1932 Bom 405; *Raman v Ayappan*, AIR 1959 Ker. 396.

[33] AIR 1941 Bom 103, cited Paras Diwan op cit, 203.

[34] Re Kamal Rudra ILR (1949) 2 Cal 374; *Begum v Begum*, AIR (1948) All 498; *Kadiappa v Valliammal*, AIR 1949 Mad 608; *Suresh Babu v Madhu*, AIR 1984 Mad 186.

[35] *Suhrabi v Muhammed*, AIR 1988 Ker 36; *Sonna v Chenna*, AIR 1950 Mad 306, and other cases. Paras Diwan, op cit 324; contra *Lakshmi v Rao*, AIR 1983 Mad 9.

[36] *Amol Singh, v Kaur* AIR 1961 Punj 51; *Jain v. The State*, AIR 1983 Del 120; *Batra v Batra*, AIR 1986 Del 149; *Reddy v Reddy*, AIR 1975 Kant 138.

[37] S 17.

[38] Paras Diwan, op cit, 435, 440, 443.

[39] *Begum v Begum*, AIR 1939 All 15.

[40] *Sukhia v Makha*, AIR 1919 All 49, and cases cited Paras Diwan op cit 438–9.

[41] *Ramzan v Taia*, AIR 1983 J & K 70, cited Paras Diwan, ibid, 439.

[42] *Rashida Begum v Shahab Din*, 1960 2 PLD Lah 1142, cited Pearl op cit 93.

[43] *Begum v Ahmed*, 1968 PLD Lah 1112, interpreting *Zohra Begum v Latif Ahmad*, 1965 PLD (WP) Lah 695, cited Pearl, op cit 96.

[44] Ibid 93.

[45] Ibid 96; *Bashir v Fatima*, 1953 PLD Lah 73, cf *Amar Ilahi v Rashida Akhtar*, 1955 PLD Lah 413.

[46] Jilani, op cit, 26–7.

[47] Paras Diwan, op cit 477–8; *Santi Devi v Gian Chand*, AIR 1956 Punj 234; *Mohini v Virehdra Kumar*, 1977 3 SCC 513.

148 SAVITRI GOONESEKERE

[48] Hindu Guardianship Act s 6. Paras Diwan, op cit 191; *Latif Tawaif* v *Prasad*, AIR 1940 All 329 (mother denied custody for prostitution), *Gairaj Singh* v *Deohlu*, AIR 1952 All 331 (immorality insufficient).

[49] *Sukhdeo* v *Ram Chandra*, AIR 1924 All 622.

[50] S 17 (2) ['age']; s 17 (3) ['intelligent preference'].

[51] *Re Agar Ellis* (1883) 24 Ch D 317 followed in cases cited Paras Diwan op cit 429 and also not followed in cases cited 427–30.

[52] Paras Diwan, op cit, 148. Islamic law, see Atia Waris Sultan Khan 1959 PLD (WP) Lah 205 at 215; Hindu law & generally for Indian law, *Skinner* v *Orde* (1871) 14 MIA 309 at 323; *Queen* v *Veeradu* ILR 18 Mad 230 at 232.

[53] Convention on the Rights of the Child, Art 14; Constitution (India) Art 25 (freedom of conscience and religion); Bangladesh Consitution Art 41 (religion); Pakistan Constitution Art 20 (religion).

[54] Family Law Courts Act 1964 Pakistan, discussed, Patel R., Socio-Economic and Political Status of Women in Pakistan (Karachi Faiza Publishers 1991) 246; Family Courts Ordinance Bangladesh (1985); Family Courts Act India (1984).

[55] Guardianship Act 1890 s 19(a); Hindu Guardianship Act 1956 s 6(c).

[56] *Subhaswami Goundan* v *Kamakshi Ammal*, AIR 1929 Mad 834; *Chetty* v *Papammah*, AIR 1948 Mad 103; Paras Diwan, op cit 199; *Gandi Kota* v *P. S. Santa*, AIR 1967 AP. 294; *Rai Chand* v *Bai*, AIR (1966) Mad 173.

[57] AIR 1960 All 479, Paras Diwan, op cit, 201.

[58] Jilani, op cit; Paniker, op cit; Bajpai, op cit.

[59] *Kanapathipillai* v *Sivakolonthu*, (1911) 17 NLR 484, and *Annapillai* v *Saravanamuttu* (1938) 40 NLR 1 (Tamil Customany law); *Kalu* v *T H Silva* (1947) 48 NLR 216 (Kandyan Sinhala law); Goonesekere, op cit, 215, note 78; Children and Young Persons Ordinance (1939), Education Ordinance (1939) Civil Procedure Code (1889), General Marriages Ordinance (1907).

[60] 1939 AD 56.

[61] *Ivaldy* v *Ivaldy* (1956) 57 NLR 568 at 571.

[62] See above 125.

[63] *Fernando* v *Fernando* (1968) 70 NLR 534 per J. Weeramantry, 538; *Weragoda* v *Weragoda* (1961) 68 NLR 83; *Kamalawathie* v *de Silva* (1961) 64 NLR 252.

[64] *Algin* v *Kamalawathi* (1968) 72 NLR 429, contra *Muthucumaraswamy* v *Parameshwari* (1976) 78 NLR 488; *Sedris Singho* v *Somawathy*, 1978–9 2 Sri LR 140 (best interests).

[65] Goonesekere, op cit, 225, 232.

[66] *Mafthootha* v *Thassim* (1963) 65 NLR 547 at 548.

[67] *Weragoda* v *Weragoda*, at 86.

[68] *Blanche anley* v. *Herbert Bois* (1945) 46 NLR 466–7; Goonesekere, op cit, 236–7.

[69] *Ranmenika* v *Paynter* (1932) 34 NLR 127; *Pemawathie* v *K Aratchi* (1970) 75 NLR 398; *Kalu* v. *T. H. Silva* (1947) 48 NLR 216; *Meenachi* v *Supremamaniam Chetty* (1898) 3 NLR 181.

[70] Goonesekere, op cit, 233–6; *In Re Evelyn Warna Kulasuriya* (1955) 56 NLR 525; *Weragoda* v *Weragoda* (1961) 68 NLR 83.

[71] Re Aysa Natchia (1860–1862) 130.

[72] *Hameen* v *Maliha Baby* (1967) 70 NLR 405 at 406 (best interests) followed in *Subair* v *Isthika* (1974) 77 NLR 397 at 402; *Mafthootha* v *Thassim* (1963) 65 NLR 541 at 548 (parental rights framework); *Haniffa* v *Rezack* (1958) 60 NLR 287 (age of discretion).

[73] General Marriages Ordinance (1907) ss 15, 20, 22; Kandyan Harriage and Divorce Act (1952) ss 4, 8, 66. *de Silva* v *Juan Appu* (1928) 29 NLR 417; J. Garvin at 420; Goonesekere, op cit, 307–10.

[74] Muslim Marriages and Divorce Act (1951) S. 23; Report of the Marriage and Divorce Commission, Sessional Paper XVI (1959); Muslim Law Research Committee Report 1978(4), Colombo Law Review 57; Goonesekere, op cit, 313–20.

[75] 54 NLR 201 (PC).

[76] *de Silva* v *de Silva* (1947) 49 NLR 73; Education Ordinance (1939) s 35(1)(4).

[77] Article 10.

[78] 1 Sri LR 25.

[79] Hindu Adoption and Maintenance Act (1956), ss 8, 9, 9(5), 10.

[80] 1987 SC 232; the guidelines were originally set out in this case in an application reported in 1984 SC 469 and later amended in AIR 1986 SC 276.

[81] Adoption Ordinance (1940), ss 3(5) and 4(b) as amended, in regard to foreign adoption in 1964, 1979 and 1992; unreported cases referred to the writer by the Commissioner of Probation and Child Care.

[82] Amir Ul Islam, op cit at 19; Bangladesh Abandoned Children's Order 1972. Education Ordinance 1939, Children and Young Persons Ordinance 1939, Adoption of Children Ordinance 1941.

[83] *Hansard* (1939) Vol. 1 and 11, (1941) Vol 1; India Juvenile Justice Act 1986, SS 27, 28, 33; Bangladesh Children's Act 1974; Sri Lanka Children and Young Persons Ordinance 1939; Punjab Children's Ordinance 1983.

[84] Ceylon Law of Adoption Sessional Paper 11 (1935).

[85] India Art 14, 15(3); Sri Lanka Art 12(1)(4); Pakistan Art 25(3); Bangladesh Art 28(1)(4); Nepal Art 11(1) and proviso.

[86] India Art 24; Pakistan Art 11; Nepal Art 20; Bangladesh Art 34(1).

[87] India Art 45, Bangladesh Art 17(a); cf Sri Lanka Art 27 (2)(h) [no specific reference to children].

[88] India Art 39(f).

[89] Art 27(2)(13).

[90] Art 18, India Art 30.

[91] India Art 21; Bangladesh Art 21, 32 (life, liberty); Sri Lanka Art 11 (freedom from torture); Nepal Art 12 (personal liberty); freedom of expression, India Art 19, Bangladesh Art 39, Sri Lanka Art 14, Nepal Art 12(2)(a).

[92] Indian Child Labour Act 1986; Pakistan Employment Children Act 1991.

[93] *Metha* v *State of Tamil Nadu* (1991) SC 283, per Renganath Mishra and M. H. Kania JJ.

[94] Nananda Redy, 'Child Labor and Legislation in India' in P. Hyndman (ed), *Lawasia Papers, Exploitation of the Child* (Sydney: Lawasia, 1987), 189 at 290.

[95] M. Gupta, 'Special Problems of Enforcement of Child Labour Laws and Regulations' in *Papers of Asian Regional Seminar on Child Labour Education and Enforcement of Legislation* (Geneva: ILO, 1992) III.

[96] U. Baxi, 'Taking Suffering Seriously' in U. Baxi (ed), *Law and Poverty Critical Essays* (Bombay: Tripathi, 1988); G. L. Pieris, 'Public Interest Litigation in the Indian Sub Continent' (1990) 40 *ICLQ* 66; P. N. Bhagwati, 'Social Action Litigation' in N. Tiruchelvom and R. Coomaraswamy (eds), *The Role of the Judiciary in Plural Societies* (London: Frances Pinter, 1987) 20.

[97] Ibid and *Salal Hydro Project Case*, 1984 SC 177.

[98] *Shiela Barse* v *Union of India*, AIR 1986 SC 1773; *Shiela Barse* v *Children Aid Society*, AIR 1987 SC 656.

[99] *Jain v. Union of India*, AIR 1990 SC 292.

[100] JT 1990 SC 263.

[101] *Mohini Jain* v *St. of Karnataka*, JT 1992 4 SC 292; *Unnikrishnan* v *St. Andhra Pradesh*, 1993 1 SCC 645.

[102] Lahore High Court Petition, *State* v *IG of Prison's Punjab* 14.02.1991; Constitutional Petition (1988), Brick Kiln Workers, Pakistan.

[103] As reported *Sri Lanka Daily News* 16 September 1993.

[104] Art 16.

[105] *Ghouse* v *Ghouse*, above n 78.

[106] L. A. Wickremeratne, 'The Emergence of a Welfare Policy 1931–1948' in K. M. de Silva (ed), *History of Ceylon* (Colombo: University of Ceylon Press, 1973) 476.

[107] Sri Lanka National Plan of Action (1991); India National Policy for Children (1974).

[108] Children's Charter (1992), Art 2 (reference only to parent), Art 14 (no reference to evolving capacities of the child).

[109] Arts 1 and 37(b) (eighteen years); Convention (fifteen years).

[110] *Chandran* v. *Venkatalakshmi*, AIR 1981 AP 1.

[111] Summit Declarations of SAARC (South Asian Association for Regional Co-operation) on children.

[112] Art 14 (freedom of religion and conscience); Minister of Education as reported in *Daily News* 23 September 1993.

[113] Shah Banu (contrary to Koranic injunctions); *Tennekoon* v *Tennekoon* (1986) 1 Sri LR 90 (ignoring that indigenous norms recognized marriage breakdown as a basis for divorce).

[114] Jilani, op cit, 29.

SCHOOL AND SADZA†: CUSTODY AND THE BEST INTERESTS OF THE CHILD IN ZIMBABWE

ALICE ARMSTRONG*

ABSTRACT

The concept of the best interests of the child in Zimbabwe must be considered not just at the level of the formal law, but also at the level of the 'living law' or the practices of the people. The formal law of custody focuses on the nuclear family and favours the mother, while in the living law, the best interests of the child are usually perceived to be congruent with those of the extended family, and the father's family is favoured. This produces a tension between the law and practice. The concept of the best interests of the child in custody decisions in practice is usually related to two basic issues: school and sadza. *Sadza*, which is the staple food of Zimbabwe, represents the child's immediate physical needs. School represents the child's long-term interests, which include education so that s/he can be self-supporting and a good relationship with the extended family. In conclusion, it is suggested that the study of the concept of the best interests of the child in its cultural context should include consideration of two key concepts, *world view* and *possibility*: world view in the sense that spiritual beliefs and values influence the content of the concept of the child's best interests and possibility in the sense that the perception of a child's best interests differs according to the opportunities and resources available to him.

> 'What would you say is the best thing for a child?'
> *'School and sadza. That is all. What else is there?'*
> 'School and sadza?'
> *'Only'*
>
> (Old man, Bikita)

Article 3 of the Convention on the Rights of the Child provides that the best interests of the child shall be a primary consideration in all actions concerning children undertaken by welfare institutions, courts, administrative authorities or legislative bodies. Similarly, the national law of Zimbabwe requires that the best interests of the child shall be the paramount consideration in all cases regarding custody. This study will explore the application of the principle of the 'best interests of the child'

---

† Maize porridge, the staple food of Zimbabwe.
* Women and Law in Southern Africa, PO Box UA 171, Union Avenue, Harare, Zimbabwe. Thanks are due to Everjoyce Win and Nabila Mohammed for helping with interviews.

with regard to custody of children in the actions of the courts, and in the opinions and actions of the people, in Zimbabwe. The objective is to come to an understanding of the meaning of the 'best interests of the child' as perceived by ordinary people in the social and cultural context of Zimbabwe, and the relationship of these perceptions to the same principle as applied by the courts.

I. BACKGROUND AND METHODOLOGY

There are two legal systems which apply in Zimbabwe: the general law, composed of Roman-Dutch common law and statutes, and the customary law, composed of the laws and customs of the indigenous people. Generally the common law and statutes are applied in the Magistrate's Courts and High Courts (hereinafter, general law courts) and the customary law is applied in the Community Courts. However, in both legal systems and therefore in both court systems, in custody cases a statute takes precedence, which provides that the paramount consideration must be the interests of the children.[1]

This study attempts to use a 'grassroots perspective'[2] to understand the meaning of the 'best interests of the child' in the socio-cultural context of Zimbabwe. Therefore, we will investigate the beliefs and practices of people at the 'grassroots' level and the relevance of the law to their situation. The discussion also draws from theories of legal pluralism,[3] which point to the significance of the 'living law' or the unofficial norms of the people, in contrast to the official, or formal, law. The discussion first considers the formal law as identified by written texts and as applied in the Community and general law courts, and then discusses the opinions and informal custody arrangements of the people at the 'grassroots' level and the responsiveness of the law to these.

The opinions of the people and their informal custody arrangements were identified from fifty-seven semi-structured interviews of men and women in one urban area and one rural area in Mashonaland, Zimbabwe.[4] The sample is shown below:

Table 1

	male	female
Harare High Income	6	8
Harare Low Income	8	12
Bikita (rural)	12	11

Only Shona people were interviewed. The interviews were conducted and taped in Shona, and transcribed and translated into English by the interviewer.

The customary law will be discussed in its *ideal* form, as recorded by an anthropologist,[5] and in its *living* form, as practised in the customary courts of Zimbabwe today. The practices of the courts have been studied in two Community Courts, one in Harare, an urban area, and one in Bikita, a rural area. Twenty court records of custody cases were chosen in each area, selecting the first custody files found beginning with August 1992 and moving backwards. Although the hearings had all been in Shona, the records are kept in English. Therefore the quotations attributed to the litigants are actually the Presiding Officer's English translation (and probably paraphrase) of what he heard in Shona.

The information on general law courts is based on court files for the first forty-seven custody/divorce cases found in the records of the High Court of Harare, also beginning in August 1992 and moving backwards. The sample includes eleven contested and thirty-six uncontested cases.

II.   GENERAL LAW OF CUSTODY

The general law of custody in Zimbabwe is similar to laws of custody industrialized countries. 'Custody' refers to the physical care and control of a child.[6] Under common law, the natural custodian of an illegitimate child is its mother[7] and in order to interfere with that natural right a third party (which includes the father of the illegitimate child) must show 'special grounds' which include 'detrimental or undesirable effects or influences on the physical, moral and psychological or educational welfare of a child.'[8]

While a couple remain married, the parents possess joint custody over their children. If married parents cease to live together, the mother has custody until an order is made by a court.[9] On divorce, a court may grant custody to either party or any other such person 'as the court may deem best fitted to have such custody',[10] subject to the proviso that the 'paramount consideration' must be the 'interests of the children concerned.'[11]

Our sample of contested and uncontested divorce/custody cases in the High Court gives an indication of the factors which are considered in determining custody under general law. This discussion will be very brief because, as will be seen, the general law considers the same factors which are relevant to custody in most industrialized countries of the north, with very little specific Zimbabwean content.[12] This discussion is offered to prove just that point, and to contrast custody in the general law courts with that in the customary courts and in the practices of the people.

In Zimbabwe, there are two types of legally recognized marriage. Civil marriage is monogamous and governed by general law. Customary marriage, which must be registered to be legally recognized (with certain exceptions), is potentially polygamous and governed by customary law. Although all divorce, whether from civil or customary marriage, is now governed by statute,[13] in the High Court, custody cases are considered only in connection with civil law marriage. Only a small proportion of the population is married according to civil law, almost always well-educated, urban dwellers (and all non-blacks). Litigation in the High Court requires representation by a lawyer, which means that the arguments made in court are constructed by lawyers rather than by the expectations and values of the parties. All arguments are framed in terms of the legislation, and therefore in terms of the 'best interests of the child.'

The following factors were considered by High Court judges to be important factors in determining the best interests of the children in custody cases:

– the wishes of the child(ren) involved, considering their age and intelligence and the suitability of each parent to be custodian

– a report from the Social Welfare officer: in one case this indicated that the child missed his siblings who were with the other parent

– reluctance to vary an existing custody arrangement

– that children of 'tender age' should not be separated from mother

– the ability of a parent to provide suitable accommodation

– who will look after child: in one case the natural parent was preferred over a domestic worker; in another the mother's 'urge for foreign travel' worked against her claim; in several others the natural mother was preferred over a stepmother

– the income of a parent

– the employment of parent and its effect on the time that parent has to spend with the child and the environment the child will live in: for example, where the father was a taxi driver working at all hours, or where the mother was a traditional healer with patients coming in and out of the house

– violence evidenced by the parent: in one case the father had a history of hitting the mother.

There are several important points to note about the general law of custody. First, in general law, disputes over custody, and the application of the 'best interests' principle, only arise in the context of marriage and divorce. There is no issue of custody if there has been no marriage between the mother and father of a child. The father of an illegitimate child is treated as any other third party, and therefore is not eligible for custody unless there are special circumstances. Thus the law implicitly presumes that it is in the best interests of the child to remain in the custody of the mother when there is no marriage to the child's father, and this presumption can only be rebutted by evidence that taking custody away from the mother is necessary to protect the child from harm.[14]

Second, custody disputes within or after marriage assume there are two interested parties: the mother and the father. Others, including other family members such as grandparents, aunts, uncles, etc, are only considered if 'the parent or parents should be deprived of custody for any reason involving harm or danger to the child's welfare'.[15] Therefore the law implicitly presumes that it is in the best interests of a child to be in the custody of a natural parent. The norm upon which the law is based is that of the nuclear family, rather than that of the larger, extended family.

Third, the general law of custody focuses on the *welfare* of the child rather than the *rights* of the parents. That is, like in the Convention, the interests of the child are paramount over the rights of the parents (or other relatives). Therefore the law may make an award custody, for instance, based on the economic position of a parent to support the child because that is considered to be relevant to its best interests, but not based on the 'right' of a father to his own blood or as a 'reward' to a mother for the amount of caring for the child that she has done in the past.[16]

III.   *IDEAL* CUSTOMARY LAW OF CUSTODY

As mentioned above, the customary law of custody no longer applies in Zimbabwe. Rather, legislation requires that the best interests of the child must be the paramount consideration in all custody cases, regardless of the system of law (ie general law or customary law) which is applicable to the case. However, the principles of customary law still influence the thinking of people in Zimbabwe to a large extent, as well as the private, negotiated settlements regarding custody at the family level. Further, since issues of custody have always been, under customary law, almost exclusively decided by families rather than by public 'courts', private arrangements of custody are by far the most common way of dealing with custody in Zimbabwe today.[17]

(a) Within Marriage

As the Shona[18] are patrilineal and patrilocal, under *ideal* circumstances the mother and children live together in a family unit, in a hut close to the father, his other wives and their children, and his extended family. Custody is not an issue in such an ideal situation. However it is worth noting that the smallest family unit is that of the *woman and her children* rather than the European notion of a nuclear family composed of mother, *father* and children. This is because customary marriages are potentially polygamous, in which case each wife establishes her own household, and the husband visits each in turn.

Further, the legal concept of 'family' is much broader than that under general law as it is comprised of the extended family which at the very least includes the paternal brothers and the grandparents of a child, and may also extend to all descendants of a specified paternal ancestor and therefore include paternal cousins, aunts and uncles.[19] One indication of this is that there is no Shona word which differentiates the meaning of the English word 'brother' from that of the English word 'cousin'. Similarly, a child will refer to a number of different persons as his or her 'mother' (*amainini*, etc), including the sisters of his biological mother.

During an intact marriage, legal custody is with the paternal family. This custody is said to arise from the fact that the family (ie, the whole family, and not just the husband/father of the child) paid the bridewealth which resulted in the marriage which produced the child. The grandparents, uncles, etc are likely to talk about the child as 'our' child.

(b) Dissolution of Marriage

If the mother of a child leaves or is divorced[20] in such circumstances, when a legally valid marriage exists and brideprice has been paid, she has no legal right to take the children with her. However, if the children are young, she may do so, and they will be claimed later by the paternal family.

When a couple 'divorces', normally

it is taken for granted that all children remain under the control of their paternal family, unless they are very young, in which case the mother or maternal family may take care of them until they are big enough to return to the father. Since the latter arrangement, which is expected to last for a number of years, may give rise to a claim for maintenance (*marero*, *uredzwa*) against the paternal family, the parties may ask the court to make a ruling on this point. The court[21] may then lay down that the child or children concerned are to be returned to the custody of the father at a certain age with or without compensation of maintenance.[22]

An exception to this norm would arise in connection with the custom of return of brideprice upon divorce. When a marriage is dissolved, there are negotiations over the return of the brideprice that has been paid, according to the number of children who are left with the paternal family. A certain number of cattle are deducted from the returnable brideprice for each child. If, however, the agreed brideprice has not actually been paid by the paternal family, or if the amount is insufficient compensation for the children born of the marriage, the maternal family may keep the children. Then later, if the paternal family wants to claim the children, they must pay compensation for the brideprice the maternal family never received. It is regarded as improper to refuse to allow the paternal family to claim the children in this way.[23]

Unlike in general law, in customary law 'divorce' is not a public legal act requiring the intervention or acceptance of a public court. To 'divorce' is simply to leave the marriage, although formal negotiations may then take place between the families on the return of bridewealth, or the custody of children. Shona-speakers talk about '*kusiyana*', which may mean either 'separate' or 'divorce'.

Similarly, the concept of 'marriage' must be differentiated from the general law concept of marriage. In Shona custom there are a number of different stages and actions which are part of the marriage process, and may take place over a number of years, or even decades. This is in contrast to general law, under which the act of registration is the legal act which determines whether a marriage exists or not. In Shona, it is possible for a person, as in one of our interviews, to say he was 'just a little bit married' to a woman, meaning they were some of the way along the process of marriage. The first of the steps which lead towards marriage, rather than an extra-marital relationship, is usually introduction to the families, which may involve payment of a token or some money. After this, it may be said that the woman 'cooks for' the man. From this relationship, negotiations may begin over bridewealth which ultimately lead towards formal marriage ceremonies. At any step along the way, the couple may refer to themselves as 'married'.

(c) 'Illegitimate'[24] Children

Normally, the maternal family has rights to a child born out of wedlock, who lives with and is cared after by its mother and her relatives. However, the father of a child born out of wedlock may obtain rights to that child by paying 'compensation' to the mother's family, or *maputiro*.[25] The most direct result of establishing these rights is the consequent right to the *roora* (brideprice) for a girl, and the duty to pay *roora* for a boy. *Maputiro* is different from *muripo*, or seduction damages, which compensate the girl's family for loss of her virginity, but do not establish rights to the child. However, once the girl's family has accepted *muripo*, the paternity of the child has been established and the girl's family cannot refuse *maputiro* if offered and must then give up the child. Both fees were traditionally paid in the form of cattle.

(d) The spiritual and ritual dimension of custody/association with family

The Shona are organized into *cizwarwa* or family groups comprised of the first and second generation descendants of one man: his sons, daughters and son's children. It is the *cizwarwa* which is responsible for important rituals regarding all its members, calling upon the common *tateguru* (father's father) ancestral spirit to assist them. These rituals are particularly important in matters of health, marriage and death.

Holleman reports that:

To be effective, *all* the members of the family group should be present at a *bira* (ritual gathering). 'Even if there is trouble between the houses of one *cizwarwa*, all should be there. Our *tateguru* would be very angry if he saw that some of his children had been left out.[26]

It is important, then, for the father of a child, and for the whole paternal family, to establish its rights to the child in order to fulfil the ritual functions of the family. Therefore the desire to obtain custody of a child is related to the best interests of the paternal family as a whole.

However, the best interests of the paternal family are identical to the best interests of the child itself:

The father is the obvious medium between his family the ancestral spirits. The idea that a son would propitiate the family spirits on his own behalf while his father is alive is considered ridiculous, as it would be quite ineffective.[27]

The son must then turn to his father for matters requiring family ritual for himself and for his children. If paternal rights over the child have not been established, the child's health, the opportunity for marriage, the welfare of his marriage and his children, and, at death, his peaceful existence, are all threatened.

As for a daughter, she must also approach the father's family in ritual matters regarding herself and therefore it may be seen as also in her best interests to be associated with the father's family. But her children will belong to the transgenerational family of their father. We see then that the mother of a child also has an incentive to allow the child to be taken into the paternal family, in that it is in the best interests of the child's health and welfare to do so. Otherwise, the child would have no access to its ancestral spirits in times of need.

(e) Discussion

It is clear from the above that 'custody' under customary law varies in major respects from the 'custody' under European-based statutes. The right to custody of a child under customary law is linked to rights and duties regarding brideprice and therefore towards descendants of the child, and to ritual functions and the ancestors. Further, the right to custody of a child is linked to rights over its productive labour, as a child was a *resource* to the family in that he/she provided labour for the family home and farm. Even though the actual living arrangement of the child may be that it remains with its mother, the father has at all times a right to demand custody and to take that child into his family.

(i) Familial vs individual right to custody

Originally western-based law conceptualized custody in terms of an *individual's* right over his/her child. Customary law, on the other hand, conceptualizes custody in terms of familial and transgenerational rights. Today, however, general law custody rights are superseded by the welfare principle which requires custody determinations to be made in accordance with the best interests of the child. However, the residue of the *individual* right to custody can be found in the general law's emphasis on the mother and father as natural custodians, to the exclusion of other family members or *family* custody.

(ii) Linking of rights and obligations

Under customary law, the right to custody brings with it the obligation to support the child materially, and a person who does not have custody, or at least the *right* to claim custody at any time, would never be obliged to provide material support for the child. This linking of rights and obligations is based on the social pattern which was prevalent in the past: co-residential families in which all parties contributed economically, including the children, and needs which could be satisfied by the common production of the family unit. Today, the social pattern is different. Families are split geographically in the search for employment and 'divorce' or separation is more common. Sexual relations are often fluid, with men having children with a number of different women, and women having children by a number of different men. Men are obliged by the courts to pay maintenance for children, even when they have no right to custody of those children, signifying a rift between right and obligation which was unknown under customary law.

(iii) Custody assumes marriage as a norm

Under the *ideal* traditional situation, 'marriage' (defined to include the various stages in the process of marriage) in co-residential units was the norm. Anthropological literature discusses what happened when a couple was *married* (assuming cohabitation) and when they were *not married*, as if these were the only two possibilities. Apparently, in custom, there were few cases of a married couple living apart or of an unmarried couple living together. Therefore traditional norms did not exist to deal with this situation. However, clearly today there are many variations of relationships between men and women which were not contemplated by traditional norms. The most prevalent is that of married couples who do not live together. In 1982, 82 per cent of the people living in communal lands in Zimbabwe were women and children,[28] with the men away presumably working or looking for work. The traditional ideal situation where a family lives together with the father's extended family is no longer the norm.

IV. CUSTODY IN THE COMMUNITY (CUSTOMARY) COURTS

In the Community Courts, we studied 20 cases in a rural area and 20 in an urban area. In the urban area 11 (55 per cent) of the applicants were mothers, and 9 (45 per cent) were fathers. In the rural area 13 (65 per cent) were mothers, 6 were fathers (30 per cent) and one was a grandmother. Table 2 shows the outcomes. Already we see that the courts prefer mothers, particularly the rural court. We also see that women appear to be aware of this, and perhaps use this knowledge to

Table 2: Outcomes in Community Courts.

Who received Custody	Bikita (rural)	Harare (urban)
Mother	16 (80 per cent)	13 (65 per cent)
Father	2 (10 per cent)	6 (30 per cent)
Other	2 (10 per cent)[29]	1 (5 per cent)[30]

strategize to obtain custody, as is indicated by the fact that the majority of court cases are brought by women.

This is in direct contrast to the ideal customary law, under which a child belongs to his or her father's family. Further, under the ideal customary law, a woman should not be allowed to approach a court independently of her family, and without a male 'guardian' to speak on her behalf. The courts then provide a dual opportunity to women: to access rights independently of their family and to acquire rights over children that they did not have, in theory at least, under the ideal customary law.

The ideal customary law, represented today mostly by attitudes and values of the people, is then in direct conflict with the law as applied in the formal 'customary' Community Courts. While the formal legal system gives women rights they did not otherwise have, it also offends against the expectations of many men and women. This tension is evident in the arguments used at the Community Courts. Further investigation of the cases at the Community Courts identifies the following factors considered, either explicitly or implicitly, by either the litigants or the court, to be relevant to the best interests of the child:

(a) Factors framed in terms of child's interests

The most central issue discussed in most cases was who cares for the child and how well they do it.

With regard to this, the following arguments were made by litigants:

The child is being looked after by a domestic worker.

No one looks after children while their father is at work.

I have another wife to look after the children.

My mother can look after the children.

The father cannot wash the clothes and bodies of the children.

The father has no wife – if he had a wife it would be better.

The child has been staying with its paternal grandparents, so I would rather take the child.

I don't want my children to be taken care of by another wife (ie, my former husband's new wife).

The children are dirty and their school uniforms have no buttons.

Since the child is staying with their uncle, I would rather take it.

Their father prepares only one meal a day for the children.

No one looks after the children during the day.

They (the children) don't have school uniforms.

There is not enough food.

Closely connected to this was the issue of accommodation and location of accommodation:

I don't want my children to stay at a growth point (ie, village designated for development) (the implication is that the girls might prostitute themselves).

There the children have to get water from sand in the river. They drink the same water as animals (. . . and my job is providing clean water for villagers!).

the work the children have to do:

At their father's my children must wake up early in the morning and fetch firewood and water.

My eldest daughter is made to go to the grinding mill bearing heavy loads and to fetch water.

issues relevant to schooling:

The elder girl is not going to school.

I am nearer to a school than he is.

I want to assist the children with homework.

and the economic resources of the parties:

She (the mother) does not have a field to keep the children. (She lost hers when he chased her away accusing her of giving him of having *mvute* which causes pain to him and venereal disease).

– (Child speaking) I want to stay with father because mother will be unable to educate me as she is not working.

Several important observations can be made about these arguments.

(i) Nuclear family orientation

First, litigants argued that it is in the best interests of a child to be in the day-to-day physical custody of a natural parent rather than a third party, even if that third party was a relative such as a grandmother. The discussion below will show that this is in contrast to the way people make their informal custody arrangements, where it is often considered to be in the child's best interests to stay with relatives other than parents, and it is often said that it is *better* to stay with *ambuya* (grandmother) because grandmothers love their grandchildren so much. Therefore litigants appear to be using the argument strategically, as a way to convince the court to grant them custody. In the Bikita Community Court this argument was used in eleven out of twenty (55 per cent) of the cases and in the Harare Community Court in seven out of twenty (35 per cent). This strategy was almost always used by women (sixteen out of eighteen) rather than men.

In seventeen of these eighteen cases, the court then awarded custody to the natural parent (in the one exception, custody remained with the grandparents), often quoting the general law principle that a child should not stay with a third party unless there are special circumstances, eg neither parent can care adequately for the child. In one case where the father had taken the child after the couple divorced and then had left physical custody with his uncle, the court granted custody to the mother on the grounds that it is better for the child to be with a natural parent. In another case, in which the father left the children with his mother while he worked in Bulawayo, the court took custody away from him because 'the best interests of the children is parental care but he will not stay with them'. In another, the children were staying with the father's sister. The Court said: 'the aunt cannot be made responsible for the children whose parents are still alive'.

It appears, then, that women, who (as will be shown below) are disadvantaged in the making of informal custody arrangements, may be using the principle of the 'best interests of the child', defined by general law to prefer natural parents, as a tool to obtain custody of their children through courts.

(ii) Gendered parenting roles

Secondly, the litigants considered the 'marital status' of the parents, particularly the presence of step-parents, to be relevant to the best interests of the child. The discussion below will show that this is also a central issue in people's informal custody arrangements. In the words of one woman:

I want custody as there would be no-one to look after my children. He intends marrying another woman and I am convinced that the woman would not be able to look after my children. If I am awarded custody I will go and stay with my children at my parent's communal home in Mutare.

Men also share this suspicion of the step-mother with its implicit assumption that it is the woman who is actually caring for the child. As one interviewee told us: 'If a child is staying with a step-mother, you, the father, will not be able to know whether the child has eaten or not'.

It appears that women strategize in the courts, by using the assumption of gendered parenting roles to their advantage, and that the courts accept this assumption. This woman assumed that the new wife would be the one 'looking after' the children, rather than their father. In only one of the eight cases in which this argument was used, did the court grant custody to the man, and that was for other reasons.

Courts reinforced the assumption of gendered parenting roles by being particularly concerned to ask about who will care for the child if custody went to the father. The following excerpt illustrates this (the applicant is male):

Court: Who will care for the children?
Applicant: I will employ a maid.
Court: How big is the house you live in?
Applicant: My children stay in a 2 roomed house with 5 elders, my children, and the lodger's children.
Court: How will you look after the very young child?
Applicant: I have my sister as well as my brother's wives.

In this case, the court decided to give custody of the six-year-old to the father and custody of the eighteen-month-old to the mother. The six-year-old was given to the father because 'applicant alleges he is denied access and has to plead with his in-laws which is extremely unfair'. The court therefore seems satisfied that a maid can look after the six-year-old, but implicitly feels that a small child is better cared for by its mother.

It is interesting that in the cases covered both the presence and the absence of a step-mother were argued to be factors militating against the child's best interests. In seven cases the mother argued that the step-mother could not care as well for her children as she could, and in one case the mother argued that the father should not have custody because he had not remarried and therefore there was no-one to care for the child. The court also assumed that it was difficult for a step-parent to care for a child that was not his or her own. As one Presiding Officer said: 'the father's second wife may find it difficult to love these extra children because she has a big family.'

It appears, then, that in the issue of the step-mother two important values may give conflicting indications of the best interests of the child. On the one hand, it is thought that a child is best cared for by his or her own blood, and on the other that a child is best cared for by a woman. A father would not be expected to care for the child himself, but to find a woman to do so. Yet that woman should not be his wife, as she is not of the same blood as the child. The result is that many children are given to the paternal grandmother to avoid this conflict.

The assumption that it will be a woman who actually cares for the child's needs on a day-to-day basis, even if custody is given to the father, and that it is in the best interests of a child to be cared for by a woman, came up repeatedly throughout the study. Gendered norms regarding childrearing are pervasive. Men are considered not to have the basic skills necessary to care for a child, such as cooking, washing, and caring. This was echoed in our interviews by one man who said:

A child wants to eat good food, to wear good clothes, a good place to sleep. All these things are found in you women, you are the ones who can see that a child has eaten properly, or is sleeping properly. We fathers fail because we can't do this business by the fire (cooking) . . . I can not be seen washing a child's 'rag'.

And a woman who said:

Ah! Does the father understand the child? Does a father stay with a child? Does he know the needs of a child? The father can say to an ill child, 'Why do you sleep all over? Wake up you are so lazy' and yet the child will be sick. A mother is the one who is bound to notice any changes in a child, whether it is sick or is upset . . . With men, a child can die while the father is there, and he won't notice.

This put men at a disadvantage in the formal courts if they did not have females in their extended family to enlist to help care for their children, as blood relatives were always preferred to paid child-carers. When coupled with increasing individualization at a number of levels – people are today less likely to live with their extended family, the nature of ties between extended family members are changing, etc – men are losing the advantage they theoretically had under the *ideal* customary law.

(iii) Economic resources

Another problematic issue raised was that of the economic resources of the parties. At the level of formal law, maintenance law is intended to compensate the custodial parent for his/her expenses in caring for the child. The courts considered the income of both parties, but stated that this in itself was not decisive because of the possibility of a maintenance order. In one case the Presiding Officer stated that the mother's 'unemployment is not relevant because father will pay maintenance'. However, in practice maintenance laws are not efficiently enforced, and are inadequate except as they are applied to people in formal employment.[31] The result of this is that, although mothers may receive custody and a maintenance order, in practice it is unlikely that she will be able to enforce this order, leaving their children with inadequate resources for food, schooling, etc.

Maintenance is clearly an important issue in custody cases, as it was raised in seven (35 per cent) of the urban cases and nine (45 per cent) of the rural cases. In most of these the man appeared to be claiming custody as a way of avoiding paying maintenance. In one case, the record reads 'the (male) plaintiff was not assisting the mother to care for the needs of the children from the time they separated in February 1990 to November 1991. When his pay was garnisheed (under a maintenance order), he started complaining about the custody of the children and brought this case'. In other cases the fathers brought up the issue of maintenance themselves:

The money I am paying for maintenance is being banked by the mother and not being used on the child

I am not willing to pay maintenance while she (ex-wife) is at her parent's home.

This connection of maintenance and custody can be interpreted in more than one way. It could be argued that men do not want to support their children financially, and therefore protest against maintenance orders by attempting to take custody of their children (in which case day-to-day custody is often given to their mothers or other female relatives). It could also be argued that men, although willing to support their children, are unwilling to give up control of their money, particularly to their ex-wives and ex-girlfriends, and therefore they prefer to obtain custody and support their children in a way in which the spending is under their control.[32] It could also be argued that since the customary law *combines* rights and obligations, men perceive the general law, which obliges them to pay maintenance without giving them the corresponding rights over their children, to be unfair.[33] In any case, the result is that the reluctance of men to pay maintenance disadvantages women as custodial parents by leaving them with fewer resources to support a child in their custody. When coupled with the socio-economic reality that women have less access to economic resources than men, it influences the attitude, discussed below, that it is in the economic best interests of a child to remain with his/her father and his family.

(b) Factors not Framed in Terms of Interests of the Child

Several other issues were raised which, although not framed in terms of the best interests of the child, give some indication of what is implicitly considered to be the child's best interests both by litigants and by the court.

(i) Behaviour of the mother

The character of mother, as evidenced by her behaviour, is put into issue, particularly where a father of a child born outside of wedlock is applying for custody, or a child is young and therefore the father faces a presumption that custody should go to the mother. In the rural sample, the Presiding Officer several times quoted the case of *Jubb* v *Jubb*[34] which held that custody should generally go to the mother provided that her character is not such as to make this course prejudicial to the moral welfare of the child. An example of how this was applied follows.

The Case of the 'Prostitute'

(Father's statement)

I separated with my wife because she brought her new and second hand clothes from a place I do not know. When I asked her where she got them she said I accused her of being a prostitute and should pay her a *mombe* (cow). I gave her the *mombe*. We reconciled and later she refused to sleep with me. She said the children were not mine but other's. Later she denied that she ever said that. Pained with the word, I beat her and sent her away with the children. She pulled a stick and threatened to beat the children if they followed her . . . She came back 12 days later with the police for the children.

(cross-exam of mother by father)

F: Did I not marry you when you were prostituting?

M: I was prostituting.

F: Are you still a prostitute?

M: If we separate, I become one.

(examination of mother by court)

PO:[35] When are you going to commence prostituting?

M: I won't do.

PO: Will you marry?

M: No.

PO: So you won't sleep with a man anymore?

M: I do not know.

PO: Who were you prostituting with?

M: Nobody.

PO: Where do you get your mealie-meal?[36]

(no answer)

PO: Why do you not want to go back to your husband?

M: He should buy me a dress.

F: If she will come back I will buy.

M: I wear size 36.

F: I can get it on Friday. If she refuses to get back home she will pay back the dress or its value.

(court postponed)

(Note to file: Plaintiff left 2 piece dress and petticoat at a value of $69.35 in custody of clerk of court)

When the court resumed, the mother still refused to go back to the father because he assaulted her. The court ordered custody to the father on the grounds of the mother's behaviour, plus other considerations regarding the children's interests.

This case is interesting because of the light it sheds on what may happen in a custody case where the mother does not live up to traditional expectations. Generally, among the Shona, the word 'prostitute' may refer to any unmarried woman, or particularly a woman who drinks beer, lives in town, goes out with men, or generally lives a lifestyle which does not conform with traditional stereotypes. It is impossible to ascertain from the court record whether this mother was a professional prostitute or simply a non-conforming woman, but there are several indications that she may be the latter. First, her husband is willing to take her back, and he and the Presiding Officer blame her more for her refusal to return to her husband than for her prostituting. Second, there is no explicit suggestion that her 'prostituting' has a bad effect on her children. Third, she states that she automatically becomes a prostitute when separated from her husband.[37] However, it is also true that some women *are* forced to prostitute when they are left without resources for themselves and their children.

In addition to actually prostituting, the issue of the mother's having boyfriends was brought up in three of the rural cases and four of the urban cases. This was considered by the husband and the court to be against the children's best interests. On the other hand, a man was assumed to have girlfriends and/or wives and, as mentioned above, in one case was disfavoured because he did not have a woman to look after the children.

In one case, the mother was accused of having a *mudzimu* (spirit) which led her to try to poison her husband. Her attempt to poison him was evidenced by the fact that she took water from a tap to bring with her when she went to hospital. The case record goes on to explain that she did not get on with husband's parents. Although not explicit from the court record, the allegation of spiritual possession may be linked to the woman's relationship with her in-laws, as witchcraft is often used to control women who are not conforming to traditional expectations.

In these cases there is an implicit argument that a woman who behaves 'badly' in terms of traditional expectations cannot be a good mother to her children, and conversely that it is in the best interests of the child to be in the custody of a person who does conform to traditional expectations. In the case of women, the traditional expectations are that she must be married, submissive, follow her husband's orders and defer to his decisions, avoid independent action, be a hard worker, etc.

In contrast to this, another issue bearing on the behaviour of the mother which was brought up three times in the rural sample and twice in the urban sample was that of a mother originally leaving her children with the father when they 'divorced'. In one case where this was considered, the Presiding Officer said that this was 'not the action of a woman who had the best interests of her children at heart'. This is an interesting conclusion due to the fact that, under customary law, a woman was supposed to leave her children with the father when they divorced. Therefore, in this instance, the Community Court appears to be applying a 'western' rather than customary notion of the best interests of the child.

(ii) Paternal rights

Male litigants made, but the court did not accept, arguments based on the customary right of the paternal family to the child. Further, the issue of *roora* (bridewealth) was raised in ten (25 per cent) of the cases. Litigants used the issue of *roora* both to claim and to deny the paternal family custody, based on whether it was paid or not. The court treated *roora* as an issue relevant to the existence of a marriage, rather than directly relevant to rights over children. In one urban case, the Presiding Officer said: 'Where (bridewealth) is not paid, the child born from such a union is born illegitimate . . . the plaintiff (father) in this matter has no right to custody as the child is illegitimate'. This points again to conflicting concepts of the best interests of the child under the formal law, even that applied in so-called 'customary' Community Courts, and the expectations of people influenced by the ideal customary law. As mentioned above, the formal law implicitly assumes that it is in the best interests of an illegitimate child to be in the custody of its mother by refusing to consider the father except as any other third party. On the other hand, the ideal customary law not only regards the father of an illegitimate child as a party to a dispute over custody, but actually prefers his family if the requisite payments have been made. Fathers who go to the courts expecting that they will be considered as relevant to their illegitimate child's best interests go away disappointed.

Although we did not find litigants arguing on the basis of ancestral spirits in the formal customary courts, there were instances of such arguments 'between the lines.'. For instance, a witness in one trial, a paternal relative, said: 'If she wants the child she should take, but if the child goes sick she should do it alone'. This may be a reference to the need to enlist the help of the paternal ancestral spirits to cure sickness. Here again we see a conflict between the formal legal system and the expectations of the people. Whereas the most important argument, according to the litigant's world view, may be the spiritual well-being of the child and the child's physical well-being which is linked to his or her spiritual connections, this argument is not used in court and would not be accepted in a court. The court's world view is that of 'modern', westernized values in contrast to the world view of the majority of its users.

(iii) Right established by caring

One mother simply made the emotional argument: 'I miss my children', and another simply argued that she had been caring for the children all along and therefore the father had no right to take them. This is the closest any woman came to making an argument based on her own right to her children, rather than using a welfare argument that it is in the interests of the children to be with her. Contrast this with the men, who often argued on the basis of their paternal right to the child(ren). As we will see below, similar arguments are made within the family.

This may indicate differing world views of men and women in which men focus on their rights, and women are more concerned about relationships, as has been argued in the north.[38] However, the insistence by men on their 'paternal rights' may also, in the context of Zimbabwe, be interpreted as a focus on relationships, particularly relationships between blood relatives within the extended family. It is more likely that women do not argue in the language of rights because the ideal customary law does not give any custody rights to women. To the extent that the ideal customary law is framed in terms of *rights* at all, it is males who have these rights, but women manipulate, negotiate and argue on the basis of their own interests and that of the larger family group.[39]

V. INFORMAL CUSTODY ARRANGEMENTS AND THE 'BEST INTERESTS OF THE CHILD'

The interview sample was chosen using preferred sampling to select cases in which non-nuclear family custody arrangements were present, and to stratify for the following variables: urban low income, urban high income, rural, male and female. The interviews were semi-structured, and asked about present household composition, past household composition as an adult and as a child, present and past residence of all natural children of the interviewee, and the interviewee's view of the reason for these arrangements. Interviewees were also probed for their views on the interests of children in custody arrangements.

In each case, the interviewee was asked to give an opinion on why the child lived or was living where s/he was. The discussion is organized around the reasons given for the different custody arrangements found.

The actual custody arrangements are not analysed for this study, since it focuses on the *reasons* for the arrangements. Ninety-three custody arrangements, other than two parents staying with their natural children, were identified from the fifty-seven interviews. The one common denominator was that all children living in households who were not paid workers were relatives of the adult(s) in the household. Other than children living with both natural parents, by far the most frequent custody arrangement was where a grandchild was living with its grandparents, either paternal or maternal. Although this most often happened when the parents of the child were 'divorced' or the child was born outside wedlock, it also sometimes happened when the parents were still 'married'.

Next came children living with other relatives: uncles, aunts, grown up sisters, brothers, etc. These children were as likely to be the children of intact marriages as from broken homes, and the reasons given for the custody arrangement often had nothing to do with the marriage but related to very practical considerations (see below).

Next in frequency was the child of separated or divorced parents, living with one or the other parent. We accepted the interviewee's own assessment that the couple was 'married' and made no attempt to distinguish between 'separated' and 'divorced' parents, or to determine the formal legality of the marriage.

Finally, came children born 'outside wedlock' (as classified by the interviewee) living with one parent or the other, either the mother or the father.

The interviews indicated that the most striking characteristic of *physical* custody in Zimbabwe today is *fluctuation*. Many, if not most children, stay with a number of different relatives for periods of their lives. This pattern, although more widespread among low-income groups who often transfer custody as a way of sharing economic resources among family members, is not restricted to the economically needy. Well-off Shona families also transfer temporary *physical* custody of their children within the extended family. Children are moved from relative to relative, usually to seize economic advantages.[40] This is in contrast to western ideas about the best interests of a child, which are based on preference for stability of parenting, and would regard the shifting custody of Shona children and the high incidence of children living apart from their mothers to reflect maternal deprivation. Shona families today appear to regard multiple mothers and fathers as desirable for their children, and by their actions contradict the western principle that a child needs one mother figure.[41] However, it has been impossible to determine definitely from this study whether this represents a shifting pattern due to economic necessity, or reflects the 'tradition' that a child belongs to a larger extended family.

(a) The Concept of 'Custody'

In choosing the sample, 'nuclear family arrangement' was defined to include all arrangements where the interviewee classified the child and both parents to be 'staying together'. However, when the data were analysed it became evident that in many families in which the father is said to be staying with the children he is actually working elsewhere and visits his wife and children in the rural areas only at month end. The same applies to 'non-nuclear family arrangements' in which a male was often described as 'staying with' a child, when he actually spent most of his time at work in another area. This is a result of the dominant social and economic pattern found in Zimbabwe, in which many males (and increasing numbers of females) migrate to the towns, farms and mines for work, but consider their 'home' to be their rural home where their family lives.

This ambiguity presents the first conceptual problem of this study of 'custody', in that the concept of custody is influenced by the concept of 'home'. A child may be said to be 'staying with' a man even when there is little day-to-day contact, if the child is staying at the man's 'home' and is supported by him.

Interestingly, this applied almost exclusively to *men* working away from home. A woman who was working away from home was seldom said to be 'staying with' a child. This indicates a profound difference in the concept of custody by a *man* and custody by a *woman*: custody by a woman implies day-to-day contact, while custody by a man does not. This gendered notion of custody will be also be evident in other aspects of the discussion below.

(b) Marriage, Divorce and Custody

Normally, in western legal systems, the issue of custody arises when the two natural parents of a child divorce. In Zimbabwe, the concept of 'marriage' is problematic, as is the concept of 'divorce'. The formal law recognizes that two persons are married when they register their marriage. In the practices of the people, however, registration of a marriage is irrelevant, and parties may consider themselves married upon the completion of any of several actions: when they live together, when they are introduced to each other's parents, when they have a child, when bridewealth is agreed, etc. The fluidity of this concept can be illustrated by an excerpt from one of the court records studied, which recorded that 'the two were married in periods between 26/2/86 and 25/2/90'. Further, whether a couple is 'married' is not always even agreed by the parties. For instance, in one case, the woman refers to the father of her children as her 'former husband' while the man refers to the mother of his children as his 'former girlfriend'. This makes it difficult to apply a law which determines the interests of the child on the basis of whether his/her parents were married.

Similarly, the concept of divorce under the formal law requires a court order while the concept of divorce in the practices of the people is more fluid, seemingly requiring only an understanding that the couple is 'divorcing'. Physical separation is not a test for divorce, as many couples separate for long periods of their lives for practical and economic reasons. Few people approach the courts for divorce, and in any event the courts only entertain divorces from registered marriages. Again, it becomes difficult to apply a law which initiates litigation over custody when the couple 'separates' or 'divorces'.

Our interviews indicated that when natural parents do divorce or separate without the assistance of a court, in practice the child goes with one or the other *family*, rather than going to one or the other parent, as is contemplated by the general law. Within this family, it is usually not the actual parent who takes physical custody of the child. This is said to be because the parent 'remarried' or might 'remarry':

(My paternal) grandmother looked after me because my mother left and my father had another wife.

The major reason given is that step-parents find it difficult to care for a child which is not 'of their blood.' Although it was universally acknowledged that some people are able to be fair and caring step-parents, it was also assumed that most people are not. In practice, most of the new spouses of the parents discussed by the interviewees *had* refused to care for any children of former liaisons, or had treated the children badly:

The child of my husband's sister (grandchild in Shona) was only one year when the mother got married and the man said he did not want the mother together with the child.

My mother was separated from my father and the new woman was not treating me properly. So I went to my uncle.

A child or children from a former liaison may also affect a woman's chances of being married, because the prospective husband or his family do not want to take on the responsibility of her children:

My daughter was 'given' the child by someone from Jinya. These people (her new boyfriend's family) said they did not want someone who had children (*mvana*: ie, her daughter already had two children from another man).

Although no-one would doubt that it is often difficult for a step-parent to form a strong emotional bond with a step-child, the reasons for refusing to care for step-children appear to be as much financial as emotional. The new spouses did not want to financially support or to care for a child which would bring them no benefit in the end:

What is likely to cause problems is when the child has grown up and the man (mother's husband, step-father) will later say 'I want money because I looked after your child'. He will want to be paid saying: 'I was giving my *sadza* to the child.'

Another woman cannot look after a child which is not hers. They think they will get nothing in the end.

Many men, in particular, are unwilling to do this, explicitly because of the financial burdens of caring for a child coupled with the knowledge that the child, when it grows up, will not remain a part of his family but will return to its natural father's family. This seems to happen in practice:

I looked after two children of my former wife because 'if you pull a branch you pull it together with its leaves'. Later those from their home came and took them.

Financial concerns are mixed with concerns for the child's welfare:

I look after my daughter's child. Her father died and her mother got married to another man. She came to me in Form 2 (+ 13 years). Because she is big it is not good for her to stay with the man (ie, the new husband). If she goes and stays with this other man, maybe she will do bad things. Also the parents (of the husband) will refuse.

Financial concerns about custody are probably a new development. Previously, children were a *resource* to their family in the immediate sense as they worked on the family farm. Therefore even though the child must be fed and clothed, the economic cost of these necessities was probably outweighed by the immediate benefit of the child's labour. Today, although a child, particularly in the rural areas, may still be a resource, most of the time that it would have been labouring is now spent in school. Further, nowadays school[42] is expensive, as are food, clothes etc. Therefore the emphasis is on the child as a future resource, in which its schooling is an investment, rather than the child as a present resource, making the step-parent (particularly the step-father) unwilling to contribute to its needs because he is unlikely to get any of this future benefit. Similarly, since the step-mother is the one responsible for the day-to-day feeding and care of the children, it is thought that she will naturally prefer her own children to her step-children, and give them the best food, etc.

It is said that according to 'old custom' a man was supposed to accept his wife along with any children she brought into the marriage. The ability to persuade a man to follow this custom may rest in part on the power and personality of the mother of the child:

I look after my daughter's child. The father died and my daughter married again and the husband did not want the child. If she (daughter) was somebody else, she would have said, *wakwena sazu, unokweva remarara aro* ('if you pull a branch you pull it together with its leaves/rubbish', ie, the child comes with the mother) but she did not say that.

Therefore the best interests of the child are seen to lie in living with another relative when his/her parents separate because each parent is expected to remarry. However, these 'best interests' are linked to the economic burden of raising the child, the custom that the child must ultimately return to its father's family, and to the power of a woman effectively to persuade her new husband to take on her child; power which is probably also linked to her strength of personality, economic independence and need for marriage economically. This last point indicates that increasing the social and economic power of women will increase their negotiating power within the family over the custody of their children.

(c) Paternal Rights

Our interviews, as well as the arguments presented by litigants at the Community Courts, indicated that it is a general belief that children belong to the man's family. Many interviewees simply echoed the principle that a child 'belongs' to its paternal family, and that children are automatically given to the paternal family when the family asks for them:

The children of my daughters are with their fathers because the 'parents' (children's grandparents) said they wanted their children.

The fathers insisted that the children be left at their home saying, 'I have divorced you, go your own way, and leave their children here'.

The father just said, 'I want you to leave my child'.

(Father) I am the one who said, 'I don't want my blood to go'.

(Father) I have a son from a woman I did not marry. I will take him when he gets big (he is now 3 years).

I would love to be with my child but the father's parents won't allow it

(I said to my wife, when she left) why then when you leave me do you want to take my child which is part of my clan?

It is not only the paternal family which believes in its right to the children, but the mother and the maternal family as well. Therefore it appears that in most cases there is no 'dispute', it is simply assumed that the children of divorced parents will go with the father's family:

At first she (the mother) went with her and then she later wrote a letter to say 'Come and take your child': that is how the child came here.

(Father) I kept the children because when we separated my wife said 'here are your children'.

(Father) My wife first took the children but the grandparents sent them back saying, 'Here is your family'.

Even when the mother is going to have custody of the child for a while, it is assumed that the child will go back to its father's family eventually. So that, even if the best interests of a child in the short term are to be with its mother, in the long term it needs to make the connection with its father's family.

Although most interviewees did not explicitly link the issue of the paternal family's rights to *midzimu*, or ancestral spirits, in a few instances the *midzimu* were said to have influenced the parent's view of the child's best interests. For instance, in one case a child (one year old) refused food when he was taken by the mother after his parents separated. It was said that he was 'demanding to be taken back to the father's' so they took him back. The family believes it was *midzimu* (ancestral spirits) making him refuse food.

A greater influence, at least as explicitly acknowledged, was rights arising from the payment of bridewealth:

My father said, 'give him back his children, because he has paid *roora* (bridewealth)'.

When we separated, the in-laws insisted on having the child because they paid *roora* (bridewealth).

How could I give him the children if my parent had not 'eaten' anything (ie, received bridewealth)?

(Father, separated from wife). The only thing I don't want is that my children should go where 'the cattle went' (ie with ex-wife, whose family received the bridewealth cattle). No! And I do not want them to go for maintenance.

Today, however, the 'custom' is linked to economic concerns. Since women have less access to economic resources than men, and find it difficult to enforce their right to child support from the fathers of their children, they often perceive it to be in the best interests of the child to go with its father:

It is better for the children to stay with their father, because I am not working. The father has a house and I am lodging. I would not manage to send the children to school. I do not have a mother I could send the children to.

(Do your children stay with their father because of 'custom'?) These days there is no *chivanhu* (custom) . . . it's simply because you are unable to look after the children. Look, I can get to a stage where I have absolutely no money. I can go and eat at a friend's house. But since I have three children, can I take them to my friend's to eat too? I can't! So this has nothing to do with *chivanhu*. It's just poverty which makes you say, since the father is working and he has a house, then let him look after his own children. That's all.

(Father) The mother could not compete (for custody), she had no money. She wanted to go and look for a job. So how was she going to look after the children?

This supports the argument, made above on the basis of court records, that since women have less access to economic resources there is a tendency to view the best interests of the child as lying with the father. This applies whether the couple has divorced or have never 'married'. If the child's material needs are seen as paramount, its best interests are perceived to lie with the parent who can better provide for the child materially.

Again, this situation is affected by the non-enforceability of maintenance laws. Taking custody of the child has, for many, become a substitute for maintenance for the child:[43]

When we were divorced I first took the children, then brought them back to their father. He said he could no longer give me money, so I should give him the children.

My son had been ordered to pay maintenance. But even though he was paying, this child was staying with its mother's *ambuya* (grandmother), and later with her uncle's wife. My son went to visit the child and said he wanted to take his child. So he was asked to pay the remaining $100 (in damages) and he paid and took the child. His wife said, 'I cannot look after somebody else's child, so take him to your mother.' So that's how the child came here.

(Father) So how can I after I gave money to her parents (bridewealth), pay money to the same people (maintenance), for their child to eat?

We see, then, that the father's right to custody of his child, as practised today, is justified by a combination of customary principles and economic realities. While the traditional concept of rights established by bridewealth and of spiritual allegiance to the father's family is still voiced in custody matters, the need for financial support for the child is increasingly the overriding factor. The first interest of the child is to have its physical needs met, and to have school fees paid. It is perceived to be in the child's interest to be in the custody of whoever can ensure that these needs will be met.

(d) Reasons Unrelated to Separation/Divorce

Although not covered by the formal law of Zimbabwe, most of the custody decisions taken by families in our sample were unrelated to separation or divorce of the parents. Custody of a child may be transferred to another relative, other than its mother or father, for a variety of reasons, some of which are articulated to be in the child's interests and others are justified by the needs of others in the child's extended family but are clearly not thought to be *against* the child's interests. This indicates that the interests of the child are generally seen to correspond with the interests of the clan as a whole. The reasons given for transfer of custody to relatives other than the mother and/or father are discussed below.

(i) Death of the parents

In Zimbabwe, there are few social services available to care for a child whose parents die. The few orphanages are overcrowded and underfinanced. For most orphans, the extended family feels committed to caring for 'their' child, and the thought of sending a relative to an orphanage is almost unheard of. It is clearly seen as a *duty* and a *right* to look after one's dead relative's child, as well as in the best interests of the child concerned:

We took the children of my father's brother because he had died.

I was looked after at my sister's when all my parents died (*all* my parents probably means including my mother's sisters and my father's brothers)

My husband's late brother's child stays with us. My husband said 'I have a big job. My brother died and left children. So these children cannot fail to go to school.'

My father's brother died and he inherited the wife and three children.

(ii) To meet the economic needs of the child

It is not only orphans who sometimes have no one who is looking after their needs, and so other relatives step in. This may also happen if the parents or a parent is alive but fails to care for the child:

My father died and my mother was a drunkard, so I stayed with my 'older brother' (my uncle's son).

Similarly, where the parents or parent is seen by the relatives to have too great a burden to bear, or simply to need help, a relative may offer to take custody of a child or children to assist:

One of my children is staying with my wife's father. He went when my wife had twins and her father saw that she couldn't stay with twins and a toddler. (the wife's father also works, and has no children at home any more).

When my father was ill I stayed for a time with a grown-up nephew.

We took my husband's young sister because my husband's parents were no longer able to send her to school.

My husband's brother's children came because uncle (*babamukuru*) had a lot of children and he was not working.

We took my husband's younger sister because my husband's parents were no longer able to send her to school.

When I was given these children of my young brother, our nephew, the one who officiated at the traditional ceremony (*kurova guva*) said he thought the teacher is the one who is able to look after the children. That is why I was given the children. And they wrote to me informing me that a decision had been reached, that I look after the children. I agreed because I realized that there was no one else to look after these children.

The mother had been made pregnant and had no one to look after her.

I took my 'grandchild' (child of my sister's first born) because the father had no money to support and left the children with my sister. She asked me to take one.

We took my two sisters. My husband was the one who was working and the one who had a house. If their parents had money and housing they would have looked after the children themselves.

When you see a child being looked after by anybody else, it is all because of poverty/need. It is all for that child's benefit.

Related to this, another reason often given for transfer of custody to a non-parent was to allow the parent to be employed. Zimbabwe is characterized by migration (particularly male) to the urban areas, commercial farms and mines for employment with family members (wives, children, parents) left in the rural areas engaged in subsistence farming. It is difficult to search for employment with a child in tow, difficult to find accommodation large enough for children, schools and necessities for children are more expensive in urban areas, and many people feel that the towns are a bad influence on children. For these reasons, a child may be left with a relative while its custodial parent(s) search for or are engaged in employment in town:

I looked after my brother's child so he could work in town. She was at an age where she could not sleep in the same room with her mother and father (and in town, there was only one room to sleep in).

If we are at home (*kumusha* ie, in the rural areas, at the traditional home) the mother is the one who should stay with the children . . . but when we are here in town, if we say the mother looks after them (when parents are separated), how will she do that if she is not given food (by the 'husband')?

Three of my four children live with my mother in the rural areas. My wife works so we thought rather than pay a domestic to look after the children, we should send them to *ambuya* and send her money.

I also have a child who stays with my mother. He stays there because my house here in town is too small.

If this is done, there may be a *quid pro quo* in terms of economic benefit:

When I divorced from my wife in 1968, I was given the children by the court. At first, when they were still young, I left them at *tete*'s (my sister's). I paid school fees for *tete*'s children.

In all these cases we see the centrality of economic considerations to custody decisions. In the socio-economic circumstances of Zimbabwe, the best interests of the child are first and foremost to have its physical needs met, and then to go to school, both of which in today's world require access to financial resources.

(iii) Schooling

Several children in the sample were sent to relatives to be near a school. Either there were no schools near enough to walk to, so the child had to stay with a relative nearby to the school, or it was not possible to get a place in a nearby school so the child was sent to a relative near to a school which did have a place, or, in the case of urban dwellers, the urban schools were too expensive so the child stayed with relatives in the rural areas attending a less expensive school. Even among our urban, high-income sample, several parents sent their children to relatives because of schooling. In the same sample, many more children were sent to the urban, high-income relatives as a way of obtaining schooling. Second only to the child's physical needs for food, clothing, etc, school is the wish of every parent for his or her child. Custody arrangements are often made on the basis of the effect on the child's schooling.

(iv) Work

One reason given for custody arrangements that is not articulated to be in the interests of the child but in the interests of other relatives, is for the child to perform chores for the relative:

Joyce is staying with grandmother so that she can fetch water for her.

We gave our son to *ambuya* so that he herds goats for his grandmother.

Sekuru (uncle) had only one son who was already grown up and had his own home, so he just wanted a *muzukkuru* to herd his cattle.

(My son, staying at his paternal grandparents) has to wash his own clothes and clean the house because they do not have a worker.

My mother looks after my sister's child's child. He is the one who looks after our cattle and other animals. This girl (his mother) was made pregnant by someone.

In Shona culture, children are expected to do chores. Therefore, in a sense, the child sent to a relative to work is doing no more than it would be expected to do in its parent's home. This parallels the discussion above that children are considered a *resource* to the family with which they stay.

Although at first glance this would appear to be a decision made without considering the child's interests, when probed further it is clear that the child's interests may play a role. Often, sending a child to a relative to perform chores is a way to redistribute the income of the extended family. The parent(s) who does not have the economic resources to support a child may send it to a relative who has a steady income, and in return the child does chores in the home:

I stayed with *sekuru* (mother's brother) because he wanted someone to cook for him and I didn't have anyone to send me to school.

When you take over responsibility for a child from within the family, it is expected that you take over everything more or less. The parents don't expect to be sending you any money or whatever. They send you the occasional parcel of food from the rural area.

However, some people think that this is changing:

Things are different now – you can't just give a child to someone to look after. You must give them soap or food.

Even when the transfer of physical custody is not a way of obtaining financial resources for the child, but simply a way of ensuring that the adult relative has help, the child is seen as contributing to the family in a way which may increase his rights in the future. In this way, then, it is considered in the child's best interest to contribute to the needs of the extended family, which will pay him or her back someday.

(v) Health

Very young children whose mothers become pregnant while they are still breastfeeding are said to suffer if they remain in their mother's home. For this reason, they are often given to other relatives:

I lived with my sister's daughter because she was ill. They brought her here '*kumsengudza*' (to remove her from the place she fell ill). I think it happened because they weaned her too quickly (ie the mother was pregnant with another child). If you do this the child cannot stay near the mother because she may be 'burnt' by the mother's pregnancy.

My oldest child was looked after by my mother. She was weaned too quickly so we gave her to ambuya to look after.

As in the general law, it is considered to be in the very young child's best interests to stay with the mother:

When we separated the child went with my wife because it was still breastfeeding.

The one that stayed with me (the mother) was only one month old.

(vi) Asking for or being given a child

It is said to be Shona custom that a newly-married woman should receive from the family a child to care for before she has one of her own, and that a childless woman should be given a child:

I stayed with *amainini* (mother's younger sister) because she had no child.

I took her when she was still very young and I was married but didn't have a child.

Tete (paternal aunt) asked us saying: 'Give me your child. I want to look after her'. *Tete* had no children, that is why she came asked for Joyce to stay with her . . . she just wanted a child to stay with her.

As you know when someone gets married she is given a child to stay with and look after.

Again, this can be seen as a method of distributing resources within the family – both economic and caring. Sometimes, but by no means always, the child is from an economically needy family.

Similarly, a child is sometimes given to a mother who already has a small child, as someone for the child to 'play' with:

I looked after my *muramu*'s child (my wife's young sister) when we just got married. She came to play with her sister's (my wife's) young baby.

One of my children stays with her uncle because *amainini* (sister-in-law) has a small child who needed someone to play with' (*Writer's note*: her uncle works and she does not, so this may be a way of redistributing income).

My four year old sister came to stay with us to play with my first born.

This is seen to be in the interests of both children, who each get the company of another child. It also further reinforces the ties of the extended family.

It is also said to be Shona custom that a couple's first born child should stay, for a while, with its mother's family, again as a way of reinforcing family connections.

Sometimes a relative simply 'asks for' the child because she likes the child, or wants to help out the mother. This arrangement occurred not only in our low-income sample, for economic reasons, but also in our high-income sample. The following is the case of a woman lawyer, married to a lecturer, who sent their daughter to a relative for a time:

My father-in-law's youngest brother is very close in age to my husband and his wife is very close in age to me, so we had, right from the beginning, a certain rapport. We were friends more than – in our culture – mother-in-law and daughter-in-law, regardless of the fact that she is married to my father-in-law's youngest brother. Because of this friendship and because my children came on very close, the second one soon after the first one, when I had my second one she thought she could help out by taking one. So we sort of agreed that she would take my daughter, because by then she did not have any young children, well, not very young. So she took my daughter who was about 2 years old and stayed with her for about a year. It wasn't because I couldn't manage financially but it was just because she was my friend and she thought she could help out because of the friendship.

Finally, sometimes a relative will simply ask for a child, sometimes because she is lonely or just likes children:

I asked for a grandchild to stay with and each of my daughters gave me one.

Although in these cases the reason for the custody may not be framed in terms of the child's interests, when asked, most people think that children enjoy staying with their grandmothers in particular, and that grandmothers like staying with children. As one man expressed it: 'At *ambuya's* (grandmother's), that's where peanut butter is found'. One reason given by some interviewees for preferring children to be in the custody of their parents is that 'grandmothers spoil their grandchildren.'

In all these cases, the transfer of custody will almost certainly be temporary, and serves the larger interests of the extended family. Based on a world view which defines the family as going beyond the nuclear family to encompass the extended family, it is also in the best interests of the child to be fully integrated into this extended family. Further, custody fluctuates, sometimes fairly often, with children spending a few years with one relative and then moving to another or back to their parents.

(e) Moral Entitlement Established by Caring

Although we found that paternal rights were emphasized in custody arrangements, the interviews also evidenced another kind of 'right' to the custody of children, based on the caring that a relative has done for the child in the past. For instance, in one case the maternal grandmother looked after the child from a very young age. Although the interviewee seemed to assume that the father's family had a 'right' to the child, the grandmother also had a right based on this caring:

When she was grown up (ie 8 or 9 and able to do chores around the house) the father said 'we won't take this child because . . . you suffered with her. So she will stay with you, ambuya, washing your dishes for you, going to the well and fetching firewood'.

This again shows that children are considered a resource in that they perform chores around the house. When a relative has *given* in terms of caring for the child before it is able to contribute to the household, then that relative has a moral entitlement to benefit from the child when it is old enough to give in return.

This may also apply in the case of a mother who gives her child up to be cared for by another when the child is very young:

My mother brought my nine-year old daughter up from the age of three weeks. When I later wanted to take her my mother's relatives said, no, she should live with *ambuya* because she brought her up. Since my mother had had a hard time with her when she was a baby, she should have advantage of her as a grown-up child. (taking the child when she was 'grown' and could do chores was taking advantage).

This concept of a *right* established by caring is interesting because it is in contrast to the law of rights generally imposed by the general law. Such an argument is likely to be used almost exclusively by women, giving them a strategic tool of negotiation within the family, which usually favours male rights. It indicates that women strategize to get custody, not just in court, as discussed above, but also at the level of the family. It also brings up again the notion of children as a *resource*, in this case allowing women to retain that resource based on their own contribution to the child.

VI.   BEST INTERESTS OF THE CHILD IN THE ABSTRACT

In our interviews, we began by asking about who lived with the respondent at various times of his/her life and why. After the interviewee told
his/her story, the last question we asked was an abstract one, 'what
would you say is the best thing for a child?' As indicated in the title to
this paper, the answers we got can be summarized as 'school and sadza.'
Almost every interviewee mentioned school in the literal sense. To give
some examples:

What I would like to teach my children is for them to have good manners and
to know that education is good. This is the most important reason why children
must be educated, so that life is easier for them and the future is brighter.

I would say the best thing for a child is to go to school.

I must plan how a child is going to be educated, as (long as I am alive).

Although school itself was important, it was also perceived as a
symbol of the future best interests of the child in the sense that school
would somehow ensure that the child would have a rosy future. As one
man told us:

For the child to have a good life, it will be because of me, the father. If I send
her[44] to school, things will go well for her . . . I was brilliant myself. I skipped
Standard 2 because I was so clever. I did Standard 1 and then went up to 3.
I was so clever. So if I had found somebody to just push me forward? Ah, I
would not be cleaning the toilets like I do now!

And one woman:

What is good for a child is to educate her, if you have educated her, the child
will enjoy life.

And another:

And also another important thing is to send the child to school. This is what
will make a child happy. So that when she completes school she will look for
work and work for herself.

In addition to the future interests of the child, basic, immediate needs
were also perceived as paramount:

The child wants enough good food, enough clothing, getting all the good things
in life. That is what is best for a child.

You must also see that a child has something to wear, and blankets, and food.
That is what is important to give to a child.

Although this is no surprise, the fact that the need for basics (*sadza*)
was so often articulated suggests a different working definition of the
best interests of the child than in social situations where food, shelter
and clothing are plentiful. The people we spoke to were not always able

to provide the basics, and therefore basic needs were at the centre of
the custody decisions they made.

Another important dimension to the concept of the best interests of
the child which arose from the answers to this question was that most
interviewees, especially when probed, stated that it is in the best interests of a child to live with his or her parents:

I think the best thing is for her to live with her parents, while they see how
she is growing up, everything she eats, where she sleeps, supporting her, everything that she needs in life, her whole life. She should live with her parents.

This is interesting because it differs so markedly from what happens
in practice. Unlike in developed countries where the major cause for
separating a child from a natural parent is divorce or separation, in
Zimbabwe children are separated from one or both parents for economic, social, spiritual and cultural reasons. However, the answers to
the abstract question about the child's best interests indicates that these
decisions are often compromises, in a less than perfect world where one
cannot always find housing, where families cannot always live together,
where there is inadequate access to schooling, etc. Choices about the
best interests of the child are made in the context of what is possible in
that child's environment, and might be made differently if the environment were changed.

Thus, in the abstract, the child's best interests are perceived in terms
of both the short term and the long term, and may be different than
best interests in the context of the real possibilities available to the child.

VII.   CONCLUSIONS

This study has identified several important aspects to the concept of the
'best interests of the child' as perceived by Shona people and as practised
in Shona custom, both in the past and today.

First and foremost, the best interests of the child are perceived to be
'school and *sadza*': *sadza* in the sense of the physical needs of the child
to be fed, to have clean water to drink and with which to bath, to have
medical care, etc, and 'school' because it is thought to be in the best
interests of every child to get an education which (it is hoped) will
enable him or her ultimately to find waged employment.

In a society where 'school and *sadza*' are not automatically available
to every child, where starvation is a real possibility and many children
cannot afford school, the concept of the 'best interests' of the child is
inevitably linked to economic interests. Although many people stated
that, in the abstract, it is in the interests of a child to be in the custody
of his/her mother and father, in practice, even in families where the
mother and father remain married to each other, alternative custody
arrangements are made for the sake of 'school and *sadza*'. A child from

a family which cannot afford school fees may be sent to stay with a relative who is working, as a way of obtaining schooling. Similarly, a child who does not live near a school, or cannot find a place in a nearby school, may be sent to a relative near a school. The same kind of arrangements may be made when parents cannot afford to feed their children, and therefore send a child to a relative to 'fetch water' or 'herd goats', with the understanding that the relative will feed and care for the child. In each case it is in the interests of the child to be in the custody of a relative rather than the natural parents because that is the way the child can obtain 'school and *sadza*'.

The child's interests can therefore only be understood in relation to the broader socio-economic circumstances of his/her family. Today, 'school and *sadza*' require money. Schooling is expensive, and is becoming more so. The rural farming sector in Zimbabwe is no longer a 'subsistence' economy. Few farmers grow all the food they eat, and even when they do, they are dependent on monetary inputs for fertilizers, tractor hire, etc. Families no longer make or collect all they need to subsist, such as soap, clothes, utensils, fuel, etc. Medical treatment costs money, whether at clinics or at traditional healers. Therefore, even '*sadza*' requires cash. The need for money to support children, coupled with an economy in which most people have little independent access to money, means that the best interests of the child will be to go where the money is.

When a custody choice is between the mother and the father, at the level of practice or the 'living law', consideration of the economic interests of the child usually favours the father. Men have greater access to wage employment, which is the primary and most reliable source of economic resources. Although the formal law requires men to maintain their children, even when those children are in the custody of another, most men object to this, the law is difficult to enforce, and enforcement of the right to maintenance may incur the wrath of the extended family which a woman needs as her own safety-net for times of need.[45] Therefore, in practice, it is usually perceived to be in the best interests of the child of parents who are separating for custody to go to the father and his family. Even when a man does not request custody, a woman may give the child to him or his family as a way of ensuring that he supports his child economically.

The legal significance of the centrality of 'school and *sadza*', or economic considerations, is that the formal law of custody, and the 'best interests' principle it applies, is at variance from the best interests as perceived and practised by the people. The formal law, as applied by the courts, prefers the natural parents to other relatives, yet when economic considerations are paramount it may be in the child's best interests to live with a relative who has more economic resources. The formal law, as applied by the courts, favours the mother above the father when the

parents separate, particularly when the child is young, and assumes
that maintenance laws provide adequately for the child's support where
there is an economic imbalance between the parents. People's practice,
or the 'living law', usually considers it to be in the best interests of the
child of separating parents for custody to be with the father's family, in
large part because the father usually has more economic resources and
because this is often the only way of ensuring that the father and his
family support the child financially. Finally, the law only addresses the
issue of custody in the context of the breakdown of marriage, while in
the 'living law' custody decisions are made in many other contexts, and
the principle of the best interests of the child is relevant in all of these
contexts.

In practice, custody may be used as a way of redistributing economic
resources within extended families and thereby enabling children to
have their needs met. The study also identified an ambiguity about the
concept of children themselves as a *resource*. On the one hand, children
are desired particularly for their contribution to the family both in the
short term by doing chores and as a long-term investment. Relatives
seem to want to care for them (sometimes as a way of accessing financial
resources from the child's parents). On the other hand, children are
also perceived to be an immediate economic burden in that financial
resources are necessary to pay for food, clothing and schooling.

Further, the study found that the child's interests usually are perceived to coincide with the interests of the extended family. A child who
is sent to a relative to perform chores for him or her is serving the
interests of the greater family unit. Similarly, the child who is given to
a relative because she is childless, or needs someone for her baby to
'play with', or is 'lonely', is meeting the needs of the larger family which
may someday be called upon for help in times of need.

Custody does not necessarily determine who actually does the day-to-
day caring for the child. This is also linked to the need for economic
resources. When the father has custody, it is almost always a female
relative of the father who cares for the child, often with the father only
visiting periodically from his workplace in town. Even when the court
grants custody to the mother, she often leaves the child with her mother
or other female relative so that she can work or seek work in the urban
centres. In the vernacular, a person may say that s/he 'stays with' a
child, even though s/he is working in town away from the child except
for a monthly visit. The same happens in intact families, with many
characterized by a pattern in which the father stays at his place of work
while the mother takes care of the children in the rural areas, visited
monthly by the father. In other families, the mother and father may
both be working in the urban areas (and may or may not be able to
live together) and leave their children with relatives in the rural areas.
This may be because there is no accommodation for the children in the

urban areas where accommodation is scarce, it may be because it is too expensive to keep the children in the urban areas where all food must be bought rather than grown and school fees are higher, there may be no one to look after the children while the parents go to work, or the parents may simply fear urban influences. The picture, then, is one of the breakdown of the nuclear family, coupled with reliance on the larger, extended family. The need to acquire the money required in today's world to support children appears be the major factor which results in separation of those children from their natural parents. This is done in the interests of the children involved, considering the socio-economic context.

Related to this is the concept of paternal rights. Most men and women appear to consider it to be in the best interests of a child to be associated with his or her paternal family. Even where the mother or maternal family wants to care for the child when it is a child, it is assumed that the child will go to the father when it is grown. This is linked to the belief that the ancestral spirits influence the well-being of a child, particularly its recovery when sick.

Unlike the concept of 'father's rights', which is emerging in the industrialized north, the concept of paternal rights emphasizes familial rather than individual rights. The paternal family refers to the child as 'our child' and treats it as such by caring for it. The needs of other members of the extended family, such as grandparents, uncles, aunts, etc, are as important as the needs of the child, but are not seen as conflicting with the interests of the child because his interest coincides with the interests of the family as a whole. Therefore, it is less accurate to speak of custody going to the father, than of custody going to the paternal family. The day-to-day caring for the child is almost always done by a woman in the paternal family, rather than by the father himself.

In this context, the importance of the connection by blood has another important influence. People almost universally consider it difficult to care for a child which is not 'of your blood'. Therefore, when natural parents separate, the child(ren) are taken by family members, who are related by blood, rather than allowing the child to be cared for by a step-parent not of his/her blood. This is usually a paternal relative if the parents have been married, if the appropriate customary payments have been made, or if the mother perceives this as the only way she can get the father's family to contribute to the child's financial needs. On the other hand, a maternal relative may take custody if the natural mother has 'been made pregnant' by a man they 'do not know', or if customary payments have not been made. In either case, when natural parents separate, it is often thought to be in the child's best interests to be cared for by people of his/her blood rather than by a 'step-parent'.[46]

However, although many people believe strongly in paternal rights, there are those that do not. A woman who wishes to keep custody of her child finds an ally in the court system, for the formal law favours the natural mother of a child in almost all circumstances. She is entitled to approach the court and request custody, without the assistance of her family. Women appear to use the court system strategically, and to formulate their arguments according to the general law to establish entitlement to their children which might not have otherwise been possible. They emphasize the formal law's preference for natural parents and assumptions about gendered parenting roles. Fathers, particularly of illegitimate children, may have their expectations dashed. On the other hand, when a family makes a custody decision, it does so through a process of discussion and negotiation in which women are inherently at a disadvantage because they are not expected to make decisions and must, traditionally, be represented by their male relatives rather than play a direct role in discussions. This produces a conflict between the formal law, in which women are favoured as custodians of children, and the beliefs and expectations of the people, based on customary law, in which the paternal family is favoured as the custodian of children. Nevertheless women may also strategize within the traditional family structures. However, a woman with the desire, resources and knowledge to pursue custody through the courts will probably be successful, and one who relies on family to acquire custody will probably not be successful, because of the differing conceptions of the best interests of the child.

In conclusion, this study indicates the importance of interpreting custody in terms of *world view* and in terms of *possibility*.

'World view' must be considered in that custody decisions can only be understood in terms of the world view(s) of the person(s) making decisions. If your world view centres on the family and maintenance of social relations, the best interests of the child may coincide with that of the family unit as a whole because his or her interests depend on the survival of that unit. If your world view includes spiritual connections which influence your health, luck and afterlife, the best interests of the child include strengthening his or her spiritual connections. In a plural society such as Zimbabwe, where people's world views are changing due to rapid economic, social and cultural change, diverse world views may also come into conflict, even within the life of and the choices made for one child.

'Possibility' must be considered, in that custody decisions are made in the real world, taking into account the existing possibilities for the child. Thus, although it may be in a child's best interests in the *abstract* to stay with his or her parents, if the parents do not live near a school, or do not have the economic resources needed to raise the child, or live in a town where they think the child will be subject to bad influences, these factors will be considered and the child may be sent to live with a relative. 'Possibility' includes the consideration of both immediate and future interests of the child. When considering the future interests of a child, particularly in countries like Zimbabwe where the economy is fragile, unemployment is massive, drought is endemic and national and international economic policies such as structural adjustment require 'belt-tightening' before improvement can be accomplished, the safety net of the extended family must be strengthened. The best interests of the child might be different in a perfect world than they are in a world of limited possibilities.

NOTES

[1] Customary Law and Primary Courts Act (No 6 of 1981) sec 3(4) which is soon to be replaced by the Customary Law and Local Courts Bill 1989 sec 5, governing the customary law and *W.* v. *W.* 1981 Zimbabwe Law Reports 243 (AD) governing common law.

[2] T. Stang Dahl, *Women's Law: An Introduction to Feminist Jurisprudence*, Oslo, Norwegian University Press, 1987.

[3] J. Griffiths, 'What is legal pluralism?' *Journal of Legal Pluralism and Unofficial Law* XXIV, 1–55, 1986; S. F. Moore, 'Law and Social Change: The Semi-Autonomous Field as an appropriate field of study' *Law and Society Review* VII, 719–46, 1978.

[4] The sample is restricted to Mashonaland, and therefore applies only to the Shona people and not to the other ethnic groups found in Zimbabwe. The Shona comprise approximately two-thirds of the people of Zimbabwe.

[5] Holleman, *Shona Customary Law* (London, Oxford University Press, 1952).

[6] Ncube, Welshman, *Family Law in Zimbabwe* (Legal Resources Foundation, Harare), 106.

[7] Ibid, 111

[8] *W* v *W* 1981 Zimbabwe Law Reports 243, 247 (AD).

[9] Guardianship of Minors Act Chapter 34, sec 4(1).

[10] Matrimonial Causes Act 33 of 1985, sec 3(4).

[11] Customary Law and Primary Courts Act (above) sec 3(4).

[12] For a full discussion of the law, see Ncube (above).

[13] Matrimonial Causes Act (above).

[14] *W* v *W* (above), 247.

[15] Ibid.

[16] See Smart, Carol, 'The Legal and Moral Ordering of Child Custody' *Journal of Law and Society*, 18, 4, Winter 1991, 485–500.

[17] See C. R. Cutshall, *Justice for the People: Community Courts and Legal Transformation in Zimbabwe* (University of Zimbabwe Publications, Harare, 1991), 93ff.

[18] Information about Shona customary law is derived from Holleman op cit, who is an anthropologist who recorded Shona custom. This information is limited, particularly by two factors: for many issues he attempted to fit Shona customs into the form of western legal concepts and his informants were largely male and royalty who may have given information that suited their interests (see Armstrong et al, 1992). This information is also supplemented by information from interviews.

[19] Holleman, op cit, A. Armstrong, et al 'Uncovering Reality: Excavating Women's Rights in Customary Law' (1993) 7 *International Journal of Law and the Family*

[20] In the vernacular, women usually 'leave' their husbands while men 'divorce' their wives.

[21] Here Holleman is referring to colonial 'native' courts rather than chief's courts.

[22] Holleman, op cit, 296.

[23] Holleman, op cit, 306–7.

[24] The term 'illegitimate' derives from general law, and may be inappropriate when referring to the status of a child born out of wedlock in customary law. Some people argue that no child is illegitimate, as every child belongs to a family – either the father's family if the proper payments have been made or the mother's family if they have not.

[25] Holleman, op cit, 244.

[26] Holleman, op cit, 25.

[27] Holleman, op cit, 61.

[28] Demographic and Health Survey 1982.

[29] In one case custody of two children went to the father and one to the mother, and in the other case custody went to the paternal grandparents.

[30] Custody of one child to each parent.

[31] A. Armstrong, *Struggling over Scarce Resources: Women and Maintenance Law in Southern Africa* (University of Zimbabwe Publications, Harare, 1992).

[32] WLSA Zimbabwe, *Who pays the Price? Maintenance in Zimbabwe* (Harare: WLSA, 1992).

[33] Armstrong, 1992, op cit.

[34] 1909 *TS* 1033.

[35] Presiding Officer.

[36] Corn meal used for making *sadza*.

[37] In another case in the rural court, the mother states: 'My husband used to chase me away and as I was unemployed I was forced to prostitute.'

[38] Carol Gilligan, *In a Different Voice* (Cambridge, Harvard University Press, 1982).

[39] For more discussion, particularly of the transformation of customary law and how this influenced the position of women, see Armstrong et al, 1993, op cit.

[40] See also Russell, Margo, 'Kinship, Homestead and the Custody of Swazi Children' (Mbabane, Report to UNICEF (unpublished) 1989), 87.

[41] Ibid.

[42] School is not free in Zimbabwe, but parents must pay school fees. In the rural areas, children often must go to boarding school, which is more expensive. In addition to school fees, parents must also buy school uniforms.

[43] See A. Armstrong, 'Different Women, Different Laws: A Study of Women and Maintenance in Southern Africa' PhD thesis University of Copenhagen, 1993.

[44] In the language of the Shona there is no differentiation between 'him' and 'her' or 'he' and 'she'. Speakers are therefore using a gender-neutral word, which I have translated 'her'.

[45] See Armstrong 1992, op cit.

[46] Whether married to the natural parent or not.

CUSTODY AND THE BEST INTERESTS OF THE CHILD: ANOTHER VIEW FROM ZIMBABWE

FAREDA BANDA*

ABSTRACT

This paper draws on research in Zimbabwe into the experiences of two groups of divorced and divorcing women, those from customary marriages and those from civil marriages. The data shows that the women's perception of their children's bests interests were related to their own social and economic strength. One important factor was the role of *lobolo* (bridewealth). In general, the customary law group had little control over what happened to their children, whereas the civil law group saw their children's interests best served by keeping them and they largely did so. The paper then considers the cultural perspectives which colour the perception of the best interests of children in the Community Courts and concludes by remarking on the rarity of the children themselves being consulted.

Although criticized for its vagueness and for not providing guidelines which courts can use in interpreting what is meant by 'the best interests of the children',[1] the principle has, by virtue of its non-specificity, the open-ended nature which is needed when applied in different cultural contexts. Indeed, the papers in this volume reflect the different ways in which societies interpret the welfare principle. Eekelaar, in an earlier work, gives primacy to the emotional relationships of the child noting,

For myself, I would argue that unless there were very good reasons to do otherwise, a child's interests are presumptively best met by retaining its present most significant *emotional* (author's emphasis) relationship (and if the child is old enough, following its wishes.)[2]

However, the contributions by Armstrong and Rwezaura in this collection suggest that within the African context, practical considerations of food, housing and schooling are considered to be of prime importance. The child appears not to have independent rights, nor does she appear to have much input into the decisions which are taken on her behalf. Nevertheless, it will be shown, using data collected in Zimbabwe in 1990 and 1991, that the lines between emotional needs and practical

* Formerly Centre for Socio-Legal Studies, Wolfson College, Oxford, UK.

considerations are not always clearly drawn. If anything, the data suggests that it is the socio-economic position of the adults which determines what they consider to be the primary consideration (emotional needs v 'school and *sadza*') when deciding what is in the best interests of their children. A brief summary of the methods used in collecting the data on which this analysis is based follows.

I. METHODOLOGY

Like Armstrong's study, the survey was conducted in the Mashonaland Central and East areas of Zimbabwe in 1990 and 1991. However, only women were interviewed.[3] This is because the main focus of the study was to examine women's experiences of law at divorce. Another distinguishing factor between this group and that interviewed by Armstrong was that all the women in the group had had contact with the courts.

In 1990 the writer interviewed seventy-six women in customary law marriages, both registered and unregistered. Twenty-one women with civil marriages were interviewed in 1991. Both rural and urban women were interviewed, the breakdown being as shown in Table 1.

Table 1: Breakdown of the Samples by Area Lived.

Area	Customary	%	Civil	%
Urban	48	63.16	19	90.48
Rural	26	34.21	–	–
Peri-Urban	2	2.63	2	9.52
TOTALS	76	100	21	100

The reason for the imbalance in the urban/rural mix can be explained by the fact that most of the customary marriage interviews and all of the civil marriage interviews were conducted in Harare. It also reflects the fact that there were not as many rural women visiting the local Community Court. A possible reason for this is that often disputes are settled within the confines of the communities concerned.

In the survey, there was a link between educational achievement and type of marriage so that it was observed that the civil group with monogamous marriages had higher educational attainments than those in the customary group (see Table 2). The educational imbalance was reflected in the employment figures of the two groups, with just 10 per cent of women in the customary group being in formal employment as against 70 per cent for the civil marriage group.

On average, the women in both samples had three children each. Children were the *raison d'etre* of the marriage and a lack of them was the reason for the men seeking divorce in two out of the three childless marriages in the customary sample. Many women said that they had

Table 2: Educational Background of the Samples.

Level	Customary	%	Civil	%
Primary	36	47.36	4	19.04
Secondary	35	46.05	12	57.14
Tertiary	–	–	4	19.04
Other	–	–	1	4.76
No schooling	4	5.26	–	–
Unknown	1	1.13	–	–
TOTALS	76	99.98	21	99.98

stayed in difficult marriages for their children's sake. Indeed, it is only when the husband's neglect of family duties began to have an adverse effect on the children's schooling or well-being that most of the women took action and sued their husbands for maintenance or custody. In this regard it is significant that the largest number of actions brought by the women were for maintenance.

The children, many of whom were of pre-school age, were the victims of the breakdown of their parents' union. They were sometimes separated from both parents and siblings. This was usually the case where the woman had children from another union. In only two of the eleven cases where the woman had children by another man were the children staying with them. In three instances the father had custody. However, in the majority of cases the children lived with their maternal grandparents.

Thirty-one couples had children outside the immediate union. Twenty-six of the men in this number had 'outside' children, as compared with eleven of the women. On average, the women had two 'outside' children each, whilst the men had three. In the study, disputes over custody and access to the children accounted for 19.73 per cent (fifteen out of seventy-six) of the actions in the customary group and for 80.95 per cent in the civil group. The large discrepancy between the two is because civil marriage divorces have to come to court and the court has to satisfy itself that adequate provision has been made for the children before it can consent to the divorce. Custody in customary cases only becomes an issue if informal agreements cannot be reached.

Armstrong's article shows clearly the impact of economic factors in making decisions about what is in the best interests of the children. This article continues along a similar vein, comparing the differences in attitude towards custody between those with economic resources of their own (the women in the civil group) and those without (the women in the customary group). It also surveys the attitude of Presiding Officers in the Community Courts, as it is they who are charged with applying the welfare principle.[4] Finally the article looks very briefly at the invisibility of children in the decision making process which so radically affects their lives.

II.   WOMEN, ECONOMICS AND 'DOING RIGHT' BY ONE'S
CHILDREN

Once the data had been analysed, differences in attitude between the
two groups manifested themselves very clearly. This analysis confines
itself to looking at those differences as they relate to the woman's attitude in custody disputes. The socio-economic and cultural factors influencing those attitudes will also be considered. From the data it emerged
that there were two factors which determined whether women were able
to participate in the debate about what was in the best interests of the
children or whether their own powerlessness (cultural or economic)
meant that decisions were in the hands of others – usually members of
their family. An important cultural factor is that of *lobolo* (bridewealth).

Although women are central to the *lobolo* contract, their role in the
negotiation of bridewealth negotiations is minimal. The contract is concluded by men and is largely for their benefit. In return for giving cash
and cattle to the family of the woman, the future husband and his family
acquire both uxorial and genetrical rights.[5] The acquisition of genetrical
rights means that any children born of the union 'belong' to the family
of the husband. The payment of *lobolo* is said to be to ensure the good
behaviour of the spouses in the marriage. This is because, should the
marriage collapse, penalties are imposed on the family of the spouse
judged to be the cause of the marital breakdown. For the woman this
means her family could be penalized by being made to return some or
all of the bridewealth received, whilst for the man it could result in
the family of the woman demanding an immediate payment of any
outstanding bridewealth or forfeiting the children until such time as the
debt is settled.

Linked to this culturally induced powerlessness is the economic
inferiority of many women. The combination of the two factors
(particularly for women in the customary group) led to the exclusion of
women from the decision-making process about both their own lives
and those of their children. This is well illustrated by the fact that when
the women were experiencing difficulties in their marriages they went
to their families for assistance.[6] In 90 per cent of cases the families told
them that there was little that they (the families) could do and told the
women to go back to their husbands. From the statements of the women
it became clear that the wish of the families to safeguard their position
in the *lobolo* contract was the reason for this advice.

The decision to return to the husband or to disregard the advice of
the family was dependent largely on the economic position of the
woman. Those women who were in employment or self supporting were
less likely to stay in unsatisfactory marriages than those without independent means. Women without means depended on their families not
only for moral support but for economic support as well. In the survey

fifty-four (71 per cent) of women in the customary group reported having returned to live with their families on the break-up of their marriages. Of these, thirty-five (46 per cent) said that it was to their families that they looked for maintenance and upkeep. The return to the family of origin often brought with it a complete loss of autonomy and became, in a sense, a return to a second childhood. The following case clearly illustrates this point (names are fictitious).

Mrs. Chipangura, aged forty-nine, with a customary law union, had been routed by her husband with whom she had nine children aged between twenty-six and nine years. Eight of the children were still in school. She takes up the story:

He made me leave the children . . . Eventually the children all ran away and came to me. (She had returned to her father's village). Even the little ones came. They said that there was no one to look after them. The houses had become dilapidated. They were hungry. I kept the children. 1985, 1986, 1987 all went and I didn't say anything. I did not hear from him and he did not provide any maintenance, or support of any kind. As I did not have any money the children did not go to school.

In 1988 I went to the Rusape Magistrates Court to ask for maintenance. He didn't come. A garnishee order for $50 was made against him, but I did not receive any money. I sued again. In January 1989 he came with his lawyer who suggested that the maintenance be increased from $50 to $80 for the children and myself. The $80 was for seven children. It did not cover the two who were already over 18. The $80 was only for school fees. It was not supposed to cover any other costs. The older children went back to their father's village. He refused to give them any money or to buy provisions for them saying that they should get the money from me. I started sending them money. I would deduct some from the $80 for school fees and send it to them.

Eventually my father said that he could no longer look after the younger children who were staying with me. He asked what would happen if they were to die. He told me to return them to their father. In June 1990 I gave him the three youngest children. I took them to Harare where he was staying. In July 1990 he sent them back to his village. Again the children (the three youngest ones) ran away and came to me protesting that there was no one looking after them. Even the five year old walked 15 kilometres through the bush to come to me.

. . . I am now staying with all of the children in his village. The older children came to see my father and explained their plight. They asked for his permission to allow me to go and live with them. My father took pity and told me that I could go back. I went back to his village with my children. (She was at court because the husband was suing for divorce and custody of four children). He hasn't been home in four years . . . As for giving him the children. He doesn't want them. He won't even look after them. I am the one who has been looking after them all these years.

By contrast, Mrs. Thebe, a university graduate who had been given custody of the three children of the marriage on divorce, had this to say;

I *allow* (my emphasis) him to visit the kids but he does that rarely.

However, even if the women did not have cultural constraints, it is unlikely that more women would have asked for custody of their children because of their inability to support them. A comprehensive project done by the Women and Law in Southern Africa project on maintenance found that, by and large, maintenance orders were ignored, so that women cannot rely on receiving child support from the fathers of their children to mitigate their inferior economic position.[7] The realization that they could not provide adequately for their children led to the women 'agreeing' to let the children go to the husband or his family in the hope that the child would be better provided for there.

Lawyers sometimes prioritized the economic advantages which a child could receive from one parent over emotional considerations. Thus one woman reported:

The lawyer told me that the children were settled in school. He said that with the housing situation as it was, I might have a hard time finding another house. He told me to let my husband keep the children and maintain me.

This 'trading off' of assets and liabilities was common to both groups so that women in each reported having 'agreed' not to claim maintenance for themselves in return for the custody of the children. A woman in the civil marriage group said:

At first he didn't say anything about the children. He only started saying that he wanted the oldest child when we started fighting over the house.

It is unclear whether, if at all, the best interests of the children were discussed.

The economic independence of women in the civil marriage group is reflected by the fact that all but three of them had custody of their children. One had agreed to let her husband keep the children because she felt sorry for him whilst the other two had children with the woman's family and in one case the man's family respectively. This is in direct contrast to custody arrangements for the customary group which were rendered complex by the fact that the children lived with their parents in the extended families of both lineages. As Armstrong shows, it is the person best able to provide for the child who is given it to look after.

While economic preoccupations crippled women in the customary group, *all* the women were united by common concern for the emotional welfare of their children. As the task of deciding what is in the best interests of the children is left to the judicial officer's discretion, it is interesting to see what use was made of that discretion. The next section

considers the attitude of Presiding Officers when making decisions about
the best interests of the child.

III.   JUDICIAL DEFINITIONS OF THE WELFARE PRINCIPLE

Eekelaar has argued that the vagueness of the welfare principle 'leaves
the judges cruelly exposed'.[8] He contends that:

The concept of 'welfare of the child' conceals very difficult value judgements,
both about our ideas about individual happiness, fulfilment and moral character and about the organisation of our society. It is therefore totally inadequate
to pass this judgement on to the judges without further spelling out how the
concept is to be understood.[9]

Within the Zimbabwean context it would seem that courts were alive
to the conflicts between cultural expectations and legal requirements
and tried to be fair and objective in making custody awards.[10] However,
a strong traditional bias in favour of the customary position of awarding
custody to men who had paid *lobolo* can still be found to operate even
though it has been overridden by statute.

The question of whether or not *lobolo* has been paid still seems to
influence the Community Courts' decisions. Under customary law, a
man cannot ask for his children unless and until he has paid *lobolo*.[11] In
making decisions about custody it seemed that the court sometimes took
this factor into account, so that in Ms Mteta's case, *lobolo* had been
asked for but the husband had not yet paid any. He tried to obtain
custody of the child.

The court said that it was giving me the child because he had not paid *lobolo*
for me and because he had rejected me. They said that if he paid *lobolo* for me
then he would be entitled to ask for and receive his child. After that he came
to speak to my brothers about paying *lobolo*.

In awarding custody to the mother, there was in this case a punitive
element in the court's decision. The issue of giving custody to the father
went beyond the fact that he had paid *lobolo* for the mother. Other
considerations included the fact that the children should not be removed
from the protection of the ancestral spirits by growing up under a different totem from their father's, for they would learn strange ways.[12] The
women themselves believed in the power of supernatural forces. Ms
Zowa was reluctant to claim custody of the children because:

I don't know what herbs he has used on the children but whenever I try to
take them back they cry at night and I have to take them back.

Moreover, if the mother re-married or saw other men then the children
would grow up in a 'foreign' house. To many men this was the 'night-
mare' scenario. Their fears were shared by Presiding Officers who saw

it as not being in the best interests of the child to grow up in another man's house. What is interesting and what emerged from the data was the differential treatment of men and women's morality. Whilst men's custody claims were not prejudiced by having children in other relationships, those of women were. No case more clearly illustrates this than that of Ms Gomo.

Separated in 1981, the husband had remarried in 1983. He had three children with his new wife. She met a new man with whom she had a child in 1988. Her husband brought an action for the custody of the four children.

He asked for custody on two grounds. One, he said that he was already keeping the children and secondly he said that I was living with someone else and he could see no reason why he should continue to pay me maintenance or why his children should stay with another man.

I explained to the court that I had only given him the children for the school holidays not knowing that he would ask for the maintenance to be cancelled. I told the court that the children were now staying with me. The court said that since he wanted his children, I should give them to him. They said that I had another husband so the children should go back to their father. I could not expect another man to look after the children since the father was willing to have them. I agreed and released the children to him. I asked the court what would happen if the children were made to suffer at their father's. They told me I could come back to tell them.

The case is revealing on many levels. The most striking of course is the court's agreement with the husband's rationale that the mother of the children cannot keep them because of her relationship with another man. In bringing this action for custody, the husband was not saying that his ex-wife was a bad mother. She had, after all, satisfactorily looked after the children for the last seven years. He was saying that in having the relationship with this man, she had become a bad wife and this made her unfit to look after the children. The court was not able to distinguish between a 'bad' wife and a 'bad' mother. However, even this labelling of her as 'bad' is questionable, for what she did was no worse than what her husband did, yet he was not labelled as being a bad husband or father. Maboreke has noted this contradiction:

A mother who leads an immoral life may be deprived of custody of her minor children, but the question of morality is rarely ever raised with relation to the father.[13]

In this case nothing was said about the fact that the father had been living with a woman with whom he had three children for five of the seven years that the two had been separated. During this time his first wife had looked after the children satisfactorily. It was only when she had a child with another man that her fitness as a parent was questioned.

While it was not good for the children to live with a man who was not their father, it was perfectly acceptable for them to live with a woman who was not their mother. The court did not see any contradiction in that. In fact it made sense to remove them from their mother because she had another child (just one, who was an infant) and move them to live with their father who had three toddlers living with him and his new wife, who doubtless had her hands full trying to look after her own children. The ages of the children of the first marriage was probably a factor taken into consideration by the court, for they were all of school age, the youngest being seven.

Paradoxically, it is worth noting that the courts appeared to favour mothers in awarding custody where the children were very young.

In court he said that he wanted his children but the court said that they were too young. (Two children aged four and twenty-one months). Moreover he did not have anyone to look after them.[14] He does not show any interest in the children. (Ms Chigudu)

The court asked how old the children had been when he had taken them. He said six, four and one. The court said that they were too young. They should be with their mother. (Ms Makanza)

The bias towards awarding custody of young children to their mothers appears to be universal.[15] A senior divorce lawyer interviewed spoke in favour of giving custody of young children to mothers, arguing:

Men don't make particularly caring parents especially if the children are very young. Men are not prepared to change nappies and powder bottoms.

Of this trend Christine Delphy has noted that, given the economic and social disadvantages associated with looking after young children, it is not surprising that custody is given to the mothers.[16]

It is significant that a social welfare officer's report was only asked for in *one* case out of a total ninety-seven cases.[17] Although it is not clear why courts do not ask for more outside input (welfare reports or psychological evaluations), one can speculate that ignorance of the availability of these options as well as a desire to deal quickly with the matter are factors which play a part.

The last section looks briefly at the consultation of children when decisions are being made about their future.

IV. 'AND HOW DO YOU FEEL ABOUT ALL THIS?'
CONSULTING THE CHILDREN

Eekelaar has come out as a strong advocate for the rights of children, arguing that children should, as far as is practicable, be consulted about matters which concern them.[18] However, in Zimbabwe, the data suggests that children's rights are subsumed within parental rights and obligations. In the data, the child's feelings were directly averred to four times (three in the civil marriage group and once in the customary group). Perhaps this reflects the cultural assumption/norm that children should be seen but not heard. It may also be, as Armstrong points out, that since children are part of a communal group, it is assumed that their interests are best served by decisions which are made for the common good. May has noted that:

The great value placed on the sanctity of family relationships and the physical presence of the extended family added to the security of the child's position in the family.[19]

Although there is provision for older children to be consulted before decisions are made about which parent is to have custody, this rarely, if ever, happens. Of the ninety-seven women interviewed, only one reported that the Presiding Officer had asked to see the children, aged fifteen, twelve and nine.

I was told to bring the children with me so that the court could interview them to find out what they wanted. The court said that they were old enough to speak for themselves. (Ms Hwacha)

Perhaps logistic and economic considerations played a part in the decision of the court not to call the children for interview. Bringing them to the court, especially in the rural areas, would involve long bus journeys and disruption to the children's schooling. Economic considerations no doubt weighed heavily on the minds of judicial officers.

V.   CONCLUSION

This analysis has considered briefly the ongoing debate in the international community about the universality of human rights. Examining the specific issue of custody, we have seen how socio-economic and cultural considerations impact upon the determination of what is in the best interests of the child. It has been shown that there is a prioritization of needs so that in situations of economic difficulty the child's physical and educational needs are given primacy. Conversely, in situations where money is less of an issue, the emotional wellbeing of the child is given greater weight. Armstrong's findings provide overwhelming evidence that, within the Zimbabwean context, it is practical considerations of 'school and *sadza*' which are paramount in determining what is in the best interests of the child.

Given the multiplicity of ways in which the welfare principle can be interpreted, how are organizations whose concern is for the well-being of all the children of the world (like UNICEF) to formulate and implement policies? Should cultural relativism always be allowed to hold sway? It is submitted that, despite the need for sensitivity and awareness of cultural differences, all of us, and organizations like UNICEF in particular, have a duty, as the guardians of future generations, to insist on a 'baseline' standard of human rights to ensure that our children are protected and are able to attain their full potential.

NOTES

[1] J. Eekelaar, '"Trust the Judges": How Far Should Family Law Go?' *MLR* 593–7 (1984); S. Cretney, *Principles of Family Law* (4th ed) (London, Sweet and Maxwell, 1984) 326

[2] Eekelaar, n 1 above, 597.

[3] Male lawyers and those charged with the administration of the law were also interviewed.

[4] Cf Eekelaar, n 1 above, 596.

[5] Although women do get token payments, most of bridewealth payments are received by the male relatives of the family of the woman.

[6] Significantly, problems about money were those most frequently cited, so that 83 per cent of women with customary marriages and 76 per cent of women with civil marriages complained of lack of financial support.

[7] Women and Law in Southern Africa, *Maintenance in Zimbabwe* (Harare, 1992).

[8] Eekelaar, n 1 above, 596.

[9] Id.

[10] Cf J. May, *Changing People Changing Laws* (Gweru, Mambo Press, 1987) 77.

[11] M. Maboreke, 'The Love of a Mother: Problems of Custody in Zimbabwe' in A. Armstrong and W. Ncube (eds), *Women and Law in Southern Africa* (Harare, Zimbabwe Publishing House, 1987) 144–5. However if the two were never married then it is still possible, under customary law, for a man to claim his child by agreeing to pay the woman's family some money.

[12] May, n 10 above, 16.

[13] Maboreke, n 11 above, 157.

[14] In giving fathers custody it is assumed that they have somebody, usually a woman, to whom they can pass on the burden of day-to-day care of the children. They are not themselves expected to look after the children.

[15] Cf S. Burman and R. Fuchs, 'When Families Split: Custody on Divorce in South Africa' in S. Burman and P. Reynolds (eds) *Growing up in a Divided Society: the Contexts of Childhood in South Africa* (Johannesburg, Ravan Press, 1986) 126–7; C. Smart, *The Ties That Bind: Law, Marriage and the Reproduction of Patriarchal Relations* (London, Routledge and Kegan Paul, 1984) 122 and 178.

[16] C. Delphy, *Close to Home: A Materialist Analysis of Women's Oppression* (London, Hutchinson, 1984) 100.

[17] It was in the customary group in a case where the husband brought an action claiming custody of the child who was living with the woman's parents. He alleged that the child was not being properly looked after and was suffering because her family did not have anything to give it.

[18] J. Eekelaar, 'The Importance of Thinking That Children Have Rights' 6 *International Journal of Law and the Family* 221–35 (1992).

[19] May, n 10 above 76.

THE BEST INTERESTS OF THE CHILD – THE CASE OF BURKINA FASO

AKILA BELEMBAOGO*

ABSTRACT

This paper examines the response of the legislature in Burkina Faso to the problem of promoting the concept of the best interests of the child in a society where traditional law and practices are strongly observed by many members of the community. It points out how the best interests of children are perceived within traditional communities and explains how the legislature has chosen to confront those traditional ideas which are seen to be inimical to modern, international notions of children's interests. How successful the legislature will be depends on the effectiveness of administrative actions and, crucially, the attitude adopted by the judiciary.

I. INTRODUCTION

(a) The Importance of New Thinking

In common with most African countries, the majority of the population of Burkina Faso is young.[1] The issue of the rights of the child is therefore particularly important. What does the future hold for the young people of Burkina Faso? What rights can the younger generation expect from the present society?

The question of the rights of the child is one of the most important challenges in the contemporary world at the edge of the third millennium. Surely the child is considered to be the future, and consequently, 'the only way available to man to shape this future from which he will be excluded'.[2] In the same manner, some have asserted that 'in the States where democracy reigns, it is to the study of the great challenges of our time that people engaged in the defence of the rights of man must dedicate themselves'.[3] It appears as if humanity is rediscovering the fundamental demands of its future: as it becomes conscious of the necessity to protect its environment in order to ensure a better quality of life for itself, so also it recognizes its responsibility towards the child by proclaiming society's duty to give the best of itself to its children.[4]

* Ministre délegué chargé de l'action sociale et de la famille, 01 BP 2216, Ouagadougou 01, Burkina Faso.

It might be thought that the proclamation of the rights of the child constitutes an assertion of a principle that is universally recognized today. The respect for the rights of all people, unanimously recognized as a duty of all democratic societies, has become inseparable from the respect for the rights of the child. Could it not be said that the degree of a society's humanism and democratic progress can henceforth be measured by the quality of the attention that it gives to its children? Apart from the diversity of societies and civilizations, each society has the duty to grant the child a privileged place. Undoubtedly, this explains the exceptional speed with which the Convention on the Rights of the Child was ratified, and its overwhelming approval by the African countries, despite their limited resources.

The 'best interests of the child' is the fundamental concept around which the Convention articulates the rights of the child. The main provision is Article 3, which provides that in all social, administrative and judicial decisions, the interests of the child must be an essential concern.[5] Therefore the interests of the child must always be taken into consideration when the State intervenes on behalf of a child. Similarly, it is the interests of the child which should guide decisions taken by the family. So also, a judge, in ruling on a conflict between parents, must treat the interests of the child as paramount. It is important therefore to determine the nature of the concept of the 'interests of the child'.

Although that concept appears in legislation and jurisprudence,[6] it has not been uniformly defined, and is, in fact, susceptible to change depending on the circumstances. At times, it will lead to the protection of the personality of the child; at other times it will be the interests of society which will be pursued. The variation will be even more sensitive when different societies and civilizations are considered. Even in western societies, the traditional authoritarian concept of family relations has prevented the emergence of the notion of the interests of the child. In this traditional conception, it would not be seen as appropriate to undermine the family – the basic structure of society, represented by the *paterfamilias* – because of a concern for the individual protection of some of its members. How will the interests of the child be interpreted and taken into consideration in the social and cultural context specific to Burkina Faso?

(b) The Socio-Cultural Context Specific to Burkina Faso

Burkina Faso is a small country in Western Africa with a population of more than eight million people. Although composed of over sixty different ethnic groups, the people live generally in relative harmony. A few large majoritarian groups,[7] however, limit the 'ethnic division' of society. Situated in the middle of the Sahelian zone, Burkina Faso is undergoing a serious ecological crisis, characterized by a shortage of rain and an increase in deserts. The ecological crisis, combined with the economic crisis, means that the majority of the population, in particular those in rural areas, lives in great poverty.

Culture rather than economic circumstances will decisively influence the future of the child in Burkina Faso. In general, the traditional societies of Burkina Faso are organized on the basis of family lineage. At the head of the line is the chief patriarch who performs social, legal and religious functions. The essential place occupied by the chief of the line reflects the gerontocratic organization of the society. At the top of the social hierarchy are the elders, and at the bottom, the children. Therefore the older one is, the more rights one has and, correspondingly, the younger one is, the less one can insist upon one's rights. The law of elders is the rule in many aspects of social life. However, the traditional society recognized the fragility of the child and the necessity to give him or her particular protection.

The traditional Burkina Faso societies are animist: animist religion deeply affects the legal and social life. Animism is based on belief in the forces of nature and in the spirit of ancestors. Animist practices affect the implementation of laws, notably the application of sanctions.

Burkina Faso has a pluralist legal system which is principally manifested through the simultaneous operation of modern and traditional rights. This pluralism is sometimes of rights (for example, when the law expressly recognizes the application of customs),[8] and sometimes of facts (for example, when despite the legislator's hostility with regard to a particular custom, it continues nevertheless to apply).

In the particular context of Burkina Faso, how can the implementation of the Convention on the Rights of the Child be assured, and more precisely, how will the interests of the child guide administrative, social and judicial actions? The universality of the Convention means that it must be applied regardless of the social and cultural contexts in question. However, its application may vary according to the diversity of the social and cultural contexts. Thus, different priorities and the means which states have at their disposal will equally affect the application of the Convention. The imprecision of the notion of the 'interests of the child' hints at this diversity in the application of the Convention. There will therefore be areas of the Convention which each society will be able to apply relatively freely, and areas – considered as the core of the Convention – which require a standard application. Part I of this case study will illustrate the influence of social and cultural peculiarities on the perception of the interests of the child, and Part II will analyse State efforts, both legislative and judicial, to make the customary practices evolve in the interests of the child.

II.   THE INTERESTS OF THE CHILD IN BURKINA FASO'S TRADITIONAL SOCIETY

Contemporary society in Burkina Faso is currently in a state of transformation. It is influenced by the traditional principles and values which derive from ancestral customs, as well as by western principles resulting, mainly, from the country's colonial heritage.[9] While stemming from the past, customs, in fact, continue to compete with the law in the regulation of essential social relations, giving way to a legal dualism *de jure* or *de facto*. Customs are reflected in a more or less indestructible manner in many domains of social life.[10] Nevertheless, it may be said that family relationships today are the main location for the application of customs.[11] This is because family relations, whether between spouses or between parents and children, are the most deeply and intimately held in society. They constitute a 'central core' of social relations, the transformation of which will be fiercely opposed. Family customs, in effect, stem not only from the realm of rights, but also from religious beliefs, from standard social values ideally held by a community, and from the collective memory of the community.

In considering how the notion of the interests of the child, essential to the Convention, will be perceived and interpreted in the social context of Burkina Faso, it is necessary to analyse the place given to the child in the traditional society and also to show the ways in which this society embraces the interests of the child (Section (*b*) below).[12] It must be remembered, however, that customary rights regulate in a specific manner certain aspects of life that affect the rights of the child (Section (*a*) below). It is not for us to justify these customary practices, but simply to try to understand them better so as to allow efficient action to be taken in considering the interests of the child.

(a) The Interests of the Child in Relation to some Aspects of the Specific Character of Customary Law

Most traditional societies of Burkina Faso are communal, patrilineal societies.[13] The communal character of the society means that it essentially relies on the group, and the patrilineal character means that the family link – that is the bond between the individual and a family – is established in the paternal lineage. Likewise, the passing down of the constituent elements of an individual's personality comes from the father. The patrilineal character of the society of Burkina Faso affects the child's right to a name and nationality, and the communal character of the society has important consequences for the child's freedom. To illustrate this, I will examine how the customary law treats the right to a name and to nationality.

(i) The right to nationality

In general, all children in the traditional society have the right to a nationality. The notion of nationality in traditional society is really linked to ethnicity.[14] It used to be in the child's best interests to assert and consolidate his or her ties to a particular ethnic group. Belonging to an ethnic group appears to be a right and a duty. It is a right in the sense that an individual from an ethnic group benefits from the protection and solidarity of all members of the group in a confrontation with another group. For example, an individual member of a group was protected from capture by other groups during the wars between tribes (which were very frequent during the pre-colonial period), or during organized raids to capture men for slave commerce. In addition to the physical protection provided by the ethnic group, there was the mystical protection that the ancestral founders of the ethnic group were supposed to provide, and the benevolence which was maintained by performing the appropriate rites and by the scrupulous observance of the interdicts proper to the ethnicity.

While ethnic belonging is a right, belonging to an ethnic group is, simultaneously, a duty: nationality is not chosen; it is imposed on an individual at his or her birth. It is not possible to resign one's nationality, nor acquire a new nationality. Thus, married women can never acquire their husbands' nationality; they are bound to their family of origin; and a child always belongs to his or her father's ethnic group.

The importance of ethnic belonging was particularly manifested by the practice of ethnic scars. Each ethnic group possessed specific marks which were known by all. So, ethnic scars, usually on an individual's face, would identify that individual as belonging to a particular ethnic group. Several justifications were given for this practice. The most advanced is that it permitted the people, at a time of frequent tribal wars, to recognize their own. For example, the Mossis, who believed that all its members should be free, used ethnic scars to prevent Mossis conquering or enslaving members of their own ethnic group.[15]

Ethnic belonging also has important consequences for the child's right to marriage. Thus, marriages are generally recommended within the ethnic group. However, a dictinction must be made between societies which practise exogamic marriage and those which practise endogamic marriage. In Burkina Faso, many societies practise endogamic marriage, that is marriage within a relatively restricted family circle. For example, the Peuhl ethnic group, a group of transhumant shepherds, practise marriage between crossed cousins.[16] Marriages between crossed cousins favour imposed marriages in the sense that families tend to determine future spouses either at the birth of a child or when the child is very young.

Other groups prefer exogamic marriage. For example, in the Mossi ethnic group, a sedentary agricultural people, marriage is prohibited if the existence of any link to a relative can be established, whatever the degree of the link might be. As soon as the hand of a young girl is asked in marriage, the two families check their genealogies to assure that there are no family links, even distant ones. Exogamic marriages have favoured unions between different ethnic groups, thus contributing in a certain way to reinforcing the sense of unity, so precious in African countries.[17] The practice of endogamic marriage creates difficulties for today's generations for whom the ethnic reference is becoming less and less essential. Constant action is required by administrative authorities to oppose ethnic obstacles imposed on marriage.

The tradition of scarring the face presented serious hardships. Not only was it unhygienic, but the scars were rarely attractive. Scarring is occurring less and less these days, with some groups ignoring the practice altogether. Scarring was banned by the authorities immediately following independence. The prohibition aimed, on the one hand, at combating a customary practice that was considered to be cruel and unacceptable; and on the other hand, the ban had a political basis: the ostentatious demonstration of ethnic belonging appeared to weaken national unity. Although the practice of ethnic scarring is progressively disappearing, other customary practices, such as excision, have not been so readily abandoned.[18]

The right to a nationality shows the differences between the customary perception of the interests of the child and the contemporary conception of the rights of the child. This difference in perception between traditional society and modern society is often expressed in a true generational conflict.

(ii) The right to a name

The determination of the child's patronymic name shows the diversity that results from custom. This diversity has led the administration to look for a way to harmonize the names transmission systems. To what degree has this harmonization responded to the need of preserving the interests of the child?

The patronymic name takes on a specific, social and religious function in traditional society. For example, in European society, a person's name unites that person to common ancestors. In effect, it expresses a descendant connection. Names can be transmitted in either a patrilineal or matrilineal line.[19] Some traditional systems of name transmission contain additional elements of identification; for example in the Gourounsi ethnic group an individual's name also identifies his or her sex.

The traditional Mossi society used to give a particular meaning to the patronymic name. In this society of warriors the patronymic name does not express a filial relationship; names were, in reality, devices or 'combat names', carried by the chief. A combat name was supposed to increase the strength of the warrior to whom it was attributed. In the praises which the Griots sang, the recall of the slogans increased the honour of a person and also the prestige which he enjoyed in society.[20] The skill of the Griots consisted precisely in knowing the combat name of everyone and being able to reveal its strength and profound significance.

An individual's name was determined, as a matter of particular concern, in a special ceremony.[21] In particular, the protective strength attributed to the name depended on 'the totem animal' that represented each clan.[22] The patronymic name was not determined immediately at the time of birth. First, the use of the patronymic name was no longer current because it was charged with a sacredness and religiosity that required a certain degree of solemnity in its use. In general, a family would determine a patronymic name when circumstances arose such that particular protection was required for a child. The choice of name was not left to chance. It was a delicate process which required the intervention of a soothsayer. The soothsayer, after completing the appropriate rites, determined the child's name. The chosen name was supposed to protect the child against evil forces. The patronymic name could be the combat name of an ancestor of the paternal or maternal line,[23] or a completely different name.[24]

The problem of the determination of the child's name has raised many legal and administrative problems because of the diversity of systems. It was not uncommon to find individuals with different patronymic names who claimed to have the same father; and, conversely, it was possible to find people with the same patronymic name who were completely unrelated. The administration adopted a suspicious attitude, even hostility, toward the transmission of the patronymic name in matrilineal lineage. It always expressed its preference for a harmonization of the transmission in favour of the majority patrilineal system. Modern administrative practices (registry office, educational system, military), based on the majority model, have created a strong pressure in favour of this model.

It is not uncommon, in urban and educated circles, to request a name change, abandoning the 'given name' and adopting that of the father.[25] It is unfortunate that a practice which has the advantage of expressing a certain idea of equality between man and woman (the matrilineal transmission of the name) has been purely and simply outlawed. It has been suggested, however, that the abandoning of original systems of name transmission, the tendency to 'assimilate' minority groups, and the harmonization of the systems of name transmission, do not express the interests of the child.

(b) The Place of the Child in a Traditional Society

The child's place in society can be examined from two perspectives: first, the child's place in family relations, and second, the child's place in wider society.

(i) The interests of the child in family relations

First, it must be remembered that the African family is organized according to a kinship classification that permits the integration of a large number of persons into the family circle. In the parental classification system, a group of people will be accorded the same degree of kinship without this designation corresponding to the real biological bond. Thus, the child will have 'fathers' and 'mothers'. All brothers of the genetic father are considered to be 'fathers' of the child. Not only sisters of the mother, but also her joint spouses are considered 'mothers' of the child. Similarly, the children of the brothers of the genetic father are considered as brothers and sisters of the child. The system of relatives prohibits all distinctions between a genetic father and 'social fathers', or between brothers and sisters who have the same father, and the other categories of brothers and sisters. Such a distinction is considered to be wrong – an attack against family unity and solidarity. The advantage of this extended circle of kinship is that the child will benefit from increased attention throughout his or her development. On the other hand, however, the child will have a greater number of obligations towards his or her family.

Parental authority is not exercised by the genetic father, but by the lineage chief who is generally the grandfather of the child. The relationship between the father and the child is very different from that between the grandfather and the child. A certain distance is established between the child and the father, and the father is treated with respect and deference. For example, in the Mossi country, the father must be addressed as 'vous'. Although all family members and all members of society, in fact, are charged with the responsibility of educating a child, the primary responsibility for a child's education rests with the father. In particular, the father possesses the right to discipline, and he exercises his right with great severity. The child has an obligation of submission with respect to his or her father, so the child must not question or oppose any decisions taken by his or her father. Submission to the father's will is valued by the society and is considered as an essential virtue to be cultivated in each child; disputes and rebellions, are seen as a parent's personal failure in the education of the child, and a bad omen for the child's future. The obligation of the child's submission to his or her father is based on the idea that parents make decisions based only upon the interests of the child. It becomes important, then, to know what is the meaning of the 'interests of the child' in the context of the traditional society.

What is certain is that the interests of the child are considered, in custom, to be subordinate to the interests of the family and society. All serious decisions affecting the child's future (marriage, placement in another family, etc) were not left to only one person. Decisions were made by a family council, generally presided over by the oldest member of the line. The child did not have the right to participate in the council's discussions, but the participation of certain people, such as the grandfather, permitted, to a certain extent, the preservation of the child's interest.

The relationship between the child and the grandfather is usually dominated by feelings of friendship and even partnership. The child will often be closer to the grandfather than to the father. While the child must address the father as 'vous', the child has the right to address the grandfather by his first name. The grandfather participates in the child's cultural education, particularly through passing on the stories, legends and proverbs of the society. Because the grandfather is very close to the child, he will often discuss important matters with the child and ask the child's opinion on major questions concerning the child. The grandfather's role protects the child against excessive behaviour by the family and moderates the customary strictness towards the child. By trying to harmonize the interests of the family with the child's personal interests, the grandfather provides some balance in the overly hierarchical social structure. The grandfather's role is particularly important with respect to the rights of the child because, ultimately, it is he who will have the last word on every important decision concerning the child.

The relationship between the mother and the child is equally important. The very young child lives principally with the mother. The relationship is as intimate with the mother as it is distant with the father. The mother is responsible for the young child's support: she must be capable of providing food, clothing and health care on her own. In traditional society, it is the mother's responsibility to lead the child to adulthood. In general, apart from their work in the family fields, women manage personal agricultural activities on plots of loaned land. They also run some small commercial activities from which they earn income. It is this personal income that permits women to provide for the needs of the young children in the family. It can safely be assumed, therefore, that it is in the child's best interests that these individual economic activities run by women be encouraged.[26]

Although the child is indissolubly linked to the paternal family, the maternal family is of no less importance. In particular, the maternal uncle, who generally resides in another village, occupies an essential place in the child's life. The child has the right to ask for help from the maternal uncle, who cannot refuse such help if the request is within his means. It is not unusual for a child to decide, with his parents' consent, to go to live and work near his maternal uncle. The maternal uncle often provides material help to a child in addition to that provided by the child's family of origin. This assistance can be important when marriage plans are being made.

The role of the mother decreases as the child reaches adulthood. The child then becomes the father's responsibility. His mission is not only to provide for the child's needs, but most importantly, to introduce the child to social life. In one word, the father's mission is to turn a male child into a 'man'.

The principle underlying the child's belonging to the paternal lineage is essentially founded on the blood link. So a family link in traditional society cannot be begun by adoption. In fact, full adoption, as recognized in modern civil law, does not exist in traditional law. It used to be quite common for a child to be 'raised' in another family.[27] However, the child was never considered to be a member of the host family, and therefore the child had no right of succession in his adoptive family. The child was not subjected to the marriage prohibitions to which the members of his adoptive family were subject, so it was possible for a 'raised' child to receive a woman in marriage in his adoptive family. Finally, the 'raised' child did not acquire any religious rights in his adoptive family: the child did not have to undergo his adoptive family's sacrifices, nor was he subject to its taboos.

The mother's lineage gives no rights to the child. For example, in a situation of divorce, custom requires that the child stay in the paternal family. Similarly, if the father dies and the mother chooses to leave the family of her late husband to rejoin her family of origin or to marry in another family, she must abandon her children to their father's lineage. Where the father dies, the only way for the mother to continue living with her children is to marry one of the brothers of her deceased husband.[28] These situations can cause extreme conflict between the interests of the child and those of the paternal lineage or the mother.

The practice of imposing the continuation of the marital link through one of the deceased's brothers is known as the 'levirate'. It seems as though this practice is essentially linked to the conception that society is founded on marriage. In traditional society, marriage is considered not as a union between two individuals, but as a union between two families. At the time of the settlement of the marriage, the wishes of the future spouses are of little importance. What is important is the consent exchanged between the two families. Thus, in certain forms of traditional marriages (the gift of the woman), the girl is given to a family without special identification of the future male spouse. The marriage therefore performs the social function of establishing or strengthening the links between two families. This is particularly true of the first marriage where the young man is obliged, by virtue of his duty of obedience to his father, to accept the spouse which the family has chosen for him. In subsequent marriages, the young man is free to marry the woman of his heart. In this conception of marriage, the death of one of the spouses would not cause the dissolution of the marriage. The marriage, defined as a link between two families by the intermediary union between children, exists beyond the actual marriage partners.

The separation of the widow from her children resulting from the institution of the 'levirate' creates a serious, and possibly traumatic, emotional loss for the children, particularly when they are very young. Because of this, authorities and feminist associations have protested against this customary practice. Nowadays, increasing numbers of women are refusing to continue the marital link with a brother of the deceased. This has happened partly as a result of the fact that families live less and less in an extended family framework, thus weakening the links established with other family members. Although action to abolish the 'levirate' is essentially being conducted from the perspective of the promotion of the rights of the woman, it also has an important effect on the rights of the child.

(ii) The interests of the child and social institutions: education and marriage

The child participates in social life through his or her involvement in age groups. These age groups include children of the same generation – all children born in the same year are part of the same age group. The age group creates the environment in which the child will develop to adulthood. Each age group performs specific social functions which change as the children advance in age. In the first stage, the age group will essentially be busy with games, which are also important as a means of education. Older children will be expected to participate in domestic chores and to become involved in agricultural activities. These include leading animals to pasture and farming individual plots of land. The age groups also organize social activities to benefit the village; collective cultivation sessions are often organized to assist people in need of extra labour.

The traditional system of educating children was not compatible with the need for children to attend formal schooling. At first, especially during the colonial period, parents had to be forced to send their children to school. This resulted in many children being hidden from the recruitment teams. Today, the majority of the population understands the need for children to attend formal schooling, although problems still exist in the north Sahelien region of the country, which is inhabited by the Peuhls – transhumant shepherds – and also with respect to the education of girls. In the Sahelien zone, schooling is fettered by the economic system of transhumant pastoral activities which is incompatible with the rhythm of school life. Formal education of girls is seen as a perversion of their role in traditional society and so is not encouraged. The interests of the child requires an innovative adaptation of the rhythm of schooling with respect to the shepherds, and constant efforts need to be made in support of the need for formal education of girls.

Initiation ceremonies mark the passage from childhood to adulthood. Initiation consists of the children undergoing a series of ordeals to prepare them for their future life. The initiation cermony is crowned by the ritual of circumcision for boys and excision for girls. In particular, excision marks the passage of a young girl to womanhood. Only a girl who has been excised could marry a man and maintain sexual relations with him.

The practice of excision was strongly opposed by the political and administrative authorities on behalf of the interests of the child. This action was justified by the numerous risks to the health and physical integrity of the young girl from excision. The pervasiveness of the practice, especially in rural environments, drove the authorities to renounce all sanctioning for the time being, despite the existence of appropriate provisions in the penal legislation.[29] Resistance to the banning of excision is still very strong today, although there has been slight observable progress in the urban environment. The attachment of the rural society to the practice can be explained by the strong link between this practice and a young woman's status. Excision of a young girl marks her integration into social life and her progression to maturity. Numerous religious beliefs are also attached to the ritual.[30] The girl's mother was equally proud of her daughter's completion of the ritual. It should be noted that the secret character of the practice makes it difficult to carry out an efficient repression. What is required is, therefore, a real change in mentality, especially amongst women.

One of the essential factors of this change in mentality is the education and schooling of young girls, and, because of the complexity of the problem,[31] legislation would also be required. In 1989, a national seminar on the practice of excision was organized; it brought together representatives of the women's associations and religious communities (Christian and Muslim) and even the leaders of custom. In 1993, a national committee to lead the fight against excision was established and a national plan to fight it was adopted.

Marriage constitutes the other essential aspect of the child's integration into society. Unlike European marriage, traditional marriage is not an act which occurs at the exchange of vows between the future spouses. It is a long process through which the links between two families are established and consolidated culminating in an alliance consecrated by the union of the young spouses. The respective families of the future spouses are very much involved in the conclusion of the marriage. In effect, in most cases, the marriage is negotiated between the two families with the children playing no essential role. The children must submit to the wishes of their respective families. Here, the interest of the family (that of building up profitable alliances with all members) seems to differ from those of the children (freedom to live with the person of one's choice). Family intervention in the conclusion of the marriage has an effect on children's freedom of consent. Intervention by the family, and the consequent effect on the children's freedom, may be more or less significant depending on the type of marriage.

Traditional marriage can be arranged in several different ways. First, it can be the result of the 'gift of a woman', which consists of a family promising one of its girls in marriage to another family. This may be as a gesture of friendship or an act of gratitude towards a person. The identity of the promised girl may or may not be pre-determined; she may be a very young child or even unborn at the date of the gift. Likewise, the future husband may not always be determined. The beneficiary family will decide who will marry the promised woman.

The traditional marriage arranged by the gift of a woman takes little or no account of the wishes of the future spouses and compromises the personal interests of the child, especially the young girl. In many cases, the girl is promised to a person older than herself. The difference in age adds to the girl's feeling of helplessness; in most cases, however, she has no alternative but to resign herself to the marriage.

Similar to this type of marriage is another form of marriage called sororate.[32] Sororate consists of giving a man in marriage to one of his wife's sisters. This could happen when the man has demonstrated his worth towards his own family and his in-laws, or when his wife has died.

Another widespread form of traditional marriage is the marriage of regular request. In this case, the family of the young man addresses another family to ask for a wife for their son. Steps are taken either at the request of the young man who has found a girl he likes, or as an initiative by the head of the family who is responsible for finding a woman for each boy in the family. In certain cases, the young man's family does not ask the hand of a particular young girl; it leaves the choice of selecting the girl to be proposed in marriage to the family to whom the request was presented. The marriage of regular request has the advantage of allowing a certain freedom to the future spouses, at least to the young man, whose opinion will often be taken into consideration. However, even this type of marriage is interventionist; it imposes great difficulties on young people who want the freedom to determine their own future, particularly with respect to their marriage.

The difficulties created by imposed marriages have resulted in the institution of a particular form of traditional marriage, called 'marriage by abduction'. It generally occurs when a young girl promised by her family already has a lover. With her consent, friends of the lover proceed to kidnap her and the two young people go and live in a distant village. After having one or more children, the young people come back to their village and seek forgiveness from their respective families through the intermediary of village elders close to the concerned families. This pardon will generally be granted, and they will be able to live in their village of origin.

There is also the form of marriage by succession – the 'levirate'. This was discussed above.

It has been seen that custom relies on principles that guard the cohesiveness and solidarity of the family or social group. In this context,

characterized by rapid change of social practices and concepts, the interests of the child, in particular, are often in conflict with those of the
group. The intervention of the judicial system and the legislature will
be necessary for the reconciliation of society with the best interests of
the child.

III. THE LAW, JURISPRUDENCE AND THE INTEREST OF THE CHILD

(a) Legislative Intervention in Favour of the Child

(i) The hostility towards customs

In a context where customs remain a reality in the everyday lives of
individuals, the elaboration of new African legislation and the consideration of the interests of the child always pose the problem of the legislature's attitude with regard to traditional law. The legislature faces a
terrible dilemma – it can either reject traditional customs in an effort
to modernize legal relations, or seek inspiration from traditional customs
and fundamental values when making new laws. A rejection of traditional customs and values would result in the law being very distant
from reality, whereas using the traditional customs and values as the
basis for new laws would have the advantage of harmonizing, to an
extent, the traditional customs and values with the new law.[33] Whatever
method is adopted, the legislature must ensure that society in Burkina
Faso evolves towards the universal principles operating internationally.

The legislators of Burkina Faso have adopted a hostile attitude
towards customary law: with the promulgation of the Persons and
Family Code, 'customs cease to have the force of laws' in the matters
they govern.[34] The legislators of Burkina Faso have therefore chosen to
put an end to the dual judicial system, a characteristic of the African
judicial systems which has existed since the colonial period (at least
concerning family law). In passing new legislation that is the only source
of rights of the person and the family, the legislature intended to extend
its control over the relations between spouses and between parents and
children. It may be said that the legislature tried to favour the evolution
of the family in Burkina Faso through the new law, characterized by an
emphasis on the nuclear family and promotion of individual freedom.

The genesis of the Persons and Family Code highlights the efforts
undertaken by the State to co-ordinate the legislative principles with
the interests of the child. A national Codification Commission was established in 1984, and was assigned the project of uniting the whole of the
population of Burkina Faso, regardless of ethnic group or religion. The
Commission was composed of legal experts, sociologists, representatives
from women's associations, and interested ministries. After defining the

guiding principles of the Code, a proposal was presented to the government in 1989. A massive information campaign was conducted by the teams of the Codification Commission through the media (radio, television, press), as well as on the road (mainly conferences in the provinces, in schools and aimed at the communities). The reactions of the people and the communities were taken into account and the project was modified before its definite adoption in the form of a government ordinance. Because of its legal innovations, the Code's implementation was expected to be deferred until a year after the date of adoption. During this delay, an information campaign and a campaign for the dissemination of new texts was organized. These precautions demonstrate the legislature's desire to change customary practices related to the interests of the child without directly confronting society. The legislature relies mainly on persuasion and time to bring about a change in behaviour patterns.

In the Code, the legislature marked its hostility toward the traditional lineage family which they described as 'parasitical'.[35] The future family of Burkina Faso will correspond to the 'biological family' which will override the 'sociological family' of the traditional society. Thus, the basic obligations, which are an expression of the solidarity of the family, only concern relations between spouses, children, brothers and sisters, and grandparents.[36] Parental authority is exercised jointly by the mother and the father, to the exclusion of the members of the extended family, who will inevitably become strangers to the nuclear family circle. The legislature has given a new value to the marriage link – it is no longer the means of establishing or reinforcing the bond between lineages, represented by the respective chiefs, but is now the core of tomorrow's society, founded on the new universal principles of humanism and the rights of humanity.

With regard to the formation of marriage, great importance is given to both the physical and psychological maturity of the future spouses. Marriage age is fixed at twenty years for a man and seventeen for a woman. Individuals who are under these ages require authorization from their parents. However, marriage is absolutely forbidden for a man under eighteen and for a girl under fifteen.

The individual freedom of future spouses is equally maintained as a fundamental principle of the new marriage law. The legislature has formally prohibited forced marriages of any type, whether it be the gift of a woman or the 'levirate'. This prohibition of forced marriages is strengthened by the recognition of civil marriage as the only valid form of marriage. Consequently, customary and religious marriages, though not forbidden, have no validity in the eyes of the law. The freedom of consent of future spouses has been the object of particular attention by the legislature of Burkina Faso. While asserting the principle of freedom of consent of the future spouses as the basic condition for the validity of a marriage, the legislature has at the same time established a procedure for the celebration of marriage aimed at controlling the freedom of engagements. Henceforth, the registrar is to play a more active role in the preparation of future spouses for their new life. The registrar is required to meet each spouse personally before the marriage ceremony and to inform them of their principal rights and obligations. This procedure is designed to ensure that the engagement is the result of the free choice of the future spouses. If, at the end of the encounter, the officer has serious reasons for believing that there has been any hindrance to the freedom of either or both spouses, the registrar may refuse to celebrate the marriage.

In its concern with limiting the intervention of the family in a marriage, the legislature has formally forbidden the payment of a dowry, which had become one of the most obvious causes for forced marriages. Non-payment of a dowry will not be grounds for opposing a marriage. Similarly, all opposition to marriage based on race, ethnic groups, or religion is forbidden.

(ii) Basis for the hostility regarding custom: the interests of the child

The opposition to custom is founded on the interests of the child's development, and on the consideration that the child has a personality which deserves to be protected. Consequently, when a customary rule conflicts with the new principles and values advocated by the legislature, it must simply be abolished. In questions of inheritance, the Persons and Family Code of Burkina Faso, in common with most modern systems, favours the interests of the child. Because of the child's position as the descendant of the deceased person, the child has priority over all other heirs. Consequently, and contrary to the custom that gave them a privileged place, the brothers of the deceased person are excluded if the deceased had children. The administration of the possessions of a deceased person will be by the surviving spouse and not by the brothers of the deceased as had been the custom.

Should it be possible to borrow from custom practices which favour the interests of the child? The legislature appears to have answered this question affirmatively. The principle of rejection of custom has not stopped the legislature from borrowing inspiration from it where it corresponded with the interests of the child. Thus, the legislature proclaims the principle of equality between all children descended from the same father, regardless of the origin of filiation. This proclamation thus removes the civil distinctions between legitimate and ex-nuptial children. Apparently this revolutionary solution by the legislators of Burkina Faso is, in reality, in perfect harmony with custom. In traditional law, primarily dominated by the polygamic marriage, no distinction is made between children on the basis of origin of filiation. Marriage gave the link of filiation no particular value. In Burkina Faso, the dominating patrilineal family framework establishes its filiation link mostly through consanguinity, whether the child has been conceived in or out of marriage. It has been objected that to establish true equality between children regardless of their filiation could weaken the marital link by depriving it of the protection of the law when confronting situations of simple fact. The legislators of Burkina Faso have remained firm in the face of these objections, maintaining that the child must not be held responsible 'for what we no longer even dare call the mistake of their parents'[37] Only the interests of the child are to be considered, even where this may be to detriment of the marriage.

It is suggested that the interests of the child could constitute a pertinent criteria for evaluating customary rights: customs that undermine the child's personality and his or her physical integrity should be abolished. On the other hand, those that contribute to the child's full maturation and preserve his or her material interests deserve to be preserved and protected in legislation. This view agrees with the African Charter on the Rights of the Child which states that 'all customs, traditions, cultural or religious practices incompatible with the rights, duties and obligations expressed in the Charter must be discouraged to the extent of this incompatibility'.[38]

At the institutional level, the legislature has undertaken a particularly useful task in re-organizing the services of the registry office. The births of many children, particularly in rural zones, were not previously registered due to the concentration of the registry offices in urban centres. To declare the birth of a child, many parents had to travel up to several dozen kilometres to the closest town. Since most parents did not see the immediate usefulness of registration, many of them did not fulfil this formality. Consequently, many children born in rural areas do not know their exact date of birth. It is often only at the time of a child's schooling, and sometimes much later, that a birth certificate is given to a child: in most cases a child is declared to have been born at about a certain year.

To remedy this prejudice to the child, the legislature has decided to establish secondary registry offices in rural villages. A local person will be given the task of maintaining the registers of the secondary registry offices. These secondary centres are to have limited operation, however: they will only keep a record of birth certificates and death certificates. Other proceedings, such as registration of marriage and declarations recognizing children, will be the responsibility of the main registry offices. The decentralization of the registry services contributes to the reinforcement of the rights of the personality of the child, and is in keeping with the African Charter which states that 'all children are to be registered immediately after birth'.[39] The actual location of these centres so as to maximize their effectiveness, has, however still to be decided.

(b) The Action of Judges in Favour of the Interests of the Child

(i) The application of the custom displaced in favour of the interests of the child

The problem of the codification and implementation of the interests of the child lies, in Africa, at the heart of societies in the course of transformation. Both the conservative forces and those seeking to reform the law are particularly concerned to ensure the protection of the interests of the child in legislation as well as in jurisprudence. At the legislative level, this confrontation is resolved in favour of the reform of laws and of the adhesion to the universal principles declared in the Convention. This is because the legislative power is in the hands of the State, and it generally supports the cause of the interests of the child. However, winning a battle is not winning the war. The conservative forces of the law, which are very much alive, will regain the advantage as the proclamation of principles gives way to the management of real life situations. In particular, family relations, in which an essential elements of the rights of the child are managed, will escape the influence of the transforming action of the legislature.[40] The task then rests with judges to restore the balance between, on the one hand, the law, which favours the evolution of the rights of the child, and custom, which is an expression of the cultural values particular to a society. When a legal dispute is submitted to a judge for decision, the judge's duty is to apply the law. The judges of Burkina Faso are constantly balancing the legislative principles founded on the rights of the child with the realities of society.

It is especially with regard to custody of children that the jurisprudence of Burkina Faso has approached the problem of the interpretation of custom in relation to the interests of the child. In most cases, the law, undoubtedly influenced by customs related to the link of kinship, awarded custody of a child to the father. Thus, in twenty-two decisions handed down by the Magistrates' Court of Ouagadougou between 1960 and 1980, twelve awarded custody to the father, six to the mother and four to the grandparents.[41]

The legal system of Burkina Faso must be understood in the context of the legal and jurisdictional dualism which has prevailed there for many years.[42] Legal dualism is manifested in the operation of a parallel system of courts. State courts decide cases according to written law,[43] and customary courts rule on the application of local customs.[44] The competence of customary jurisdiction and written law regarding an individual's status, marriage or divorce, was determined by the civil or customary status of the individual parties. The jurisdiction of customary law operated in disputes between people who had kept their customary status (or particular status),[45] while the written law dealt with disputes between persons coming under the registry office. An individual's status will therefore be important to the judge since this will determine if it is custom or the modern legislation which should be applied in cases regarding custody of children or succession. Modern legislation gives greater protection to the rights of the child, while custom favours the rights of the extended family over those of the child.

In Burkina Faso, the judicial system regarded the customary status as the rule and the civil status, the exception.[46] However, in interpreting an individual's lifestyle, judges commonly affirm that the individual has implicitly placed himself or herself under a system of written law with respect to the rules relating to marriage and divorce. This departure from the application of custom is specifically to guarantee the interests of the child.

In a decision of the Supreme Court[47] involving a widow (N) against the brothers of her deceased spouse, and related to the determination of the rules (modern or customary) to be applied in a decision concerning the custody of the children and the administration of the property involved in the inheritance, the judge first recalled the principle of the application of the custom of N's family's ethnic group. According to this custom,[48] when the head of the family dies, his estate returns to his 'little brother'. The latter, in charge of the guardianship of the children, should also conduct the administration of the estate in the interests of the children. The widow was either to marry one of the brothers of the deceased person or to leave her children with her husband's family. Consequently, this custom – the law of the parties – should have applied to regulate custody of the children and the devolution of succession.

However, the judge raised a series of issues as to the lifestyle of N and her spouse so as to contest that N was still under customary status. The judge suggested that 'by their common quality as agents of the civil service . . . and by their life style', N and her spouse had shown their mutual will to lead a 'modern life'. Specifically, the widow N was a teacher and her spouse had been a veterinarian. They were both Catholic and had benefited from a property loan provided by a commercial bank, and their children pursued advanced studies. Taken together, the judge held that these facts established that the spouses had agreed to avoid the application of customs in respect of their marriage. Consequently, displacing the application of custom by the application of the principles of civil law, the court decided that the surviving spouse, N, should be awarded custody of her children and the administration of her husband's estate.

This case provides an example of how the judicial system has assessed a person's lifestyle to displace the application of custom, which is considered to be too harsh. This finding would apply to a certain group in the population, for example intellectuals and city dwellers. Nevertheless, the position of the judicial system remains mainly subjective, in the sense that custom would have been applied if the elements of the individuals' lifestyle had revealed their attachment to traditions and their adherence to those values. It is therefore not a value judgment that the judge delivers but a selective application of custom according to the status which can be implicitly imposed on an individual.

In a ruling in 1974, the Supreme Court was even more explicit in its attitude. It considered that custom may vary in as much as it is dependent on the people to whom it applies; consequently, the judge was at liberty 'to differ in accordance with what is considered to be a subject of rural environment which is still attached to the integrity and rigour of the original conceptions or of people more affected by the standards of modern life . . .'.[49]

(ii) Moderation of the rigour of custom in the interests of the child

Nevertheless, judges have not been satisfied to use judicial means only to disapply the application of customs in the case of certain people. In acknowledging their application, judges have attempted to moderate the rigour of the original conceptions of customary law.[50] In the case of spouse N, discussed above, the Supreme Court, in considering arguments based on tradition, held that custom is itself subject to numerous exceptions, 'justified by the concern to humanize the sometimes harsh customs, to raise the value of the human person, to protect his/her corporal integrity and individuality'. In other words, one cannot apply a custom 'to the letter' because what characterizes the custom is its flexibility, its dynamism and its capacity to adapt. The adaptation of custom can be perceived, notably in urban centres, to be the result of a combination of the political life, economic situation and the imported religions of Islam and Christianity. Furthermore, the Supreme Court maintains that custom remains open to the new principles of humanism and of respect for individual freedom, and that it knows how to submit to them. In the case of N and her deceased spouse, the court decided that in customary matters, the notion of the interests of the child applies with the same force as in modern law.

The Supreme Court is most certainly justified in adopting this point of view, since the Constitution had provided that the recognition of customs be limited to matters which were not in conflict with constitutional principles.[51] Moreover, by virtue of this constitutional disposition, 'customs which gravely contravene the principles of civilization will not be applied . . .'. Together with the necessity to take into account the evolution of customs in accordance with the lifestyle of the people, the interests of the child gives judges the means to displace or moderate their application. This is, in fact, what occurred in the case of N and her deceased spouse, where the Supreme Court decided that it was in the interests of the children, and in particular for the better continuation of their studies, that, contrary to the spouses' custom, custody of the children should be granted to their mother. At the same time, the mother was considered as the appropriate person to administer the estate in the interests of the children. In its ruling of 10 April 1981, the Supreme Court reversed the judges' earlier decision on the basis that they had ignored the evolution of custom, and consequently had made an erroneous assessment of the appropriate customary rules.

Since the adoption of the Persons and Family Code, judges are in a better position to decide matters according to the interests of the child. Since they no longer have to reconcile written law and custom (custom no longer having the force of law), a judge can consider the interests of children in applying the written law. With respect to custody, in particular, the law states that a judge's decision must be based only on the interests of the child. A judge enjoys considerable freedom in his or her assessment of a custody matter to the extent that the law has not defined the content of the notion of the interests of the child.[52] So the Court of Appeals of Ouagadougou, in a 15 November 1991 judgment, decided that the 'the interest of minor children is determined discretionarily by the judge with respect to the elements of fact'.[53] The case concerned the custody of minors in the context of a divorce. The judge, taking into consideration the lifestyle of the wife, a businesswoman whose job involved frequent travel, as well as the situation of three children born before the marriage, decided that the goal was to safeguard the interests of the children, particularly to guarantee them a good schooling. With this in mind, the judge granted custody to the father. In the same case, the judge decided that the husband should stay in the family home – this was also on the basis of its being in the best interests of the minors. Custody of the child was again awarded to the father in a judgment in 1992.[54] In this case, the judge assessed that the life led by the wife (notably an assortment of lovers) justified granting custody of the minor to the father.

Some important restrictions exist, however, with regard to the ability of the judge to control or displace the application of custom. First, it is necessary for the competent jurisdiction to have the opportunity to apply the law; that is for the conflict to be submitted to the judge. It is only extreme cases, where solutions have not been found in the familial framework or the customary structures, which will be taken to court. The majority of cases will bypass the judges' control. This may not necessarily be undesirable since judicial intervention must be contemplated only when social relations are disrupted. The second restriction on the action of jurisprudence in favour of the rights of the child is the problem of the continuous training of magistrates. Most magistrates do not have adequate resources or access to materials and are continually overworked.[55] The magistrates of Burkina Faso have very few occasion to observe legislative evolution and to familiarize themselves with the range of international conventions such as the one related to the rights of the child. Therefore, they will play little part in the bold application of new dispositions.

IV. CONCLUSION

The notion of the 'interests of the child' constitutes an essential principle for the implementation of the Convention on the Rights of the Child. In Burkina Faso, the interests of the child occasionally contradict customs and tradition. The legislators took a hostile attitude towards custom, basing themselves on the child's interests. The legislative texts enacted in the years following 1984 exhibit an obvious consideration for the interests of the child. However, the liveliness of custom and tradition presents a problem in making the legislative norm, and consequently the Convention, effective. In this context, the role of judges is significant. In certain cases, the judicial system displaces the application of custom by means of the civil status of the family. In other cases, judges will apply custom, but they may use their discretion to ease its effect where a rigorous application would cause hardship. At times, in an even more radical attitude, the judiciary may consider that, although the formal conditions of the application of custom are met, the custom should be rejected as being inconsistent with the fundamental principles of the Constitution.

The decisive role of the legislature and jurisprudence will not be able to influence the situation of children effectively unless certain accompanying actions are taken. These include particularly the training of magistrates with regard to the Convention on the Rights of the Child and new national laws which take into consideration the interests of the child. Equally, there needs to be support for effective creation of institutions, such as the secondary registry centres, which are presently delayed as much on account of the limited means of the State as of administrative burdens. The interests of the child in the development of societies in African States will be catered for as much by the adaptation and creative application of customs and traditions as by new laws. In Burkina Faso, the action of judges undoubtedly constitutes a vital means of reconciling the interests of society with the best interests of the child.

REFERENCES

Compaore, A. *The legal situation of the married woman*. Mémoire ESD, University of Ouagadougou, 1982.
Diallo, S. *The Rights of the Family in Mossi Custom*. Mémoire IHEOM, Paris, 1964.
Donnier M. *The Interests of the Child*. Dalloz, 1959, chron. p 179.
Lompo, F., Yarga, L. *Customary Courts in Upper Volta*. Ouagadougou, African presses, 1980
Meyer, P. 'Note on the Supreme Court 24 July 1981' *Rev burk de Droit*, N° 8, 1985, 177 s.
Nuytinck, H. 'The Principles of the New Family Law in Burkina Faso', *Rev Penant*, N° 805, 1991.
Ouedraogo, H. 'The New Succession Law of Burkina Faso', *Rev burk de Droit*, N° 22, 1992.
Pageard, R. 'The Private Law of the Mossis: Tradition, Evolution'. Ouagadougou, Rech Volt, N° 10, 1969, t. 1 & 2.

NOTES

[1] Nearly 50 per cent of the population is under eighteen years of age.

[2] M. Donnier, 'The Interest of the Child', D 1959, Chron., 179.

[3] Declaration of Mr. Malhuret, Secretary of State to the Rights of Man (France), J. O. Deb, Ass, Nat, 8 May 1987, 949.

[4] From this point of view we can establish a parallel between two important meetings which were held recently: the Earth Summit held in Rio, in June 1992, and the Chief of States Summit on the Right of the Child held in New York in September 1990.

[5] The same principle is also evoked by the African Charter of the Rights of the Child, article 4: African Charter on the Rights and the Well Being of the Child, adopted in July of 1990 by the conference of the Chief of States and of the OUA government. The document is not yet in force.

[6] See in particular, article 302 of the old civil code applicable in Burkina Faso and above all the articles of the Persons and Family Code. However, it is mostly *jurisprudence* which inculcated the rights of the child, notably in family institutions.

[7] The major group is the Mossi group, which represents a little less than half of the population. Then come the Peuhl and Gourmantche groups.

[8] Custom itself is an expression of plurality, since each ethnic group applies specific local customs.

[9] Burkina, formally called Haute-Volta, was a territory of the old colony of French Western Africa. The country attained independence in 1960.

[10] In particular, the land property system constitutes one area where customs continue to operate.

[11] Next to family relations, land law is another context where custom continues to be manifested. This is not surprising since land ownership is closely related to the family: in effect land in a traditional society is more a place of identification and space for development than a possession having economic value.

[12] At times the traditional conceptions contribute to the protection of the child but at other times they sacrifice the interests of the child to other social considerations considered to be more important.

[13] There exist a few societies of matrilineal organization, for example the Dagara society in the southern region of the country.

[14] It can be said that the Burkinabe nation still remains to be forged. The actual population of Burkina is, in effect, an assembly of several ethnic groups, more or less important and more or less structured, which formerly existed independently of one another. It is only the colonial process that, in the creation of the colonial administration territories, permitted the actual national regrouping while favouring the breaking-up of certain communities.

[15] The Mossi chiefs only captured their servants and slaves in the neighbouring communities which were less organized and less militarily powerful.

[16] Marriage between crossed cousins gives preference to the union between a young man and the daughter of the maternal uncle.

[17] It should be pointed out that the problem of castes imposes many obstacles on the marriage. For example, in the Mossi culture the caste of blacksmiths is marginalized; elsewhere its the griots who are marginalized.

[18] It is easier to fight the practice of ethnic scarring than that of excision which is presently kept relatively secret.

[19] The transfer of name in the matrilineal line is particularly practised by the Dagara ethnic group.

[20] Even today, the evocation of the 'motto' of a person evokes great satisfaction and pride, leading the person praised by the Griot to give the latter gifts, usually money, though at times goods.

[21] This ceremony was called the 'sigre'.

[22] The animal totem was very important in the traditional societies. It determined the clan name of the group. If in a family there were different patronymic names, the 'clan name' was the same for all members of the lineage. For, example, a young Mossi could ignore his patronymic name, but he always knew his 'clan name': this knowledge was quickly inculcated to the child through education of totemic taboos which generally consisted of an absolute prohibition by all members of the lineage against eating the meat of the totem animal.

[23] In principle, the child only carried the name of ancestors already deceased. When the determined name corresponded to that of a living relative, the child had to carry a substitute name until the relative's death gave him the right to carry the attributed name. See S. Sambo Diallo, *The Rights of the Family in the Mossi Custom.* Memo of the Institute of Hautes Studies of Outremer, Paris, 1964.

[24] See R. Pageard, Number 10, 1969, t. 1, 49 s.

[25] It did not seem very acceptable to some, with the modern judicial concepts of the legitimate and natural child, to use any other name than the father's.

[26] It was due to this that a fund was established for the support of the remunerative activities of women.

[27] Quite often a person entrusts a child to be raised by a relative or a friend. The 'adoptive father' must treat the child as his own. He particularly has the responsibility of finding a woman for the child and of organizing his marriage.

[28] In general, the remarriage is not imposed on the spouse: she has the choice of staying, by marrying into the deceased's family, or leaving, thereby leaving her children. The widow is consulted on the choice of brother with which the marriage link might be pursued.

[29] A national committee to combat excision was established; it is presided over by the wife of the Head of State. This committee has taken action which should develop in two main phases: first, a public awareness programme has been undertaken, mainly in rural areas, with the support of the religious and customary authorities; and second, the committee advocates the application of the sanctions allowed for by the legislation.

[30] The belief that non-excised women are exposed to serious risks at the time of birth is deep-rooted. Those who escape the ritual are usually excised later, generally after one or more miscarriages.

[31] Note the recent debate resulting from the sentencing by the French justices of women who practised this operation within the milieu of West-African immigrants in France.

[32] Practised by the Gourounsi ethnic group in particular.

[33] The problem is more complex than this, because contemporary African society is not homogeneous; although the majority of the population, especially the rural population, lives according to custom and adheres to its essential values, a strong minority, composed of the intellectual elite and the urban populations, opposes the customary rules.

[34] Article 1066, Persons and Family Code (CPF).

[35] See document of the presentation of the project of the CPF.

[36] See article 685, CPF.

[37] Hubert M. G. Ouedraogo, 'The New Burkinabe Successional Law'; Rev Burk Droit, No 22, 1992, 185.

[38] African Charter on the Rights and Well Being of the Child; article 3.

[39] Article 6. 2, African Charter.

[40] It is what certain authors describe as the phenomenon of loss of the rule of law, referring to the lack of respect in the practice of legal dispositions in family matters: V. H. Nuytinck, 'The Principles of the New Family Law in Burkina Faso', in Penant, No 805, 1991, 258–75.

[41] A. Compaore, 'The Legal Situation of the Married Woman Through the Divorce Cases in Voltaique Law. Report of Expertise, ESD, University of Ouagadougou, 1981–2. 74 and 75.

[42] In fact, until the adoption of the Persons and Family Code in 1989, in matters of family relations.

[43] It consisted of the Courts of First Degree, Court of Appeals and the Supreme Court. See the law of 10 May 1963. See F. Lompo, and L. Yarga, The Customary Courts in Haute-Volta, Ouagadougou, African Press, 1980.

[44] The court of first instance is responsible for all lawsuits relating to 'the status of people, family, and divorce' (Dec. December 3, 1931, modified many times). The court of second instance hears appeals from decisions from courts of first instance (V. Arr. March 7, 1975).

[45] Meanwhile, in certain cases the legislation allows the parties to subject their relationship to the system of the written law.

[46] This principle resulted from the interpretation of article 82 of the Constitution of 1946 which provided for the maintenance of the customary status of local natives except for those who had expressly renounced it.

[47] Supreme Court, Ouagadougou, 10 April 1981, Rev Burk., of Law, No 10, 1981, 181.

[48] It consists of the 'Gourounsi Nouna' custom of Leo.

[49] Supreme Court, ch jud, 11 January 1974, Bull Supreme Court, 1978, 31.

[50] P. Meyer, noted under Supreme Court, 24 July 1981, and Court of Appeals Ouagadougou, 20 May 1983. Rev Burk of right, No 8 1985, 177 s.

[51] The current Constitution takes the same precautions, by providing that the law will define the conditions in which the customs will be ascertained and harmonized with the fundamental principles of the Constitution.

[52] Exceptionally, the law provides that custody of a child under seven years of age must always be granted to the mother, except under particular circumstances where such a decision would be detrimental to the child.

[53] Court of Appeals of Ouagadougou, 15 November 1991, unpublished.

[54] Court of Appeals of Ouagadougou, 17 January 1992, unpublished.

[55] Of the thirty courts of first instance which legislation deems necessary, only eleven are functional due to the lack of personnel.

MODALITIES OF THE BEST INTERESTS PRINCIPLE IN EDUCATION

ADEL AZER*

ABSTRACT

Abstract concepts and formulations of policy standards, such as the best interests principle (article 3 CRC), are only fully understood when perceived dynamically within a concrete historical-social setting. Moreover, the substantive content of formal policy in a particular sector is often further qualified or delimited by interacting forces, parallel socio-economic policies and executive decisions. Taking account of these issues in studying the best interests principle within the context of basic education in Egypt indicated that the historical roots of education, maintained by contemporary forces, have contributed to the co-existence of plural education systems serving different interest groups. Apart from elitist foreign education provided for the few, the majority of children are channeled into the mainstream government system, which faces numerous constraints which negatively affect the rates of enrolment and sustainability. In addition, considerations of affordability and functionality have far-reaching impact on the family's perception of the best interests of the child, which is in some cases in conflict with official policy perception. These and other indications demonstrate the complexities and the various modalities of the best interests principle when perceived concretely within a particular social context.

I. INTRODUCTION

The search for policy standards and criteria, such as the best interests of the child, in the field of basic education, goes far beyond the identification of abstract concepts. It entails the understanding and analysis of the policies themselves within concrete historical-social settings. Moreover, policies and policy standards are not to be conceived as static self-contained norms which exist in a vacuum,[1] but rather as dynamic concepts interrelated and interacting with other policies and forces within a particular socio-economic and political reality.[2] Adopting this approach in the analysis of educational policy in Egypt would entail various levels of investigation.

* 1075 Corniche El Nil, Garden City, Cairo, Egypt. Deep gratitude is expressed to Mr. M. Baquer Namazi, UNICEF Representive and to UNICEF Cairo office for the valuable support and encouragement given during the preparation of this study.

A. The first level would focus on the right to education *per se*, as it is regulated in the national legislation. In this context, three aspects could be investigated:

(i) The formal aspect would entail an examination of whether the basic principles of the ordering of human relations have been observed by the national legislation. Foremost among them are the principles of impartiality, equity and justice[2] Other derivatives are the principles of exclusion of arbitrariness and discrimination.

(ii) The substantive aspect, on the other hand, would require an analysis of the content of educational policies as they are embodied in legislation. The principles contained in the constitution, the laws and the ministerial decrees, would be studied analytically. The identification of the underlying as well as the professed rationale of these policies would also shed light on the social ends which are sought by the policymaker.[4]

(iii) The executive contribution to the policy can have serious impact on the substance of the policy. This takes various forms:

* Often the legislator allows the executive discretionary power to interpret and to implement the law according to the prevailing social realities, or in accordance with considerations such as feasibility, adequacy and affordability. In these cases the executive's contributions should promote the policy objectives; however, this is not always the case.

* During the implementation phase, the substantive policy may be adulterated, impeded or changed in many ways. Decisions or actions on the local level may fall short of, or even contradict, policy intent. More serious are the covert or concealed strategies which the executives adopt with the purpose of changing or restricting the impact of legislation. Such attempts have been recorded in many countries and take the form of selective implementation or of strategies designed to reduce accessibility to a certain right.[5] In such cases, actual changes in the standards and criteria of declared policies are witnessed and experienced.

B. A second possible level of investigation would take account of the interaction between the main focus of the study, namely the right to basic education, and other related rights of the child. This approach is supported by the United Nations General Assembly resolution (No. 421 V, reaffirming resolution No. 543 VI), which stipulates that the 'enjoyment of civil and political freedoms, and of economic, social and cultural rights are interconnected and interdependent'. This view was also endorsed by the Teheran proclamation (1977): 'All human rights . . . are indivisible and interdependent'.[6]

Moreover, an assessment of the interaction between related rights may reveal a case of dependency, reinforcement or conflict. On the other hand, the structure of certain rights may disclose a case of complexity. In other words, the composition of a certain right may presuppose and necessitate the provision of other rights. In such cases understanding policy standards would entail an assessment of the interrelationship of the different rights within the complex structure.

II. METHODOLOGY

The approach adopted in undertaking this study required a combination of socio-legal methods and tools. In addition to an analytical study of legislation regulating basic education, field studies have been undertaken in three governorates, Cairo, Qaliubia and Assiut (Annex I), with the purpose of assessing the perceptions, decisions and actions of the executives. The perceptions of parents were also assessed.

Furthermore, experts and senior officials in the field of education were asked to write papers on various related issues (Annex II). The group met in a two-day workshop to discuss the findings of the fieldwork and the papers. Their cooperation has contributed valuable insight to the study.

III. HISTORICAL ROOTS

As previously stated, a dynamic understanding of the policy of adherence to a human rights principle would entail an analysis of the policy in question within a particular socioeconomic and political context. Such an understanding would be enhanced by taking account of each society's historical experience,[7] particularly the significant historical causal factors which clarify the raison d'être of the situation involved.

However, a comprehensive historical study of education is clearly beyond the aims and the scope of this work. Thus, our attempt will be limited to depicting a few significant historical factors which have had impact on the education system in Egypt. Such an attempt would reveal that:

– Several features of contemporary education in Egypt have been acquired, and have survived, over centuries of historical developments.

– These historical roots still colour certain aspects of the perception and the choices of present-day policies.

1. *Religious versus secular roots*: Archeological studies reveal that a duality has existed in the educational system ever since the early stages of the Pharaonic era.[8] Ancient carvings show that around the years 3000 until 2000 BC, education among the 'populace' was handled totally by the parent and concentrated on practical, occupational teaching and religion. Reference is also made to an 'élitist school' in the Pharaoh's

palace. An alternative for the élite was to send the child to live with an 'educator'. Later carvings show a school built by Ramses II annexed to a temple in Thebes. Higher education was provided in the temples.

The contributions of religious institutions to education continued during the Christian era (60–641 AD) through the churches and monasteries. After the Arab invasion, the teachings of Islam became the major influence and component of education, provided in mosques and Kottabs. Another important development was the establishment of Al Azhar mosque by the Fatimides in 970 to spread the faith, and later to provide education. Ever since, Al Azhar has had far-reaching impact on both the cultural and political spheres.[9]

The dyadic nature of the education system, religious and secular, persisted over the years, though the balance oscillated occasionally in favour of one or the other. For instance, in the nineteenth century, the ruler Mohamed Ali, wishing to build a strong army and administration, neglected religious education in favour of secular schools. However, the dyadic nature of education still survived.

2. *Foreign versus Arab roots*: Arab education, with its dyadic religious – secular roots, did not maintain its authenticity in Egypt for long: foreign invasions by the French (1798) and the English (1882) introduced élitist foreign education tailored to provide politicians and administrators to run the country in collaboration with the foreign power. Thus, a more complex plural system of education came into being, yielding a hybrid of cultural influences which still permeates decision making on the policy level, and contributes to a variegated social fabric on the societal level.

3. *National movement versus elite privileges*: With the turn of the twentieth century,[10] the plural nature of the education system became even more pronounced as four different, unrelated and unco-ordinated systems of education coexisted, each serving a particular function. The religious Kottabs continued to serve the poorer sectors, especially in rural areas. Parallel to this traditional form, primary schools were introduced as a secular alternative for the education of the masses. On the other hand, fee-paying schools were established to educate the better off. These schools were favoured by the occupying power, which desired to staff government departments needed to run the country. Lastly, foreign schools were set up to serve the foreign communities and their counterparts among the ruling élite.

Later years witnessed a build up of strong nationalistic feelings, which were eventually embodied in the 1919 revolution calling for an end to foreign occupation and the inception of democratic government. The movement gradually gained ground: a modern constitution was introduced in 1923, accompanied by some popular measures, including an attempt to 'democratize' education. In 1926 the Government proclaimed that primary education would become compulsory. However, the plan faltered due to lack of resources.[11] Meanwhile, the national movement continued to pressure for reform and democracy; and gradually the government introduced some reforms. In primary public (government-run) schools the following measures were taken: the introduction of free meals (1941), the abolition of school fees (1944), and the discontinuation of the teaching of foreign languages in the primary stage. The aim was to promote the Arab culture and language and to eliminate cultural disparities in society.

The Egyptian revolution of 1952 was another significant turning point in the country's history. After initial successes in ridding the country of feudalism and of foreign occupation, the revolutionaries set out to achieve the ambitious goal of restructuring a modern nation based on principles of nationalism, democracy and equity. An attempt was made to 'nationalize' and to unify the education system. Foreign schools were placed under sequestration and the foreign administrations were expelled. However, these measures had limited impact: the foreign schools were transformed into government-run foreign language schools. These continued to function as private fee-paying schools for the élite – both the surviving old and the emerging new – who managed to maintain privileges, including the 'interest' in providing for their children a privileged foreign language education.

To democratize education, the revolution sought to broaden its availability all over the country. However, the drive was too hasty and the quality of the service suffered. Moreover, these efforts were hindered by the financial burdens of consecutive wars during the 1960 and 1970s.[12] Meanwhile, a study undertaken in Cairo University in 1966 claimed that the background of the students indicated that the education system after the revolution had maintained its élitist nature. The majority of university students were sons of professionals (33.2 per cent), businessmen and landowners (29.3 per cent). Much smaller percentages of labourers' children (5.6 per cent) and peasants' children (5.8 per cent) managed to continue to university level.[13]

IV. HISTORICAL ROOTS MAINTAINED BY CONTEMPORARY CONSTRAINTS

Various contemporary factors represent serious constraints on the country's resources and its effort to provide basic needs. An understanding of the pressures involved would contribute to the realization of the difficult choices which the government is faced with.

1. *Rapid population increase*: Consecutive censuses reveal that, whereas the size of the population doubled during fifty years (1897–1947), it has nearly doubled again in about thirty years (1947–76). The annual growth rate during the latter period ranged between 2.31–2.54 per cent. The latest population census, however, recorded a rise in the rate of population growth to 2.8 per cent and accordingly the total size reached

50,455049. Recent estimates of the Central Agency for Public Mobilization and Statistics (CAPMAS) record a rise to 56,915000 individuals in
1991. Moreover, the geographic distribution reveals a dense population
concentration in the narrow Nile Valley and the Delta, which represents
4 per cent of the total size of Egypt. The population density was estimated at 48 individuals to every square kilometer of the total territory,
and 1170 individuals to every square kilometer of the inhabited areas.[14]

The territorial limitations and the rapid population growth represent
serious constraints, worsened by an on-going rural-urban migration
causing serious pressures on the cities and the services, particularly
education.

2. *Age composition*: A high proportion of the population is young: those
who are under twelve years (the minimum legal age for employment),
figure as 34.1 per cent of the population (1986). This unproductive
category represents a burden on the country's economy and its services.
Another limiting factor is the small size of the work force not exceeding
27.7 per cent of the total population.[15]

3. *Educational status*: Census figures (1986) indicate that the percentage
of illiterates was at a high of 49.4 (37.8 per cent males, 61.8 per cent
females); those who read and write (without qualifications), 24.4 per
cent; holders of a certificate below university level, 21.8 per cent; and
university graduates, 4.4 per cent.

4. *Wealth and poverty*: Various factors have contributed to an inadequate and imbalanced economy:[16] the financial cost of consecutive wars
in the 1960s and 1970s; the malfunctioning of public enterprises; and
the increase in public spending, including the provision of subsidies to
alleviate poverty, were all conducive to an ailing economy. The country's gross domestic product was estimated in 1988 at just below 31
billion US dollars, while external debts soared to over 52 billion US
dollars; thus the ratio of debt to GDP was estimated at 167.9 per cent.
Strains on the economy brought growth nearly to a halt by 1990. The
partial debt relief in 1990 reduced the ratio of debt/GDP to 106.9 per
cent.[17] This situation accounts for the low level of GNP per capita estimated at 640 US dollars, worsened by an annual inflation rate of 11 per
cent.[18]

Moreover, the income distribution has traditionally been inequitable,
with a wide gap between the rich and the poor: the GNP per capita for
the lowest 40 per cent of households was estimated in 1987 at 280 US
dollars.[19] World Bank estimates of families classified as poor ranged
between 20–25 per cent, and the very poor between 10 and 13 per cent
of the total number of families.[20] Though the Government faced ever
growing demands for services, job-creation and subsidies, it had to
accept, rather reluctantly, the World Bank's prescription for economic
adjustment, privatization, removing subsidies and shifting the burden

to consumers. This policy also entailed serious cuts in public spending, including investments in basic services.

– The outcome in the field of education was restrictive. The budgetary provisions (1990–91) totalled LE 2307 million, representing 6.1 per cent of the total budget and 5.2 per cent of GNP.[21] These resources are insufficient for expansion and for the provision of new school facilities to keep up with the growing population. Private initiatives and donations have been encouraged, but had limited impact.

– Al Azhar schools had been for many years restricted in resources and have come to depend, to a large extent, on private initiatives and funding.[22]

– Private education, on the other hand, has benefited from the trend towards privatization and is expanding. Statistics of the MOE indicate that the number of classes in private primary schools increased in 1990–91 by 20.5 per cent.[23]

– The traditional Kottab has been encouraged by the Ministry of Awkaf, responsible for religious affairs, to combat illiteracy among the poorest.

Thus, the historical roots are maintained and plural educational systems still coexist.

V.   THE RIGHT TO EDUCATION

Egypt's Constitution (1971), founded on socialist democratic principles, indicates that its economic structure is based on 'sufficiency and justice in a manner preventing exploitation, conducive to liquidation of income differences, protecting legitimate earnings and guaranteeing the equity of the distribution of public duties and responsibilities' (article 4). In accordance with these principles the Constitution stipulates that 'education is a right guaranteed by the State (article 18); it shall be free of charge in the various stages of State educational institutions' (article 20). Moreover, education is 'obligatory in the primary stage and the State shall work towards extending obligation to other stages' (article 18).

Meanwhile, the obligatory stage had, in fact, been extended to nine years of basic education (the Education Act No. 139/1981) but was eventually reduced to eight years (Act No. 233/1988). Accordingly, the present Basic Education System includes eight years of compulsory education, divided into two stages: a primary stage for five years, followed by a preparatory stage for three years. Basic education is followed by three years of secondary education (general or technical), or by five years of advanced technical education.

Equal Opportunity in Education

It is generally conceded that all individuals have equal rights to education, guaranteed by the following constitutional stipulations. 'All citizens are equal before the law. They have equal public rights and duties without discrimination between them due to race, ethnic origin, language, religion or creed' (article 40). And 'The State shall guarantee equality of opportunity to all citizens' (article 8). Both legal and educational practitioners concede that equality before the law and equal opportunity are basic principles which qualify entitlement to education; however, views differ widely in their interpretation of these principles, particularly in relation to the extent and content of the right to education.

The diverse views represent, in fact, two main trends of thought, well expounded in Unger's differentiation between formal and substantive ideals of justice. 'An ideal of justice is formal when it makes the uniform application of general rules the keystone of justice, or when it establishes principles whose validity is supposedly independent of choices among conflicting values'. On the other hand, substantive justice governs the actual outcome of distributive decisions, and how most effectively the purposes ascribed to the rule would be achieved.[24]

(i) Judicial decisions

Judicial precedence in this context has been clear and constant. The Supreme Administrative Court in defining the principle of equality of opportunity indicated: 'equality means non-discrimination between individuals of the same category or of similar legal status or position'.[25] The Constitutional Court upheld the view that: 'equality, inferred in the principle of equality of opportunity, is guaranteed by the universality and abstraction of the legal norms which regulate rights'.[26]

(ii) Educational interpretations

Educationists in Egypt have adopted the principle of equality of opportunity as a basic qualification of the individual's right to education; however, their interpretations indicate two diverse stances.

● The prevalent trend among educationists is influenced by the judicial interpretation of the principle of equal opportunity: equality is subject to similar status or position. Thus, everyone would have 'an equal chance (access to educational opportunity) according to his ability'.[27]

● Inversely, other views claim that equal accessibility to educational opportunities does not adhere to, or realize the requisites of, the principle of equal opportunity to education. Other additional requisites are deemed necessary:[28]

– Children in basic education (in the various sub-systems and schools) should receive the same standard of education. This would entail similar school buildings, facilities, equipment and teacher's qualifications.

– Equal opportunities would also require diversity in the curriculum to accommodate the different abilities, inclinations, environments and community needs. However, diversity should not lead to the provision of a lower standard of education for some children. This view is in accordance with the UNESCO Convention of 10 December 1960.

– Guaranteeing equal opportunities for those who cannot keep up with mainstream education, due to personal or social factors, would entail the provision of compensatory education.

VI. DIVERSITY IN EDUCATION POLICY

The 'best interests' concept – as an ideal standard for all actions concerning children, as stated in article 3 of the Convention on the Rights of the Child – arose originally in a situation of simple choice within the context of judicial decision-making in cases of custody.[29] Obviously, its implications within the context of socioeconomic policies are not so simple. The concept's bearing on the educational field is even more complex, and would probably be controversial – especially in developing countries. This has, in fact, been recognized by the Jomtien World Conference[30] which indicated that the 'scope of basic learning needs and how they should be met varies with individual countries and cultures, and inevitably changes with the passage of time' (Article 1 of the World Declaration). Moreover, the intricate Egyptian scene contributes to the complexity of the issues involved. The Education Law (Act No 139/1981) provides a general umbrella for various forms of pre-university education, and consequently several sub-systems coexist alongside mainstream basic education, each seeking to further a particular interest in addition to the mainstream goals. An analysis would reveal the diverse particularities and interests involved.

(a) Objectives of Mainstream Basic Education

The Education Law (Act No. 139/1981) which regulates both state and private educational institutions, specifies the following objectives: basic education aims at 'developing the pupils' abilities and potential, fulfilling their inclinations and aptitudes, instilling values and manners, and teaching practical and vocational skills consistent with the prevailing conditions in their communities. Thus, those who complete basic education would be enabled either to pursue their education to further higher levels, or to face life after intensive vocational training, the purpose being to prepare the individual to be a productive citizen in his environment and in society (article 16).

The guidelines to achieve these goals include the following principles (article 17):

– Integrating the religious, national, moral and physical aspects of education.

– Taking account of the relationship between education and productive work.

– Strengthening the relationship between education and the community through the diversification of the educational and the occupational components of the curriculum, in accordance with the requirements of the different local communities and their needs for development.

– Integrating the theoretical and practical components of the curriculum.

– Drawing on the local environment and the socioeconomic activities within it as sources of knowledge and activities in all the courses.

An impressionistic interpretation of the previous text may conclude that basic education is a unified system which licenses diversification. This is only partially true. However, an in-depth investigation would also reveal the existence of parallel sub-systems, and in a few instances semi-autonomous systems of education.

Meanwhile, the task of diversifying the curricula according to the different environments and communities has not been accomplished and at present unified, centrally designed curricula are taught in State schools throughout the country. The High Council of Education had previously indicated the unfulfilled need for diversification.[31] On the other hand, diverse forms of education coexist, catering to serve particular sectors of the population. Two main umbrellas shelter diverse forms of education: private education and Al Azhar education.

(b) The Objectives of Private Education

A private school is defined as a non-governmental institution whose function is to provide education or occupational and technical instruction prior to the university stage (article 54, Education Act). The Education Act indicates that private schools fulfill some or all of the following objectives (Article 55, Education Act):

– Assisting in basic or secondary education (general or technical) in accordance with the plans and curricula of equivalent 'formal schools'.

– Broadening the sphere of teaching foreign languages, in addition to the formal curricula.

– Teaching special curricula licensed by the Minister of Education, after the approval of the High Council of Education. Each school prescribes its bye-laws and sets the fees to be paid. The bye-laws are ratified by decree of the governor concerned.

In practice, the private education system functions as an umbrella which provides legitimacy for various sub-systems. Among them are:

* Arabic private schools which are similar to State schools, apart from being fee-paying.

* A category of diverse schools known as 'language schools' which teach a basic foreign language in addition to the unified government curriculum of Arabic, religion and social studies. The explanatory notes of the Education Act state explicitly that some courses may be taught in a foreign language. However, all courses, apart from the stated unified courses, are taught in foreign languages, and are in fact derived from foreign curricula. The schools themselves are offshoots of the foreign roots which had influenced the education system. Though this influence had diminished during the initial stages of the Revolution, it had still survived. The last two decades have witnessed a strong revival of foreign education – much sought after by the upper-middle and upper classes.[32]

According to official statistics the percentage of students in the pre-university stage of education, who are enrolled in private schools, is 5.9 per cent of the total number of students in this stage.

A further development towards the provision of élitist foreign education is the permit given to a few schools to teach the British curriculum leading to taking the IGCSE examination. The fees for the courses and for the examination are excessive according to local standards. Similar permits have also been granted to other foreign language schools.

(c) The Objectives of Al Azhar Basic Education

Al Azhar is the bearer of religious Islamic education in Egypt and the provider of religious teaching for Islamic countries. Following the Egyptian Revolution, university education in Al Azhar was extended to include various disciplines in addition to religious courses. The aim of education in Al Azhar *Institutes*, which provide pre-university education, is to provide for the Arab and Islamic countries teachers specialized in religious and Arabic studies.[33] Originally, Al Azhar *schools* were established for the purpose of teaching the Koran. In 1961, the general primary and preparatory curricula (now basic education) were introduced in these schools, in addition to the original religious courses. However, these schools still retain their autonomy as a sub-system of education fulfilling its historical mission.[34]

VII.   HARD CHOICES IN MAINSTREAM BASIC EDUCATION

Official statistics indicate that over 12 million students are enrolled in pre-university education. Whereas about 5.9 per cent attend private schools, the majority are in the mainstream formal education system. The Government faces considerable difficulties in providing basic education to over ten million students (see table in Annex III) and catering for about 1.5 million new entries annually. The policy issues which confront the decision-maker are enmeshed in numerous constraints,

deficiencies and pressures. In fact, the decision-maker faces a complicated situation in the field of basic education: 'because basic learning
needs are complex and diverse, meeting them requires multi-sectoral
strategies and action'.[35] Moreover, goals, strategies and action must be
adapted to the specific realities of the country in terms of priorities,
feasibility, and availability of resources.[36]

To emphasize the importance of the previous statement, one might
postulate that these multi-sectoral strategies and actions represent
'arteries' leading to the heart of the education system. Carrying the
simile further, the analysis of actions taken in the context of education
policy, especially in developing countries, should not overlook the possibility that one of the 'arteries' may be blocked, but that still a 'by-pass'
may be possible. In such a case an alternative sub-system or measure
may be introduced to overcome the difficulties encountered and to
secure the interests of a certain category of children.

Taking account of these complex issues, and within possible alternatives, hard choices and decisions are made.[37] The crucial question in
each case is whether the best interests of the child, within a concrete
situation, had been given sufficient consideration, or had these interests
been sacrificed in favour of other priorities. Only through in-depth analysis of the system and the actions taken to implement it would such
complex issues be determined. Such an attempt is made under the following sub-sections.

(a) Accessibility

Enrolment rate: Though basic education is a right for every child of school
age and is also a compulsory stage of education, nevertheless not all
six-year-old children actually attend school. The Ministry of Education's (MOE) statistics for the scholastic year 1990/91 recorded that
1,452,582 children had enrolled in the first year of basic education: 93.6
per cent in primary schools (government and private), and 6.4 per cent
in Al Azhar Institutes (primary stage). However, official sources in
MOE indicate that these figures include some children below six years,
the age of entry into basic education (about 81,636 children). It was
also indicated that actual enrolment falls short of accommodating all
six-year-old children, and that those who had actually enrolled represent
97.6 per cent of that age group.[38] However, it is also conceded that this
percentage is an overestimate, since enrolment does not necessarily
mean attendance. In fact, a recent ministerial document stated that
actual enrolment figures could not exceed 80 per cent of six-year-old
children.[39]

The pressure on the educational system to accommodate all children
of basic education age has proved insurmountable. According to official
statistics, the pupils who were registered for the five year primary stage

(1990–91) totaled 6,402,472 pupils, representing 88.5 per cent of the total category of children aged six to eleven years.

Shift system: Moreover, due to the shortage of school buildings, the government was faced with a crucial policy consideration – in fact a dilemma – which required making hard choices. The matter boiled down to whether it would be 'better' to educate half, or less, of the number of children who are entitled to basic education or to adopt a two-shift system which would cut down the school hours, but would accommodate at least double the number of those who would normally attend a full-day school system. The choice made was to educate a larger number of children. Consequently, most school buildings are used to accommodate two shifts, and only 31 per cent of primary school children attend a full-day school system.[40]

Class crowding: A related issue is the problem of class crowding. The average density of the classroom is forty-five pupils; however, fieldwork in Shubra El Kheima (a district in Greater Cairo) revealed that in many cases the class density is as high as sixty pupils.[41] The Government realizes the difficulties involved, and its plans for the future envisage a gradual increase of school facilities, working towards an extension of the full-day system. The estimated sum required for five years in order to make basic education accessible to all children of school age, ranges between £6–10 billion.[42]

(b) Sustainability

As a principle, the accessibility of a service, and in fact any other human right, is not the decisive factor in guaranteeing the provision of that service or right. Assuring the substantive content of a right entails going beyond the mere provision of an opportunity (in other words accessibility) and would require working towards sustainability.

This issue is of special significance in providing the content of particular rights. For instance:

* The structure of a certain right may reveal a case of complexity, in other words the composition of that right may presuppose and necessitate the provision of other rights. A typical example is the right to an adequate standard of living (article 27 CRC).

* Another instance is indicated in the Jomtien framework for action (1990): target goals may be achieved and/or maintained through intermediate goals. This is of special importance in the case of education. For instance, its provision to deprived groups would require an understanding of the nature of deprivation as a multi-faceted phenomenon. Consequently, the targeting process, and its sustainability, would entail multi-sectoral strategies and action. This issue has been explicitly stated in the MOE's strategy document.[43] The strategy indicates that 52 per cent of the children in basic education suffer from anemia and 20 per cent have vitamin and protein deficiency. The document points out

in detail the outcome and the dangers which threaten the health and development of these children, including the negative impact on their mental and physical abilities.

Case studies in underprivileged areas bear witness to the vulnerability of children. During a visit to a school in Shubra El Kheima, the nurse in charge of the school clinic pointed to the white spots on the faces of some children as an indication of malnutrition. To the researcher's question of why the drop-out rate was so high, the headmaster answered testily: 'let them first feed properly! Can't you see the poor living standards?'[44]

Meanwhile, the official strategy outlines two courses of action:

– Reinforcing preventive health services for children in kindergarten and basic education. For this purpose a new scheme for school medical insurance has recently been drafted (Act No. 99/1992). Each student will pay an annual contribution of LE 4. Students in private schools will be charged 10 per cent of their annual fees (not exceeding LE 50). A degree of equity is thus realized, though the poor would find their small contribution an additional burden on their strained budget.

– The other proposed course of action is that of introducing nutrition programmes into kindergartens and basic education. However, because of budgetary limitations, though provided mostly through foreign aid, the provision will be gradual, starting with rural areas and depressed urban areas.

Noteworthy in this context are the findings of the study in Cairo and Shubra El Kheima, which revealed that attendance rates were noticeably higher in schools which provided biscuits during the school-break.[45] Moreover, nutrition is used in some cases as an incentive to encourage students to enlist in technical elementary schools.[46] However, MOE statistics indicate that the numbers of students in the primary and the preparatory stages who benefit from the nutrition programme are 2,354107 (representing 38.5 per cent) and 86011 (representing 2.5 per cent) respectively, out of the total number of students in basic education.[47]

(c) Affordability

The Egyptian Constitution stipulates that 'education in government institutions shall be free of charge in all stages' (Article 20). However, as previously stated, the budgetary provisions for education (representing 6.1 per cent of the country's total budget and 5.2 per cent of GNP) are insufficient for expansion to keep up with the growing population. Consequently, free education has proved to be a heavy burden for an ailing economy. This background would shed light on a clause in the Education Act (No. 146/1981) which grants the education authorities the discretionary power to require payments for 'additional services' and for 'insurance on the use of school equipment' (Article 3).

A decree of the MOE (No 187/1992) followed requiring the payment of an annual fee for 'additional services' amounting to LE 9 in the primary stage and LE 13.2 in the elementary stage. However, the fees can be paid in two instalments.

Another decree (No 149/1986) introduced semi-obligatory private group tuition for a monthly payment for each course attended: LE 2 in primary and LE 3 in preparatory for each course attended per month. The parents-teachers school councils are entitled to double these fees. Those in the fourth and fifth grades of primary school and in preparatory school pay a fee to sit for the end of year examinations.

Here several issues are at stake:

– As a principle, the prescribed payments rescind, in actual fact, the constitutional stipulation which guarantees free education.

– Moreover, this universal prescription of fees payment is another instance of the formalistic approach which does not leave room for considerations of substantive justice or purposive policy. Discussing this issue in the seminar, the participants stated that the negative aspects in education policy cannot be remedied without taking cognizance of the 'social map', which indicates that the lowest stratum of society includes 40 per cent of the population, and that a high percentage of the rural population, in addition to those who live in urban squatters, are 'socially handicapped'.[48]

– Research findings bear witness to the inability of poor families to shoulder the burden of school expenses and fees. In a study on child labour, 42 per cent of the families of children who dropped out of school stated that education expenses represented a heavy burden on the family budget.[49] Other research findings indicated that the highest drop-out rates are among the lower strata of society, namely poor farmers followed by labourers.[50]

– In our present study, a parent who was interviewed indicated that the family monthly income was LE 200 and that it fell short of meeting the basic needs of his family of five. To illustrate he said that he could not afford to buy meat more than once a week; the family had to eat vegetables and beans most of the week and explained why his son had dropped out of school: 'I cannot afford school expenses, a pencil which used to cost 1.5 piastres, now costs 20 piastres'. A recent study estimated that a poor family's expenditure on education in 1990/91 as compared to its expenditure in 1980/81, has increased on average by 580 per cent. It was indicated that this increase had exceeded the rise in a poor family's average total expenditure, estimated at 358 per cent.[51]

Various interviews in the three research areas confirmed the inability of poor families to meet school expenses.[52] In this context, it is of interest to note that some religious associations in poor communities offer assistance and pay the school fees of underprivileged children. A particular example was witnessed in Shubra El Kheima, where an association

provided orphans with special cards that grant them the right to free
services such as medical treatment, free schooling and even a free hair-
cut.[53] A decree of MOE (No 173/1992) has taken account of humanitar-
ian considerations by exempting orphans and the children of military
personnel who die in combat from school fees. In these cases the provision of assistance would also be possible. Exemption and assistance are
not extended, however, to other categories such as the poor.

(d) Executive Initiatives

As indicated earlier, the substantive content of policies is often modified,
or even adulterated, during implementation. In the case of education,
the policy is laid down at the central level and local authorities are
not granted much discretionary power. Moreover, the limited physical,
material and financial resources leave hardly any room for flexibility
in implementation.[54] However, and despite all odds, the fieldwork has
revealed cases in which the executives have shown ability in overcoming
difficulties and in solving some problems facing education policy. Of
special relevance were the attempts made to tackle the issue of affordability, though they were controversial.

– When the poor fail to pay school fees, the headmaster would often
investigate possible channels to provide financial support. Resources
may be obtained from the limited funds of the school or the local educational authority, or as a last resort, the headmaster may seek donations
from religious associations and charities.[55]

– In many schools the researchers were informed that the headmaster
had often sought or accepted donations from local religious associations
to cover poor children's fees. Such cases illustrate the ongoing interaction between the formal and informal support systems in developing
countries. Where and when the formal system fails to achieve an 'individual interest', the informal support system often intervenes to provide
an alternative.[56]

– However, the skeptics are suspicious and caution that such solutions
may not be in the best interest of the child. The headmaster of a technical preparatory school, fearing fundamentalist influence, refused
donations from religious associations: 'I will not sell my boys to anyone'.
He added: 'resources must be provided from school or government
funds'.[57] The governor of Damietta took a similar stance and prohibited
unlicensed private tuition by private associations.[58]

– The headmaster of the technical school also decided not to implement the Ministry's directive allowing schools to charge fees for private
group tuition. Private tuition was to be gratuitous as a form of social
solidarity.

– In another school, an association for the care of students was established; each student was to pay 75 piastres monthly to contribute to

paying the fees and the price of spectacles or other equipment needed by poor children.

However, many educationists insist on the need for radical changes: 'It is the state's duty to allocate resources for the provision of free basic education'.[59] This view has been endorsed by the MOE's strategy (1992) which calls for the restructuring of free education. The proposal envisages that:

– Basic education would be totally free of charge as it represents the 'essence of national security and of the formation of a productive citizen capable of contributing to the comprehensive development and defense of the country'.

– Secondary and university education in government institutions would be free if the student is 'committed', otherwise payment would be required.

– Those who opt for private education in the first stage should be charged payments in further stages of education, including university, thus they would contribute to social solidarity.

However, these proposals are still under consideration within the context of economic adjustment policies and government affordability.

VIII.   FUNCTIONALITY OF EDUCATIONAL POLICY

For many years education has been criticized on various grounds. Since the nineteenth century, Egyptian education has been influenced by various Western systems. However, this influence was limited to the adoption of foreign curricula, which were not, however, assimilated or integrated into the national context and culture. Thus, the children learned, but did not relate what they learned to their lives, their needs and their problems.[60] With the advent of the 1952 Revolution, education policy was claimed to be outdated, maintaining a traditional socio-economic and political structure. Apart from élitist education, the curriculum of mainstream education was biased towards middle class values and an anachronistic historical function – namely to provide administrators and clerks for the government.[61]

Though far-reaching changes were introduced after the Revolution, the changes in education, however, were limited to broadening the sphere of opportunities, without changing the content or the quality of the system.[62]

Prominent intellectuals and researchers pointed out the failings of the education system.

* In the education process the student continued to be on the receiving end, expected to learn and to be examined on what he has memorized.[63]

* Consequently, the curriculum provided educational material in the form of 'abstract truth' and statements of facts, not as issues for deliberation.[64]

* Special emphasis was given to the teaching of the Arabic language, concentrating on syntax, structure and grammar. In some cases 'the beauty of the language seemed to have an effect similar to a drug; thus its function was transformed from being a tool of communication to being a goal in itself'. Teaching the language predominated over ideas and thought; the study of the literary and cultural heritage prevailed over performance and achievements in the sciences.[65]

Education in Egypt is understood to be a process which includes two components: instruction or teaching and nurturing (used as a synonym of upbringing). It is generally conceded that the process of nurturing is shared by the family and the school, to instill in the child 'moral, aesthetic and social values, a sense of identity, self-respect and a sense of belonging'.[66]

In this context the following points are of special concern to the issue of the best interests of the child.

(i) Here again emerge the strong religious roots which influence culture and education. It is generally conceded that the moral basis required for nurturing the child is provided by religious teaching. Evidence of the strength of this conviction is the fact that it has become a constitutional stipulation: 'Religious education shall be a principal subject in the courses of general education' (article 19).

(ii) Educationists indicate, however, that there is a need to appoint psychologists in schools – in addition to present social workers – to contribute to the nurturing process.

(iii) Within the context of the nurturing process, reference is usually made to the negative effects of language and foreign schools. Though foreign languages are an asset, teaching foreign curricula in all courses is considered to be a negative factor during the 'formative' years which contribute to shaping the child's character, mind, sense of belonging and identity.[67]

Moreover, the plurality of the education system contributes to a diversity in world views, outlooks and inclinations. Educationists indicate the main goals of basic education, namely that it is intended to be the 'basis of national unity . . . to guarantee a common language and a common value system'.[68]

IX. NON-FUNCTIONALITY OF THE SYSTEM FOR THE POOR

As a principle the provision of a basic right presupposes its substantive functionality for the beneficiaries; hence, the requisite that education would be targeted towards the development of the child's personality, talents and abilities. However, as previously indicated, the education system had been limited in its content and objectives. To the underprivileged sectors of society, the issue was even more problematic, reflected in the high rates of school drop-out.

(a) School Drop-Outs

There have been several estimates of the drop-out rates from primary education. Monitoring a cohort group of children enrolled in primary schools in Sharkiya governorate showed that, after six years, 23 per cent of the children had dropped out. The figures were highest for the second, fourth and sixth grades, as a result of failure in examinations. A parallel study in the governorate of Daqahlia revealed a drop-out rate of 29 per cent. The highest rates were among farmers' children (45.6 per cent), followed by labourers' children (32.6 per cent). The two main reasons for dropping out were educational failure (60.1 per cent) and the family's need for extra income (31 per cent)[69]. In a study undertaken in collaboration with the World Bank, the National Council for Education Research estimated the drop-out rate among males at 19.4 per cent and among females at 20.7 per cent, representing a combined total of 20 per cent.[70] Another estimate by the Ministry of Education recorded a drop-out rate of 15.2 per cent.[71]

(b) School Drop-Out and Child Labour

A study on child labour in the region of Greater Cairo[72] sought to assess the factors which contribute to the proliferation of the phenomenon and its connection with school drop-out. The educational level of a sample of working children (N = 566), indicated that 90.8 per cent of the children had either not enrolled in schools or had dropped out before completion of the primary level. Only 9.2 per cent had completed the primary state, but had thereafter discontinued. Table 1 indicates these findings.

Table 1: Working children's educational level.

Educational Level	N	Percentages
Never went to school	114	20.1
Attended in primary school, but dropped out	400	70.7
Completed primary school	4	0.7
Did not complete preparatory school	48	8.5
Total	566	100

School drop-out is closely correlated to child labour. In fact it is the main source of recruitment. Despite legal prohibition of child labour before the age of twelve, the phenomenon has been on the increase. CAPMAS statistics show that the employment of children aged six to twelve years has been regularly increasing: from 3.5 per cent (in 1979), to 5.3 per cent (in 1980) and 7 per cent (in 1984) of the total labour force (6 + years). The number of working children in 1984 was 1,104,000; 71 per cent were working in rural areas. Working children below 15 years totalled 1,472,600, representing 10.3 per cent of the labor force (six + years). A CAPMAS labour force sample survey (1988) indicates higher rates of child labour in the agriculture sector (77.8 pe cent). The sex distribution reveals a higher percentage of female child employment in rural (47.9 per cent) than in urban (30.5 per cent) areas (Annex V).

(c) Factors Contributing to Child Labour

Until recently, hardly any attempts were made to understand why families forewent education in favour of child labour. Controversial views were stated ranging from lack of awareness, negligence of child upbringing to child exploitation, etc. Investigation revealed the following findings:

(i) Family background

It was often claimed that child labour is a product of an unsuitable or a broken family background.[73] Our study disproved this: the vast majority of the children lived in a cohesive well-integrated family; cases of divorce did not exceed 1.4 per cent among the children's families. Though the family background was not a contributing factor, nevertheless an understanding of the dynamics which influence choice and often determine conduct among the underprivileged is deemed necessary.

(ii) Understanding the experience of the poor

In tackling the issue of individual experience, Unger pointed out that a person's conduct is comprehensible only if 'we are able to see why he acted in a certain way, at a certain moment, given his beliefs about the circumstances in which he had to act'.[74] Embedded in a person's perception and subsequent conduct are his experiences, beliefs and values. It would be conceivable, however, that a person would experience conflict between his ideals and his life experience.[75] Earlier research sought to comprehend the dynamics of choice among the poor in Egypt. The study concluded that the poor often envisage, and do seek, betterment. Foremost among their aspirations is the desire to educate their children. However, this desire is often in conflict with the need to maintain their status quo – invariably around subsistence level. Given this conflict, an additional negative experience would usually outweigh their ideals and aspirations.[76]

(iii) Initial choice favouring education

Going back to the study on child labour in Greater Cairo, the findings revealed that the vast majority of the parents (80 per cent) had desired to educate their children. Moreover, a significant percentage of children had persevered for several years before dropping out: 8.5 per cent had completed the primary stage (dropping out of the preparatory stage); 27.2 per cent dropped out of sixth form and 14.6 out of fifth form of primary education.[77]

(iv) The determining factors

Investigating the factors which actually lead to child labour, the children's responses revealed the causes which contributed to their employment and the corresponding scores of each cause as shown in Table 2. (Respondents were permitted to state more than one cause.)

Table 2: Factors leading to child labour.

Factor	N	Percentages
Educational failure	281	49.6
Learn a profession	256	45.2
Contribute to family income	226	39.9
Earn own money	187	33.0
Other	38	6.7

It is evident from the table that the main factors which contribute to child labour are either educational or economic in nature. Educational failure in conjunction with the desire to learn a profession as a substitute for education had greater impact. This was followed by the family's need for financial assistance (33 per cent) and the child's desire to earn his/her own spending money (33 per cent). Altogether, the economic factors amounted to 36.7 per cent of the responses. Other diverse factors collated in the table under the item 'other' included: the death of a parent; the need to prepare for marriage (girls); 'it is better to work than to stay at home or to play in the street'. Thus, the two main decisive factors were unsatisfactory education experience and the need to supplement the family income. An in-depth study of the two factors revealed the following findings:

(v) Unsatisfactory experience in education

* The study on working children in Greater Cairo included eighteen in-depth case studies, which revealed that various children had had unsatisfactory experiences during the early stages of basic education. Parents who were interviewed reported that the child had 'failed repeatedly', or that he 'hated school', or that he was 'uninterested in education'.[78]

* The field study undertaken in the first district of the governorate of Assiut, which is an underprivileged area inhabited mostly by peasants, craftsmen and other labourers, included interviews with fifty-four heads of families. The interviews were illustrative of underprivileged parents' perception of education.[79] The vast majority of the parents (92 per cent) believed that mainstream education is suitable for the 'rich categories' of society. For most (83 per cent), basic education is a terminal stage. This attitude is reinforced (as stated by some respondents) by the high rates of unemployment among graduates of different levels of education.

A high percentage (89 per cent) stated that the best interests of their children in education would combine basic knowledge (reading, writing and maths) with training in local industries. Thus the students would 'feel the relevance of the courses'.

The negative feelings towards education are not peculiar to the Egyptian scene as the same experience has been recorded in various Third World countries. A UNESCO report indicated that when a gap exists between the school environment and the child's social background and no attempt is made by the school to bridge that gap, school failure would be probable. Moreover, the educational curriculum might not be relevant to low-income families. Primary education, particularly, might not be relevant to the social realities and to the experience of a poor child, not to mention his/her felt needs. Consequently, these factors contribute to the family's decision to discontinue the child's education.[80] The UNESCO Forum on Education for All asserted that in such cases parents are not likely to send children to school for the inherent value of literacy.[81] On the other hand, 68.5 per cent of the working children's mothers in Shubra El Kheima complained of the high costs of education; 56.2 per cent among them singled out the cost of private group tuition.[82]

(vi) Supplementing family income

The child labour study in Greater Cairo indicated[83] that the families have a limited income: on the average LE 48.680 per week to be divided among 7.1 family members. The vast majority (94.9 per cent) received financial assistance from their children and 81 per cent of the mothers said that the family cannot do without this assistance. On average 2.2 children contributed a sum representing 22.8 per cent of the total family income. Case studies have revealed that for some families, the child's wages are vital for survival:

– A fifty-year-old service labourer working for the local authority received a monthly salary of LE 50. As the sum was insufficient to maintain five children, two children went out to work, thus raising the family income to LE 130.

– An elderly incapacitated parent who had not been insured had to rely for sustenance and medication on his children's income.

– Among the most needy are the female-headed families, for whom the child's wages are a principal source of income.

In contrast to the children's school experience, 84 per cent of working children expressed satisfaction with work. However, 16 per cent said they disliked it. Working children (91.7 per cent) also expressed a high sense of responsibility and commitment to contributing to the family income.[84]

X.   RESTRUCTURING EDUCATION POLICY

Several attempts have been made to tackle the problems which have foiled educational efforts for many years. Foremost among them is the issue of the non-response of the underprivileged to the system and the high drop-out rates.

As previously stated, the Education Act of 1981 introduced a new system of basic education. However, because of the difficulties encountered in the initial stages of implementation, the Minister of Education presented the 1992 strategy document spelling out and refining the objectives of basic education and expounding more concretely the new policy initiatives. These are on two levels: (a) the introduction of functional changes in mainstream basic education; (b) the provision of alternative educational opportunities for those who fall out of the mainstream. Each level indicated criteria to meet stated goals and felt needs.

(a) Functional Changes in Basic Education

The strategy calls for a total renewal of basic education within the framework of stated guidelines for the education system as a whole.[85] Each stage of education shall be comprehensive but may be terminal. Thus a student who drops out of the system after completion of basic education would be able to find work opportunities. For this purpose introductory courses in technical education will be provided to develop both the manual and technical abilities of the children. Modern methods of teaching such as audiovisual and computer equipment are to be introduced. The philosophy, the curricula and the methods of teaching are to undergo total transformation. First, from quantity to quality: the strategy indicates that the children were burdened by vast amounts of information, beyond the limitations of age and the requirements of education. During the scholastic year 1991–92, the curricula of basic education were reduced by 15–20 per cent of their previous size. Second, from negative recipience to positive participation: the curricula and the methods of teaching tended to view the function of education as the provision of necessary information and knowledge, which the child memorized. Accordingly, teaching was basically the transmission of truths or factual material, which left little room for deliberation of possible alternatives. A total change is suggested aiming at developing the different abilities of the child, including his/her critical and analytical abilities. This would mean that the child would be an active participant in the education process; and that examinations would be problem-oriented rather than merely testing the child's ability to memorize information.

Because of the shortages in school buildings and facilities and the adoption of a multi-shift system, extra-curricular activities suffered. The strategy calls for the urgent resumption of these activities, but points to the financial difficulties involved in building sufficient and suitable schools, estimated at LE 6–10 billion. As is the case with traditional systems, education had been stereotyped and rigid. However, some flexibility was introduced in 1981 and was further increased in the 1992 strategy. For instance, the transfer between different channels of education became possible, especially from mainstream basic education to technical education. Governors were given some flexibility in deciding the dates for starting and ending the school year and also in allowing some days off school, in accordance with local needs. This is usually related to the employment of children in agricultural activities such as cotton picking.

The comprehensive changes include the gradual provision of nutrition in primary schools, starting with rural areas and poor urban quarters. The scheme seeks to achieve several related objectives: to improve health conditions and school performance and to encourage school attendance among poor children.

(b) Alternative Opportunities for the Underprivileged

Parallel to the efforts to remodel mainstream basic education, the Government adopted a pragmatic approach in an attempt to provide alternative opportunities for the benefit of the underprivileged.

(i) Elementary occupational schools

A report of the Education and Scientific Research Committee in the People's Council (Parliament) indicated in 1988 that 'figures of success and failure and of drop-outs from basic education reveal that a large number of students do not aspire to continue their basic education to the elementary stage, and many of them fail or drop-out before the completion of the primary stage. Moreover, these children cannot enrol in an occupational training centre before the age of sixteen – which is wasteful. To tackle this intricate issue the Education Law was amended (by Act No. 233/1988) allowing those 'who terminate successfully the primary stage and show occupation inclinations, to continue compulsory basic education in occupational training centres or in occupational schools or classes'. Those who succeed are awarded a certificate of occupational basic education, and may enrol in occupational secondary schools.

(ii) One classroom schools

This system was devised in 1975 to provide education for deprived areas, especially for remote villages. A three-year programme of non-formal education equivalent in content to the primary level, is targeted to serve three main categories of children aged six to fourteen years; those in the compulsory age of education who had not enrolled; those who dropped out of the primary stage; and those who have had some education, but are still semi-illiterate.

The system is not bound by the structure or the practice of formal schools. Thus the school location may be in a mosque, church, village club, a flat etc. No school furniture is required, apart from blackboards. Teaching is provided for three and a half hours daily, for five days per week. Fridays and market days are excluded. A simplified version of the primary school curriculum is taught by local teachers, supervision and examinations are undertaken by the nearest 'mother' primary school. The learners are usually divided into two groups and the teacher, who works simultaneously with the two groups, alternates explanation and exercises to each group during the same teaching session.

In recent years several governorates have shown a lack of interest in this system, in favour of formal education.[86] Despite its flexibility, the main criticism leveled at it is that it has failed to provide practical occupational training which is required for this category of children.[87]

(c) Community Schools

This is a new initiative which started in 1992 on an experimental basis, and is undertaken jointly by MOE and UNICEF in the governorate of Assiut.[88]

Similar to the one-classroom school, the community school is targeted to serve remote rural areas deprived of educational services. Basically the system seeks to involve local community participation in providing the school premises – which may be built specially or set up in an existing building. Community involvement in the administration of the school is also required in order to relate school activities to the needs of the community. UNICEF contributes furniture and equipment, and the MOE provides books, teachers' salaries, and medical care and nutrition for the children. School hours are flexible in order to provide opportunities for deprived children aged 8–14 years, some of whom would be working children. Rural girls are especially encouraged to enrol. 90 per cent of enrolments in 1993 were of girls. The school curriculum is provided by the MOE, but the approach to teaching and the additional training courses encourage self-learning. The teaching process is another innovation: the classroom is divided into 'corners'; in each corner a group of children is helped to self-learning 'facilitated' by a teacher/facilitator (aided by assistants) chosen from the local community. Teaching includes the development of abilities and involves the rudiments of occupational training, suited to community needs.

This approach has been propagated by the Jomtien framework for action which sees the learner as a resource for the educational system, who should not be taken for granted. Rather he must be actively encouraged to participate in the learning process.[89]

XI. CONCLUSION

The point of departure of this study was the assumption that an understanding and interpretation of a legal text in abstraction would be misleading. Moreover, it sought to demonstrate that policy standards, as embodied in legislation, are very much the product of interacting historical and contemporary forces. This is of particular relevance to understanding the plural nature of the education system in Egypt. A realistic understanding of children's rights would concede that the provision of children's rights may vary between cultures or sub-cultures. Such variations may be functional and beneficial, as long as they do not restrict or preclude one of the principles of the Convention; children's rights are often interrelated or interdependent, and a seemingly universal right may be biased in favour of a certain sector of society, and may prove non-functional for a less privileged group. Thus, as a principle, one should not assume that learning needs are uniform. Quite the contrary, as pointed out in Jomtien, the scope of varying learning needs should be recognized.

This approach was appropriate for the task of grasping the different modalities of the best interests principle in education, not precluding the complexities involved. During centuries of Egypt's history, several educational systems came into being to serve political goals and group interests. However, contrary to expectations, instead of merging into a unified universal system, plurality survived and continued to serve different interest groups. Contemporary developments have contributed to sustaining the status quo, and thus the plurality of education continues to generate a social divide and to weaken the unity of the social fabric.

Meanwhile, each sub-system seeks to achieve particular goals and interests for its recipients. For instance, although religious teaching is a common denominator in the different schools' curricula, Al Azhar Institutes lean strongly towards religious teaching as a primary goal. This education achieves the interests of those pupils who seek a career in teaching or religious affairs. Graduates may choose further education in Al Azhar colleges for higher education, where these graduates are given priority. There can be a conflict of interests between the graduates of different systems. For example, graduates of the Faculty of Law and Sharia in Al Azhar University have limited access to appointments in Personal Status courts, but are barred from other judicial posts. Private education is an umbrella for a wide spectrum of sub-systems of fee-paying schools which realize the interests of different sectors of society. Arabic private schools provide the mainstream official curriculum to children of middle class families. A better standard of teaching is provided in these schools to prepare students for further higher education, and for a probable career in the civil service.

Private education also includes a wide range of language schools which provide 'privileged' educational opportunities. A wide choice of foreign curricula is available, in addition to modern extra-curricula activities promoting the development of children's abilities. However, within this category of privileged private education, a hierarchy of schools has emerged. Predominant is an élitist system which prepares students for taking 'foreign certificates' examinations, based on foreign curricula. Not all well-off families choose this channel. Two factors influence their choice, the extortionate fee required, sometimes to be paid in foreign currency, and the 'interest' and the status which some seek to achieve by identifying with foreign cultures. A 'privileged world' is opened for these graduates who are prepared to communicate on the international level and to govern and control on the national scene.

The majority of children are channelled into mainstream government education. The system is fraught with complexities: increasing numbers of eligible children, economic constraints and economic adjustment policies, all contributing to serious pressures and the rates of non-enrolment and non-sustainability. Consideration of the issue of affordability has been one-sided: the government cannot provide all the resources needed for education, consequently some fees for 'extra services' are to be shouldered by the family. However, the circumstances of the poor have not yet been given sufficient consideration. That the poorest, if not aided financially, should at least be exempted from school fees, was one of the recommendations of the symposium on the best interests of the child in education.

Another factor is the functionality of the education system. As in the case of the rich, who opt out in favour of private education, those among the poor who make the initial choice of plodding on in mainstream education often find the system non-functional and consequently opt out in favour of early child employment. Thus, in both cases, the family's perception of the system's functionality, and consequently the best interests of the child, would be in conflict with the official policy perception.

It is generally conceded by educationists that the best interests of the child would entail the adoption of a unified system which licenses diversification according to the child's abilities and inclinations, taking account of community needs. A child's interests in education are also dependent on his ability to perform and to sustain this ability throughout the stages of basic education. Comparative research has demonstrated the close correlation between ability and school performance on the one hand, and health and nutrition on the other, revealing a typical instance of the interrelatedness of children's rights.

ANNEX I

Three field studies were undertaken in three governorates: Cairo, Qaliubia and Assiut.

1. The Cairo study was undertaken by Dr. Rasmy Rustum Abdel Malek and a team of researchers. Structured interviews included: ten primary schools headmasters, five preparatory schools headmasters, twenty-five teachers and social workers in primary schools and ten teachers and social workers in elementary schools.
2. The Qaliubia study was undertaken by Prof. Elham Afifi and a team of researchers. The methodology included an anthropological study

using observation and interviews with school personnel. In addition a questionnaire was submitted to mothers (N=100) of children who had dropped out of basic education.
3. The Assiut study was undertaken by Prof. Wasfy Aziz Boulos and a team of researchers in a low-income sector of Assiut. The tools used included:
 – A questionnaire submitted to a sample of heads of school children's families (N=54). The parents' professions included carpenters, clerks, plumbers and other non-skilled labourers. Moreover, thirty-five school officials were interviewed (headmasters, teachers and social workers).

ANNEX II:

Papers Presented in the Workshop on the Best Interests of the Child in Education 18, 19 May 1993.

Mr. Prince Ahmad Radwan Undersecretary Ministry of Education	Basic Education – Goals and Problems
Prof. Wasfy Aziz Boulos Head Faculty of Education Assiut	Views of the Underprivileged on Basic Education (Field Study)
Mr. Said Heikal Director General Ministry of Education	One-class Schools and Community Schools
Prof. Ibrahim El Lakkany Faculty of Education Tanta	Curriculum of Basic Education and its Role in Developing Abilities
Prof. Mohamed Seif El Din Fahmy Faculty of Education Al Azhar	Democratic Education
Mr. Awad Tawfik Professor Center of Education Ministry of Education	Services Delivered in Basic Education
Dr. Rasmy Rustom Assistant Professor Center of Education Ministry of Education	Best Interest of the Child in Basic Education (Field Study)
Dr. Elham Afifi Professor NCSCR	Best Interest of the Child in Education (Case Study)
Dr. Saneya Saleh SRC American University	Schools of the Year 2000 (an experiment in Basic Education)

ANNEX III:

Growth Rates and External Debt

Year	Growth GDP	Rates % GNI	GDP at current Prices	External Debt	Ratio % Debt/GDP
1970	6.0	5.4	7645	1831	24.0
1975	5.1	4.5	11343	4792	42.2
1980	10.9	11.3	22913	20384	89.0
1985	7.0	4.9	34513	41836	121.2
1986	2.6	−2.3	35847	46041	128.4
1987	2.5	−0.9	35629	50783	142.5
1988	3.9	4.1	30996	52027	167.9
1989	2.4	1.5	33344	51159	153.4
1990	0.5	−0.3	37304	39885	106.9

Source: World Bank: *World Tables 1991.* Values in 000's U.S.$

ANNEX IV:

Statistics of Pre-University Education (1991–92)

Stage	Schools and Department	Classes	Students	Teaching Staff
Pre-School (nurseries)	1196	5673	223051	9162
Primary	15361	150467	6541725	25258
Elementary	5853	84917	3593365	11010
Secondary	1185	16032	571997	4738
Industrial	411	14961	521670	2644
Agricultural	100	3773	132787	716
Commercial	808	12571	455727	2392
Teachers Education	121	804	25335	448
Special Education	234	1485	14428	
One Classroom Schools	338	741	21732	
Total	25615	291424	12,101,817	

Source: Statistics of the Ministry of Education, 1991–92.

ANNEX V:

Per cent Distribution of Employed Children Age (6–14) by Place of Residence, Sex, Type of Economic Activity and Educational Level in 1988

Items	Urban	Rural	Total
Male	69.5	52.1	53.8
Female	30.5	47.9	46.2
Educational Level			
Less than 10	12.2	19.7	18.4
Illiterate	53.4	49.5	49.7
Read and write	20.6	18.3	19.3
Intermediate	13.8	12.5	12.6
Economic Activity			
Agricuulture	26.3	36.5	77.8
Manufacturing	25.3	6.2	8.9
Construction	2.6	4.4	1.6
Trade	23.2	4.2	7.0
Services	22.6	1.7	4.7
Occupation			
Sales	22.1	3.0	6.0
Services	5.3	0.8	1.4
Agriculture	26.3	86.6	77.7
Production	46.3	9.6	14.9
Total	100.0	100.0	100.0
No.(000)	189	1120	1309

Source: CAMPAS, Labor Force Sample Survey 1988.

NOTES

[1] P. Heck, *The Jurisprudence of Interests*, translated by M. Schock, (Harvard University Press, 1948) 31 at 35.

[2] K. Mannheim, *Ideology and Utopia*, translated by L. Wirth and E. Shils (New York: Harvest, 1936) 85 at 87.

[3] M. Ginsberg, *On Justice in Society* (London: Heinemann, 1965).

[4] P. Townsend, *Sociology and Social Policy* (Middlesex: Penguin Education, 1976), 12 at 13.

[5] A. Doron, 'The Welfare State, Issues of Rationing and Allocation of Resources' in S. Spiro and E. Yuchtman-Yaar (eds), *Evaluating the Welfare State* (Jerusalem: The Academic Press, 1983).

[6] T. Van Boven, 'Distinguishing Criteria of Human Rights' in K. Vasak and P. Alston (eds), *The International Dimensions of Human Rights* (Connecticut: Greenwood Press, 1982), 49.

[7] N. B. Tarrow, *Human Rights and Education* (New York: Pergamon Press, 1987), 4.

[8] M. Khafagy and I. Hafiz, *Shedding Light on the History of Education in the United Arab Republic* (published in Arabic; Cairo: The Ministry of Education, 1963), 10 at 15.

[9] The Kottabs provided informal teaching, basically religious teaching, reading and writing, nowadays mostly in villages: M. K. Harby and E. M. Al-Azawy, *The Development of Education in Egypt during the Twentieth Century* (published in Arabic; Cairo: The Ministry of Education, 1958), 9.

[10] Khafagy et al, op cit, 96.

[11] Ibid.

[12] Due to limited resources after the 1967 war, a school nutrition programme was stopped and its budget was transferred to the upkeep of schools: S. Nessim, Equal Educational Opportunities During the Period 1952–1980, in A. Azer (ed), *Equal Opportunity in Education Policy in Egypt* (Published in Arabic; Cairo: The National Center for Social and Criminological Research, 1991), 71.

[13] S. Badran, *The Making of the Mind* (published in Arabic; Cairo: Al Ahaly, 1993), 165.

[14] Central Agency for Public Mobilization and Statistics (CAPMAS), *Statistical Yearbook* (Cairo: CAPMAS, 1991).

[15] UNDP, Human Development Report (Oxford: Oxford University Press, 1992).

[16] Ibid.

[17] M. Imam, 'The National Context' – paper presented in the Situation Analysis of Children in Egypt (Cairo: UNICEF, 1992, unpublished).

[18] UNDP, op cit.

[19] Ibid.

[20] World Bank, 'Poverty Alleviation and Economic Adjustment in Egypt' (executive summary in Arabic, No 8515, 1990, unpublished).

[21] Imam, op cit.

[22] National Specialized Council (NSC), Report No 74 on Al Azhar Schools (published in Arabic; Cairo: NSC, 1990), 60 at 66.

[23] P. A. Radwan, 'Basic Education in Egypt – The Present Situation and the Future', Paper presented in the Symposium on the Best Interests of the Child in Basic Education. UNICEF, Cairo, 1993 (unpublished).

[24] R. M. Unger, Law in Modern Society – Towards a Criticism of Social Theory (London: The Free Press, Macmillan, 1976), 194.

[25] The Supreme Administrative Court, Case No 161, 29 June 1957, A. S. Abu Shady and N. Attia (eds), The Collection of Principles Issued by the Supreme Administrative Court (published in Arabic; Cairo: Al Nahda, 1960).

[26] The Constitutional Court, Case No 3, 6 March 1971, in the Collection of Principles Issued by the Constitutional Court (published in Arabic, Cairo, Matbaa Amirya, 1976).

[27] A. F. Sorour, Strategy for Developing Education in Egypt (published in Arabic, Cairo, Ministry of Education, 1987), 41 at 42.

[28] M. S. Fahmi, 'Democratic Education', Paper in the Symposium on the Best Interests of the Child, op cit.

[29] S. Parker, 'The Best Interest of the Child: Some Theoretical Considerations', at 26 in this volume.

[30] Jomtien Declaration on Education for All and Framework for Action to meet Basic Learning Needs (New York, UNICEF House, 1990).

[31] High Council of Education, in the National Specialized Councils (NSC) Report No 103, Vol 6 (Cairo, NSC, 1974), 451.

[32] Nessim, op cit, 71.

[33] High Council of Education, in the National Specialized Council's Report No 74 (Cairo, NSC, 1990) 53 at 60.

[34] Ibid.

[35] Jomtien Declaration, op cit.

[36] UNICEF, First Call for Children – World Declaration and Plan of Action from the World Summit for Children (New York, UNICEF, 1990).

[37] Jomtien Declaration, op cit.

[38] Radwan, Paper in the Symposium on the Best Interests of the Child, op cit.

[39] Ministry of Education (MOE), Mubarak and Education (published in Arabic, Cairo, 1992).

[40] Radwan, op. cit.

[41] E. Afifi, 'Basic Education – The Philosophy and Application, A Field Study', Paper in the Symposium on the Best Interests of the Child, op cit.

[42] MOE, op. cit.

[43] Ibid.

[44] Afifi, op cit.

[45] R. Abdel Malek, 'The Rights of the Egyptian Child in the Basic Education System: The Law and the Implementation – A Field Study', Paper in the Symposium on the Best Interests of the Child, op cit.

[46] Afifi, op cit.

[47] A. Tawfik, 'Services Delivered in Basic Education', Paper in the Symposium on the Best Interests of the Child, op cit.

[48] Discussions of the participants in the Symposium on the Best Interests of the Child, op cit.

[49] A. Azer and N. Ramzy, Child Labor in Egypt – A Field Study, the National Center for Social and Criminological Research (in Arabic, Cairo, UNICEF, 1991) 41.

[50] National Council for Education (NCE), Report on the Reform of Primary Education (published in Arabic, Cairo, MOE, 1979).

[51] M. El Baradei, 'The Effect of Economic Adjustment Programs on Equal Educational Opportunities in Egypt', Paper presented in the Conference on the Effects of Economic Adjustment on Justice in Distribution, Faculty of Economics, Cairo University, 1992 (unpublished).

[52] Fieldwork findings in the research areas.

[53] Findings of the fieldwork in Shubra El-Kheima.

[54] Abdel Malek, op cit.

[55] Afifi, op cit.

[56] A. Azer and E. Afifi, *Social Support Systems for the Aged in Egypt* (Tokyo, The United Nations University, 1992).

[57] Interview in Shubra El-Kheima.

[58] Akhbar Al Yom Newspaper, 12 June 1993.

[59] Discussions in the Symposium on the Best Interests of the Child.

[60] The National Center for Education and Development (NCED) Symposium on Egypt's Problems and the Role of Education (Cairo, NCED, 1987).

[61] Nessim op cit, 47 at 53.

[62] S. Badran, 'Education and Dependency in Egypt', Article in *Al Tarbya Al Moasera* (Periodical) (Cairo, Dar Al Isha'a Lil Tibaa, 1985), 23.

[63] T. Hussein, *The Future of Culture* (published in Arabic, Beirut, Dar Al Ketab Al Lebnani, 1973), 115, 203.

[64] S. Saleh, 'Schools of the Year 2000 – An Experiment in Basic Education', Paper in the Symposium on the Best Interests of the Child, op cit.

[65] Z. N. Mahmoud, *Renovating Arab Thought* (published in Arabic, Cairo, Dar El Sherouk, 1978), 234 at 251.

[66] A. Gindy, 'Children's Needs in the Different Stages of Development and the Priority Needs in Each Case', Paper presented in the Conference on the Future United Nations Convention on the Rights of the Child (Cairo, UNICEF, 1988), 75 at 77.

[67] Discussions in the Symposium on the Best Interests of the Child, op cit.

[68] Technical Office of the MOE, *Education Policy in Egypt* (published in Arabic, Cairo, MOE, 1985), 4.

[69] National Council for Education, op cit.

[70] S. Saad, 'Dropping Out of Basic Education', Paper in the Symposium on Child Labour, The National Center for Social and Criminological Research, Cairo 1986 (unpublished).

[71] Ministry of Education, 'Child Labor', Paper presented to the Ministerial Committee set up to study the phenomenon of child labour, the National Center for Social and Criminological Research, Cairo, 1988 (unpublished).

[72] Azer and Ramzy, op cit, 39.

[73] National Center for Social and Criminological Research, Symposium on Child Labour, op cit.

[74] Unger, op cit, 246.

[75] Unger, op cit, 258.

[76] C. Van Nieuwenhuijze, M. Al-Khatib and A. Azer, *The Poor Man's Model of Development* (Leiden, Brill, 1985), 132 at 139.

[77] Azer and Ramzy, op cit, 39.

[78] Ibid.

[79] Boulos, Paper presented in the Symposium on the Best Interests of the Child, op cit.

[80] International Institute for Educational Planning, Seminar on Planning Education for Reducing Inequalities (Paris, UNESCO Press, 1981).

[81] UNESCO, *Final Report of the International Consultative Forum on Education for All* (Paris, UNESCO, 1991), 12.

[82] Findings of the Fieldwork in Shubra El-Kheima.

[83] Azer and Ramzy, op cit, 42 at 46.

[84] Ibid.

[85] MOE, op cit.

[86] M. S. Helkat, 'One-Class Schools and Community Schools', Paper in the Symposium on the Best Interests of the Child, op cit.

[87] Ibid.

[88] Ibid.

[89] Jomtien Declaration, op cit.

THE BEST INTERESTS PRINCIPLE IN FRENCH LAW AND PRACTICE

JACQUELINE RUBELLIN-DEVICHI*

In all actions concerning children, whether undertaken by public or private social welfare institutions, courts of law, administrative authorities or legislative bodies, the best interests of the child shall be a primary consideration.

Convention on the Rights of the Child, art 3, para. 1.

L'intérêt de l'enfant, c'est la notion magique. Elle a beau être dans la loi, ce qui n'y est pas, c'est l'abus qu'on en fait aujourd'hui. A la limite, elle finirait par rendre superflues toutes les institutions de droit familial. Pourtant, rien de plus fuyant, de plus propre à favoriser l'arbitraire judiciaire.

Jean Carbonnier[1]

ABSTRACT

This article examines the history of the principle of the best interests of the child in French law. The author explains that, although its nature changed over time, it has been a pervasive influence in French law from the early nineteenth century. In keeping with its traditional championing of human rights, France enthusiastically embraced the UN Convention on the Rights of the Child, but it is wrong to think that this introduced radical change into French law. Nevertheless, the 'best interests' principle, as proclaimed in the Convention, has been appealed to by a number of persons with influence in the legal process with regard to changes in the law regarding parentage and parental authority. The author concludes that the most significant effect which the Convention is likely to have in French legal practice will be to enhance the child's right to be heard, especially in legal proceedings. However, the French courts have been ambivalent in the degree to which they have been prepared to treat the Convention as directly applicable in French law, and the author believes France may be at risk of censure before the European Court of Human Rights.

I. INTRODUCTION

France, which claims to be the country of human rights *par excellence*, was one of the first countries to sign, ratify and implement the UN Convention on the Rights of the Child.[2] The media,[3] as well as a number of public and private institutions, immediately voiced their opinions

* Centre de Droit de la Famille, Université Jean Moulin, 1 rue de l'Université BP 638 69239, Lyon Cedex 02, France.

regarding the Convention, its import, and the extent of its application.[4] To non-jurists, the Convention appeared extremely innovative since it provided the child with what he or she had always lacked – rights; and, most importantly, the right no longer to be treated as an object, but as a subject whose best interests would at last be taken into account. However, this is in two respects a misconception.

First, the child is a subject in law; he or she has judicial existence from birth and even from the moment of conception. Second, the child's best interests have long been present in codified law and in case-law. The enthusiastic reception which the Convention received has given somewhat mythical proportions to the concept of the child's best interests and one might fear that, paradoxically, French law, going beyond the Convention, is so preoccupied with the child's best interests that it runs the risk of conjuring away the child's rights.

In this article, I will examine on the one hand analyses of the child's best interests prior to the adoption of the Convention and, on the other, the way in which French law has reacted to the principle of the child's best interests as expressed in the text of the Convention.

II.   THE CHILD'S BEST INTERESTS IN FRENCH LAW PRIOR TO THE ADOPTION OF THE CONVENTION.

(a) The Appearance of the Principle of the Child's Best Interests in French Law.

In France, as in many countries, family policy and legislation have long been centred on the child's best interests, which have rightly been described as 'a general principle in law'.[5] It is no doubt true that the child's best interests have never been absent from the legislature's preoccupations but it was originally the best interests of childhood rather than of the child as such, perceived as serving the general interests of society, which inspired nineteenth century laws to protect children in the areas of child labour, apprenticeship contracts, control of wet-nurses and also compulsory schooling.[6] Historians see the emergence of the best interests of the child considered as an individual as having occurred in the nineteenth century.[7] The law of 24 July 1889 allowing courts to deprive a father of his paternal power (déchéance de puissance paternelle) is unanimously interpreted as being less a sanction against the parent than as a measure taken to protect the child. Taking into account the best interests of the minor meant that he or she should be educated rather than punished, and this led to the creation of specialized institutions[8] well before the adoption by juvenile criminal law, in the ordonnance of 2 February 1945, of the same fundamental principle.[9]

The best interests of the child are also at the foundation of educative assistance. If the health, safety or morality of a minor are in danger, reference to a judge responsible for children (*juge des enfants*) can be made. This judge has been accurately described by Professor Malaurie as a 'magistrate guardian whose powers are practically discretionary, dejuridicized and delegalized'.[10] One may also underline the growing intervention of the state in family law,[11] but note that the state now intervenes to compensate for inadequate solidarity within the family and to ensure that the family or welfare agencies work in the child's best interests rather than to act as the upholder of public order.[12]

It is in civil law that the child's best interests were first and most clearly taken into consideration. The Code of 1804 enshrined paternal power as an apparently discretionary prerogative entrusted to the father,[13] but commentators considered that paternal power was to be understood as being in the best interests of the child, which the father could use as he saw fit.[14] Demolombe, one of the most famous commentators on the Civil Code, having affirmed that paternal power was established neither in the father's best interests, as in the earlier law in Southern France (*le droit romain*), nor in the best interests of the children, as in the earlier law of Northern France (*le droit coutumier*), concluded that it had been established in the best interests of all concerned: 'principally in the best interests of the children, no doubt, since their weakness requires protection and their inexperience requires guidance; in the best interests of the father and the mother, since for them it is not merely a duty, but also a right to bring up their children . . .; lastly, in the best interests of the state itself, since the healthy functioning of the family is the first and most important guarantee of the healthy functioning of society . . .'.[15]

As far as divorce is concerned, the Napoleonic Code expressly sought to promote, if not the best interests of children, at least their advantage, by providing a beneficial exception to the rule which it formulated in article 302: 'Children will be entrusted to the spouse who has obtained the divorce, unless the court, at the request of the family or the Imperial Director of Prosecutions, orders, to the best advantage of the children, that all or some of them shall be entrusted to the care either of the other spouse, or of a third party'. Case-law quickly applied the text broadly, the *Cour de cassation* considering that the courts had discretionary powers in this area, which they used to give priority to the child's best interests even by entrusting guardianship to the guilty spouse without this having been sought by the family or the Director.[16]

In the period immediately following the Second World War – roughly in the period when the United Nations Organisation was working on the Declaration of the Rights of the Child, proclaimed on 20 November 1959 – the child's best interests came to be seen as the most important factor in all legislation. In the eighth edition of his Civil law manual, Dean Carbonnier wrote that family law had become 'pedocentric' and that the notion of the best interests of the 'minor' child was treated as a magic formula. 'It is a question of particular interests, specific to the child as a young person, sometimes described as his or her educational interests . . . The child is not able to appreciate his or her own interests on his or her own and on top of that, it is not his or her interest at the present moment, but at some later date, his or her interest as an adult at some undetermined future moment'.[17]

While many commentators tried to define the child's best interests more precisely,[18] courts emphasized the idea that paternal power was more the recognition of a function than of a right, since it was a right which should be exercised in the best interests of the child. Two decisions, famous perhaps because of their commentator, are always cited, but they are only examples of an abundant case-law. The first is a judgment of the *Cour de Paris* of 30 April 1959[19] which gave visitation rights to a child's godparents where the parents objected, taking, in the judges' view, 'a narrow and improper conception of parental authority'. The judgment affirms that 'it is traditionally accepted that the various rights of parents as far as their children and their children's property are concerned are entrusted to them by law not in their own personal interests, but in the best interests of the child and to the extent to which they are necessary for the accomplishment of the duties which the parents have assumed . . . paternal power, a power for protection finds in such a definition its justification and its limits'.

The second judgment, by the *Tribunal de Versailles* on 24 September 1962,[20] in the area of educative assistance, was in a case where parents wished to force upon their child the practices of the Protestant church, and affirmed 'that paternal power is not an absolute, discretionary right; that it should above all be exercised in the best interests of the child and have as its aim to ensure the harmonious development of the personality; that no essential attribute of the child should, in the case of conflict, be outside the control of the judge, the latter having the competence to decide what are the best interests of the minor'.

So, before the law of 4 June 1970, which abandoned the expression 'paternal power' in favour of the expression 'parental authority' (*autorité parentale*), case-law had already adopted a definition similar to that now provided in article 371–2: 'Authority belongs to the father and to the mother to protect the child in its safety, health and morality. They have the right and duty to look after, supervize and educate their child'.

(b) References to the Child's Best Interests in French Law

Even before the Convention on the Rights of the Child was signed, French law openly included numerous references to the child's best interests. For example, in the case of the adoption or legitimation of a child by court order,[24] the court pronounces the adoption or legitimation only if it considers it to be justified in the child's interests, even if the necessary conditions are fulfilled (articles 353 and 333–3).

It is of course in the area of the exercise of parental authority when parents are separated that the question of the child's best interests is most urgent. The position of French law in this matter, and in particular, recent changes in the law, is fully explored later in connection with the law of 8 January 1993.

French commentators have frequently wondered how to evaluate the best interests of the child. Dean Carbonnier, observing that it was even more difficult to define children's interests than those of an adult, who can express what he or she takes to be his or her best interests, accurately remarked: 'What, then, should be done? The presumption upon which law continues to work generally is not so stupid: that the child's best interests coincide with those of the parents; and that the parents will decide on the matter. However, the presumption can only be effective if the family holds together. If not, it is for the judges to evaluate from the outside where the best interests of the child lie. And one can anticipate that they will take as their criteria the precepts of current educational thinking'.[25]

The attribution of parental authority on divorce, which is carried out with express reference to the child's best interests,[26] has provoked much criticism. According to Professor Malaurie,[27] article 290 of the Civil Code provides three indicators of the 'relatively mysterious' best interests of the child. 'The judge takes into consideration: 1° Agreements made between spouses; 2° Information which has been gathered during the social investigation and counter-investigation laid down by article 287-1; 3° The feelings expressed by minors . . .'. Everything relevant has been said about the way in which judges interpret these best interests,[28] about the way in which social workers carry out their enquiries or ascertain the feelings of children, and about the constraints imposed by the '*Droit du Savoir*' and the practices of 'psy' experts.[29] It would seem more important to underline the quality of the the social workers' expression of the opinions of the children, which has led the *Cour de Cassation* to rule that the requirement that the child should be heard is fulfilled even if the judge himself has not heard him or her, but rather that the child has been heard in the course of a social investigation,[30] and to recall that commentators unanimously recognize that in the 80 per cent of custody cases where parental authority is jointly exercised and residence of the child is granted to the mother, this is more because fathers do not dare to seek the child's residence or do not know that they can do so.[31]

Clearly, recourse to the child's best interests is sometimes a convenient pretext for the judge to disregard a legal rule, even if this is carried out in good faith.[32] I have argued elsewhere[33] that the best interests standard should only be applied when there is no other applicable rule: the criterion of the child's best interests is above all a legal right. But Dean Carbonnier writes: 'To decide the child's best interests is a [diffi-

cult] question of fact, which should, for this reason, be determined only
by the trial judge,[34] and he classifies this 'notion cadre' (a sort of conceptual framework) as a 'notion à contenu variable'.[35]

No one would deny that the best interests of the child constitute a
worthy policy aim. Nevertheless, if the child has rights, or if it is possible
to empower him or her with rights, it is important to avoid 'judicial
paternalism', and taking decisions away from children. This observation
applies as much to parents who tend not to notice that their children
grow up, as to judges who are generally more accustomed to applying
specific principles of law than to determining what the best solution
might be, and who often lack the objectivity necessary to realize that
their decisions are influenced by their own background and who thus
apply their own personal criteria when making a decision.

The best way to summarize the situation on the eve of the Convention
on the Rights of the Child is to cite Professor Hauser's commentary,
which shows both realism and a sense of humour: 'The idea of the "best
interests of the child" was constantly invoked by the generations of the
sixties and seventies, but the best interests of the child, even after the
age of eighteen, were always decided by other people, by the father, the
mother, judges, lawyers, and so on, but never by the child himself or
herself'.[36] Even if French law has long used the notion of the best interests of the child, the principle did not have quite the same meaning as
that which it possesses in article 3 of the Convention. The report on the
application of the Convention made to the Committee on the Rights of
Children by the French government in virtue of article 44 of the Convention, which mentions 'anticipatory measures' taken by France in the
two or three years prior to the Convention, does not take into account
that this referred to the best interests of the child as evaluated by persons
other than the child himself or herself, despite the fact that the child
was at the centre of the measures concerned.

It is nevertheless true that the French child has not been endowed
with superrights[37] by the Convention, as suggested in the report of the
non-governmental organizations,[38] which claims that the best interests
of the child 'must systematically have priority over those of adults or of
society, over economic or cultural considerations'. We shall see that one
of the Convention's merits, with respect to French law, was to accord
the child, alongside the rights that he/she possesses from birth, some
rights which will not come into full effect until he or she comes of age,
and some specific rights, which he or she can exercise alone. Without
question, what was most lacking in the French system was the right to
be heard. This right indeed encountered much resistance and has not
yet been fully incorporated into national law. With his customary fore-
sight, Dean Carbonnier affirmed: 'It is clear that the many freedoms
that it [the Convention] attributes to minors will not be born in a

vacuum and that they can only be created by cutting into the authority of fathers and mothers'.[39]

III.   FRENCH LAW AND THE PRINCIPLE OF THE BEST
INTERESTS OF THE CHILD IN THE WAKE OF THE
CONVENTION

(a) The Reception of the Convention on the Rights of the Child by the French Authorities

France actively prepared for the introduction of the Convention, but the results do not seem the match the efforts then undertaken. On 29 August 1988, the Prime Minister asked the *Section du rapport et des études du Conseil d'Etat* for a 'Report on the adaptation to the evolution of our society of the rules and principles of our family law as well as of our child protection system', considering that '1989 was heralded as the International Year of the Child and would be the year when an International Convention on Children's Rights would be considered'. This report, entitled *'The protection of children and their status'* was published by La Documentation française in February 1991. The *Haut Conseil de la population et de la famille* was also asked to examine the Convention's impact on the future of the family.[40] In March 1990, this same organisation gave its opinion on the introduction of the Convention in French law.

The important report on bio-ethics, ordered by the Prime Minister to assess the current situation and define the direction of public policy,[41] takes into account the Convention and refers to it every time the question of the child's rights or best interests is raised. Another report regarding the application of the Convention was ordered by the former Secretary of Family Affairs, of the Elderly, and of the Repatriated. This report was published recently by La Documentation française. Its title, *'Affirming and Promoting the Rights of the Child after the International Convention on the Rights of the Child'*,[42] is indicative of the underlying political will. A further informational report on the rights of the child, prepared by Madame Cacheux, a deputy, was published by the Law Commission of the *Assemblée Nationale* in November 1989.[43]

In addition to the official reports described above, a great number of conferences (academic and otherwise), often multi-disciplinary, were held in France concerning the significance and application of the Convention.[44] Moreover, several academics have written articles on the subject.[45] The *Institut international des droits d'expression française* devoted its 22nd annual conference in Montreal in October 1992 to the national and international protection of children. The application of the Convention in the respective countries was the focus of discussion.[46]

In France, which considers itself the champion of children's rights, after having been that of human rights, the political will was clear: on 10 June 1989, the President announced, at a conference sponsored by the National Association of Family Associations (UNAF): 'It is my hope that France will be one of the first signatories [of the Convention] and that the implementing legislation will be passed quickly. It is often difficult to adapt internal law, which represents all of our traditions and ways of thinking – to a new international law. Nevertheless, we must do so. It is imperative that we reconsider the legal status of the child. Children must be respected in their own right. Whoever loves freedom, whoever dreams of it, whoever wishes to see it spread throughout the entire planet knows well that such a phenomenon begins with the clear conception that the child is a person who must not be deformed and submitted to what other individuals or collective bodies would like to impose upon him or her'. Similarly, at the world summit on children which took place on 29 and 30 September 1990, the Prime Minister, referring to the Convention, declared that: 'My country signed and ratified it without the slightest hesitation, and our presence bears witness to our common will to apply it fully. But the meaning of this Summit, France's solemn mission is that we must go further, we must reinforce international cooperation in favour of the child. Children, all children, ours as well as those of others, have rights to which we are bound and which we must constantly affirm and defend'.[47] The various ministries have also taken great pains to inform both specialists and the public at large,[48] and our legislators have flooded the ministries with questions concerning the application of the Convention.[49] A draft law to designate 20 November the National Day of the Rights of the Child has been proposed.[50]

The Convention has of course been strongly criticized, but by non-lawyers for the most part: the philosopher, Alain Finkielkraut, was amongst those who expressed disapproval of the fact that the Convention treats the child as an adult, thus not protecting children from those who might manipulate them.[51] Many others criticized the Convention for 'reducing parental responsibility even more, as though the child had all the rights and the parents all the duties'.[52] Finally, there were those who insisted on the weakness of our current law on the subject when compared with the lofty principles reflected in the Convention.

Apart from the fact that this last accusation is misconceived (whatever the government in power, family policy in France regarding children has always been very active), it is incorrect to claim that the protection of children is incompatible with the recognition of genuine rights, or that privileging the role of the family with respect to the child's upbringing is irreconcilable with acknowledging that certain rights may exist even against the will of the family.[53] Article 3, paragraph 2 of the Convention illustrates perfectly that reconciliation is not only possible, but considered highly desirable: 'States parties to the Convention undertake to ensure that the child is afforded such protection and care as is necessary for his or her well-being, taking into account the rights and duties of his or her parents, legal guardians, or other individuals legally responsible for him or her, and, to this end, shall take all appropriate legislative and administrative measures'. If it is true that, in accordance with a widely-held view and in keeping with the need to grant children rights and thus responsibilities, we must preserve their right to be children, this simply means that we must find the appropriate balance between the rights which the child possesses and the protection to which, as a bio-dependant being, he or she is entitled.[54]

(b) The French Legislature and the Convention on the Rights of the Child

The legislature was well aware of the need to pass implementing legislation quickly so as to avoid the humiliation of a moral sanction, and even a possible legal sanction by the European Court of Human Rights on the basis of a violation of the child's human rights. The Government's sense of urgency was demonstrated by the proposal of five draft laws, the first two of which, concerning inheritance rights and parentage rights,[55] were proposed to the *Assemblée nationale* on 23 December 1991. The three others were proposed on 25 March 1992.[56] These were motivated by an alleged necessity to 'close a gap in our law', and to affirm the existence of 'biological rights' in addition to 'civil rights' and 'welfare rights', to complete, in the words of the Minister of Justice in a speech given on 23 December 1991 at the National Conference on Ethics, the 'trilogy of fundamental rights'.

The need for legislation to ensure free and informed consent, to protect the genetic materials of human beings from the abuse of medical or biological techniques, and to ensure the respect of the human body, was created by major scientific advances in the areas of assisted procreation and organ transfers. As regards parentage rights, notably the parentage of the child born as a result of medically assisted procreation techniques, it is clear that, although the Convention on the Rights of the Child was invoked to support the establishment of certain limits, the Convention had in fact very little to do with the matter. It is, however, disturbing that the right to know the biological truth of parentage by genetic fingerprinting should only be allowed by bringing judicial proceedings, a provision introduced in the draft law on bioethics on the basis of a somewhat surprising consensus manifested by such institutions as the Order of Physicians, the *Conseil d'État* and the National Ethics Committee. This provision is both ineffective (it would be easy to send samples to laboratories in other countries), and incompatible with a sensible judicial policy (a law which forbids the seeking of evidence is difficult to justify).

Moreover it is contrary to article 3 of the Convention on the Rights of the Child.

In any event, these draft laws have not yet been presented to the *Assemblée Nationale*, which is fortunate since the provisions concerning the parentage of a child born pursuant to an assisted procreation are, in my opinion, poorly drafted. They unnecessarily modify parentage law, which is based on biological reality.[57] As for the first two draft laws, they were initially to have been voted upon in Spring 1992, but there were more urgent matters, notably the votes on the Maastricht treaty on Europe and on the new *Code pénal*. For this reason, the Government, steadfast in its desire to pass at least one of the draft laws, worked with great single-mindedness to accomplish its goals. To this end, it temporarily sidelined draft law 2530, despite the fact that it was already in its final form[58] and submitted draft law 2531, which had more media appeal, dealing as it did essentially with parentage rights,[59] as well as creating a family judge, the *juge aux affaires familiales*.

After public debates, the *Assemblée Nationale* voted in favour of the bill in May 1992. The version passed by the *Assemblée Nationale* included amendments which, thanks to the report prepared by Deputy Denise Cacheux for the Law Commission of the Assemblée Nationale, improved the text with regard to the anonymity of the birth-mother, step-parent adoption, parental responsibility and the right of the child to be heard in judicial proceedings. The bill was thus entitled 'draft law amending the Civil Code with regard to the family and to children's rights, and creating the family judge'. After the report prepared by Senator Luc Dejoie for the Senate Law Commission, the Senate passed the bill at first reading, in December 1992. That same month, the bill went to a second reading in both Chambers. There was a subsequent Senate/Assembly Conference on the draft law (presented by Deputy Denise Cacheux and Senator Luc Dejoie). The bill was finally adopted on 23 December 1992, and promulgated on 8 January 1993.[60]

The law's history reveals that the Convention was often cited, both to support a provision under discussion (for example the right of the child to be heard in judicial proceedings as provided for in article 12 of the Convention) and to argue against certain provisions (for example the right of the child to know his or her parents, as provided for in article 7). But interviews conducted with those I considered to have played the most important role in the creation of the law – both legislators and judges[61] – show a very strong division between those who decide or act on the basis of the Convention, and those who ignore the Convention, with which they are sometimes hardly familiar, but refer directly to the child's best interests. The most astonishing is the attitude of the courts. When called upon to make a decision in a case where the Convention is invoked, they either apply it without difficulty or, on the contrary, resort to surprising arguments to avoid doing so.

(c) The Law of 8 January 1993 and the Convention on the Rights of the Child

It will suffice to mention the most important of the provisions of the law of 8 January 1993 which are more than just technical modifications and which directly concern the best interests of the child as expressed in the Convention.

(i) Maternity outside of marriage is not automatically established under French law, at least in theory, simply by declaring the birth of the child to the mother on the state register. This is no longer a principle of great import, since *possession d'état* (a sort of de facto parentage) is now sufficient to establish biological parentage, especially when the mother allows her name to appear on the birth certificate.[62] It is nevertheless true that the law continues to discriminate between maternity outside of marriage and maternity within marriage (legitimate maternity) – where the maxim *mater semper certa est* is applied. Moreover, after heated parliamentary debates, the new law incorporated, in articles 341 and 341–1 of the Civil Code, the right for the woman to request, upon giving birth, that her identity and her admission to the hospital be kept confidential.[63] The child's right to know and be raised by his or her parents, provided for in article 7 of the Convention, is subject to the important restriction: 'as far as possible'. The right of the child (after coming of age) is in direct conflict with that which the law guarantees the mother, and there does not appear to be any legitimate reason to deny the privilege accorded to the woman, even if one accepts the hypothesis that to do so were in the best interests of the child.

(ii) With respect to paternity outside marriage, judicial establishment of paternity prior to the new law was only possible if the conditions imposed by article 340 of the Civil Code (*cas d'ouverture*) could be met,[64] because the available evidence was always open to doubt. Similarly, a support action (*action à fins de subsides*, which allows a judge to order a man who had intimate relations with the mother and who cannot prove that he is not the father to pay child support), had to be dropped if the defendant established that the mother was promiscuous. The certainties provided by genetic fingerprinting have led the deputies to remove these obstacles, articles 340 and 342–4 seeming to be directly at odds with the best interests of the child, which are to establish his or her biological parentage. Surprisingly, the Senators were reluctant to agree, fearing for 'family tranquillity' and declaring themselves horrified at the prospect of 'exhuming corpses' in order to obtain evidence to establish paternity. The Senators failed to see that the best interests of the child should not be sacrificed for family tranquillity in fact based on a lie.[65]

Eventually, the Sénat/Assemblée conference produced a compromise in accepting the removal of these unnecessary obstacles, but deciding that proof of paternity outside marriage could only be brought if there was sufficient evidence to establish a presumption, or serious indication, of paternity: this limitation, inspired by the fear of scandal, makes little sense, and should not impede the child in his or her quest to establish paternity or to bring a support action.

(iii) The best interests of the child are again taken into consideration by a reform in the area of parental responsibility.[66] The Law Commission of the *Assemblée Nationale* and its representative, Madame Cacheux, invoked the necessity of making the law conform to the Convention[67] to justify the introduction, in the text of the draft reform, of what Monsieur le Haut-Conseiller Massip elegantly calls 'the irresistible ascension of joint parental responsibility'. The debates prior to the vote on the law illustrate perfectly the way in which the legislators intended to apply the Convention in this area. According to Madame Cacheux, the legislature wished to give expression to 'the preoccupation of the UN Convention on the Rights of the Child to retain a parental responsibility shared by both parents in matters concerning the upbringing of their child',[68] but the Senate Law Commission observed that, under current law, the effect of the Malhuret law of 22 July 1987 was that the best interests of the child were already the basis of judicial decision.[69] With respect to divorcing parents, the earlier law allowed the judges discretion, after consulting the parents, to decide whether to confer parental responsibility jointly or on one or the other of the parents, but considered that, as a general principle, the solution chosen by the parents should be accepted.[70] The law of 8 January 1993 simply codified judicial practice, confirming the principle of joint parental responsibility and conferring the choice of the child's habitual residence on the parents; the judge is to intervene only in the absence of agreement by the parents or if such agreement appears to the judge to be contrary to the child's best interests.

As for unmarried families, the 1987 law maintained the principle of conferring sole parental responsibility on the mother, but facilitated access to shared parental responsibility by allowing the two parents to make a joint declaration before a judge (who does not have authority to consider the desirability of this choice) and by leaving to the parents the opportunity to resort to the family court (*juge aux affaires matrimoniales*) in case of disagreement. While maintaining these options, the law of 8 January 1993 extends the concept of shared parental responsibility to the unmarried family, incorporating in the same text, article 372, the principle relating to parental responsibility in both the married and the unmarried family. Under the *Assemblée Nationale* version, the two parents simply had to acknowledge the child as theirs within six months of the birth, which corresponds to the practice of most unmarried couples.[71] This version excluded cases where the father acknowledges his child long after his or her birth, or only when obliged to do so. The Senate, however, reluctant to put unmarried and married families on an identical legal footing, prevailed in its insistence that joint responsibility be conditional upon a double acknowledgement, made within a year of birth, and when the parents are living together.

(iv) Once again, it was the Law Commission of the *Assemblée Nationale* which introduced into the initial draft law, texts designed to enable French law to conform to the Convention by granting the child the right to be heard and represented in legal proceedings with a degree of autonomy. Nevertheless, the final version represents a very timid step towards providing the child direct access to the courts and in this sense it does not fully conform to the Convention, even if the legislature was careful, in the 1993 law, to replicate, almost literally, the terms of article 12.

For several years, children's rights specialists have noted that minors cannot intervene in cases directly affecting them, with the sole exception of *assistance educative* proceedings (for children in danger or in need of special protection), where children could address themselves directly to the children's judge, but in practice had no possibility of being represented by a lawyer. As far as divorce is concerned, and solely in relation to the consequences for the children, the judge had the discretion to consult the children and, since the Malhuret law of 1987, which amended article 290 of the Civil Code, the judge was required to consult children over thirteen years of age, unless he or she provided a specific justification for not doing so.

Two draft laws were proposed in May 1989,[72] and approximately thirty bar associations, some with the help of the Ministry of Justice, initiated specialized training in child advocacy with the goal of providing children with adequate legal representation. Meanwhile, numerous commentators were reflecting upon the situation.[73] Citing the Convention, certain lawyers insisted on the rights of the child to be heard and represented, independently of their parents, especially in the case of divorce. The courts reacted variably to these efforts. Some found that article 290 of the Civil Code adequately protected the child's right to be heard; others, increasingly numerous, allowed the testimony of the child or of his or her representative on the basis of the Convention.[74]

The new law enunciates general principles in articles 388–1 and 388–2 of the Civil Code. A minor capable of forming his or her own judgement may now be heard in all proceedings affecting him or her; a child's request to testify may not be denied without a special justification; a minor has the right to be accompanied by a lawyer or any other person of his or her choosing, and is entitled to legal aid. When the interests of the child appear to be at odds with those of his or her legal representatives, the judge must appoint a *guardian ad litem* to represent the child. Prior to the new law, such representation was only provided for under limited circumstances.[75] A circular from the Ministry of Justice of 3

March 1993[76] observes explicitly that Chapter V of the law introduces into current law the principle of the recognition of the right of the minor to express his or her views established in article 12 of the Convention.

These provisions are satisfactory, and conform to the spirit of the Convention as well as to the letter of article 3. Despite the fears expressed by certain practitioners, they do not appear to me to grant the judge unlimited discretion. Who is better placed than the judge, given his or her function and knowledge of the facts of the case, to make the necessary findings? This represents great progress. A child may now be heard in all proceedings affecting him or her, even in a case concerning a modification of his or her parents' marital property regime, according to the commentators, or in a case concerning termination of a lease for the family dwelling, as the Versailles court of appeal[77] held on 4 December 1992; and especially, in my view, in a case regarding the parentage of a minor.[78] But the legislature did not foresee all of the implications of its ratification of the Convention. In the existing state of French law, as the courts have often noted, minors do not have the power to initiate a law suit. The French, convinced that parents know best what is good for their children, tend to consider that parents are better placed than the children themselves to discern their aspirations, their interests, as well to defend their rights.[79] Nevertheless, denying the child direct access to the legal system is probably contrary to the UN Convention. The guarantee of such a right can be found in article 6 of the European Convention on Human Rights. At the very least we must grant the minor the right to resort to the legal system in conflicts between the child and his or her parents – as is already permitted in several countries.[80] Under present French law, a young person is allowed to initiate proceedings only when he or she is eighteen. It is probable that the courts will soon be faced with arguments based on the Convention on the Rights of the Child in these matters, as the Convention has already been invoked on a number of other points.[81]

(d) Uncertainties in the Courts

There is no doubt that the UN Convention on the Rights of the Child, ratified as an international treaty, has precedence over all other laws, by virtue of article 55 of the French Constitution. Accordingly, the provisions of the Convention supersede conflicting national laws, as do the provisions of the European Convention on Human Rights, which is often invoked before the French courts.[82] Indeed, invoking the European Convention confers an obvious advantage since individual appeal may be made to the European Court. As a human being, the child possesses the rights guaranteed by the European Convention. Discriminatory treatment, denial of direct access to the legal system, and lack of impartiality, to name a few, are prohibited by both Conventions.

Certain judges have even shown excessive zeal in this area. The *juge aux affaires matrimoniales* of Rochefort held, on 27 March 1992,[83] that article 374 of the Civil Code conflicts unnecessarily with the European Convention because it attributes parental responsibility of an illegitimate child to the mother, on the sole basis of her sex. The judge could have held otherwise, as the possibility of considering the child's best interests empowered the judge to adopt the solution which he or she found most appropriate to the situation. In another case, the Court of Appeal of Reims[84] held that the composition of the children's court, presided over by the children's judge who had prepared the case, contravened article 6–1 of the European Convention of Human Rights, which guarantees to all an independent and impartial judge in criminal matters. The decision was overturned by the *Cour de Cassation*[85] on 7 February 1993. That Court was right, in my opinion, to hold that the European Convention was not violated, given that the ordonnance of 2 February 1945, regarding juvenile delinquents, stresses the importance of the educational orientation of the juvenile justice system. Moreover, the presence of two lay judges on the panel, as well as the possibility of appeal, guaranteed the impartiality of the system.

I must also mention an unpublished decision by the trial court of Nîmes, on 21 January 1993, that the halving of the inheritance of an adulterine child when there are legitimate children, conflicts neither with the European Convention nor with the Convention on the Rights of the Child, since such a reduction represents a compromise between two principles of French law, the equality of all children regardless of their parents' marital status and the importance of monogamy. The court held, accordingly, that the reduction in inheritance rights was 'a provision necessary for the protection of the rights of others and of the public order principle of our law'.

On 19 March 1992, the Court of Appeal of Reims (Jurisdata no 47130) held that a minor could not rely on article 12 of the Convention to bring his unmarried parents before the court in an effort to have the judge declare that he reside with his father. On 12 June 1992, the Court of Appeal of Colmar (Jurisdata no 47160) denied a child's request for a lawyer to represent him in his parents' divorce, reasoning that article 12 could not be invoked in the absence of specific implementing legislation. The Court of Appeal of Paris reached the same conclusion (Jurisdata no 22752). The Court of Lyon followed suit on 9 December 1992 (Jurisdata no 48495) on the grounds that the Convention leaves an option to the signatory states parties between a child's direct access to legal proceedings and his or her right to intervene in proceedings. The Montpellier trial court invoked article 18 of the Convention on 24 March 1992 (Jurisdata no 48501) and again on 28 April 1992 (Jurisdata no 48502) to hold that the court was required to receive petitions requesting the joint exercise of parental responsibility.

But in all these cases, the new law of 8 January 1993 made the provisions of the Convention directly applicable. In contrast, the trial court of Dijon[86] cited article 3 of the UN Convention to uphold the adoption of a child from Bangladesh despite that country's prohibition of adoption because 'it is clearly in the best interests of a child who has no biological family to be accorded the status of a legitimate child with respect to those who, in taking him or her in, undertake to give him or her affection and to permit him or her, as best they can, to develop fully his or her personality'.

Two other decisions are worthy of mention. The Court of Appeal of Chambéry, on 20 February 1992 (Jurisdata no 48803), and the Montpellier Court of Appeal, on 5 March 5 1992 (Jurisdata no 34141), refused to apply the Convention. In the first case, the court held that it was not in the child's best interests to award visitation rights to the grandmother. The other court ruled that it was not necessary to hear the testimony of a six-year-old child (who normally would not be capable of expressing his or her own views) to determine whether custody be awarded to the child's maternal grandparents, over the objections of the child's father.

On 27 November 1992,[87] the Court of Appeal of Paris, adopting the arguments of the state's prosecutor, who relied heavily on provisions of the UN Convention, held that article 26 of the Convention obliged the social security system to cover those children over sixteen who have left school, thus superseding the provisions of the Social Security Code (which confines certain beneficiaries to those under sixteen years of age). 'The relevant provisions of the Convention on the Rights of the Child concern only private interests, they do not interfere with international public order nor the relations between States parties; it is thus for the court to interpret both the meaning and the extent of the Convention's provisions'.

The major surprise came in a decision of the first civil chamber of the *Cour de Cassation* on 10 March 1993.[88] The case was brought by an unmarried father who appealed against the trial court's refusal to grant him visiting rights. Although the child in question had been interviewed by both a social worker and a medical expert, the father argued that the judges could not fairly decide the best interests of the child without inviting the child to testify before them. According to the petitioner, the Court of Appeal violated articles 1, 3, 9 and 12 of the Convention by refusing to hear the child. It could perhaps be argued that the last two texts are not directly applicable because they impose obligations upon the contracting States Parties.[89] Article 1, however, simply establishes the age of majority; article 3 states a directly applicable rule: 'In all actions concerning children – the best interests of the child shall be a primary consideration'. The *Cour de Cassation* made no distinction between the articles of the Convention. It simply stated that 'the provisions of the Convention on the Rights of the Child, signed in New York on 26 January 1990, cannot be invoked before the courts, [because] this Convention, which only creates obligations on the part of the States Parties, [is] not directly applicable on the national level'.

Initially, I thought that the Judges of the First civil chamber were simply reacting to a fear that future plaintiffs might continue to ask judges to disregard the law until the provisions of the new Article 388–1 came into force. The *Cour de Cassation* could quite properly have decided that the provisions of the Convention were satisfied, since the young girl in question had adequately expressed her views by way of the social worker investigation.[90] On 2 June 1993, however, an unmarried father, invoking article 8–1 of the Convention, appealed a decision by the court of appeal which had sanctioned the residence of a child with his mother in Mexico, requiring the father to exercise his visitation rights in that country. The *Cour de Cassation* reached the same conclusion. In both cases it could have been shown that the Convention was in fact observed; but the court preferred to assert that it bound only states in relation to one another.

In my view, this broad formulation, which fails to distinguish between different provisions of the Convention, is unsound. By article 2 of the Convention 'The states party to the Convention [undertake to] respect and ensure the *rights* set forth in this Convention to each child within their jurisdiction'. This view has been reinforced by a judgement of the *Conseil d'Etat* of 30 June 1993[91] in which it was assumed that the Convention applied so as to confer rights on individuals.

As far as the *Cour de Cassation* is concerned, if an appeal is brought before the European Court on Human Rights, France runs the risk of being sanctioned because of the decisions of its First civil chamber.[92] After the condemnation of France by the European Court on the issue of transsexualism on 25 March 1992, the *Cour de Cassation* did an abrupt about-turn in a decision in plenary session on 11 December 1992. Is a further condemnation the only way to ensure that the UN Convention on the Rights of the Child is fully applied in the French legal system?

NOTES

[1] Commentary on a decision rendered by the Paris Court of appeal, 10 April 1959, Dalloz 1960, p 673. Dean Carbonnier is one of the most famous French legal scholars.

[2] Signed 26 January 1990 by Minister Edwige Avice; ratification authorized by law No 90–548, 2 July 1990 (Journal Officiel 5 July, 1990), approved by the Assemblée Nationale, 561 votes out of 564, ratification carried out on 7 August 1990 (publication by the Decree of 8 October 1990 (Journal Officiel 12 October 1990). It must be emphasized that France was amongst the earliest signatories, about the twentieth. As of April 20 1993, there were 134 States-Parties, and 24 States which had signed the Convention but which were not yet party to it (Source: *Défense des enfants International*).

[3] See especially *Le Monde*, 22 November 1989, which includes an interview with Madame H. Dorlhac de Borne, Secretary of Family Affairs, and J. -P. Rosenczveig, director of the Institut de

276 JACQUELINE RUBELLIN-DEVICHI

l'Enfance et de la famille, F. Rousseau-Lenoir, general Secretary of the Fédération internationale des Droits de l'Homme, A.-A. Giscard d'Estaing, Président of the Fondation pour l'Enfance.

[4] The Institut de l'enfance et de la famille (IDEF), then under the direction of Judge J. P. Rosenczveig, published a special issue of their journal, the *Lettre de l'IDEF* (November 1989), organized a symposium entitled Les Messagers de la Convention, produced a pamphlet, coordinated the group of sixty-four associations and French affiliates of non-governmental organizations which presented Madame Dorlhac de Borne, then Secretary of State, with a report entitled '73 idees pour l'application en France de la Convention des Nations Unies sur les Droits de l'enfant'. This group has since become the COFRADE, and it holds an annual meeting on the application of the Convention in France. Deputy Denise Cacheux (who in 1993 became director of IDEF, replacing Judge Rosenczveig) presented the Assemblée nationale with a 'Rapport d'information sur les droits de l'enfant', *Journal Officiel*, n° 1013, 1989–1990; the Direction de la Protection judiciaire de la Jeunesse (from Minister of Justice) published a special issue of its journal *Droit de l'Enfance et de la Famille* on the UN Convention of the Rights of the Child (n° 29, 1990–1).

[5] See A. C. Van Gysel, 'L'intérêt de l'enfant, principe général de droit', *Revue générale de droit belge* 1988, 2, 186.

[6] See for example S. Bernigaud, 'La protection administrative et judiciaire de l'enfant. Etude comparative en droit français et québécois', thèse Lyon, 1992.

[7] M. Perrot, 'Sur la notion d'intérêt de l'enfant et son émergence au XIXème siècle'; see also M. Chauvière, 'L'introuvable intérêt de l'enfance', Le droit face aux politiques familiales, 'Evaluation et contrôle de l'intérêt de l'enfant dans et hors de sa famille', symposium in Université de Paris VII, 30 January 1982.

[8] The Duchâtel circular, of 2 December 1840, on, already stated that the child's interests should not be the concern of the judiciary alone.

[9] See also M. -S. Dupont-Bouchat, in *Droit et Intérêt*, Publications des Facultés Universitaires Saint-Louis, 1990, 47; J. Costa-Lascoux, in *De quel droit? De l'intérêt – aux droits de l'enfant*, Cahiers du CRIV, 1988, n° 4, et and on juvenile criminal law before the ordonnance of February 2 1945, J. -F. Renucci, *Enfance délinquante et enfance en danger*, CNRS, 1990, 16 et *seq*, and refs cited.

[10] P. Malaurie, *Cours de droit civil, La famille*, Cujas ed, 1989, n° 789.

[11] P. Malaurie, op cit n° 762.

[12] The law of 6 January 1986 law reveals this well, again citing this definition of the mission of the Aide sociale à l'enfance in Article 40 of the Code de la famille et de l'aide sociale: 'To bring material, psychological, educative support to minors and their family to provide all that is necessary to minors placed in service and to supervize their vocational guidance, in collaboration with their family and their legal representative'.

[13] See H. Fulchiron, Rép. Dalloz, 1992, V° Authorité parentale.

[14] See P. Malaurie, op cit n° 762.

[15] C. Demolombe, Cours de Code Napoléon, (2ème éd, 1861, t. VI, De la puissance paternelle, n° 266).

[16] See decisions list, dating from 1821, in the famous *Traité pratique de droit civil français* by Planiol, Ripert et Rouast, tome II, La Famille, LGDJ 1926, n° 652.

[17] J. Carbonnier, *Droit civil* t 2, La famille, les incapacités, PUF, coll Thémis, 370.

[18] Marc Donnier, D 1959, chr, 179; Y. Leguy, 'L'intérêt personnel de l'enfant et les relations familiales', thèse Rennes, 1974; R. Le Guidec, 'L'intérêt de l'enfant en droit civil français', thèse Rennes 1973.

[19] Paris, 30 avril 1959, D 1960, 1, 673, note J. Carbonnier.

[20] Trib gr Inst Versailles 24 sept 1962, D 1963, 52, note Carbonnier.

[21] Civ. 16 déc 1980, D. 1981, note J. M. But the refusal to consent must first be judged improper.

[22] Civ 6 janvier 1981, D 1981, 495 note P. Raynaud.

[23] Since the 1972 law, not only are actions to contest false acknowledgements by any interested party permitted (Article 339 of the civil code), but also actions by a mother to contest legimate fatherhood (article 318) and actions by any interested party to contest legitimate parentage when the birth certificate is in contradiction with *possession d'état* of the child (article 322 *a contrario*). There can also be a parentage contest where a child has a birth certificate indicating that he or she is legitimate, but his or her father does not treat him or her as his own child and another man acknowledges the child (article 324–9 *a contrario*).

[24] This gives a natural child legitimate status in relation to one or both of his or her parents according to article 333 of the civil code: 'If marriage between the two parents is impossible, the judicial authority may provide legitimate status where the parent applicant has treated the child as his or hers'.

²⁵ J. Carbonnier, Droit civil, prec 370.

²⁶ See R. Bendacha, 'La notion d'intérêt de l'enfant dans la jurisprudence récente relative au divorce', *Mémoire de doctorat en droit de la famille*, Lyon 1992.

²⁷ P. Malaurie, op cit, no 327.

²⁸ See I. Théry's study of 235 dossiers relating to custody procedure after divorce at the *Tribunal* of Paris in 1989, 'La référence à l'intérêt de l'enfant dans la modification du droit de garde après divorce', thèse démographie 3ème cycle 1983, or 'la référence à l'intérêt de l'enfant: usage judiciaire et ambiguïtés, in *Du divorce et des enfants*, Cahier no 111 de l'INED, PUF 1985.

²⁹ See for example M. King et C. Kratz, 'La notion d'intérêt de l'enfant en droit: vecteur de coopération ou d'interférence', *Droit et Société*, no 22 1992.

³⁰ Cass civ 2ème 5 juin 1991, Bull civ II, no 173.

³¹ See for example H. Fulchiron, 'Autorité parentale et parents désunis', CNRS éd, 1985; Rép. Dalloz, Vo Autorité parentale.

³² M.-S. Dupont-Bouchat remarks pertinently: 'It is striking to observe the tenacity in legal discourse of abstract expressions practically devoid of content, for instance the notion of the child's best interests'. ('L'émergence de l'intérêt de l'enfant', in *Le divorce*, Université des femmes, Bruxelles, 1992, 35).

³³ 'Critique de l'idéologie de l'intérêt de l'enfant', in *Le divorce*, Université des femmes, Bruxelles, 1992, 143.

³⁴ *Droit civil*, tome 2, La famille, 14ème éd 1991, 271.

³⁵ J. Carbonnier, 'Les notions à contenu variable dans le droit français de la famille', in *La notion à contenu variable en droit*, Bruxelles, éd., Bruylant, 1984.

³⁶ At the symposium 'Autour de l'enfant', Lyon 6 May 1993.

³⁷ See M. Dovy, 'La convention internationale des droits de l'enfant: l'intérêt de l'enfant français', *Mémoire de DEA de droit de la famille*, 1993.

³⁸ See above, n 4.

³⁹ J. Carbonnier, *Droit civil, Personnalité, Incapacités, Personnes morales*, 1990, 13ème et 17ème éditions, no 124; see also no 109 et no 110.

⁴⁰ Directed by Jacques Commaille, 6–7 avril 1990, La documentation française, 1992.

⁴¹ Noëlle Lenoir with M. Bruno Sturlèse, *Aux frontières de la vie: une éthique biomédicale à la française* (tome 1); *paroles d'éthique* (tome 2), La documentation française, 1991.

⁴² By E. Alfandari, F. Dekeuwer-Defossez, F. Moneger, P. Verdier, P. Y. Verkindt.

⁴³ Report by Mme Cacheux, JO Ass nat. n° 1013, annexe au Procès-Verbal de l'Assemblée Nationale du 16 novembre 1989.

⁴⁴ See for example: 'Les droits de l'enfant, quelle protection demain?', Lierre et Coudrier, May 1991; 'Colloque européen des droits de l'enfant: le social par cÏr' Amiens, Novembre 1991; 'Autorité parentale, responsabilité parentale et protection de l'enfant', Confrontations européennes régionales, éd Chronique sociale, Lyon, Déc 1992; 'Enfance et violences' (2ème partie, Les droits de l'enfant), ed PUL, Lyon 1992; 'Autour de l'enfant', 6 May 1992, Actes Centre de droit de la famille, Lyon; (Autour de l'enfant, 6 May 1993, Actes Centre de droit de la famille, Lyon.

⁴⁵ See for example J. L. Clergerie, 'L'adoption d'une convention internationale sur les droits de l'enfant', *Rev dr public*, 1990, 446; F. Moneger, 'La Convention des Nations-Unies sur les Droits de l'enfant et le droit français de l'enfance', *Rev dr san et soc*, 1990, 276; J. -M. Bret, 'La Convention des Nations-Unies sur les droits de l'enfant: un texte applicable et appliqué en France', Gaz Pal. 1991, 10 déc.; J. Rubellin-Devichi, 'L'apport de la Convention sur les droits de l'enfant dans le droit de l'enfance et de la famille', *Premières journées d'études transdisciplinaires de Rouen*, juin 1991, Actes éd, ANPASE, 1991. See also F. Dekeuwer-Defossez, 'Les Droits de l'enfant', PUF coll. Que sais-je?, 1991, et C. Neirinck, 'Le droit de l'Enfance après la Convention des Nations-Unies', Delmas, 1993, and a thesis by M. Lopato, Lyon, June 1992.

⁴⁶ The questions to which the authors of the reports had to reply were: 'Has your country adopted the new United Nations Convention on the rights of the child? Has the adoption of this text had the effect of modifiing the laws, regulations, or case law of your country in the subject area? See my forthcoming report, in the Acts of the Conference.

⁴⁷ Report on the Convention's application, 2. This report was made in accordance with article 44 of the Convention on the Rights of the Child, to be presented by the government to the Committee for the Rights of the Child, which was formed in accordance with article 43.

⁴⁸ The full text of the Convention, widely diffused by the French UNICEF Committee, is equally the subject of leaflets produced by the Secretary of State for the Family, of which over 600,000 copies were distributed.

[49] Question n° 45 937 of July 22 1991 to Madame Prime Minister 'concerning the consequences of French ratification of the Convention on the Rights of the Child in July 1990: very concrete proposals have indeed been made in fiscal, social and civil legislation. The Deputy wishes to know what measures have already been taken as well as those foreseen for an effective application of the said Convention' (JO Ass Nat 24 Feb. 1992, *Questions et Réponses*, 857).

[50] Recorded at the Assemblée nationale on 8 June (JO Ass Nat. Doc. n° 295).

[51] See for example. *Le Monde*, 9 January 1990; in an article entitled 'La Convention de l'ONU, une potion magique', (I. Théry, *Esprit*, March-April 1992, 5), a sociologist speaks of 'the extraordinary legal confusion which gives this text a character which goes well beyond traditional UN-style compromises'. For an elegant defence of the Convention on a philosophical plane, see A. Boyer, 'L'enfant, être humain, citoyen en herbe', in *Esprit*, forthcoming.

[52] L. Roussel (one of the most important French demographers) in 'L'enfant dans la famille incertaine', (Les droits de l'enfant, quelle protection demain, above n 44, 233). Nevertheless, the preeminence of the role of the parent is clearly emphasized: the Convention stresses the importance of the family in the child's well-being and education (arts 3, 5, 9, 10, 18), and affirms that, accordingly, the State has the obligation to help parents to exercise their parental responsibilities, as well as that of protecting the child against parental shortcomings, voluntary or not (arts 3, 19, 20). According to the accurate formulation of S. Ambry, at the symposium of Rouen, the child is a subject of law, but a subject of law within the family.

[53] French law has long operated under a system that protects minors because they are not legally competent, whilst also according the minor a certain legal autonomy which increases proportionately as the individual approaches the age of eighteen.

[54] And from which, for the most part, he or she benefits in his or her capacity as a human being: see Rubellin-Devichi, 'Les droits de l'enfant et de sa famille dans le droit positif français de 1989', in 'L'enfant et la justice', *Rev de la Sauvegarde de l'enfance et de l'adolescence*, 1990, no 2/3, 152 et s.

[55] Projet no 2530 'modifiant le Code civil et relatif aux héritiers' (draft law no 2530 amending the Civil code and concerning heirs) and Projet no 2531 'modifiant le Code civil, relatif à l'état civil et instituant le juge aux affaires familiales' (amending the Civil Code, on the état-civil and instituting the judge of family affairs).

[56] Projet no 2599 'relatif au corps humain et modifiant le Code civil' (draft law on the human body and amending the Civil Code); Projet no 2600 've à l'informatique, aux fichiers et aux libertés' (draft law on the use of personal and identified data with the object of protecting and improving health and amending law no 78–177 (6 January 1978) in relation to computers, files and civil liberties).

[57] It will prohibit legal action for denial or contesting of paternity if the husband or partner of the mother consented to the AID. But in France, by accepting the action, case law has imposed important damages against a party initiating the action for going back on his word: see Rubellin-Devichi: Procréations assistées et stratégies en matière de filiations', *JCP*. 1991. I. 3505, and ref cited.

[58] Essentially, this draft law abolishes any remaining discrimination against adulterine children, and reforms the rights of the surviving spouse which, under French law, have remained notoriously inadequate.

[59] It is also true that family law specialists considered a reform of law no 72–3 on parentage to be highly desirable. Although this was undoubtely the most elegant, the most harmonious, and the most far-sighted of Carbonnier's laws, it was rendered obsolete both by scientific advances and changed attitudes. The law of parenthood had once again become incoherent (See Hauser et Huet-Weiller, *Traité de droit civil*, vol 1, LGDJ no 448, 206).

[60] See commentaries by J. Rubellin-Devichi, 'Une importante réforme en droit de la famille,' *JCP* 1993. I. 3659; J. Massip, 'Les modifications apportées au droit de la famille par la loi du 8 janvier 1993', *Rép Defrénois 1993*, 609 et Seg; G. Sutton, 'La filiation au fil d'une loi en patchwork', D. 1993, 163; J. Hauser, 'La filiation et la loi du 6 janvier 1993' Papers of the symposium 'Autour de l'enfant', 6 May, 1993, forthcoming.

[61] Luc Dejoie, responsible for the report of the Commission des lois du Senat; Mme Denise Cacheux, responsible for the report of the commission des lois de l'Assemblée Nationale; Mme Catherine Chadelat, chef du Bureau des affaires civiles de la Chancellerie; M. Michel Allaix, chef du Bureau des affaires judiciaires à la direction de la Protection Judiciaire de la Jeunesse; M. Pierre Drai, Premier président de la Cour de cassation; M Jacques Massip, Conseiller-doyen à la Cour de cassation; M. Paul Bouchet, Président de la Commission nationale consultative des droits de l'homme, who presided over one of the working groups of the Section du rapport et des études of the Conseil dEtat; Mme Madeleine Sabatini, Président of the Cour d'appel de Reims and

member of the abovementioned working group; M. Jean-Pierre Rosenczveig, Président of the Tribunal pour enfants of Bobigny, and past president of IDEF; Mme Geneviève Sutton, Vice-Président honoraire of the Tribunal de grande instance of Paris. It must be noted that some members of Parliament have considered themselves inadequately qualified to answer us, even if they have had an important part in the law drafting, because they know the law concerning children intimately, but not the Convention.

[62] See articles 334–8 and 337 of Civil Code.

[63] Previously, this right was only codified in the Code de la famille et de l'Aide sociale. Certain authors deduced from this, wrongly I believe, that the woman was only guaranteed the right to be cared for free of charge: see Rubellin-Devichi, Droits de la mère et droits de l'enfant. Réflexions sur les formes de l'abandon, Rev. trim. dr. civ. 1991, 695.

[64] Article 340 listed particular situations in which proceedings may be commenced: 'Paternity out of wedlock may be judicially declared: 1) in case of abduction or rape when the offence took place during the period of conception; 2) in case of seduction achieved by fraud, abuse of authority, promise of marriage or betrothal; 3) where paternity can be unequivocally established by means of letters or other writing originating from the putative father; 4) where the putative father and the mother have lived, during the period of the conception, in a state of cohabitation, that is to say in stable and continuous relationship, if not actually as a common household; 5) where the putative father has maintained or contributed to the maintenance of the child, as father'.

[65] See for example the report by Senate Law Commission (representative Luc Dejoie) J. O. Doc. Sénat, no 76, 23, 68, 73, 82 et 87.

[66] See also on this point H. Fulchiron, 'Une nouvelle réforme de l'autorité parentale, commentaire de la loi no 93–22 du 8 janvier 1993 à la lumière de l'application de la loi Malhuret', D. 1993, chr, 117

[67] See the intervention of Mme Cacheux in the debates in l'Assemblée nationale, 1291 et seq.

[68] L. Cacheux, JO déb Ass nat 16 May 1992, 1292 et seq.

[69] L. Dejoie, report prec, JO doc Sénat, no 76, 100, and the heated debates provoked by the issue, JO déb Sénat, 9 Dec 1992, 3761.

[70] See 'Rapport pour le Ministère de la justice sur l'exercice en commun de l'autorité parentale, bilan d'application de la loi du 22 juillet 1987', under the direction of H. Fulchiron, Centre de droit de la famille, 1993, 263 et seq.

[71] In 1979, 30 per cent of children were born out of wedlock, France being in this respect in second place amongst countries of the European community: two-thirds of them are acknowledged by their father, very often before the birth. (V. B. Rabin, Economie et Statistiques no 251, February 1992).

[72] 'Proposition tendant à instituer un avocat de l'enfant', JO Ass Nat, n° 666, 1989; 'Proposition tendant à instituer les défenseurs d'enfants', JO Ass. Nat, 1989, n° 762.

[73] See for example Judge Y. Benhamou, 'Réflexions en vue d'une meilleure défense en justice de l'enfant', D. 1993, 103.

[74] See O. Matocq, 'chronique de droit de la famille', JCP 1993. I. 3639 n° 52 and ref cited.

[75] Article 388–1 of the Civil Code states:
'In all proceedings affecting a minor capable of forming his or her views, he or she may, without compromising those provisions providing for him or her to intervene or consent, express those views before the judge or the person designated by the judge for such a purpose.
If the minor asks to be heard, his or her request may not be denied without a specifically justified decision. The minor may be heard alone, or in company of a lawyer or any other person of his or her choosing. If he or she considers that the choice of this representative is not in the minor's interests, the judge may appoint another person.
Testifying does not confer upon the minor the status of party to the proceedings'.
Article 12 of the UN Convention states:
1. States Parties shall assure to the child who is capable of forming his or her views the right to express those views freely in all matters affecting the child, the views of the child being given due weight in accordance with the age and maturity of the child.
2. For this purpose, the child shall in particular be provided the opportunity to be heard in any judicial and administrative proceedings affecting the child, either directly, or through a representative or an appropriate body, in a manner consistent with the procedural rules of national law'.

[76] Circular of 3 March 1993, JO Ass Nat, 24 March 1993, 4551. The decree inforcing the applicatioon of the law of 16 September 1993 raises more questions than it resolves by removing the possibility to contest the refusal to listen the child who wants to be heard.

[77] Cited by par Me O. Matocq, 'La parole de l'enfant en justice', Journée du 6 mai 1993, above.

[78] *Contra*: G. Sutton, above n 60: '. . . Is it in the child's best interests to ask him or her questions relating to the genuine or false nature of the ties which link him or her to his or her legal father or of the paternity of a man who the mother claims to be his or her biological father?' Our reply is affirmative, the child's best interests in this situation being undoubtedly to establish his or her real parentage and to be free from the whims of his or her parents, or of those who claim to be such. In the decision of the *Cour de cassation* of 25 June 1991 (JCP 1992. I. 3593 note Rubellin-Devichi and ref quoted), the husband had his fatherhood reinstated against the will of the mother and of her second husband.

[79] The law of 8 January 1993, requiring the opinion or consent of a minor over 13 before changing his or her Christian name (Article 60 of the Civil Code), or surname (Article 61–3 and 334–2) and before adoption, even if simple adoption (Article 360) is an important step in the right direction.

[80] Under the Children Act 1989, the English courts have heard applications from children who do not wish to return to their family home (See *The Times* 6 and 7 November 1992). It was on the basis of the child's right to have recourse to justice (and not on the basis of the right to divorce from his parents) that in September 1992 Gregory Kingseley (aged twelve) obtained authorization from a Judge in Florida to be adopted by his host family against the will of his parents, and that in August 1992 Kimberley Mays (aged fourteen), substituted accidentally at birth by another baby girl, at the Wauchula County hosppital (Florida) persuaded the Judge to declare that her biological parents no longer had rights over her, given that her psychological father was the man with whom she had lived since birth. In France, it would have been necessary to obtain a placement decision based on assistance educative from the Juge des enfants. The child can request such a decision (Article 375 of the Civil Code) or a decision of the Tribunal de grande instance declaring improper a refusal to consent to adoption (Article 348–6). But such action would only be available to the adopting parents and would presuppose that the biological parents had relinquished interest in the child voluntarily, which clearly did not occur in the Kimberly Mays case.

[81] See Rubellin-Devichi, 'L'état de la personne et les Conventions internationales', symposium in Montpellier, 5 et 6 February 1993, Acts forthcoming, Engels éd.

[82] Not always successfully. On the subject of surrogate mothers' associations, see decisions by the Conseil d'Etat, 22 January 1988 and by the Cour de cassation 22 December 1989 and 31 May 1991; see Rubellin-Devichi, above n 81.

[83] JAM Rochefort, 27 March 1992, *JCP* 1992. II. 21885, note T. Garé ; D. 1993, 174, note Flauss.

[84] Reims, 30 July 1992, *Rev Droit de l'enfance et de la famille*, 1992/2, 180, note Allaix.

[85] Cass crim, 7 February 1993, *JCP* 1993 II. 22141 note M. Allaix.

[86] TGI Dijon, 8 November 1991, Clunet 1992, 367, note E. Loquin.

[87] Paris, 27 November 1992, *Gaz Pal* 15 April 1993, concl Domingo.

[88] Cass civ. 10 March 1993, 'Chronique de droit de la famille', *JCP* 1993, I, 3688, obs J. Rubellin-Devichi ; C. Neirinck et P.-M. Martin, 'Un traité bien maltraité', *JCP* 1993, I. 3677 ; M.-C. Rondeau-Rivier, 'La Convention des Nations-unies devant la Cour de cassation: un traité mis hors jeu', D 1993, 203 et J. Massip, Rép; Defrénois 1993, 852, et D 1993, 361.

[89] See for example M.-T. Meulders-Klein, 'Les droits civils de l'enfant à la lumière de la Convention des Nations-Unies', in *La Convention sur les droits de l'enfant et la Belgique*, Story-Scientia, 1992, 99.

[90] See the position previously taken by the Cour de cassation in its decisions of 18 December 1990, (chronique de droit de la famille, *JCP* 1992. I. 3547, obs. H. Fulchiron) and of 5 June 1991 (Rép. Defrénois 1992, 302, obs Massip).

[91] CE 30 juin 1993, *Journal du droit des Jeunes*, no 129, 33.

[92] At least if the European Convention is violated. If the case decided by the Court of Nîmes on 21 January 1993 is not reversed by the Court of Appeal, and if the Cour de cassation maintains its unbroken line of precedents, France will certainly be censured, as was Belgium in the *Marcks* Judgment of June 1979, and in the *Vermeire* Judgment of 29 November 1991 and Austria in the *Inze* decision of 28 October 1987 (See Rubellin-Devichi above n 82).

THE BEST INTERESTS OF CHILDREN AND CHILDREN'S SCHOOL EXPERIENCE IN JAPAN: THE PARENTS' PERSPECTIVE

SATOSHI MINAMIKATA*

ABSTRACT

This article gives an account of the current Japanese education system, paying particular attention to the oppressive prevalence of examinations which determine the educational careers of children from an early age. The consequence of this system is the widespread subjection of children to intense regimes of study, especially through preparatory and cram schools. Drawing on survey material, the author examines how parents conceptualize the process in terms of the 'best interests' of the children. He argues that the system is a function of a cultural perception that affluence has not truly been attained and an ethos where it is thought attainable through individual effort and sacrifice in a milieu of equal competition, which leads people to adapt their perception of their children's best interests to the social realities of modern Japan.

I. INTRODUCTION

Children in Japan experience a unique childhood as regards education. In order to gain access to what are deemed 'good' schools at all levels (elementary, junior and high school) children are subjected to such intense monitoring and examination pressures that the whole process has been termed by the media 'an examination hell' (*jyuken jigoku*).

A comparative Japanese-US survey by the Yomiuri Shimbun (5 November 1991) showed that Japanese children spend a great deal more time at school than their American counterparts. Japanese children attend school for an average of 240 days a year, compared to 180 days for US children (Kato 1992, 83). Elementary schoolchildren in Japan spend forty-six hours a week studying, compared to the twenty-seven hours spent by US children. These include eight hours a week (for Japanese children) and two hours a week (for US children) of study outside school. As for high school students, those in Japan devote sixty-one hours a week to study, whilst US high schoolers study only thirty

* Faculty of Law, Niigata University, 8050 Ikarashi 2-nocho, Niigata 950–21, Japan.

hours a week. Japanese children spend nineteen of these hours studying outside school, compared to four hours by US children.

A survey by Somucho (1993: 54–55) revealed that 51.6 per cent of children between eleven and fifteen attend cram schools, that 24.3 per cent of elementary and junior high school students spend between two and three hours a week at cram schools (with 6.3 per cent spending more than ten hours a week in this way). Other research has shown that the average sleeping time for elementary school children went down from 9.23 hours in 1970 to 9.03 in 1990, while the average time spent studying increased from 7.03 hours to 7.19 hours (Keizaikikakucho 1992: 109). However, there are regional and class variations regarding the extent to which parents wish their children to attend university, which would affect these figures. Somucho (1991–1: 37) found that 35.8 per cent of parents in rural areas had this wish, compared to 52 per cent of parents in cities with a population under 100,000, and 63.5 per cent in Tokyo. There are similar distinctions related to parental income; the desire for university educated children increases according to income.

Many parents are caught up in the intense lives of their children. In order to send their children to 'good' schools, they need to send them to 'cram' schools, hire private tutors, or buy special books and educational materials. This economic burden often becomes too great to be borne by the father's income alone. It has been claimed that the primary reason for married women working outside the home is the need to support their children's education (Inoue and Ebara 1991: 161).

While in developing countries the relationship between children's educational requirements and the 'best interests' of the child is often centred around the conflict between education and engaging in labour which is necessary for the family's survival, it is rarely necessary in Japan for a child to contribute towards the family's resources to ensure its subsistence. Children therefore have the opportunity to live as children. Nevertheless, as will be discussed later, Japan is an overheated, consumption-oriented, society in which people's *sense* of privation remains quite high. In this respect, the problems raised by Japan's 'examination hell' can be said to be those of children of an affluent society.

In these circumstances, how do parents perceive what is in the best interests of their children? For most parents, the choice whether to subject their children to this pressurized regime is important because it is very relevant to what is thought to be in the children's best interests. Put simply, the choice is between giving them more free time to spend as they please or thrusting them into a vicious race where judgements are made on the basis of 'test' results, with the purpose of gaining entrance into 'good' schools. According to Campbell (1992: 1), a child's interest lies in the process of growing up as well as in their future as an adult. In the Japanese context, one may ask whether the education system is damaging to the child's maturation process, or to the interests of the child as a future adult.

This paper will be able to produce some answers to the first question. But whether the system is damaging to future adults cannot easily be answered, although, as will be seen, some parents have expressed views about that. Instead it has been possible to provide evidence of the way parents articulate their perceptions of the system. However, these parents will not, for the most part, themselves have experienced the pressures, which have been at their most extreme in recent years. The longer-term effects of the system on adults will only become evident at some time in the future.

Before examining the views of parents, it is necessary to give a brief description of the Japanese education system.

II. THE JAPANESE EDUCATION SYSTEM

Education in Japan is organized as follows:

1. *Nursery*: Entry from ages zero to five. The primary objective is child care, not education, although it may provide an educational programme similar to a *kindergarten* (below). Only the children of parents who cannot provide care themselves (eg working parents) are allowed admission.

2. *Kindergarten*: The primary objective is pre-school education. Children are admitted at four, and there are no requirements for admission.

3. *Elementary School*: This is a six-year compulsory education institution for children aged between six and twelve. State schools have a unified national curriculum. Private schools are also regulated, but are allowed some freedom to develop unique curricula.

4. *Junior High School*: This is a three-year compulsory education institution for children aged twelve to fifteen. State schools operate a national unified curriculum; private schools may provide a unique curriculum, within limits.

5. *High School*: A non-compulsory segment of the education system, for children aged fifteen to eighteen. Admission is by entrance examination. Schools may be general or vocational (eg agricultural schools).

6. *University*: These provide four-year courses (six for medicine) for people over eighteen. Entrance examinations vary; state universities (and some private ones) determine admission on the basis of a nationwide entrance examination as well as their own entrance examination.

7. *Junior College*: A two-year institution similar to a university.

8. *Professional Schools*: Five-year educational institutions for children over fifteen.

9. *Vocational Schools*

10. *Cram Schools and Preparatory Schools*: These exist to assist children to pass examinations. In reality, they enable students to achieve higher 'ability' scores. Some *kindergartens* with a good reputation require applicants to take an entrance examination and there are cram schools and preparatory schools to prepare children for these examinations and for entrance examinations for elementary, junior high and high schools as well as universities. All are private institutions (Okamoto 1992: 102).

The basic structure thus consists of nine years' compulsory elementary and junior high school education, to which is added high school and university education. Some national and private universities operate affiliated primary and secondary schools. Private 'escalator' schools make it possible for some students, having been admitted to a kindergarten or elementary school, to move up the school system without taking examinations. For this reason, many parents hope to send their children to such schools, and, as a result, cram and preparatory schools preparing children for entry to such schools (including *kindegartens*) are very popular. (Nihonkodomowomamorukai 1993: 190–191).

The *University Certificate Examination* is available for students who do not have a high school diploma but would like to be eligible for university entrance examinations. Students who obtain the certificate and pass the university entrance examinations are admitted to university. It has been reported that the number of high school drop-outs and other students taking this examination has increased recently, the number of applicants growing from 3,116 (1980) to 19,293 (1991). On the other hand, the pass rate has dropped from 40.0 per cent to 28.8 per cent, suggesting that once students have dropped out of the examination race, their chances of gaining access to university are much reduced (Nihonkyoikunenkankankokai 1987: 243, 1993: 22).

The numbers of university students have risen since 1945, especially after 1960, when the total was 630,000. By 1992 it had risen to 2.3 million. On the other hand, with the exception of the post-war baby boomers, the number of elementary schoolchildren has fallen, so that the percentage of children gaining entry to university has been increasing. In 1960, 8.2 per cent of high-school students went on to university, but the figure was 26.4 per cent in 1990 (Asahishimbun 1993: 240). The number of universities and junior colleges has increased likewise. There were 245 universities in 1960; in 1992 there were 523 (Asahishimbun 1993: 239. Nihonkyoikunenkankankokai 1993: 25). This might be thought to have alleviated the pressures of examinations. However, university 'ranking' became more conspicuous during the 1970s, and competition to enter 'good' universities was all the keener.

The consequence was that the number of students wanting to enter particular universities grew, making competition more intense. One device developed by cram and preparatory schools to assist students in monitoring their chances of entry was the 'deviation score', a method widely believed to have had adverse educational consequences. When developed in the 1960s, the original purpose of the device was to guide students in their decision as to which school they might most successfully apply. But the objective changed and became a measure of educational achievement, and an important standard in determining the child's academic future. Universities came to be ranked according to their 'deviation score' and society began to evaluate schools in accordance with their 'deviation score'. Children were therefore pressured to aim at schools with the best 'deviation scores', thereby devoting more and more time to study. We must now consider the effects of these pressures on parents and on children.

III. CONSEQUENCES OF THE EXAMINATION SYSTEM

(a) Effect on the Household Economy

The most visible consequence of this system on families has been its cost. A research report on the costs of education conducted by the Ministry of Education compares the following annual costs in 1980 and 1990. The direct cost (ie school tuition) of elementary state education for one child rose from 44,754 yen to 54,230 yen, while the indirect costs (ie for cram schools and tutors) rose from 78,899 yen to 120,463 yen. For junior high schools students, the direct costs rose from 80,371 yen to 107,728 yen, and indirect costs from 56,570 yen to 125,268 yen. For high schools students, the direct and indirect costs rose from 166,923 and 38,025 to 260,726 and 70,648 yen respectively. For private high school students, the increases were from 467,620 (1981) and 53,421 (1981) to 563,480 and 88,780 yen (Mombusho 1987: 148; 1993: 160). These figures must be set against a rise in the average monthly household income from 349,686 yen in 1980 to 563,855 yen in 1992, whereas the consumer price index for education rose from 754.8 to 1302.4 over the same period (Asahishimbun 1993: 192, 198).

According to a 1993 survey (AIU Hokenkaisha 1993: 2), the average cost of educating a child from nursery school through university was 8.71 million yen per child in the state system, and 17.2 million yen per child in the private sector (42.09 million for medical school). This must be seen against an average annual income for conjugal families of 5.13 million yen (in 1990) (Koseishojidokateikyoku 1990: 5). One survey gives the proportion of the wife's income within the household economy as having risen from 4.3 per cent in 1965 to 9.0 per cent in 1988, while education-related expenses rose from 3.9 to 4.7 per cent over the same period (Inoue and Ebara 1991: 31). In a family of four, with two children, the elder being a university student, education-related expenses amounted to 11.9 per cent in 1974 and 20.0 per cent in 1984 (Jinkomondaishingikai 1988: 32). Hence the main reason why married women seek paid employment is to help meet these expenses (Inoue and Ebara 1991: 161). The percentage of married women who work outside the home increased from 32.7 in 1962 to 58.2 in 1992 (Inoue and Ebara 1991: 89; Keizaikikakucho 1992: 67), a clear indication of the effect of education expenses on the household economy.

(b) Effects on Children

Of course, the overall household economy indirectly affects the children. But more direct consequences for children can be seen in increased vandalism, bullying and other deviant behaviour. However, here we will look mainly at truancy.

The number of elementary schoolchildren who were absent for more than 50 days in the year rose from 2,651 in 1974 to 9,652 in 1991. Among junior high school children the increase was from 7,066 in 1972 to 43,794 in 1991, a massive rise during the period in which 'examination hell' intensified. Of the two main reasons given for these absences, 'illness' and 'dislike of school', the former decreased significantly, while the latter rose greatly. For elementary school children, absences due to illness decreased from 75.6 per cent to 51.2 per cent between 1970 and 1991, while those due to 'dislike of school' rose from 11.6 to 32.3 per cent. In junior high school, absences attributed to illness dropped from 57.1 to 24.2 per cent, while absences attributed to dislike of school increased from 28.5 to 60.9 per cent (Seitoshidokenkyukai 1993: 39). However, a possible dramatic consequence, a rise in children's suicide, is *not* shown in the statistics, which have decreased from 534 cases in 1990 to 454 in 1992, when 27.5 per cent were reported to be connected with school or education (Nihonkodomowomamorukai 1992: 94; Somu-cho 1993: 248).

IV.   THE VIEWS OF PARENTS — THE BEST INTERESTS OF THE CHILD 'NOW' AND 'IN THE FUTURE'

For the purposes of this project, questionnaires were mailed to thirty-eight conjugal households in Tokyo and its surrounding areas. Respondents were aged between thirty and fifty. In all surveyed households, either both parents were in employment or the mother had previous employment experience. The majority had either university or junior college education. Such a sample cannot claim representativeness. Instead, the purpose was to obtain qualitative data from a segment of the population on their views about the best interest of their children in relation to their children's education experience.

(a) Desirability of University Education

Not surprisingly, those parents who had themselves experienced university education thought this should be provided for their children, either because they saw this as a 'natural' duty, 'necessary to prevent the child having an inferiority complex in the future' or because they wished to give the child the same educational experience they had received. The desire was very strong: 'A university education is virtually a necessity to our minds'.

These parents saw such education as being vastly beneficial to the child. Some gave practical reasons:

Not only does the lack of university education greatly limit my child's opportunities for employment; I have hopes that a university education will help my child find an area of study he wants to pursue.

One of the basic premises of modern society is the idea that one's academic career can make or break one's social career or status. I am exposed to this at my office every day, and would therefore like my child to receive a university education.

Others put the matter in terms of the child's personal well-being:

I myself learned a great deal and made good friends at university, so I would like to give my child the same experience.

At university I finally met a professor under whom I wanted to study and discovered an area of study I wanted to pursue, and was able to immerse myself in study for four years. I would like my children to have the opportunity to spend a few years of their lives in the same way.

There is a perception of universities as places for relaxation, for forming friendships and enjoying a period of respite between the examination 'hell' and entering the hard world of employment.

(b) Views on the Examination System

Some parents saw the system narrowly in terms of the training and skills they considered it provided for their children.

When studying for examinations, children acquire knowledge that ties them directly to the area they wish to pursue in the future as well as information which will be of no use in the future. But, even if it is crammed into them, children acquire a wide variety of information, which is beneficial to their future. In addition, studying for examinations helps to nurture a mental concentration that will be useful in future studies.

Another view was that children actually enjoy it.

In families where both parents work . . . some children may find cram schools a more enjoyable way of spending their time. While studying for entrance examinations has the disadvantage of taking away time for playing video games or reading comics, there are advantages in being able to make friends at cram school, learning interesting ways to study, or enjoying their progress in scores and test rankings.

Others thought the experience of competition was a good preparation for life. But while these parents seemed to believe in the ultimate beneficial effects of the system, some had doubts about its immediate effects. Few were as completely dismissive about the importance of the interests of the children as the respondent who said:

The issue is not whether or not the system is in the interests of children; rather, it is a process of natural selection in modern society.

More expressed reservations in terms such as these:

Junior high school and high school years are when children should be learning the most important things of life – forming close ties with friends, developing communicative skills, learning ways to play, and compassion to others. It is a problem that these years must instead be devoted to studying for examinations. It is frightening to think that the children who lead this sort of childhood will some day grow up to become élites with important roles in society.

Notwithstanding such reservations, parents felt trapped within the system: examinations were just a fact of life that had to be accepted.

The current examination system is abnormal, but a certain amount of competition cannot be avoided.

I do not think that all aspects of the examination system are in the interests of the children. But, academic or otherwise, it is not possible to avoid competition. Examination hell is one of the many hurdles we face in life, and we must clear it in order to move on.

Some parents, however, were very critical of the system. They thought it was antagonistic the the children's interests. Some expressed this in terms of its unsuitability as a form of education:

Children have to acquire biased jumping techniques in order to jump over warped hurdles.

The examination system crams techniques into children; it does not encourage individuality. In this respect, it is contrary to their interests.

Examination studies are only helpful for passing entrance exams and are often of no practical use in society after college.

Other parents, however, saw more profound disadvantages:

Because the main emphasis is on techniques of passing tests, children acquire knowledge in fragments; they are not given an opportunity to develop their view of the world or a sense of values.

Children who get caught up in the system lose their child-like characteristics and cannot experience the fun and play of childhood. I doubt that children brought up in this way will become well-balanced adults.

It is difficult to judge what is in the interest of children. If their 'interest' is interpreted as preventing them from sustaining disadvantages when they enter society as adults, then examination studies which emphasize intellectual and rote memory do not provide sufficient moral training and might therefore be said to be in conflict with the interest of children. Moreover, a childhood that is immersed in competition is not in the interest of children.

From childhood, we are taught that as long as we study we will grow up to become well-balanced adults. Essential ideas such as having compassion towards others are neglected in the examination hell system.

Nevertheless, worries about 'reality' intruded even on these ideas. One parent, who had not subjected his children to the system, commented:

. . . when I come across advertisments for cram schools, I cannot help but feel slightly uneasy. I am worried whether their school is providing them with adequate academic skills to succeed in society after graduation. But studying at this school provides them with the opportunity to develop the ability to do things of their own will, the ability to have compassion towards others, and other abilities not expressible in figures, and that is why I want them to continue at this school.

In summary, we can say that, while parents tend to stress that ultimately the decision lies with the child, they certainly feel that their children should go to university; not simply because this will have a beneficial effect on the child's life, but because in Japan a person's academic background plays a large part in determining his or her opportunities in life. A 1991 survey showed that 53 per cent of parents believe that a university education is of great assistance in obtaining employment (Keizaikikakucho 1992: 105). Parents have different perspectives, however, of the effect on their children's interest of the examination system. Some see the restrictions it imposes on their children's enjoyment of childhood as an unfortunate sacrifice which is not, however, sufficiently serious to outweigh the advantages to the children's interests in submitting to the system. Others give greater weight to their children's 'personal' development, and see the goal of achieving a 'good' university as insufficiently significant to outweigh the damage to this development they think is inflicted by the examination system. However, the majority are prepared to accept the sacrifices as a concession to social reality (Nihonkodomowomamorukai 1993: 186–187). They seem to wish to minimize the harmful effects by rationalizing that competition is a necessary feature of growing up. In this way, parents seem to be attempting to reconcile the realities of Japanese society with the children's best interests.

V. CONCLUSIONS

If we try to place the parents' views in a broader context, it seems that most seem not to want to force their views on their children: they appear to respect individualism. Although some said that 'education is in itself coercion', this should not be interpreted as advocacy of coercion, but rather as a cynical comment on a particular mode of education. Rather, they tended to underline that the choice for university should lie with the child. However, despite this recognition of the value of self-determination, parents found themselves in a dilemma because it is of course true that children seldom enter the examination system through their free choice. The two are rationalized, and reconciled, by a concept of the interests of the child which sees it as being necessary to equip the child to face the realities of Japanese society.

It is also important to recognize that these views have been developed in a period of high economic growth. Therefore it can be said that one of the underlying premises is an effort to maintain a standard of living, not just for the parents, but for the children as well. The period of high economic growth began in the 1960s. People began to equate wealth with the purchase of consumer goods (Somucho 1993: 8). But this was achieved under working conditions – in terms of effort and time – unthinkable in the West. This led to an intensely competitive spirit and a determination to maximize one's own benefits. Despite all this, the inferior housing situation and underdevelopment of social infrastructures prevented people from *feeling* truly affluent. In a 1992 survey, a surprising 76.2 per cent of people did not think of Japan as being an 'economic giant' (Yomiurishimbun (Yomiuri Newspaper) 10 March 1992). Thus people strive to attain even more wealth, beginning the process over again. The Japanese have even been referred to as a people who are capable of only having 'wealth without happiness' (Dower 1988: 27).

During this period, the habitat of the individual, the family, became more isolated as relatives moved away and nuclear families became dominant. An ethic developed which saw the major objective of a person's efforts as being to acquire wealth for oneself and one's family (Samucho 1991–2: 129). Sacrifices might therefore be necessary to provide one's children with a 'good' school, and a 'good' job; and the subjection of children to the examination system was one of them. This ethos was encouraged by the sense of superficial equality that pervaded Japanese society. This was the 'myth' that, regardless of your background, you could achieve wealth and high social status through effort alone. Since effort and sacrifice brought results, any effort and sacrifice was worth making (Okamoto, 1992: 99). Of course, competition had to be fair, and objective 'testing' of ability became an important element in this. The concept of 'objectivity' led to the use of 'deviation' scores described earlier.

In conclusion, it may be thought that even if the compromise most parents reached over their perception of the interests of their children may have served the interests of the children in the past, if affluence begins to decline, even these sacrifices will fail to secure the desired lifestyle and high status outcomes. In that event, it would not be surprising if more parents did not begin to question whether they should so relentlessly pursue 'good' schools and 'good' jobs for their children. Furthermore, if the idea that creativity and individuality are important facets of personality becomes more important, an increasing number of parents may begin to think more critically about the examination system. Japanese social and cultural patterns are showing signs of change. What these changes will do to perceptions of children's interests in the future will be interesting to observe.

REFERENCES

AIU Hokenkaisha (1993), *Gendaikosodateko*, 1993 ed, AIU Hokenkaisha, Tokyo. (How to bring up children)

Asahishimbun (1993), *Japan Almanac 1994* Asahishimbunsha, Tokyo.

Campbell, T. (1992), 'The Rights of the Minor: as Person, as Child, as Juvenile, as Future Adult' 7 *International Journal of Law & the Family* 1; also in P. Alston, Parker S. and Seymour J. (eds) (1992), *Children, Rights and the Law* Clarendon Press, Oxford, 1.

Dower, J. (1988), *Konnichi no Beinichikannkeiniokeru Shinritekisokumen 1* 336 Kokusaimondai 1. (Psychological Aspects of Current US-Japan Relationships).

Inoue, T. and Ebara, Y. (1991) *Josei no detabukku* Yuhikaku, Tokyo. (Women's Data Book).

Jinkomondaishingikai (1988), *Nihon no jinko nihon no kazoku* Toyokeizaishimposha, Tokyo. (Population and Family in Japan).

Kato, T. (1992), *Shakai to kokka* Iwanamishoten, Tokyo. (Society and State).

Keizaikikakucho (1992), *Kokuminseikatsuhakusho* Ookurashoinsatsukyoku, Tokyo. (White Paper on Japanese Living Standards).

Koseishojidokateikyoku (1990), *Zenkoku boshisetaitochosakekka no gaiyo* Koseisho, Tokyo. (Report on Single Parent Families).

Mombusho (1987), *Mombutokeiyoran 1986* Daiichihokishuppan, Tokyo. (Main Statistics on Education 1986).

Mombusho (1993), *Mombutokeiyoran 1993* Ookurashoinsatsukyoku, Tokyo. (Main Statistics on Education 1993).

Nihonkodomowomamorukai (1992), *Kodomohahusho* Sodobunka, Tokyo. (White Paper on Children 1992).

Nihonkodomowomamorukai (1993), *Kodomohahusho* Sodobunka, Tokyo. (White Paper on Children 1993).

Nihonkyoikunenkankankoiinkai (1987), *Nihonkyoikunenkan 1987* Gyosei, Tokyo. (Japan Almanac on Education 1987).

Nihonkyoikunenkankankoiinkai (1993), *Nihonkyoikunenkan 1993* Gyosei, Tokyo. (Japan Almanac on Education 1993).

Okamoto, K. (1992), *Education of the Rising Sun*, Ministry of Education, Tokyo.

Seitoshidokenkyukai (1993), *Detanimiru seitoshido heiseigonenban* Daiichihoki, Tokyo. (Data on School-children 1993).

Somucho (1991–1), *Chugakusei no hahaoya* Ookurashoinsatsukyoku, Tokyo. (Junior High School Children and their Mothers).

Somucho (1991–2), *Gendai no seishonen* Ookurashoinsatsukyoku, Tokyo. (Young People in Current Society).

Somucho (1993), *Seishonenhakusho* Ookurashoinsatsukyoku, Tokyo. (White Paper on Young People 1993).

INDEX

Human rights (*cont.*)
UN Convention on the Rights of the Child
1–25
universality *see* Universality
World Conference 2, 8, 9, 16

indeterminacy theory 26–41
India *see also* South Asia
adoption of children 137, 138
antislavery 142
child labour 141–3
children's rights 142
Constitution 140, 142, 145
education 142, 143, 145
Juvenile Justice Act 139
public interest litigation 142
Internal discourse
dynamics 68–70
participation 69
universality 79
International Covenant on Civil and Political
Rights 4, 16
International Year of the Child 6

Japan, education in 281–91
best interests of the child 281–91
cost of 285, 286
cram schools 282, 289
examination system 285, 287–9, 291
'good' schools 282
parents' views 286–291
sacrifices for 290
structure 283, 284
suicide 286
time spent at school 281, 282
truancy 286
university 284, 285, 286, 287, 289

Legal reasoning
conventions 34
distributive justice 36–9
inclination 33–6
rational choice 29, 31, 36, 39, 40
scepticism 31–4, 36, 39, 40
utilitarianism 37, 38
values 36

Minority
status 43–5

Nepal *see also* South Asia
Constitution 141
education 141
Norms
universality *see* Universality

Organisation of African Unity 83

Pakistan *see also* South Asia
child labour 141, 143
children in prison 143
Constitution 140, 143
education 142
public interest litigation 143

Rational choice theory 29, 31, 36, 39, 40

Scepticism 31–4, 36, 39, 40
Self-determinism 42–61
decision-making by children 53–7
impulse 51–2
legal competence 54–7
liberalism 50
licence 50–1
objections to 50–3
self-destructive 52–3
subjectivism, and 49
South Asia
adoption of children 121, 123, 137–9, 146
affirmative action for women and children
140
best interests of the child principle 118–34, 145
bride sale 121, 122
child abandonment 124
child abuse 131
childhood, right to 142
child marriage 120–2, 124, 130–1
child-rearing practices 120
child trafficking 131
colonial laws 119–20, 122, 123, 146
custody of children 119–21, 125–31
Directive Principles of State Policy 140, 141
divorce 123
dowry 122, 124
education 141
equality and freedom, right to 140, 141
freedom of conscience and religion 130
guardianship law 125–31
access rights 128
child's welfare 125–8
child's wishes 129, 130, 145
Islamic principles 127–8
maternal right 126–8
non-marital children 128
paternal right 125–9
personal law 125, 126, 129
religion 125, 127, 129, 130
statute 125, 126, 128, 130
human rights norms 140, 145, 146
indigenous systems 118–24, 146
infanticide 124
life, right to 141
maintenance of children 120, 121